P9-DME-220

▶ Raptors ◀

RAPTORS

▾ ▾ ▾ ▾ ▾ ▾ ▾ ▾

THE BIRDS OF PREY

Scott Weidensaul

LYONS & BURFORD, PUBLISHERS

Printed in Hong Kong

Design by Howard P. Johnson, Communigrafix, Inc.

Composition by Ling Lu, CompuDesign

10 9 8 7 6 5 4 3 2 1

Library of Congress Cataloging-in-Publication Data

Weidensaul, Scott.
    The raptor almanac: birds of prey.
        p.   cm
    Includes bibliographical references and index
    ISBN 1-55821-275-2 (cloth)
    1. Birds of prey.   I. Title.
    QL696.F3W443   1995
    598.9'1—dc20   95-21839
                      CIP

The author wishes to thank the following publishers for permission to reproduce illustration, maps, charts or text:

Birder's Handbook, by Paul R. Ehrlich, David S. Dobkin, and Darryl Wheye, Simon & Schuster Inc., © 1988.

Dictionary of American Bird Names, Rev. ed., by Ernest A. Choate, The Harvard Common Press, © 1985.

Falcons of the World, by Tom J. Cade, Cornell University Press and Nicholas Enterprises Ltd., © 1982.

Field Guide to Birds' Nests, by Hal H. Harrison, Houghton Miffin Co., © 1975.

Field Guide to Hawks, by William S. Clark and Brian K. Wheeler, Houghton Miffin Co., © 1987.

Field Guide to Western Birds' Nests, by Hal H. Harrison, Houghton Mifflin Co., © 1979

Flight Strategies of Migrating Hawks, by Paul Kerlinger, Chicago University Press, © 1989.

Handbook of North American Birds, Vols. 4 and 5, by Ralph S. Palmer, Yale University Press, © 1988.

Harrier: Hawk of the Marshes, by Frances Hamerstrom, Smithsonian Institution Press, © 1986.

Hawks, Eagles & Falcons of North America, by Paul A. Johnsgard, Smithsonian Insitution Press, © 1990.

Manual of Ornithology, by Noble S. Proctor and Patrick J. Lynch, Yale University Press, © 1993.

Ospreys: A Natural and Unnatural History, by Alan F. Poole, Cambridge University, © 1989.

Woodworking for Wildlife: Homes for Birds and Mammals, by Carrol L. Henderson, Minnesota Department of Natural Resources, © 1984.

Photo credits on page 382.

CONTENTS

INTRODUCTION
VII

FOR MY FATHER, CHARLES WEIDENSAUL

▼

INTRODUCTION

It is hard to find anyone who is apathetic about raptors—especially after they have seen a wild hawk up close. One of my most vivid memories of childhood is of my first visit to Hawk Mountain, not far from my family's home in the rumpled Appalachians of eastern Pennsylvania. Here, each autumn, a cascade of migrating hawks, eagles, falcons, and vultures surges south, following the long hills—to the delight of thousands of people who climb to the ridgetop of this world-famous sanctuary to watch them.

I was twelve, already a committed naturalist of the snake-collecting, toad-grabbing sort—the kind of boy whose room his mother hates to clean, never knowing what manner of living creature she'll find under the bed. I loved birds and bird-watching, too, but hawks were just a minor thread in the big tapestry.

That brisk fall day at Hawk Mountain changed my outlook forever. By sheer happenstance, we arrived the day after a stormy cold front had pushed through the state, dragging its train of chilly northwest winds behind it. The sky was full of hawks—sharp-shinneds and Cooper's hawks, redtails and redshoulders, harriers and kestrels (which everyone still called marsh hawks and sparrowhawks in those days).

I sat on the rocks, enthralled, watching the fleet shapes hurtle through the air. I couldn't identify more than one out of ten of them, although I loudly volunteered my guesses until one of the experienced hawk-watchers sitting nearby gently corrected me. But the die was cast. I had been caught up in the spell of raptors, and remain contentedly so now, almost twenty-five years later. I still climb the ridges each autumn, often to catch and band the hawks in my small contribution to science, but always to marvel at their grace and stirring beauty.

I am hardly alone in this obsession. Birds of prey have exerted a powerful grip on the human imagination for almost as long as we have been human, at least judging from the prehistoric rock art found in many corners of the globe. We have worshiped raptors, enshrined them as totems, and ridden to battle beneath war standards cast in their shapes or flags sewn with their silhouettes.

We have ascribed healing powers to their feathers and bones, praised them as symbols of freedom, and harnessed their speed and agility to do our hunting for us. At the same time, paradoxically, humans have scorned birds of prey as wanton killers of innocent creatures, or reviled them as competitors, and we have killed them in vast numbers down through the generations with ever-increasing efficiency.

Only in this century have we begun to reconcile these opposing visions of raptors, recognizing that the world of nature allows for no moralistic judgments, and that birds of prey fit neatly—and necessarily—into the functioning whole. In fact, in some ways the pendulum has swung well to the opposite side; raptors have never been more popular, and the potency of their symbolism—of freedom and wild beauty—has never been stronger.

There are some 310 species of diurnal birds of prey worldwide—the hawks, eagles, falcons, and vultures. These range from the tiny falconets of Asia, weighing scarcely two ounces, to the condors of the New World, which may weigh twenty or thirty pounds and fly on wings that span ten feet or more. They include the "classic" raptors like the red-tailed hawk and peregrine falcon, but many unusual, even bizarre species—vultures that feed on the marrow of bones they smash from the air, cranelike secretary-birds that stalk about on long legs, massive harpy eagles with claws the size of a grizzly bear's. There are raptors that feed mostly on bats, or wasp grubs, or palm nuts, or sea snakes.

A broad overview of this astonishing diversity of predatory life, *Raptors* explores the physical and evolutionary attributes that make a raptor a raptor; details the ecology and natural history of these aerial hunters, including their behavior, reproduction, and lifestyles; explains the history and techniques of conservation, and describes the challenges still facing many of the world's raptors; and examines the many ways these remarkable creatures have affected human lives and cultures down through history, suggesting ways you can enjoy and help birds of prey yourself.

Biologists are still working out the precise relationships among raptors, including the fundamental question of how many species there are. Wild animals do not come with convenient labels, and specialists may argue for years over whether a particular form is a full species, a subspecies, or merely a local race. I say there are "about" 310 species of diurnal raptors because the question is still somewhat open. Likewise, many of the old, familiar names of raptors have changed with the years, like the monkey-eating eagle that is now the Philippine eagle. These changes, although proper for accuracy, can be confusing. For the sake of consistency, the English names of raptors used in this book conform with the fourth edition of James Clements' authoritative text, *Birds of the World: A Checklist.*

Finally, I extend my sincere thanks to the staff, board, and volunteers of Hawk Mountain Sanctuary. For almost two and a half decades I have been watching hawks with them and learning from them, and on occasion I have been privileged to work beside them on exciting research projects. The sanctuary's marvelous research library was put at my disposal, and my endless questions have always been treated with patience and interest. Particular thanks are due Laurie Goodrich, Hawk Mountain's conservation ecologist; director of research Dr. Keith Bildstein; and executive director Cynthia Lenhart. Keith and Cynthia graciously reviewed portions of this book for accuracy.

My thanks go as well to my editor, Lilly Golden, for her patience and professionalism.

As I write this, a female American kestrel is sitting on a wire just outside my office window, bobbing in the wind as she watches the meadow for an incautious rodent. A moment ago she flashed into view, a masterwork of tapered wings, sharp claws, and dark, brilliant eyes. In that instant, she transformed a quiet afternoon into one of high drama and excitement—exactly the kind of fire that raptors of every description add to the natural world.

—Scott Weidensaul

Fall 1995

1

HUNTERS

ON THE

WIND

1

WHAT IS A RAPTOR?

Often the simplest questions can be the hardest to answer. Bird-watchers and naturalists know a raptor when they see one—but they often find it hard to say just how they know.

"Raptor" is the blanket term used by ornithologists for hawks, falcons, eagles, vultures, and owls. Owls are *nocturnal* (or night-active) raptors, while the rest are *diurnal* (or day-active) raptors; this book will deal with diurnal raptors only.

Also known as *birds of prey*, raptors feed almost exclusively on meat, and, except for carrion-eaters, pursue and kill the animals on which they feed. But although all raptors are carnivorous, not all birds that eat meat

▶ *What defines this Cooper's hawk as a raptor isn't the fact that it eats meat— many birds are carnivorous— but its specialized claws and sharp, hooked beak.*

are raptors; in fact, the vast majority of bird species, from robins to herons, feed on other animals.

It is anatomy, more than diet, that defines a raptor. Raptors possess feet and beaks specially adapted for hunting. The feet have long, curved talons, which grasp and kill the prey, and the beak is sharply hooked for tearing meat. The bills of some raptors, particularly falcons, have a notch along the cutting edge of the upper mandible that fits neatly between the neck vertebrae of their prey, severing the spinal cord once the animal has been brought to the ground.

Vultures, which have traditionally been classified with the other diurnal raptors, are an obvious exception to the rule about diet and anatomy. For the most part they feed on carrion, and lack the strongly taloned feet of other raptors; their bills are hooked, although not as severely. Genetic evidence has now convinced the scientific community that New World vultures are, essentially, short-legged storks with only a coincidental resemblance to raptors. (Old World vultures, on the other hand, are still thought to be closely related to hawks.) Because they have so long been lumped with raptors, however, American vultures will be discussed with them in this book.

Raptor Classification

No doubt from the time we invented language we had names for animals, but each part of the world had its own names. That made it almost impossible for a scientist from one region to know what another scientist from a different region was talking about. Who would guess, for example, that a windhover and a killy-hawk were the same bird, the one we know today as the American kestrel?

The taxonomic system used today was created by an eighteenth-century Swedish naturalist, Carolus Linnaeus,* as a way to clear up the chaos of local names and bring a measure of order to human understanding of the natural world. His taxonomy still stands as one of the stellar achievements of biology.

Linnaeus drew up a hierarchical system that starts with the great kingdoms of plants and animals and with each level, or taxon, becomes progressively more and more specific. Closely related species are assigned to the same genus; related genera to the same family; related families to the same order; and so on through class, phylum, and finally kingdom. At every level, the organisms within a taxon are more closely related to each other than to other taxa.

Linnaeus created what is known as binomial nomenclature—those often tongue-twisting "scientific names" that are based on Latin and Greek. Each organism is assigned a genus, or generic, name (always capitalized), which is shared by its close relatives, and a lowercase species, or specific, name. The combination is unique, and universally recognized by scientists.

By tradition, the person who first describes a new species is accorded the honor of giving it its scientific name. Linnaeus, in his 1757 masterwork *Systema Naturae*, set down the classification and scientific names of the creatures known at that time, including the turkey vulture *(Cathartes aura)*, bald eagle *(Haliaeetus leucocephalus)*, and American kestrel *(Falco sparverius)*.

Scientific names are not chosen arbitrarily. For example, the genus name *Haliaeetus* comes from the Greek word *haliaetos*, meaning sea-eagle, while the specific name *leucocephalus* is a combination of the Greek *leukos* (white) and *kephale* (head). "White-headed sea-eagle" is a rather good description of a bald eagle.

HAWKS THAT AREN'T

*T*he word "hawk" has often been applied to birds—even to certain insects—that are obviously not raptors. Sometimes, as with the insect-eating bird known as the nighthawk, the name arose because these birds catch their prey in flight, "hawking" it out of midair. Other creatures, like the large wasp known as the cicada-hawk, were named because of their hunting abilities.

"Hawk" is also often used in a general, imprecise sense to refer to all diurnal raptors. In the heyday of falconry, for instance, the sport was also known as "hawking," even when the bird being flown was a falcon rather than a true hawk.

▸▸▸ MORPHOLOGY VS. BIOCHEMISTRY

Traditional classification systems, including that of Linnaeus, were based on physical, or *morphological*, characteristics, on the assumption that birds with similar features were most closely related. Scientists realized that some features, like feather

---

*Carolus Linnaeus was born Carl von Linné, but in keeping with his own taxonomy he Latinized his name, and that is how history knows him.

Raptor Classication

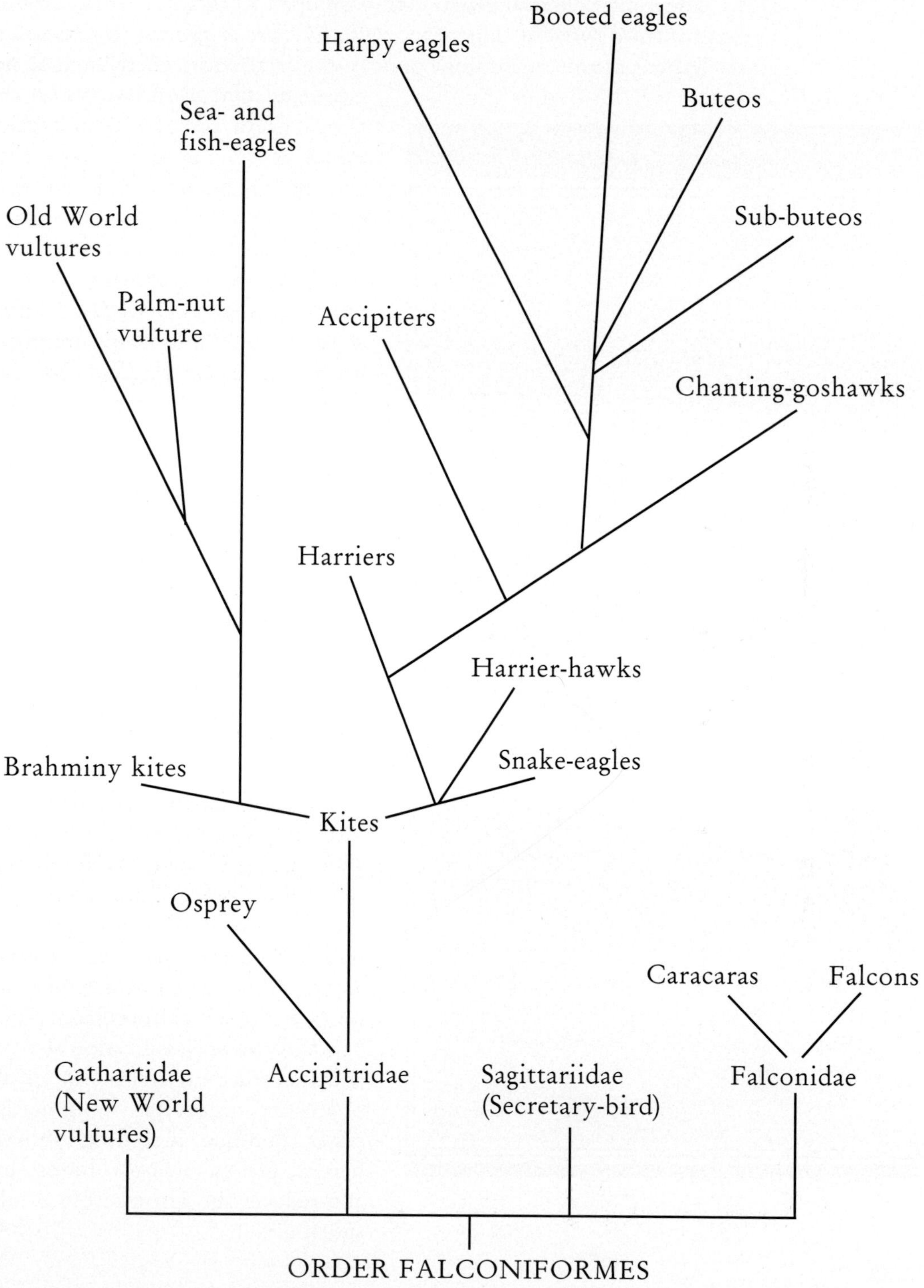

Harpy eagles

Booted eagles

Buteos

Sub-buteos

Sea- and
fish-eagles

Chanting-goshawks

Old World
vultures

Palm-nut
vulture

Accipiters

Harriers

Harrier-hawks

Brahminy kites

Snake-eagles

Kites

Osprey

Caracaras   Falcons

Cathartidae
(New World
vultures)

Accipitridae

Sagittariidae
(Secretary-bird)

Falconidae

▶ *Evolutionary
relationships
between raptor
groups, based on
the traditional
classification sys-
tem, rather than
biochemical clas-
sification.*

ORDER FALCONIFORMES

(Adapted from Hawks, Eagles & Falcons of North America, *Johnsgard, 1990)*

color, bill shape, or leg length can change easily, so they focused instead on a variety of more subtle structures, many of them internal.

The morphological classification grouped all the diurnal raptors into the order Falconiformes. Within that order were five broad groups, known as families—the *New World vultures,* including condors; the *accipitrids,* which include hawks, eagles, kites, and Old World vultures; the *osprey;* the *secretary-bird* of Africa; and the *falcons and caracaras.*

But appearances can be deceiving. Just because two birds share similar features, it doesn't necessarily mean they are closely related. More recently, scientists have turned to the process known as *DNA-DNA hybridization* for clues to the relationships among species. This method relies on the fact that each strand in the double helix of DNA is a long sequence of four nucleotides that each bind only with one other of the four—guanine only with cytosine, adenine only with thymine—so that the two strands are reverse mirror images. The order in which these pairs appear on the double helix forms the genetic code.

DNA is removed from bird tissue, boiled until it splits into separate strands, then mixed with DNA from another species of bird that has been similarly treated. Where the nucleotide sequences match, the strands rejoin. The degree to which the strands match is an indication of how closely related the two species of birds are—closely related species will match to a higher degree than less closely related species.

DNA studies have shaken the traditional taxonomy of birds, and many of the results remain controversial. The most radical change among raptors is the reassignment of American (or New World) vultures from raptors to storks. The alternative classification also places vultures and the other raptors in the greatly expanded order Ciconiiformes (along with twenty-five other families including shorebirds, gulls, herons, grebes, pelicans, loons, and penguins), and reduces the osprey from a full family to a subfamily.

BUZZARDS

Many of the common names given to raptors are confusing, because their usage varies from continent to continent. A sparrowhawk in Europe is a small accipiter, for instance, while in North America "sparrowhawk" is an old name for a falcon, the American kestrel.

Buzzard is another confusing name. It comes from the French word busard, *or hawk, and is used in the Old World to describe a number of soaring hawks in the genus* Buteo. *The word "buzzard" still properly refers to buteos. Early settlers in North America, however, transferred the name to vultures, and it remains an inaccurate slang term.*

Strictly speaking, North American buteos should be referred to as buzzards— red-tailed buzzard instead of red-tailed hawk, for instance. This book holds with general practice, however, by applying the name buzzard to Eurasian buteos only. Therefore, the single species of buteo found across the entire Northern Hemisphere, Buteo lagopus, *may be referred to as a rough-legged hawk or a rough-legged buzzard, depending on whether the context is North American or European.*

► The term "buzzard" comes from the French word busard *(hawk),* and properly refers to buteos like this common buzzard— a convention followed in Europe, but not in North America.

Biochemical Classification of Raptors

Superorder Passerimorphae

Order Columbiformes
(Pigeons and doves: 313 species)

Order Gruiformes
(Cranes, rails, coots, bustards, and allies: 196 species)

Order Ciconiiformes
(1,027 species)

 Suborder Charadrii
 <u>Infraorder Pteroclides</u>
 (Sandgrouse)

 <u>Infraorder Charadriides</u>
 (Shorebirds, gulls, terns, skimmers, auks, and puffins)

 Suborder Ciconii
 <u>Infraorder Falconides</u>
 (Osprey, hawks, Old World vultures, eagles, caracaras, falcons)

 <u>Infraorder Ciconiides</u>
 (Grebes, tropicbirds, gannets, anhingas, cormorants, herons, flamingos, pelicans, New World vultures, storks, frigatebirds, penguins, loons, petrels, albatrosses)

Order Passeriformes
(5,712 species)

(Adapted from Manual of Ornithology, *Proctor and Lynch, 1993; after Sibley, Ahlquist and Monroe)*

► *Based on analysis of DNA rather than morphological attributes, this classification places New World vultures in the infraorder Ciconiides, with storks, penguins, loons and a number of other genera.*

ARE VULTURES STORKS?

The idea that New World vultures are most closely related to storks may seem unlikely to the average bird-watcher, but scientists have suspected as much for years. Ornithologists long ago noted physical and behavioral similarities between the two groups, including the vultures' habit of defecating on their legs in hot weather to cool themselves, something storks also do.

Biologists also noted the dissimilarities between New World vultures and all other raptors—the small, raised hind toe of a vulture, for example, which is very different from the powerful hallux of a hawk, and the vulture's "perforate" nostrils, with

an opening through the beak from side to side. Most American vultures also have a fairly good sense of smell, which is lacking in other raptors, including Old World vultures. Finally, like storks, New World vultures lack a syrinx, the organ of sound production in birds; the best they can do is hiss and grunt.

Only recently have scientists found proof for the theory, however. Studies of DNA show that New World vultures are much more closely related to storks than to Old World vultures, and they have been reassigned with storks to the same order as pelicans, loons, and penguins, among other birds.

◄► *Although New World vultures like this black vulture (left) have traditionally been classified as raptors, recent genetic research has confirmed that they are more closely related to storks, like this wood stork (right), than to hawks, eagles and falcons.*

▼ *Old World vultures, like this Rueppell's griffon from Africa, are directly related to eagles and hawks. Similarities of anatomy and behavior between Old and New World vultures are the result of convergent evolution, not a close taxonomic relationship.*

TRADITIONAL CLASSIFICATION OF DIURNAL RAPTORS

Order Falconiformes—310 species worldwide

FAMILY	NAME	NUMBER
Cathartidae	New World vultures	7 species
Pandionidae	Osprey	1 species
Accipitridae	Kites, hawks, eagles, and Old World vultures	237 species
Sagittariidae	Secretary-bird	1 species
Falconidae	Falcons and caracaras	64 species

CLASSIFICATION BASED ON DNA-DNA HYBRIDIZATION

Order Ciconiiformes (also includes 25 other families)

FAMILY	NAME
Accipitridae	
Subfamily Pandioninae	Osprey
Subfamily Accipitrinae	Kites, hawks, eagles, and Old World vultures
Sagittariidae	Secretary-bird
Falconidae	Falcons and caracaras
Ciconiidae	
Subfamily Carthartinae	New World vultures
Subfamily Ciconiinae	Storks

▶ *Kites, like this Mississippi kite, are slim, lightly built raptors that feed heavily on insects and small vertebrates.*

Major Raptor Groups

Most North American and Eurasian raptors fall within one of five major groups—the kites, accipiters (forest hawks), buteos (soaring hawks), eagles, and falcons.

••• KITES are generally slim, buoyant, relatively light bodied raptors that feed primarily on insects, reptiles and amphibians, and small mammals. Kites tend to be highly migratory (although the snail and hook-billed kites are sedentary), rather social during the breeding season, and predominantly southern in distribution. Number of breeding species in North America: five; Europe: three.

▶ *The American kestrel is a typical falcon, with long, pointed wings and a long tail.*

••• ACCIPITERS are mainly forest hawks, built for a dash-and-grab style of hunting. There are three species in North America, ranging from the dove-sized sharp-shinned hawk to the crow-sized goshawk of the northern conifer forests. Accipiters have long tails and fairly short, rounded wings, a combination that allows for quick acceleration and snap turns. They feed largely on birds and mammals. Number of breeding species in North America: three; Europe: three.

••• BUTEOS are the soaring hawks that wheel across limitless skies on broad tails and fan-shaped wings. They are also the most diverse group of diurnal raptors in North America, and have the greatest diversity of habitats. While most (such as red-tailed, Swainson's, and ferruginous hawks) inhabit open country, some, like the broad-winged and red-shouldered hawks, are forest-dwellers. Their diet ranges from small mammals and birds to insects and other invertebrates. Number of breeding species in North America: twelve; Europe: three.

··· EAGLES are so named because of their size, rather than a close taxonomic relationship. The bald eagle is a member of the fish-eagle clan, which also includes the Stellar's sea-eagle of Asia, the African fish-eagle, and the white-tailed eagle of Eurasia. The golden eagle is a booted eagle, a group nearest to buteos and considered more evolutionarily advanced than any other raptors save falcons. Number of breeding species in North America: two; Europe: eight.

··· FALCONS are fast-flying, streamlined aerialists, supremely suited for taking prey in the air. They are long-winged and -tailed, similar in shape to kites but with a greater sense of power. The falcons include one of the smallest of North American hawks, the robin-sized American kestrel, and the gyrfalcon of the Arctic. Their diet is mostly birds, although smaller species take large numbers of rodents, reptiles, and insects. Number of breeding species in North America: six; Europe: ten.

··· OTHER RAPTORS—NORTH AMERICA Of the remaining six species that breed in the United States and Canada, three are vultures, which, as already noted, are unrelated to the other raptors. The rest are:

—**Northern harrier,** the sole North American representative of a genus with nearly worldwide distribution, marked by a peculiar facial disk reminiscent of owls.
—**Crested caracara,** a member of the falcon family but distinctly unfalconlike, with its long legs and chunky appearance. The crested caracara is restricted to a few pockets in Florida and the Southwest; it and related caracaras are widespread in the New World tropics.

▼ Decidedly unfalconlike in its bulky appearance, the crested caracara is classified with the falcons on the basis of internal features.

—**Osprey,** a single species found as a breeding bird or migrant on every continent save Antarctica. Its long, crooked wings, held in a shallow M-shape, are characteristic, as is its plunging dive for fish. The soles of its feet are covered with tiny, sharp tubercules to prevent fish from slipping away.

··· OTHER RAPTORS—EUROPE

—**Harriers.** Unlike North America, which has only one kind of harrier, Europe has four species, including the northern harrier, known in Great Britain more commonly as the hen harrier. The northern harrier, western marsh-harrier, and Monatgu's harrier are all widespread through Europe, while the pallid harrier is restricted to eastern Europe and southwestern Asia.

—**Old World vultures** are generally restricted to southern Europe, where four species are found—the Eurasian griffon, cinereous (black) vulture, Egyptian vulture, and lammergeier (bearded vulture).

—**Osprey,** which is found widely across northern Europe, as it is in the New World.

NORTH AMERICAN RAPTORS

E = East, **S** = South, **W** = West, **N** = North, **SW** = Southwest, **A** = Arctic, **C** = Continental

SPECIES	LATIN NAME (GENUS/SPECIES)	DISTRIBUTION
NEW WORLD VULTURES		
Turkey vulture	*Cathartes aura*	C
Black vulture	*Coragyps atratus*	S
California condor	*Gymnogyps californianus*	W (California)
OSPREYS		
Osprey	*Pandion haliaetus*	C
KITES		
Mississippi kite	*Ictinia mississippiensis*	S, SW
American swallow-tailed kite	*Elanoides forficatus*	S
White-tailed kite (formerly black-shouldered kite, *E. caeruleus*)	*Elanus leucurus*	W, SW
Snail kite	*Rostrhamus sociabilis*	S (Florida)
Hook-billed kite	*Chondrohierax uncinatus*	S (Texas)

SPECIES	LATIN NAME (GENUS/SPECIES)	DISTRIBUTION
▼		
FISH-EAGLES		
Bald eagle	*Haliaeetus leucocephalus*	C
▼		
HARRIERS		
Northern harrier	*Circus cyaneus*	C
▼		
ACCIPITERS		
Sharp-shinned hawk	*Accipiter striatus*	C
Cooper's hawk	*Accipiter cooperii*	C
Northern goshawk	*Accipiter gentilis*	N, W
▼		
BUTEONINES		
Harris' hawk	*Parabuteo unicinctus*	SW
Common black-hawk	*Buteogallus anthracinus*	SW
Gray hawk	*Asturina plagiata* (formerly *Buteo nitidus*)	SW
Red-shouldered hawk	*Buteo lineatus*	E (also Calif.)
Broad-winged hawk	*Buteo platypterus*	E
Red-tailed hawk	*Buteo jamaicensis*	C
Swainson's hawk	*Buteo swainsoni*	W, SW
Rough-legged hawk	*Buteo lagopus*	A (C in winter)
Ferruginous hawk	*Buteo regalis*	W (SW in winter)
White-tailed hawk	*Buteo albicaudatus*	SW (Texas)
Zone-tailed hawk	*Buteo albonotatus*	SW
Short-tailed hawk	*Buteo brachyurus*	S (Florida)
▼		
BOOTED EAGLES		
Golden eagle	*Aquila chrysaetos*	W, A (E in winter)

continued

NORTH AMERICAN RAPTORS

E = East, **S** = South, **W** = West, **N** = North, **SW** = Southwest, **A** = Arctic, **C** = Continental

SPECIES	LATIN NAME (GENUS/SPECIES)	DISTRIBUTION
▾ **FALCONS**		
Crested caracara	*Caracara* (formerly *Polyborus) plancus*	S (Florida), SW
American kestrel	*Falco sparverius*	C
Merlin	*Falco columbarius*	N (S in winter)
Aplomado falcon	*Falco femoralis*	SW (reintroduced)
Prairie falcon	*Falco mexicanus*	W, SW
Gyrfalcon	*Falco rusticolus*	A
Peregrine falcon	*Falco peregrinus*	A, W (rare E)

EUROPEAN RAPTORS

E = Eastern Europe, **CE** = Central Europe, **M** = Mediterranean basin, **I** = Iberian Peninsula, **N** = Northern Europe, **S** = Southern Europe, **A** = Arctic, **C** = Continental

SPECIES	LATIN NAME (GENUS/SPECIES)	DISTRIBUTION
▾ **OSPREYS**		
Osprey	*Pandion haliaetus*	N
▾ **HONEY-BUZZARDS**		
European honey-buzzard	*Pernis apivorus*	C (except N, M)
▾ **KITES**		
Black-shouldered kite	*Elanus caeruleus*	I
Red kite	*Milvus milvus*	C (except N)
Black kite	*Milvus migrans*	C (summer only)

continued

SPECIES	LATIN NAME (GENUS/SPECIES)	DISTRIBUTION
▾ **FISH-EAGLES**		
White-tailed eagle	*Haliaeetus albicilla*	N, E
▾ **OLD WORLD VULTURES**		
Lammergeier	*Gypaetus barbatus*	S (local in mts.)
Egyptian vulture	*Neophron percnopterus*	S
Eurasian griffon	*Gyps fulvus*	S, I
Cinereous vulture	*Aegypius monachus*	I, S (local)
▾ **SNAKE-EAGLES**		
Short-toed eagle	*Circaetus gallicus*	I, S, E (summer)
▾ **HARRIERS**		
Western marsh-harrier	*Circus aeruginosus*	C, except N (M in winter)
Northern (hen) harrier	*Circus cyaneus*	C
Pallid harrier	*Circus macrourus*	E
Montagu's harrier	*Circus pygargus*	C, except N (summer)
▾ **ACCIPITERS**		
Levant sparrowhawk	*Accipiter brevipes*	M (summer)
Eurasian sparrowhawk	*Accipiter nisus*	C (N in summer)
Northern goshawk	*Accipiter gentilis*	C
▾ **BUTEOS**		
Common buzzard	*Buteo buteo*	C (except A)
Long-legged buzzard	*Buteo rufinis*	M, E
Rough-legged buzzard	*Buteo lagopus*	A (E, CE, N in winter)

E=Eastern Europe, **CE**=Central Europe, **M**=Mediterranean basin, **I**=Iberian Peninsula, **N**=Northern Europe, **S**=Southern Europe, **A**=Arctic, **C**=Continental

SPECIES	LATIN NAME (GENUS/SPECIES)	DISTRIBUTION
EAGLES		
Lesser spotted eagle	*Aquila pomarina*	E, CE (local)
Greater spotted eagle	*Aquila clanga*	E
Spanish eagle	*Aquila adalberti*	I (local)
Imperial eagle	*Aquila heliaca*	M, E (local)
Golden eagle	*Aquila chrysaetos*	A, N, E, I, S
Booted eagle	*Hieraaetus pennatus*	I, S
Bonelli's eagle	*Hieraaetus fasciatus*	I, M
FALCONS		
Lesser kestrel	*Falco naumanni*	M, I (summer only)
Eurasian kestrel	*Falco tinnunculus*	C (N, E in summer only)
Red-footed falcon	*Falco vespertinus*	E, CE (summer only)
Eleonora's falcon	*Falco eleonorae*	M (summer)
Merlin	*Falco columbarius*	A, N (C in winter)
Eurasian hobby	*Falco subbuteo*	C (except A)
Lanner	*Falco biarmicus*	M
Saker	*Falco cherrug*	E, CE (M in winter)
Gyrfalcon	*Falco rusticolus*	A
Peregrine falcon	*Falco peregrinus*	C (local except N, A)

▶ *One of the most graceful raptors in the world, the American swallow-tailed kite was once found as far north as Minnesota, but is now restricted to the Southeast and tropics.*

▸▸▸ NEW SPECIES, MISSING SPECIES

Bird populations are never static, and that includes raptors. The ranges of several species have changed dramatically over time. Until the 1880s, for instance, the American swallow-tailed kite was found up the Mississippi basin as far north as Minnesota and Wisconsin. But in the space of just fifty years—and for reasons that are still a mystery—its range shrank to a few patches along the Southeast coast. Now there are signs that the kites may be expanding back into parts of their old range once more.

The hook-billed kite, a tropical species that reaches its northern range limit along the Rio Grande, has only recently begun breeding on the U.S. side of the border. While it is possible that hookbills may have bred in the United States prior to European settlement, the first recorded nests were found in extreme southern Texas in 1964, and a few pairs have bred fitfully in the area ever since.

The flamboyantly colored king vulture of the American tropics may also once have inhabited the United States. Eighteenth-century naturalist William Bartram, who traveled along the St. John River in the 1770s, reported that the "painted vulture" was commonly seen scavenging for scorched carrion in the wake of grass fires. Bartram's *Travels Through North & South Carolina, Georgia, East & West Florida* gives a meticulous description of an adult king vulture, although he mistakenly claims the white tail has a brown tip. His report has been dismissed by modern experts, partly because of the error about the tail, and partly because no other naturalist reported seeing the species in the United States. But others, including respected raptor biologists Noel and Helen Snyder, accept Bartram's claim, and have even suggested reintroducing king vultures to central Florida.

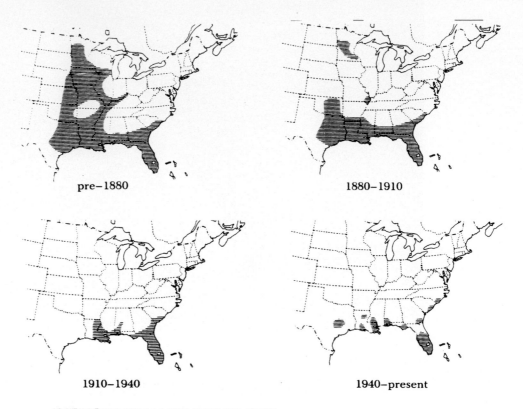

pre–1880

1880–1910

1910–1940

1940–present

AMERICAN SWALLOW-TAILED KITE
Elanoides forficatus

 Breeding range in U.S., from maps compiled by J. M. Cely
(map on lower right slightly modified)

Total range of the species includes various islands and much of South America

(Adapted from Handbook of North American Birds, *Vol. 4, Palmer, 1988)*

▶ *Prior to the 1880s, American swallow-tailed kites bred across much of the Great Plains, a range that inexplicably shrank over the next half-century.*

▸▸▸ SPECIES AND SUBSPECIES

Many raptors are found over wide areas of the globe. Some, like the peregrine falcon and the osprey, occur on almost every continent, while others, such as the red-tailed hawk, are restricted to single continents but nonetheless occupy enormous areas within them.

Raptors of the same species that inhabit far-flung regions often show differences in size and color—differences that are not significant enough to warrant designation as separate species, but which deserve scientific notice.

For instance, peregrine falcons are all members of the species *Falco peregrinus;* all have the trademark black "helmet" markings on the face, dark back, and light,

► *The golden crown feathers on this immature peregrine falcon are characteristic of the Arctic subspecies,* Falco peregrinus tundrius.

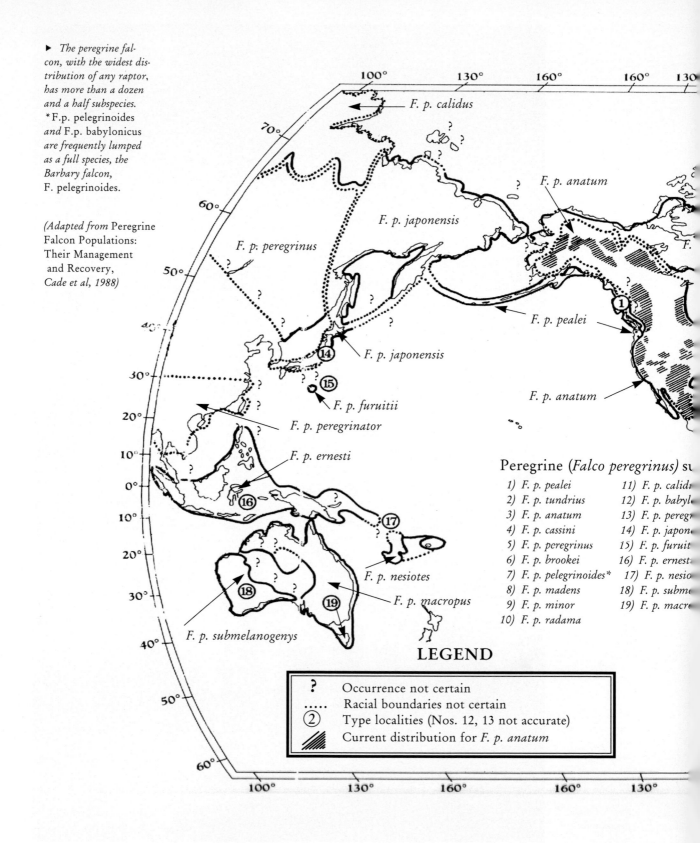

▶ The peregrine fal-
con, with the widest dis-
tribution of any raptor,
has more than a dozen
and a half subspecies.
*F.p. pelegrinoides
and F.p. babylonicus
are frequently lumped
as a full species, the
Barbary falcon,
F. pelegrinoides.

(Adapted from Peregrine
Falcon Populations:
Their Management
and Recovery,
Cade et al, 1988)

F. p. calidus

F. p. anatum

F. p. japonensis

F. p. peregrinus

F. p. pealei

F. p. japonensis

F. p. anatum

F. p. furuitii

F. p. peregrinator

F. p. ernesti

F. p. nesiotes

F. p. macropus

F. p. submelanogenys

Peregrine (*Falco peregrinus*) su

1) F. p. pealei	11) F. p. calid
2) F. p. tundrius	12) F. p. babyl
3) F. p. anatum	13) F. p. peregr
4) F. p. cassini	14) F. p. japon
5) F. p. peregrinus	15) F. p. furuit
6) F. p. brookei	16) F. p. ernest
7) F. p. pelegrinoides*	17) F. p. nesio
8) F. p. madens	18) F. p. subme
9) F. p. minor	19) F. p. macre
10) F. p. radama	

LEGEND

?	Occurrence not certain
....	Racial boundaries not certain
②	Type localities (Nos. 12, 13 not accurate)
▨	Current distribution for *F. p. anatum*

Breeding distribution of
Peregrine Falcon subspecies

barred undersides. But those that breed in the Arctic tend to be very pale as adults, and the immatures have a distinctive golden crown, while peregrines from the Pacific Northwest and Aleutians are almost chocolate when young and very dark blue-gray as adults. Inland peregrines are roughly midway between these plumage extremes.

Distinct populations like these may be given the rank of subspecies, indicated by a third scientific name after the usual generic and specific Latin names. Ornithologists have divided North America's peregrines into three subspecies—the pale *Falco peregrinus tundrius* in the Arctic, dark *F.p. pealei* on the Pacific Coast, and *F.p. anatum* inland. Worldwide there are seventeen peregrine subspecies generally recognized by scientists, although there is spirited disagreement over the validity of some of the subspecies.

Other raptors are even more diverse. While the peregrine has seventeen subspecies worldwide, the red-tailed hawk has fourteen just within North and Central America and the islands of the Caribbean. They range from the nearly black Harlan's hawk, *Buteo jamaicensis harlani*, which was for years considered a separate species, to the very pale prairie form known as Krider's hawk, *B.j. kriderii*, in which the usual browns and rusts appear bleached.

Not all widespread raptors show a lot of subspecific variation. The northern harrier, which breeds over most of the Northern Hemisphere, has just two subspecies—one in North America (*Circus cyaneus hudsonius*), the other in Europe and northern Asia (*C.c. cyaneus*).

▶ *While most raptor subspecies differ only slightly in appearance, some are dramatically different, like the all-dark Harlan's hawk, an Alaskan form of the red-tailed hawk.*

Breeding ranges of subspecies from U.S., Canada, Mexico, and Central America only.

SPECIES	BREEDING RANGE

BLACK VULTURE

Coragyps atratus atratus—North America south to central Mexico
C.a. brasiliensis—southern Mexico, Central America

TURKEY VULTURE

Cathartes aura aura—American Southwest through Central America
C.a. septentrionalis—eastern North America
C.a. meridionalis—western North America

CALIFORNIA CONDOR

No subspecies recognized.

OSPREY

Pandion haliaetus carolinensis—most of North America
P.h. ridgwayi—Cuba, Bahamas, Belize

HOOK-BILLED KITE

Chondrohierax uncinatus uncinatus—Texas through South America
C.u. mirus—Grenada
C.u. wilsonii—Cuba

AMERICAN SWALLOW-TAILED KITE

Elanoides forficatus forficatus—southern U.S. to southern Mexico
E.f. yetepa—Central America to Argentina

WHITE-TAILED KITE

Elanus leucurus majusculus—North and Central America

SNAIL KITE

Rostrhamus sociabilis plumbeus—Florida, Cuba
R.s. major—southern Mexico to Belize
R.s. sociabilis—Belize through South America

SPECIES	BREEDING RANGE

MISSISSIPPI KITE

No subspecies recognized.

BALD EAGLE

Haliaeetus leucocephalus leucocephalus—southern U.S.
H. l. alascanus—Alaska to Newfoundland, south to Pennsylvania and Oregon

NORTHERN HARRIER

Circus cyaneus hudsonius—North America south to northern Colombia

SHARP-SHINNED HAWK

Accipiter striatus velox—most of Canada and U.S.
A.s. perobscurus—Queen Charlotte Islands, British Columbia
A.s. suttoni—southern New Mexico south through central Mexican highlands
A.s. madrensis—Guerrero State, Mexico
A.s. fringilloides—Cuba
A.s. striatus—Hispaniola
A.s. venator—Puerto Rico

COOPER'S HAWK

No subspecies recognized.

NORTHERN GOSHAWK

Accipiter gentilis atricapillus—most of Canada and northern U. S.
A.g. laingi—Queen Charlotte Islands of British Columbia and temperate rain forests of southeastern Alaska

COMMON BLACK-HAWK

Taxonomy is controversial; following usually assigned:
Buteogallus anthracinus anthracinus—extreme Southwest to South America
B.a. gundlachi—Cuba

continued

Breeding ranges of subspecies from U.S., Canada, Mexico, and Central America only.

SPECIES	BREEDING RANGE

HARRIS' HAWK

Parabuteo unicinctus harrisi—Texas to South America

P.u. superior—California and Arizona to Baja and western Mexico (sometimes included with *P.u. harrisi*)

GRAY HAWK

Asturina plagiata plagiata—extreme Southwest to southern Mexico

A.p. micra—Central America

RED-SHOULDERED HAWK

Buteo lineatus lineatus—eastern North America

B.l. alleni—southern Plains to northern Florida

B.l. extimus—southern Florida and Keys

B.l. texanus—southern Gulf Coast to eastern Mexico

B.l. elegans—coastal California

BROAD-WINGED HAWK

Buteo platypterus platypterus—eastern North America

B.p. antillarum—Lesser Antilles

B.p. brunnescens—Puerto Rico

B.p. cubanensis—Cuba

B.p. insulicola—Antigua

B.p. rivierei—Dominica, St. Lucia, Martinique

SHORT-TAILED HAWK

Buteo brachyurus fuliginosus—Florida, Mexico, Central America

SWAINSON'S HAWK

No subspecies recognized.

SPECIES	BREEDING RANGE

WHITE-TAILED HAWK

Buteo albicaudatus hypospodius—Texas through South America

ZONE-TAILED HAWK

No subspecies recognized.

RED-TAILED HAWK

Buteo jamaicensis alacensis—Alaskan panhandle

B.j. harlani—central Alaska to British Columbia

B.j. calurus—western U.S. and Canada

B.j. kriderii—northern Plains

B.j. borealis—eastern Plains, eastern U.S. and Canada

B.j. umbrinus—Florida

B.j. fuertesi—Texas, northern Mexico

B.j. fumosus—Tres Marias Islands, Mexico

B.j. socorroensis—Socorro Island, Mexico

B.j. hadropus—Mexican highlands

B.j. kemsiesi—Central America

B.j. costaricensis—Central America

B.j. jamaicensis—West Indies

B.j. solitudinus—Cuba, Bahamas

FERRUGINOUS HAWK

No subspecies recognized.

ROUGH-LEGGED HAWK

Buteo lagopus sancti-johannis—Arctic and subarctic from Alaska to Newfoundland

GOLDEN EAGLE

Aquila chrysaetos canadensis—northern and western North America south to central Mexico

SPECIES	BREEDING RANGE

CRESTED CARACARA

Caracara plancus audubonii—extreme southern U.S. through Central America

C.p. lutosus—Guadalupe Island, Mexico (extinct)

C.p. pallidus—Tres Marias Islands, Mexico

AMERICAN KESTREL

Falco sparverius sparverius—most of U.S. and Canada

F.s. paulus—extreme southeastern U.S.

F.s. sparvoides—Cuba

F.s. dominicensis—Jamaica, Hispaniola

F.s. peninsularis—Baja California

F.s. guadalupensis—Guadalupe Island, Mexico

F.s. tropicalis—southern Mexico through Central America

F.s. nicaraguensis—Nicaragua, Honduras

F.s. caribaearum—Puerto Rico to Lesser Antilles

F.s. brevipennis—West Indies

SPECIES	BREEDING RANGE

APLOMADO FALCON

Falco femoralis septentrionalis—northern Mexico to Central America; formerly southwestern U.S.

F.f. femoralis—southern Central America through South America

MERLIN

Falco columbarius columbarius—Canada and extreme northern U.S., including interior Alaska

F.c. suckleyi—coastal British Columbia and Alaska

F.c. richardsonii—northern U.S. Canadian prairies

PRAIRIE FALCON

No subspecies recognized.

GYRFALCON

No subspecies recognized.

PEREGRINE FALCON

Falco peregrinus anatum—originally mountainous areas of eastern and western U.S. and Canada, north to arctic coastal plain

F.p. tundrius—Arctic coastal plain from Alaska to Greenland

F.p. pealei—coastal southeastern Alaska and British Columbia

SUBSPECIES OF EUROPEAN RAPTORS

Includes breeding ranges of subspecies found in Europe west of the Urals.

SPECIES	BREEDING RANGE

OSPREY

Pandion haliaetus haliaetus—eastern and northern Europe, including Britain; Mediterranean basin

EUROPEAN HONEY-BUZZARD

Pernis apivorus apivorus—Europe and northern Asia

SPECIES	BREEDING RANGE

BLACK-SHOULDERED KITE

Elanus caeruleus caeruleus—Iberian Peninsula; also Asia, Africa

RED KITE

Milvus milvus milvus—Europe to western Russia, eastern Mediterranean, northwestern Africa

Includes breeding ranges of subspecies found in Europe west of the Urals.

SPECIES	BREEDING RANGE

BLACK KITE

Milvus migrans migrans—Eurasia west of the Urals, northwestern Africa

WHITE-TAILED EAGLE

Haliaeetus albicilla albicilla—Eurasia from Iceland and Norway to Japan

H.a. groenlandicus—Greenland

LAMMERGEIER

Gypaetus barbatus aureus—Eurasia

EGYPTIAN VULTURE

Neophron percnopterus percnopterus—southern Eurasia, Africa

EURASIAN GRIFFON

Gyps fulvus fulvus—southern Eurasia from Spain to India; Africa

CINEREOUS VULTURE

No subspecies recognized.

SHORT-TOED EAGLE

Circaetus gallicus gallicus—western Eurasia, northern Africa

WESTERN MARSH-HARRIER

Circus aeruginosus aeruginosus—Eurasia east to Lake Baikal

NORTHERN (HEN) HARRIER

Circus cyaneus cyaneus—Eurasia east to Sea of Okhotsk

PALLID HARRIER

No subspecies recognized.

MONTAGU'S HARRIER

No subspecies recognized.

LEVANT SPARROWHAWK

No subspecies recognized.

SPECIES	BREEDING RANGE

EURASIAN SPARROWHAWK

Accipiter nisus nisus—Europe

A.n. wolterstorffi—Sardinia, Corsica

NORTHERN GOSHAWK

Accipiter gentilis gentilis—Europe and western Russia to northern Turkey

A.g. buteoides—northern Scandinavia and Russia

A.g. schvedowi—southeastern Russia to China

COMMON BUZZARD

Buteo buteo buteo—Europe east to Finland and Ukraine

B.b. vulpinus ("steppe buzzard")—Russia east through western Siberia

B.b. menetriesi—Caucasus

LONG-LEGGED BUZZARD

Buteo rufinis rufinis—northern Africa, Greece, and Turkey east to central Asia

ROUGH-LEGGED BUZZARD

Buteo lagopus lagopus—Norway east to central Siberia

LESSER SPOTTED EAGLE

Aquila pomarina pomarina—central Europe from Poland and Baltics southeast to Caucasus

GREATER SPOTTED EAGLE

No subspecies recognized.

SPANISH EAGLE

Aquila adalberti—no subspecies recognized (formerly considered subspecies of *Aquila heliaca*).

IMPERIAL EAGLE

Aquila heliaca—no subspecies recognized (*Aquila adalberti* formerly ranked as subspecies *A.h. adalberti*).

GOLDEN EAGLE

Aquila chrysaetos chrysaetos—northern Britain, Alps, Apennines, Corsica, and Sicily; Norway and Baltics east to central Russia

A.c. homeryi—Spain and northern Africa, Sardinia

BOOTED EAGLE

Hieraaetus pennatus pennatus—southern Europe east to Caucasus

H.p. harterti—Caucasus east to central Asia

BONELLI'S EAGLE

Hieraaetus fasciatus fasciatus—western Europe

LESSER KESTREL

No subspecies recognized

EURASIAN KESTREL

Falco tinnunculus tinnunculus—Europe, northwestern Africa to central Asia

RED-FOOTED FALCON

Falco vespertinus vespertinus—central Europe east to Siberia

ELEONORA'S FALCON

No subspecies recognized.

MERLIN

Falco columbarius aesalon—northern Europe from Britain to Siberia

F.c. subaesalon—Iceland

F.c. pallidus—western Kazakhstan to central Russia

EURASIAN HOBBY

Falco subbuteo subbuteo—Europe and northern Africa east to Kamchatka Peninsula

LANNER

Falco biarmicus feldeggi—southern Europe to Greece

SAKER

Falco cherrug cherrug—eastern Russia east to central Asia

F.c. cyanopus—central Europe to eastern Russia

GYRFALCON

No subspecies recognized.

PEREGRINE FALCON

Falco peregrinus peregrinus—Europe except Mediterranean basin

F.p. brookeri—northern Mediterranean basin

F.p. calidus—Eurasian Arctic

▸▸▸ LUMPERS AND SPLITTERS

Taxonomists struggle constantly with the question of what is and is not a species. Those who tend to divide populations into separate species are known informally as *splitters,* while those who join varieties that resemble each other (or which interbreed) are called *lumpers.*

In the nineteenth century the splitters held sway, and dozens of dubious "species" were recognized based on often minor differences of plumage or size. In

the twentieth century the pendulum swung the other way and the lumpers took over; most of the suspect species were shown to be merely geographic variants of widespread types, and were relegated to subspecies status.

The tide may again be turning, thanks in part to growing DNA evidence, and a number of raptors once considered subspecies have been elevated to full species status. For example, the white-breasted hawk, the rufous-thighed hawk, and the plain-breasted hawk were considered distinct species until the 1950s, when they were lumped as subspecies of the widespread sharp-shinned hawk. But by the early 1990s, the three were again split off from the sharp-shinned hawk when there was enough evidence that the birds are reproductively isolated—the test of a species.

Other species that have been split recently include the common black-hawk, whose coastal Mexican form is now known as the mangrove black-hawk, and the gray hawk, whose Central and South American subspecies are now named the gray-lined hawk.

▸▸ COLOR PHASES AND FORMS

Color variation is common among raptors, a fact that can make identifying similar species even more frustrating for beginners. Color phases are especially frequent among buteos. In North America, red-tailed, Swainson's, rough-legged, ferruginous, broad-winged, and short-tailed hawks routinely have dark phases, which range in frequency from fairly common among roughlegs to extremely rare in broad-wings. In Florida, dark short-tailed hawks actually outnumber "normal" light-phase birds. The white-tailed hawk also has a dark phase, which is rare in the United States but more common in the tropics; likewise, there are two distinct phases of American kestrels, one with a striking white face, the other with a dark gray head, both found only in Cuba and the Bahamas.

◀ Scientists recently split the common black-hawk (opposite page) into two species, as they did with the Central and South American form of the gray hawk (left).

▼ The beautiful Harlan's hawk, a subspecies of the red-tailed hawk, nests in interior Alaska, British Columbia, and Alberta, and winters in the southern Plains.

♂ variant

♂ common;
4 tail bars

♂ variant

♀ variant

♀ dorsal

common: two-toned
dark area in tail

♀ dark
variant

melanistic
(all flying ages)

Juv. ♂ ♀
common patterns:
wing darkens toward trailing edges, one-toned wide
tail band distinct dorsally

▶ Plumage variations in rough-legged hawks, showing how both males and females have light and dark phases. *(From* Handbook of North American Birds, *Vol. 5, Palmer, 1988)*

Phase is a deceiving term, as the plumage color remains constant throughout the bird's adult life (some scientists prefer the word *morph* to avoid confusion). Phases are unrelated to age and, in most cases, to gender, and a nest may contain siblings of both dark and light phases.

It is not uncommon for color phases to have a geographical link. Dark-phase red-tailed hawks are rare in the eastern subspecies, but much more frequent in the West. Dark-morph broad-winged hawks are virtually unknown in most of the species' range, but do occur very rarely in Alberta. Gyrfalcons exhibit three highly variable color phases—white, gray, and dark charcoal gray. White is most common in northern Greenland and northeastern Canada, while darker birds dominate in Labrador and shades of gray almost everywhere else. There is such a range of intergrades within gyrs, however, that many experts avoid using the words "phase" or "morph" to describe them.

In Australia and Tasmania, the gray goshawk has a spectacularly lovely pure-white phase—the only raptor in the world that is normally completely white (other mostly white raptors, like the white hawk of the American tropics, have dark flight-feather edges). The "dark" phase of this species is a pale gray above with light gray barring on the chest.

Gyrfalcons come in a variety of colors, which grade from almost pure white to gray to charcoal-black.

SPECIES	COLOR PHASES	SPECIES	COLOR PHASES

HOOK-BILLED KITE
Black phase in adults and immatures, not recorded in U.S. range.

BROAD-WINGED HAWK
Very rare dark phase found in Alberta only.

RED-TAILED HAWK
Variable phases, primarily in western subspecies; "dark morph" usually dark brown, "rufous morph" deep chestnut color, Harlan's hawk deep black with mottled gray tail.

SWAINSON'S HAWK
All-brown dark phase rare, except common in northern California; also rufous or "intermediate" phase.

ROUGH-LEGGED HAWK
Light- and dark-plumage morphs, each phase with three types (immature, adult male, and adult female); dark phase relatively common, especially in eastern range.

FERRUGINOUS HAWK
Uncommon dark phase, retaining normal light flight feathers and tail; rufous individuals sometimes are considered a separate morph.

SHORT-TAILED HAWK
Light and dark phases; dark most common in Florida.

GYRFALCON
Poorly defined phases intergrading from white in Greenland and northeastern Canada to dark gray in western range; darkest gyrs in Arctic of Labrador and Quebec.

▸▸▸ HYBRIDS

Hybrids—the offspring of parents from different species—are normally rare among wild animals. Differences not only in appearance but also in voice, courtship behavior, habitat, and range all help keep the species distinct.

Among birds, hybridization is most common among groups that form brief pair bonds, like grouse, ducks, and hummingbirds, and least common among those like raptors that generally form monogamous, long-term pairs. Hybridization does happen rarely, however; captive-reared peregrine and prairie falcons have been seen to mate after their release in the wild. A possible Cooper's hawk–goshawk hybrid was reported from New England, although many experts discount it as badly documented; and a black vulture–turkey vulture hybrid often mentioned in books turned out to be a fraud—a black vulture whose head had been painted red.

In Europe, Africa, and Asia (the Old World), hybrids have been found between black kites and red kites, rough-legged hawks and common buzzards, peregrine falcons and lanner falcons, and merlins and Eurasian kestrels. Possible hybrids between harrier species have been seen in Eurasia. In Australia, the white phase of the gray

EUROPEAN RAPTORS WITH COLOR PHASES

SPECIES	COLOR PHASES

EUROPEAN HONEY-BUZZARD
Highly variable plumage ranging from dark chocolate overall to very pale below.

SHORT-TOED EAGLE
Variable amount of dark in plumage; extreme light morph rare.

COMMON BUZZARD
Extremely variable, from black-brown to creamy, with greatest variability in northern populations; "steppe buzzard" (*B.b. vulpinus*) with three distinct phases, including rufous morph.

LONG-LEGGED BUZZARD
Also highly variable, although light birds predominate.

ROUGH-LEGGED BUZZARD
Light- and dark-plumage morphs, each

SPECIES	COLOR PHASES

phase with three types (immature, adult male, and adult female).

BOOTED EAGLE
Light morph most common; dark morph shows light on tail and at base of primaries.

ELEONORA'S FALCON
Three general forms: "black" phase charcoal gray overall, common "normal" phase resembling large hobby, and intermediate "dusky" phase.

GYRFALCON
Poorly defined morphs intergrading from white in eastern Siberia to light gray in Iceland and dark gray in Scandinavia and Russia; "black" phase of Canadian Arctic not found in Europe.

---

goshawk has hybridized with brown goshawks as its habitat has fragmented and its population has declined. While most hybrids are between raptors in the same genus, there is a record of an infertile hybrid between a buteo-accipiter pair—a common buzzard and a northern goshawk.

Perhaps the oddest North American example of a hybrid mating involved a female red-backed hawk, a species native to the Andes that had never before been recorded north of Colombia. In 1987, however, one appeared in central Colorado, setting off shock waves among birders. Her origin was open to debate, although she showed no signs of having ever been in captivity. The next spring she mated with a male Swainson's hawk, and by 1993 had completed her sixth breeding season, producing several young over the years.

Rare as natural hybrid raptors are, they are increasingly common in captivity. Falconers, using artificial insemination, have created a kaleidoscope of hybrids, especially among falcons. The hope is that the hybrid will exhibit the best traits of both parent species. Unfortunately, the reverse is often true, leaving the falconer with, say, a bird possessing the ill temper of a prairie falcon and the wandering tendencies of a gyrfalcon.

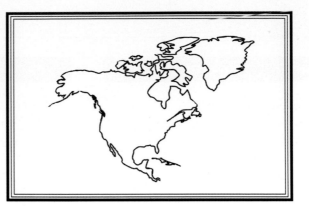

ÉVOLUTION AND DISTRIBUTION

RAPTOR EVOLUTION

Birds, because of their thin-walled, hollow bones, have a notoriously spotty fossil record. That they arose from reptiles is clear, but whether birds evolved from the crocodilelike thecodonts (also ancestors of the dinosaurs), or from small, predatory dinosaurs themselves, continues to stir debate among paleontologists.

Many of the arguments have focused on the famous Jurassic fossil *Archaeopteryx,* which, with its feathered wings and tail, reptilian teeth, and clawed wings, would seem to be the perfect intermediary between reptiles and birds. Yet in most senses, *Archaeopteryx* was closer to modern birds than to a primitive ancestor. Its feathers, so perfectly preserved in the fine-grained German limestone, are asymmetrical, just like those of modern birds, turning each feather into a small airfoil for maximum lift in flight.

Whatever their ancestry, archeornithes like *Archaeopteryx* died out at the close of the Cretaceous period in the mass extinction that also claimed the dinosaurs. Other victims of the great dying were the odontognathes, or toothed birds, which included the loonlike waterbird *Hesperornis.*

With the dinosaurs out of the way, mammals and birds in the Tertiary period were free to expand. Raptors (both diurnal hawks and eagles, and owls) appear rather early in the fossil record of the Tertiary, as does a group of unrelated hunters, the diatrymas—huge, flightless predators with meat cleaver–like beaks.

As incomplete as the fossil record is for birds in general, it is even less revealing for birds of prey. The first modern raptors show up as fossils from the Eocene epoch some fifty million years ago, specifically sea-eagles (kin to modern bald eagles) and booted eagles of the genus *Aquila,* like the golden eagle. The Eocene also saw the first appearance of the genus *Milvus,* which today includes the Old World kites such as the red kite. Falcons evolved considerably later, in the Miocene epoch.

New World–style vultures also first appeared in the early Eocene in the Western Hemisphere with *Paracathartes howardae,* a bird very similar to modern turkey vultures. A vulturine species with no modern counterpart, however, was the strange, long-legged "stilt vulture," *Neocathartes grallator,* which was discovered in Wyoming fossil beds formed along what was once tropical shoreline habitat. Although some specialists dispute its place in the vulture family tree, *Neocathartes'* legs and obvious ground-dwelling habits further support recent DNA evidence that New World vultures are actually descended from storks.

Interestingly, Old World vultures, which descended from accipitrine eagles, were once common in the New World—in fact, a close relative of the modern Egyptian vulture turned up as a fossil in California.

▸▸ Fossil Raptors

Some of the most dramatic raptors appeared during the Pleistocene epoch, which encompassed the periodic ice ages that have gripped the world in the last two million years. This epoch saw the rise of huge land mammals, the Ice Age "megafauna" like mammoths, giant ground sloths, and herds of horses, bison, and camels. These, in turn, supported a cast of enormous avian scavengers, including the teratorns, giant condorlike birds.

Tar pits like Rancho La Brea in California have produced the bones of teratorns like *Teratornis merriami,* which had a wingspan of about twelve feet, two feet larger than modern condors. Other teratorns were even bigger, including *T. incredibilis* from Nevada, with an estimated wingspan of more than sixteen feet. The grandest of all was *Argentavis magnificens,* a late Miocene teratorn from Argentina that stood as tall as a small man and had a wingspan of some twenty-five feet—the largest flying bird ever. (Huge as the teratorns may have been, they were surpassed by the flying reptile *Quetzalcoatlus,* which had an astonishing wingspan of thirty-six feet.)

The La Brea tar pits have been especially productive for raptor fossils, which make up more than half of the total number of bird fossils recovered from the petroleum seeps. Among the extinct species found were teratorns, a condor, a caracara, an Egyptianlike vulture, and two species of eagles—one, the Daggett eagle, unusually long-legged and possibly ground-dwelling. Modern species found in the pits were California condors; sharp-shinned, red-tailed, and rough-legged hawks; northern harriers, kestrels, and prairie falcons; and bald and golden eagles.

With the mass extinction of the giant Ice Age mammals at the close of the Pleistocene, the teratorns were presumably deprived of their food supply, and died off as well. The somewhat smaller California condor survived the Pleistocene extinctions, although its range shrank dramatically. During the ice ages it was found as far east as New York State and Florida, and fossils have been found in caves along the Grand Canyon. By the modern period, however, condors were restricted to a narrow band along the Pacific Coast, from Baja to the Columbia River.

The world's largest eagle is also known only from fossil remains, but it was lost much more recently than the teratorns. Native to New Zealand, Haast's eagle weighed an estimated thirty pounds—compared with fifteen to twenty pounds for a harpy eagle, the largest surviving eagle today, and about nine pounds for a golden eagle. The island was also home to an eagle-size goshawk weighing about seven pounds.

The monstrous eagle apparently fed on moas, the giant, flightless birds of New Zealand—and like the moas, it disappeared about one thousand years ago when the ancestors of the Maori culture arrived on New Zealand. But unlike the moas, which were hunted for food, the eagles may have been killed in self-defense. "What do you think that eagle, specialized at crippling and killing two-legged prey between three and ten feet tall, did when it saw six-foot Maoris?" writes biologist Jared Diamond, who studied New Zealand's birdlife. The answer, for anyone who has seen a smaller hawk or eagle take its prey, cannot fail to bring a chill to the spine.

DISTRIBUTION

It's hard to find a habitat without a resident raptor. While a few travel over open water, none is truly pelagic; likewise, no raptors inhabit Antarctica, or the arctic ice cap.

But aside from those exceptions, raptors of one form or another populate the world from end to end. Climb the Himalayas to twenty-five thousand feet, where the air is so thin a human has a hard time breathing, and you may see a lammergeier vulture soaring even higher. In the extreme heat of the North African desert, sooty falcons fly through the scorching air, while gyrfalcons hunt ptarmigan through the gloom of the months-long winter twilight in the Arctic.

Most of the eighty-one genera of diurnal raptors are restricted to a single continent or region. A few, however, including falcons, buteos, true harriers, and accipiters, have enjoyed more widespread success.

The tropics hold some of the greatest diversity of raptors—which is not surprising, since these fertile regions support the greatest diversity of life in general. In tropical rain forests especially, raptors have expanded to fill an amazing variety of ecological niches, those combinations of habitat and lifestyle that allow species to avoid direct competition with each other.

In the lowland forests of the western Amazon, for instance, a naturalist may find more than thirty species of raptors, from the diminutive, appropriately named tiny hawk, an eight-inch accipiter that appears to specialize in catching hummingbirds, to the enormous harpy eagle, which captures sloths, large monkeys, and other

ERA/PERIOD/EPOCH	DURATION (MILLIONS OF YEARS AGO)	MAJOR EVENTS
MESOZOIC ERA		
Late Cretaceous Period	ending 65 M	Mass extinction at close of Cretaceous wipes out toothed birds, dinosaurs.
CENOZOIC ERA		
Paleocene Epoch	65–53 M	Major divergence of modern birds; many groups first appear. Flightless hunter *Diatryma* evolves.
Eocene Epoch	53–37 M	Sea-eagles (*Haliaeetus*), booted eagles (*Aquila*), kites (*Milvus*) first appear in fossil record. First New World–style vultures appear in North America in early Eocene. "Stilt vulture" *Neocathartes* living in Wyoming in late Eocene.
Oligocene Epoch	37–26 M	New World vultures appear; *Buteo* hawks found in North America.
Miocene Epoch	26–7 M	First falcons found in fossil record. Old World vulture *Paleoborus* living in South Dakota. First true osprey, *Pandion homalopteron*, in California. Huge teratorn *Argentavis magnificens* in Argentina.
Pliocene Epoch	7–2 M	Most modern bird genera in existence.
Pleistocene Epoch	2–.01 M	Giant teratorns in New World; seven species of North American eagles, including ground-dwelling Daggett eagle. California condors and closely related species present across Pacific Coast, southern U.S., New York, and south to Peru.
Recent Epoch	.01 M–present	Teratorns become extinct at close of Ice Age, along with all but two North American eagles. Giant Haast's eagle, New Zealand, extinct c. 1,000 A.D.

heavy treetop prey. Crane hawks poke into tree cavities for lizards, chicks, and frogs using their long, unusually flexible double-jointed legs. Double-toothed kites habitually follow monkey troops, snatching up the lizards and insects the primates scare up, and red-throated caracaras seek out wasp nests, perhaps relying on chemical protection, for the caracaras have a terrible odor, and are rarely stung by even the fiercest wasps.

While species vary from continent to continent, many of the ecological niches that they occupy are fairly similar. A ferruginous hawk in the American West and a tawny-eagle on the Russian steppes both inhabit open grasslands with patches of scrubby trees; both nest in trees if they are available, and on the ground if not; both feed heavily on small mammals.

Similar environmental pressures tend to prod evolution in the same directions regardless of ancestry, a phenomenon known as *convergence*. The most striking example is the close parallel between New World and Old World vultures, the similarities of which even extend to the shape of the skull bones. Vultures on both sides of the Atlantic have bare heads, not because they are closely related, but because they feed on carrion. Feathered heads would become matted with blood from feeding inside large carcasses, while bare skin is much easier to keep clean.

True harriers display a pronounced convergence with owls in the shape of the face and the style of hunting. Often hunting early or late in the day, harriers course low over grasslands or marshes searching for rodents and small birds. They use their eyes, of course, but harriers are unusual among hawks in that they also hunt by sound; they have even evolved distinct facial "disks" of feathers around the face, like an owl's, which serve as twin parabolic reflectors to concentrate sound waves in their ear openings, which are unusually large, also like an owl's.

In fact, northern harriers and short-eared owls hunt much the same prey, in the same habitat, in the same low, quartering fashion. The only difference is that the hawk hunts mostly by day, and the owl mostly by night.

▶ *The hooded vulture of Africa has adapted well to human society, making a living feeding on carrion and scraps of food near villages.*

RAPTOR DIVERSITY
BY CONTINENT

Because many species are found in more than one region, the total exceeds 310.

REGION	NUMBER
▼ Asia (east of Ural Mts., incl. India)	90 species
Africa (incl. Madagascar)	88 species
South America	76 species
North America (incl. Mexico and Central America)	58 species
Australia (incl. New Guinea and surrounding islands)	45 species
Europe (west of Ural Mts.)	39 species
Antarctica	0

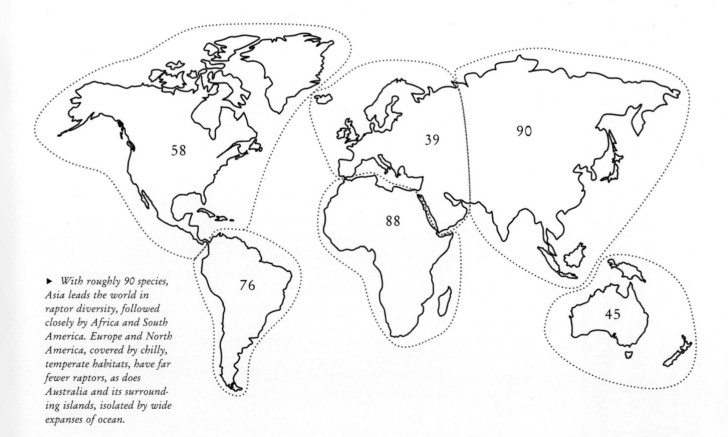

▶ With roughly 90 species, Asia leads the world in raptor diversity, followed closely by Africa and South America. Europe and North America, covered by chilly, temperate habitats, have far fewer raptors, as does Australia and its surrounding islands, isolated by wide expanses of ocean.

Anatomy and Physiology

Physical Structure

▶▶▶ Skeleton

The most remarkable aspect of any bird skeleton is its astonishing delicacy and light weight. Even a sturdily built bird like a golden eagle has a skeletal frame that looks almost wispy—long, thin leg and wing bones, and compact, partially fused bones in the shoulder and pelvic regions. The skull has a solid beak, but the rest is more airs than bone, with huge eye sockets and a brain case that can be crushed easily between a man's fingers.

Nor are the major limb bones any more substantial. The long bones of the wings and legs are hollow, braced from within by crisscrossing support struts. Even the deeply keeled sternum, or breastbone, which provides the foundation for the flight muscles of the chest, is a thin layer of bone through which you can shine a bright light.

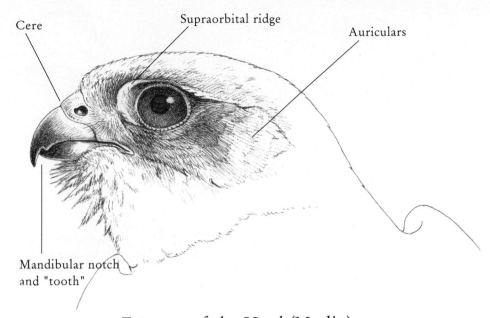

Cere   Supraorbital ridge   Auriculars

Mandibular notch
and "tooth"

Features of the Head (Merlin)

Flying birds must strike a fine balance, structurally speaking. The skeleton must be strong enough to withstand the tremendous stresses exerted by powered flight but be light enough to permit the bird to get off the ground. The thin walls, interior supports, and "pneumatization" (the process that produces the many hollows and air sacs) give the bird strength without excessive weight.

Raptors, which need their feet in order to kill, put an additional demand on their skeletons. The leg bones of most raptors display the ridges and knobs necessary to anchor the powerful muscles that control the feet and talons, and these bones are more substantial than in nonraptors of comparable size.

▸▸▸ BEAK

A raptor's beak is one of its defining features, sharp and deeply hooked for tearing meat that is held down by the feet. The beak is a core of bone covered by a sheath of keratin, the same variety of skin that produces human fingernails, reptilian scales, and cow horns.

The keratin layer continues to grow throughout the raptor's life, constantly being worn back (and the edges and point sharpened) by the normal wear and tear of eating. Raptors in captivity usually require periodic beak coping with a clipper and file, partly because they aren't exposed to the same wear as a wild bird's, and partly because rich captive diets may promote beak growth.

The cutting edge of the upper mandible is rarely straight, and in many raptors forms a sharp, tight S-curve. Often called a "tooth," it is more accurately known as the *mandibular notch,* and is particularly well developed on falcons and some kites. The notch slips easily between the neck vertebrae of the prey to neatly sever the

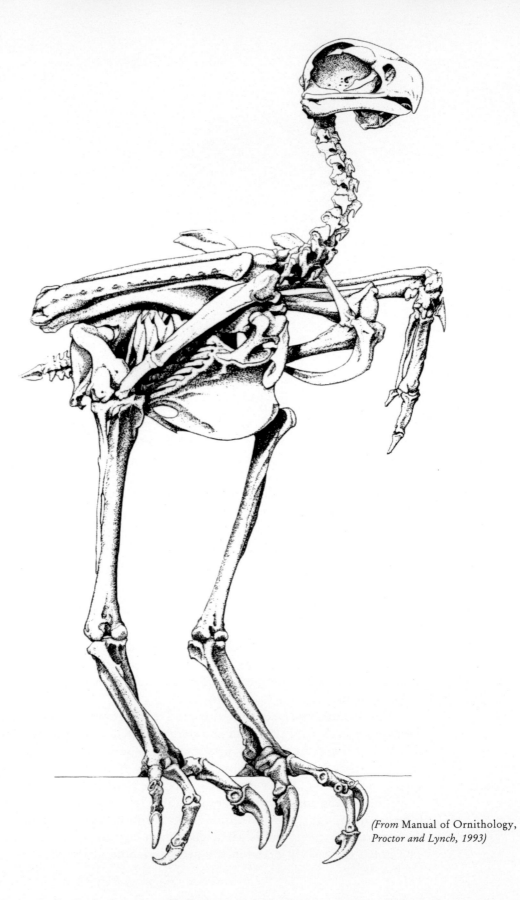

▶ *Stripped of feathers and muscle, the skeleton of a golden eagle shows the long, powerful legs and feet, as well as the delicacy of the bony framework.*

(From Manual of Ornithology, *Proctor and Lynch, 1993)*

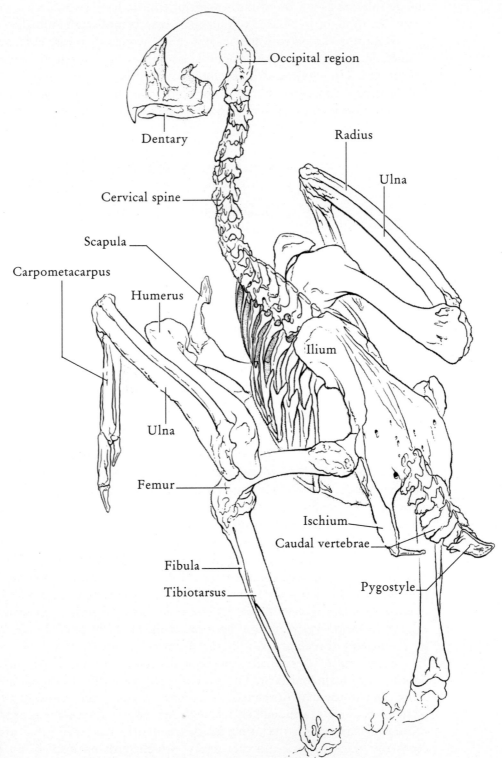

Occipital region

Dentary

Radius

Ulna

Cervical spine

Scapula

Carpometacarpus

Humerus

Ilium

Ulna

Femur

Ischium

Caudal vertebrae

Fibula

Tibiotarsus

Pygostyle

▶ *This view
from above and
behind shows the
major bones of a
golden eagle.*

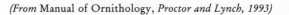

(From Manual of Ornithology, *Proctor and Lynch, 1993*)

spinal cord—an efficient way to administer a *coup de grace*. As their name indicates, the double-toothed kites of the American tropics have two notches on each side of the beak, thought to be used to pull apart insects and small animals.

Raptors, like parrots and several other groups of birds, have an area of bare skin at the base of the upper mandible known as the *cere;* this is where the nostrils are located. The cere is usually brightly colored (yellow or orange in the vast majority of cases) and may change color with age. Immature peregrine falcons, for instance, have a pale bluish cere that becomes lemon yellow with adulthood.

▸▸▸ FEET AND TALONS

▲ *The right foot of a northern goshawk shows the huge, curving talons that are used for grabbing and killing prey. (Credit: Scott Weidensaul)*

Generally speaking, raptors have powerful leg muscles, sturdy toes, and long, curved claws known as talons. Three toes on each foot face forward, while the hind toe, or *hallux,* often sports the longest and heaviest talon.

The tarsometatarsus, the long "leg" bone that rises from the juncture of the toes, seems analogous to a human shinbone, but it is actually a fused, elongated foot bone. And the thigh—the drumstick—is usually hidden up under the feathers. (If this seems confusing, squat down and raise yourself up on your toes, knees close to your chest. That's roughly how a bird stands.)

The strength of a raptor's foot is prodigious. Over the years, in banding hawks or working with injured raptors, I have been "footed" (as the accident is known) more times than I can count, from the needlelike pricks of sharp-shinned hawks to the wound made by a captive redtail that drove one hallux through the side of my left hand so that it curved up through my palm. Once, an associate on a banding project got careless with a large female goshawk he was measuring; the hawk grabbed his upper thigh with all four talons of one foot, bunching up a mass of muscle as big as a tennis ball. It took three of us to pry the claws out.

But a raptor's feet are a food-gathering device first, and a defensive weapon only second. By grabbing rather than biting, a hawk can kill potentially dangerous prey while holding it away from its body; if it used its beak, it would expose its vulnerable eyes and face to attack. The toes are covered in keratin scales, which may expand to form large plates on the front of the *tarsi* (the keeled edges of these plates on the insides of its legs gives the sharp-shinned hawk its name).

Some raptors, especially the booted eagles, tropical hawk-eagles, and some buteos, have feathered tarsi. The rough-legged hawk, for example, has dense feathering right to the base of the toes. This may provide some protection from the bites of small mammals, although this is far from certain. Raptors that feed regularly on venomous snakes, on the other hand, frequently have tarsi that are plated with especially thick scales. And the osprey, which feeds exclusively on fish, has tiny tubercules on the soles of its feet, providing a natural nonslip surface for gripping its wet, wriggling prey.

▶ *With flattened claws and little ability to grip, a black vulture's feet are typical of both New World and Old World vultures.*

Vultures, on the other hand, have nonspecialized feet with fairly short, blunt nails rather than curved talons; some New World vultures cannot even close the foot completely to grab. Since their prey doesn't require killing, this isn't surprising.

As with the beak, the talons are a growing keratin layer over a core of bone, and like the bill they are kept in check by constant wear.

TALE OF THE TOE

One reason why ospreys are usually assigned to their own family is their unusual feet. Unlike most hawks, which have the three long toes pointing forward, and the shorter hallux pointing behind—an anisodactyl arrangement—ospreys have a foot arrangement known as zygodactylus, in which two toes point forward and two back, and all four are roughly the same length.

This is a common arrangement among owls, woodpeckers, parrots, and cuckoos, but is unique among raptors.

What's more, an osprey's talons are exceptionally curved, forming about a third of a circle, and in cross-section they are round. The talons of other raptors form shallower curves, and in cross-section they are flattened or concave on the underside.

METABOLISM

A raptor's warm-blooded body burns fuel like a furnace, at a metabolic rate considerably higher than in most mammals. Metabolic rate depends to large degree, however, on size—smaller birds have a faster metabolism than larger species.

Being warm-blooded—biologists prefer the term *endothermic*—has big advantages. Unlike a lizard or a frog, a raptor can be active at any time, regardless of the air temperature; this opens up many frigid habitats that would otherwise be off-limits. The cost of endothermy is high, however; birds must eat considerably more than cold-blooded vertebrates, like reptiles and amphibians, just to keep fuel in the furnace.

Like most birds', a raptor's heart is markedly larger than that of a mammal of comparable size, and is more efficient at pumping blood; this is especially true for smaller species and those living at higher elevations. But while a bird's heart rate is generally higher than a mammal's of the same size, its respiration rate tends to be lower. This is because birds have evolved a complex, sophisticated network of air sacs and bronchial tubes that complements the lungs, allowing a more complete exchange of fresh and depleted air with each breath. In fact, when a bird inhales, the fresh air bypasses the lungs completely, going first to the abdominal air sacs, and only then recirculating up through the lungs, to the anterior (front) air sacs, and finally back out the trachea to be exhaled.

DIET OF WINTERING FEMALE MERLIN

Estimated diet of a wintering female merlin along Pacific Coast, based on observations from October through February. Figures in parentheses indicate the number of kills actually observed.

112 Least sandpipers (51)
108 Dunlin (49)
 26 Western sandpipers (12)
 18 Sanderlings (8)
  9 Yellow-rumped warblers (4)
  7 Water pipits (3)
  7 Savannah sparrows (3)
  4 Northern phalaropes (2)
  4 Red-winged blackbirds (2)

(Source: Cade, 1982)

FOOD CONSUMPTION

Like all birds, raptors must eat a great deal in order to supply their prodigious energy needs. The amount of food eaten varies with body size. While an eagle obviously consumes a greater amount of meat each day than a small hawk, it actually eats less in proportion to its body size. For example, diminutive raptors like sharp-shinned hawks and American kestrels must eat between twenty and twenty-five percent of their body weight in food each day, while a massive species like a Stellar's sea-eagle can get by with eating less than five percent of its weight.

How often and how much a raptor eats also depends on its age, whether or not it is in breeding condition, the time of year (cold weather requires more food energy than warm), and so on.

▶ *After a heavy meal, a raptor's crop bulges noticeably, as in this merlin. The crop serves as a food storage area, allowing the bird to eat quickly.*

DAILY FOOD CONSUMPTION

SPECIES	GRAMS OF FOOD DAILY	PERCENTAGE OF BODY WEIGHT
Turkey vulture	140 (captive)	10
Stellar's sea-eagle	240 (captive)	3.5
Sharp-shinned hawk	25 (male)	25
Broad-winged hawk	14–23 (summer)	3.5–5.5
Red-tailed hawk	147 (male in winter)	10.2
	136 (female in winter)	11.2
	82 (male in summer)	7.4
	85 (female in summer)	7
Golden eagle	448 (adult)	5.5–6.6
American kestrel	24 (male in winter)	21
Peregrine falcon	104 (cold weather)	11.5
	83 (warm weather)	1

(Source: Palmer, 1988; Brown and Amadon, 1968)

▸▸ DIGESTION

When a raptor eats, food moves from the mouth down the esophagus to the crop, an enlargement of the esophagus that serves as a food storage area. The crop allows the raptor to feed heavily when food is available, and to do so quickly, shortening time spent feeding on the ground when the raptor is vulnerable to attack from other predators. Later, when the bird is perched in safety, the crop passes the meat to the stomach at a more leisurely pace.

A full crop makes a visible bulge, just where the neck and chest meet. It is especially noticeable in flying birds; a sharp-shinned hawk that has just eaten will look as though it has swallowed a golf ball. In some species, such as the striated caracara of the Falkland Islands, when the crop is full, it pokes out of the chest feathers in a skin-covered ball.

A raptor's food is an important source not only of nourishment, but also of water. Many species get a large portion of their daily water needs from the body fluids of their prey, and raptors that live in arid climates, like the desert-dwelling sooty falcon, may get virtually all their water from their prey.

▪▪▪ EXCRETION Birds excrete far less liquid than do mammals, thus conserving water. Instead of liquid urine and solid dung, raptors excrete a viscous, white fluid that quickly dries to a chalky consistency—the "whitewash" that is frequently seen around raptor nests and perches.

▸ An immature red-tailed hawk defecates, ejecting a concentrated, nitrogenous substance known as urates that conserves water.

One unusual benefit of excretion is cooling, employed by New World vultures and their cousins the storks. These birds defecate on their bare legs, which helps to keep them cool as wind blows over the damp surface. (For this reason New World vultures must be marked with wing tags rather than the normal leg bands researchers usually use—the excreta builds up in a heavy, dangerous ring.)

··· PELLETS Compared to owls, diurnal raptors are rather fussy eaters, and most ingest relatively little roughage—bones, fur, and feathers from their prey. The powerful gastric juices in a raptor's digestive system can usually dissolve what is swallowed, but any indigestible bits will be regurgitated as a pellet. While owl pellets usually contain the nearly complete skeleton of small prey animals, pellets among hawks, eagles, and falcons are neither as large nor as informative. Pellets are virtually unknown among New World vultures.

The size of the pellet depends on the species and the size of prey, but generally speaking, pellets are an inch or two long, oblong, and dark gray. Any indigestible item may be included. One golden eagle pellet from Oregon contained an aluminum leg band originally placed on a male wigeon months earlier.

Experiments with captive redtails showed that pellets were regurgitated an average of about eighteen hours after a meal; but in wild raptors, a pellet is expelled roughly once a day, usually early in the morning. A raptor's digestive system, especially that of the falcon, is capable of dissolving complete bones.

Size and Weight

Raptors range in size from the petite to the enormous. The smallest diurnal birds of prey are the sparrow-size falconets of India and Indonesia, which weigh less than two ounces; at the other end of the scale is the Andean condor, with a wingspan of about ten feet and weighing up to twenty-five pounds. (The California condor has a slightly smaller wingspan, but a reputed maximum weight of thirty-one pounds.)

The most massive predatory raptors, all weighing twelve to twenty pounds, include the huge harpy eagle of the American tropics, the Philippine (monkey-eating) eagle, and the spectacular Stellar's sea-eagle of the northeastern Asian coast.

The northern race of the bald eagle is the largest predatory raptor in North America, but although its maximum wingspan of 7.5 feet is close to that of a Stellar's sea-eagle, its weight rarely exceeds ten pounds. American kestrels are commonly called North America's smallest raptors (males weigh 3.5–4 ounces), but in reality, male sharp-shinned hawks are both shorter (averaging about 10 inches versus the kestrel's 10.5) and slightly lighter in weight, often under 3 ounces. West Indian races of sharpshins are even smaller.

Most raptors occupy the middle ground, roughly from the size of a dove to that of a crow. Individual size and weight are largely the results of genetics, of course, but the average size of a species is also affected by environmental factors, including food availability and climate. Small warm-blooded animals have a difficult time retaining body heat, for instance, so it is logical that the smallest raptors tend to be found in temperate or tropical regions.

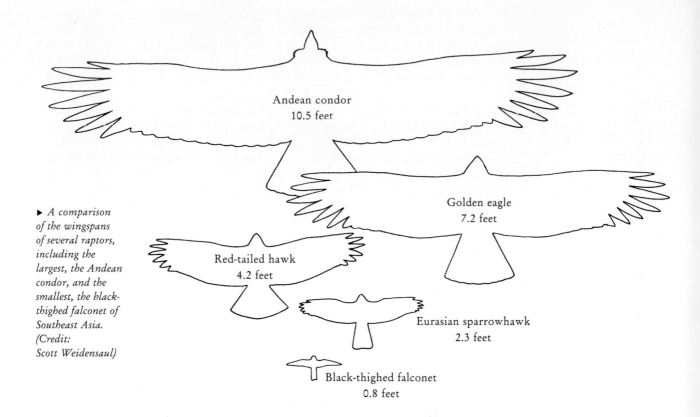

Andean condor
10.5 feet

Golden eagle
7.2 feet

▶ *A comparison of the wingspans of several raptors, including the largest, the Andean condor, and the smallest, the black-thighed falconet of Southeast Asia. (Credit: Scott Weidensaul)*

Red-tailed hawk
4.2 feet

Eurasian sparrowhawk
2.3 feet

Black-thighed falconet
0.8 feet

▸▸ DIFFERENCES BETWEEN THE SEXES

Differences in color, size, or other physical attributes between males and females within a species are known as *sexual dimorphism.* Raptors are unusual among birds in that the females of most species are noticeably larger in size than the males, a phenomenon known as *reverse sexual dimorphism,* or *RSD.* It also occurs in owls, and in a few predatory, nonraptor birds like skuas.

RSD is most evident in active, bird-eating groups like accipiters and falcons, and least in more sluggish raptors like buteos and eagles. In both Old and New World vultures the sexes are either roughly the same in size, or the males tend to be slightly larger than the females.

The differences can be pronounced. Consider sharp-shinned hawks, the most dimorphic species in North America. Females average about 174 grams, or 6 ounces, and range in weight from 144 to 208 grams (5.0–7.2 ounces). Males, on the other hand, average just 103 grams (3.6 ounces), and range from 82 to 125 grams (2.8–4.4 ounces). It's not unusual for a female sharpie to weigh nearly twice as much as her mate.

Dimorphism can vary even among closely related species. Size differences between male and female goshawks are noticeable, but not as extreme as among sharpshins, even though both are accipiters; likewise, among falcons, peregrines and prairie falcons are more strongly dimorphic than American kestrels. Harris' hawks

▶ *Female sharp-shinned hawks are considerably larger than their mates, a phenomenon known as reverse sexual dimorphism that is most evident among active, bird-eating raptors.*

show fairly significant size differences between the sexes, while rough-legged hawks—fellow buteonines—do not.

The reason for the size difference has been debated for years, with competing theories that focus on hunting requirements, reproductive strategies, the demands of migration, and a host of other possible factors. These are considered among the most probable explanations of RSD:

••• EXPANDING THE LARDER   According to this theory, the male and female in a pair can take different sizes of prey, expanding the variety and amount of food available for their chicks, and reducing competition between themselves. A small male Cooper's hawk, so the reasoning goes, could hunt smaller, more agile birds and mammals, while his larger mate could catch heavier prey beyond his ability. There is research to show that this really does happen, at least among accipiters—but this evidence does not explain why males are smaller than their mates.

••• RULING THE ROOST   A number of top raptor authorities believe that females of the most aggressive species, like accipiters and falcons, might choose smaller mates because they represent less of a threat to the females and their chicks. Over time, this phenomenon might produce smaller males overall.

••• BEATING RIVALS   In another reproductive approach, the theory suggests that males that are fit enough to hold a good territory are a scarce "resource," for which females must compete. Bigger females have a better chance of dominating smaller females, and so most often succeed to reproduce, passing on their genes to the next generation.

••• PADDING THE NEST   Laying eggs is an expensive proposition for birds, energetically speaking, so larger females should have an edge over smaller ones. The larger size may also permit bigger clutches, and may even provide more physical padding, so to speak, to protect the egg before it is laid.

No one is sure which theory—if any—is right, although recent studies suggest that the theories pertaining to pair bonds and reproduction, rather than hunting, are more likely.

COMPARISON OF RAPTOR WEIGHTS (IN GRAMS)

SPECIES	MALE Average (weight range)	FEMALE Average (weight range)
NORTH AMERICAN RAPTORS		
Turkey vulture	(2,079–2,387)	(1,990–2,347)
Black vulture	(2,016–2,688)*	
California condor	(8,170–14,070)*	
Osprey	1,403 (1,200–1,600)	1,568 (1,250–1,900)
American swallow-tailed kite	441	423
White-tailed kite	273 (250–297)	330 (305–361)
Mississippi kite	245 (216–269)	311 (278–339)
Bald eagle	4,123	5,244
Northern harrier	364 (298–372)	529 (473–595)
Sharp-shinned hawk	103 (82–125)	174 (144–208)
Cooper's hawk	349 (297–380)	529 (460–588)
Northern goshawk	912 (735–1,099)	1,137 (845–1,364)
Harris' hawk	735 (634–877)	1,047 (913–1,203)
Red-shouldered hawk	555	629
Broad-winged hawk	357 (310–400)	440 (389–460)

Not classified by sex.

SPECIES	MALE Average (weight range)	FEMALE Average (weight range)
Swainson's hawk	808 (693–936)	1,109 (937–1,367)
Red-tailed hawk	1,028	1,224
Ferruginous hawk	1,059	1,231
Rough-legged hawk	1,027	1,278
Golden eagle	3,924 (3,550–4,400)	4,692 (4,050–5,720)
Crested caracara	834	953
American kestrel	114 (94–126)	147 (132–160)
Merlin	155 (129–187)	210 (182–236)
Peregrine falcon	581 (453–685)	817 (719–952)
Gyrfalcon	1,170 (960–1,304)	1,752 (1,396–2,000)

(Sources: Primarily Johnsgard, 1990, citing many sources; also Brown and Amadon, 1968; Terres, 1980; Clark and Wheeler, 1987)

▼

EUROPEAN RAPTORS

SPECIES	MALE Average (weight range)	FEMALE Average (weight range)
Osprey	1,403 (1,220–1,600)	1,568 (1,250–1,900)
European honey-buzzard	684 (510–800)	832 (625–1,050)
Black-shouldered kite	235*	
Red kite	877 (780–950)	1,030 (960–1,100)
Black kite	733 (660–850)	884 (750–1,076)
White-tailed eagle	4,025 (3,075–4,985)	5,116 (3,650–6,560)
Lammergeier	(4,568–5,720)*	
Egyptian vulture	1,889 (1,584–2,180)*	
Eurasian griffon	(6,850–8,200)*	
Cinereous vulture	(7,000–11,500)	(7,500–12,500)
Short-toed eagle	(1,815–1,982)	(1,304–2,324)

* Not classified by sex.

continued

COMPARISON OF RAPTOR WEIGHTS (IN GRAMS)

SPECIES	MALE Average (weight range)	FEMALE Average (weight range)
Western marsh-harrier	520 (427–580)	(600–1,100)
Northern (hen) harrier	367 (362–388)	483 (370–588)
Pallid harrier	313 (235–416)	379 (255–453)
Montagu's harrier	(230–305)	340 (254–435)
Levant sparrowhawk	——————	——————
Eurasian sparrowhawk	137 (117–186)	256 (210–305)
Northern goshawk	865 (571–1,110)	1,414 (820–2,054)
Common buzzard	806 (535–985)	938 (700–1,200)
Long-legged buzzard	(590–1,281)	(1,147–1,543)
Rough-legged buzzard	872 (730–990)	1,040 (845–1,152)
Lesser spotted eagle	(1,340–1,455)	1,500
Greater spotted eagle	1,664 (1,585–1,770)	1,747 (1,670–1,820)
Spanish eagle	(slightly smaller than imperial eagle)	
Imperial eagle	1,954 (1,900–2,100)	2,071 (2,050–2,110)
Golden eagle	3,924 (3,550–4,400)	4,692 (4,050–5,720)
Booted eagle	(1,162–1,210)	——————
Bonelli's eagle	(1,712–2,386)	2,500
Lesser kestrel	129 (92–176)	(145–190)
Eurasian kestrel	180 (113–230)	223 (170–271)
Red-footed falcon	150	167

SPECIES	MALE Average (weight range)	FEMALE Average (weight range)
Eleonora's falcon	350	390
Merlin	186 (150–215)	231 (187–255)
Eurasian hobby	180 (131–222)	225 (141–325)
Lanner	(500–600)	(700–900)
Saker	(730–990)	(970–1,300)
Gyrfalcon	1,170 (960–1,304)	1,752 (1,396–2,000)
Peregrine falcon	622 (550–660)	1,010 (740–1,120)

(Sources: Primarily Brown and Amadon, 1968; also Newton, 1979; Cade, 1982)

▸▸ REGIONAL SIZE DIFFERENCES

Even within a species, regional populations may be quite different in size. As a rule, the more northerly populations tend to be larger (because a larger body makes it easier to stay warm in cold weather), but there are less easily explained differences.

For instance, scientists examining accipiters from four regions of the United States—New Jersey, Wisconsin, Nevada, and California—discovered that Cooper's hawks from the western locales were significantly lighter than eastern birds but had longer wings and tails.

Why? The most likely theory is that when western Cooper's hawks are migrating, they are more reliant on soaring in thermal air currents than are eastern birds, which use deflection currents in the Appalachians or along the coast. The lighter weight and overall larger flight surface would be an advantage under those circumstances.

FEATHERS

Feathers, not flight, define a bird. Many other organisms have evolved powered flight, but no other creatures possess feathers. Likewise, some birds have lost the power of flight, but they are still birds.

The reptilian ancestry of modern birds is fairly clear, so it is a safe guess that feathers evolved from reptile scales; both are made of keratin, and both cover the body in overlapping shingles. But the fossil record is almost completely mute on

TYPES OF FEATHERS

CONTOUR FEATHERS
Surface feathers of body, wings, and tail.

RECTRICES
Long contour feathers of tail.

REMIGES
Flight feathers of wings; primaries extending from "hand," secondaries from "arm," tertiaries located closest to the body.

DEFINITIVE DOWN
Fluffy, insulating layer beneath contour feathers.

SEMIPLUMES
Downy feathers, also forming insulating layer.

POWDER DOWN
Specialized, scattered feathers that disintegrate into fine powder, possibly important for preening.

BRISTLES
Feathers with long, thin quills but no vanes; usually found around mouth, nostrils, and eyes.

FILOPLUMES
Hairlike feathers embedded in nerve bundles; used to monitor position of other feathers.

---

the sequence of events—what intermediate steps were involved to turn solid scales into airy feathers. The change may have come much earlier than once thought, however, and proponents of warm-bloodedness among dinosaurs theorize that feathers would have been of more value initially as insulation than as a means of flight.

Raptors are typical birds in the structure of their feathers. A *contour* (body) feather has a stiff central shaft surrounded by the soft, flexible *vane;* toward the base of the feather, the vane becomes downy to increase insulation.

The vane is made up of individual barbs, like tree branches, which in turn have very fine barbules running their length like fuzz. Barbules have microscopic hooks, which allow the barbs to be smoothed back into a single surface, whether by your fingers or the beak of a preening bird. Restored to its original condition, the feather is ready to deflect water or wind.

Of course, the exact design of a feather depends on what part of the body it comes from. While most body feathers have some downiness at their bases, raptors (like virtually all birds) also have very fluffy down feathers that grow close to the body, beneath the water-repellent layer of the contour feathers. By trapping air, the down layer provides unmatched insulation. The flight feathers of the wings—the primary feathers on the "hand," and the secondary feathers along the "arm"—are elongated and very stiff, with thickened shafts. There are bristles around the eyes and mouth, and specialized feathers known as *filoplumes* that help the bird's brain monitor its flight. The bases of these long, fine quills are embedded in nerve packets, and transmit information about the position of nearby feathers.

Feathers are not distributed randomly on a raptor's body. Most are grouped in eight distinct concentrations known as *feather tracts,* which run (on most birds) down the back of the head along the spine, from the throat down both sides of the chest and stomach, along the leading edge of the wings, and behind the legs. While the function of the feather tracts is still debated by ornithologists, some practical applications for the birds are obvious. While feather tracts are permanent, a temporary gap known as a *brood patch* forms in females (and males, in some species) during the breeding season, allowing the incubating hawk to nestle its eggs directly against its warm skin.

Each contour and flight feather is anchored by a set of tiny, interlocking muscles that allow the bird to move the feather—fluffing the feathers when it's cold, flattening them to increase heat loss or make its body shape more aerodynamic. Many raptors will also raise their body feathers, especially those around the face, when confronting a predator or an intruder. The effect is to make these raptors seem even larger and more formidable than they already are.

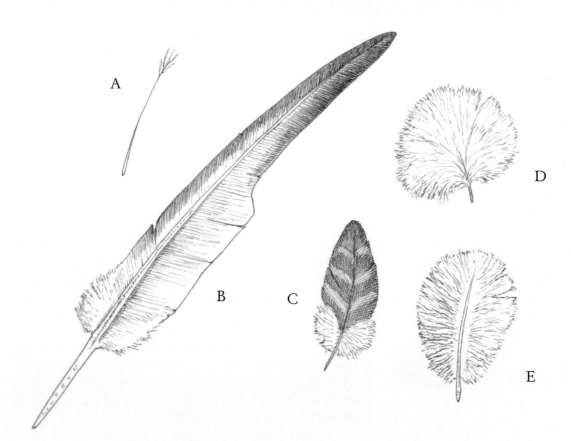

▲ *Five major feather types: A) Filoplume. B) Contour feather (primary feather). C) Contour feather (body feather). D) Down. E) Semiplume. (Credit: Scott Weidensaul)*

▶ *A peregrine falcon chick still wears a crown of juvenile down, which is rapidly being replaced by contour feathers.*

▲ *A young red-tailed hawk's overall color—brown back, brown barred tail, and light underside—is determined by genetics.*

▸▸▸ FEATHER COLOR

Raptors are not among the most colorful of bird families. None has the brilliant greens, blues, or crimsons found on many songbirds; most are a combination of browns, grays, and white that can make them maddeningly difficult to identify.

Feather color is determined primarily by genetics and, to a much lesser degree, by the environment. Barring a genetic glitch, a young red-tailed hawk will always be dull brown above, creamy white with varying amounts of streaking below; the tail will be brown or some shade of rust, with thin brown bands.

But as the young bird ages, and its juvenile feathers become exposed to months of sunlight and rain, they change subtly. The edges of the flight feathers and larger contour feathers become ragged from wear, and the sun bleaches much of the richness from their color. When the hawk begins to molt, the new feathers stand out dramatically from the old, and until the molt is complete, the hawk may have a patchy, piebald look.

The drab colors of most raptors probably help camouflage them, both from their prey and from their enemies (roosting or nesting hawks are at risk from other raptors, including owls). The most common pattern in raptors—indeed, in all animals—is known as *countershading*, in which the upper parts are dark and the under parts light. Sunlight striking the back lightens the upper parts, throwing the under parts

into darkening shadow. The result is that the colors even out, and the bird "flattens"
to the eye, thus becoming less noticeable. Countershading is not a perfect camouflage, however. Even a hawk with a pure white stomach, backlit while soaring
overhead, is going to be silhouetted against the sky.

Feather pigment is valuable for more than just color, however. The dark pig-
ments known as *melanins* actually make the feather barbs stronger and more resistant to abrasion—the reason so many otherwise white birds have black wing and tail
tips.

··· ALBINISM AND COLOR ABNORMALITIES   Because of a genetic
quirk, raptors are sometimes born with color abnormalities, ranging from an
absence of pigmentation (*albinism*) to greater than the average amounts of
melanin pigment (*melanism*).

Complete albinos—those lacking all pigmentation, including in the eyes—are
relatively rare. Not only are such birds very conspicuous, but they often suffer
from poor eyesight, which reduces any raptor's chances for survival.

Partial albinism, which affects only part of the body, or leaves the entire
plumage looking bleached, is much more common in raptors, especially in red-
tailed hawks, in which it ranges from birds with patches of white on the body to
birds that are all white except for the eyes and, perhaps, the quills of the feathers.
Because the eyes in partial albinos are usually pigmented, sight is better and survival rates are much higher. One albinistic red-tailed hawk near my home—an
all-grayish-white bird except for dark eyes, dark cheeks, and a faintly pink tail—
survived for at least eleven years, raising chicks most summers with a normally
pigmented male. The chicks, although they carried the recessive gene for albinism,
were also normally pigmented.

ABNORMAL PLUMAGES OF CERTAIN SPECIES

TURKEY VULTURE
Complete and partial albinism, bleaching

BLACK VULTURE
Complete albinism

OSPREY
Limited partial albinism

SHARP-SHINNED HAWK
Partial albinism, bleaching

COOPER'S HAWK
Bleaching

NORTHERN GOSHAWK
Partial albinism

RED-SHOULDERED HAWK
Complete and partial albinism

BROAD-WINGED HAWK
Complete and partial albinism

SWAINSON'S HAWK
Limited partial albinism

RED-TAILED HAWK
Partial albinism; melanism

BALD EAGLE
Partial albinism, bleaching

GOLDEN EAGLE
Partial albinism

AMERICAN KESTREL
Complete and partial albinism

MERLIN
Partial albinism

PEREGRINE FALCON
Complete and limited partial albinism

PRAIRIE FALCON
Partial albinism, bleaching

(Sources: Clark and Wheeler, 1987; Terres, 1980)

Melanism, the condition in which too much pigment renders the hawk gray or black, is much less common than albinism. Even rarer are *erythrism,* an excess of red pigment, and *xanthochromism,* an excess of yellow. Rarest of all is the condition known as *gynandromorphism,* in which the bird has a mix of male and female plumage; this has been recorded in American kestrels.

▸▸ MOLTING AND PLUMAGE SEQUENCES

An individual feather has a life span, and when it wears out, it is replaced, a process known as *molting.* The replacement feather begins growing inside a feather sheath, a thin, pencil-shaped structure poking out of the skin. Also known as a *blood quill,* the sheath is soft and engorged with blood supplying the growing feather inside. As it grows it displaces the old feather, and when mature the sheath splits, revealing the new feather rolled up inside. The length of time it takes a new feather to grow varies, requiring up to seventy-five days in large species like golden eagles.

Raptors molt in a predictable sequence, starting a few weeks after hatching when a chick's first juvenile feathers begin poking through their natal down. In its first years, a chick may also undergo a radical change of color as it moves from juvenile plumage to adult plumage.

For adult raptors in North America, the molt generally begins during the breeding season and ends sometime in autumn. They obviously cannot molt all their flight feathers at once, as waterfowl do—even the loss of a few wing and tail feathers may affect their flying ability. To minimize flying problems, wing and tail feathers generally molt symmetrically, with matching feathers from the left and right sides falling out at roughly the same time. Small and medium-size raptors generally replace all of their feathers annually, while the biggest, such as eagles, may take two or three years to accomplish the task.

►►► SEXUAL DIFFERENCES IN PLUMAGE

Only in a relatively few species of raptors are males and females colored differently. In the United States and Canada, only the northern harrier, snail kite, American kestrel, and merlin have noticeably different plumages for males and females, although in adult rough-legged hawks males generally have tails with multiple bands, and females generally a single wide, terminal tail band. With these and other raptors that show sexual color differences, the females tend to be colored like the immatures of that species.

Like size differences between males and females, color differences are a form of sexual dimorphism. But unlike reversed dimorphism for size, the causes of which are unclear, most scientists agree that color differences stem from mate selection.

NORTH AMERICAN RAPTORS with SEXUAL PLUMAGE DIFFERENCES

SPECIES	ADULT MALE	ADULT FEMALE
Osprey	Plain chest.	Faint "necklace" in most females.
Snail kite	Sooty gray, white at base of tail; legs, facial skin bright red.	Streaked with brown; legs and face yellow-orange.
Hook-billed kite	Gray barring on undersides.	Rufous barring on undersides; rusty collar on nape of neck.
Northern harrier	Pale gray with black wingtips.	Brown and buff streaking overall.

continued

SPECIES	ADULT MALE	ADULT FEMALE
Sharp-shinned hawk	Back bluer than female; only slight difference.	Back browner than male, less barring on belly, skin color fainter; only slight difference.
Cooper's hawk	Back bluer than female; only slight difference.	Back browner than male, less barring on underside; only slight difference.
Northern goshawk	Barring finer, few vertical streaks; only slight difference.	Heavier barring on undersides, more vertical streaks; only slight difference.
Rough-legged hawk	3–4 dark bars on tail, belly usually white or mottled; highly variable.	Usually dark band at tail tip, belly usually heavily barred; highly variable.
Golden eagle	Several thin gray bands across dark tail.	One wide, one thin gray band on tail.
American kestrel	Bluish wings; rusty tail with dark terminal band; belly spotted or clear.	Rusty wings; rusty tail with thin barring; belly streaked.
Merlin	Upper parts bluish.	Upper parts brownish.
Aplomado falcon	More white streaking in dark belly band.	Little streaking in belly band.
Peregrine falcon	Under parts generally whiter; less barring.	Under parts more richly colored; upper parts with brownish cast.

SPECIES	ADULT MALE	ADULT FEMALE
Osprey	Plain chest.	Faint "necklace" in most females.
Western marsh-harrier	Dark back; rusty undersides; gray wings and tail.	Dark brown overall; cream forehead, throat, and shoulders.
Northern (hen) harrier	Pale gray with black wingtips.	Brown and buff streaking overall.
Pallid harrier	Very pale gray with small area of black on wingtips.	Brown and buff streaking overall.
Montagu's harrier	Pale gray with black wingtips; black line at base of primaries.	Brown and buff streaking overall.
Levant sparrowhawk	Blue-gray above; white undersides finely barred with rust.	Browner above; more heavily barred below.
Eurasian sparrowhawk	Bluer above; undersides barred with rust.	Browner above; undersides barred with gray-brown.
Northern goshawk	Generally grayer than female.	Somewhat browner than male.
Rough-legged buzzard	3–4 dark bars on tail, belly usually white or mottled; highly variable.	Usually dark band at tail tip, belly usually heavily barred; highly variable.
Bonelli's eagle	Darker brown above.	Somewhat lighter brown above.
Lesser kestrel	Gray head, wing patches, tail; unmarked chestnut shoulders.	Rusty, heavily barred upper parts, wings, and tail.

continued

EUROPEAN RAPTORS WITH SEXUAL PLUMAGE DIFFERENCES

SPECIES	ADULT MALE	ADULT FEMALE
Eurasian kestrel	Grayish head and tail; back and shoulders rusty with some barring.	Rusty, heavily barred upper parts, wings, and tail.
Red-footed falcon	Dark gray except for reddish thighs, undertail coverts.	Rusty head and belly; gray back with barring.
Merlin	Upper parts bluish.	Upper parts brownish.
Eurasian hobby	More brightly colored than female; little streaking on thighs and undertail coverts.	Browner than male; heavier streaking on thighs and undertail coverts.
Lanner	Back and wings bluer than female.	Browner overall than male.
Peregrine falcon	Under parts generally whiter; less barring.	Darker on lower back; undersides more heavily barred.

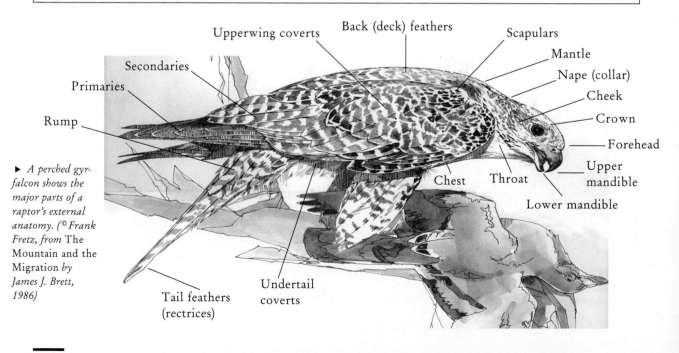

▶ *A perched gyr-falcon shows the major parts of a raptor's external anatomy. (© Frank Fretz, from* The Mountain and the Migration *by James J. Brett, 1986)*

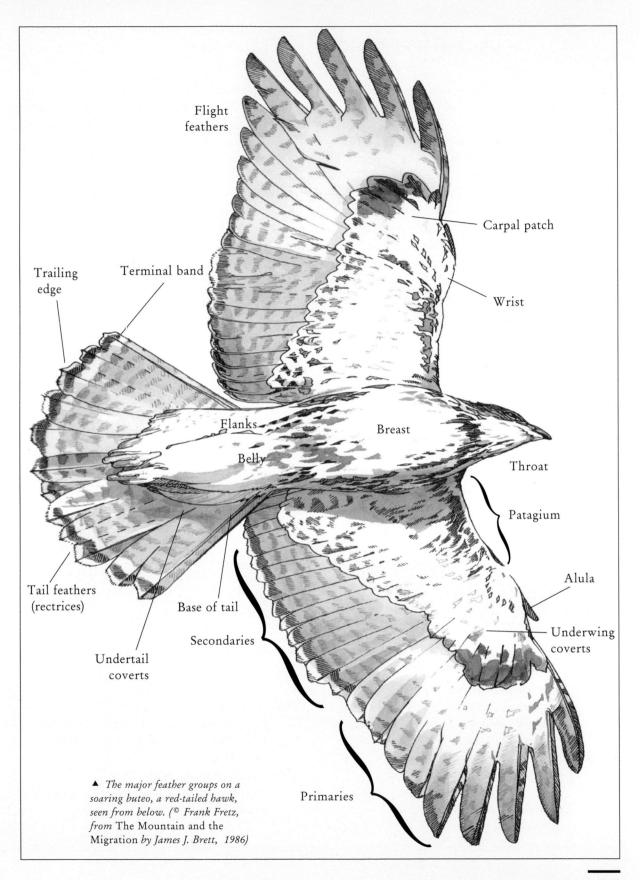

Flight
feathers

Carpal patch

Wrist

Trailing
edge

Terminal band

Flanks

Breast

Belly

Throat

Patagium

Alula

Tail feathers
(rectrices)

Base of tail

Secondaries

Underwing
coverts

Undertail
coverts

Primaries

▲ *The major feather groups on a
soaring buteo, a red-tailed hawk,
seen from below. (© Frank Fretz,
from* The Mountain and the
Migration *by James J. Brett, 1986)*

▸▸ AGE DIFFERENCES IN PLUMAGE

Most raptors have distinct immature and adult plumages, which may be so completely different that people have mistaken the birds for entirely separate species. Even John James Audubon made such an error; when he shot an all-brown, immature bald eagle of the huge northern race on the upper Mississippi in 1814, he assumed it was a new species, which he named the Bird of Washington in honor of the late president.

Immature and subadult raptors are usually a cryptic mix of browns, buffs, and black and white; and many juveniles of both sexes resemble the adult female if the species is dimorphic—which is perhaps a way for them to avoid territorial disputes with breeding adults. Bold or noticeable plumage characteristics in adults—a red-tailed hawk's brick red tail, or the widely barred tail of a broad-winged hawk—are usually missing from youngsters, presumably for the same reason. As adult flight feathers molt in, they give the trailing edge of the wings and tail a ragged, chewed look.

An immature's flight feathers are often somewhat longer than an adult's of the same species, perhaps to compensate for their unpracticed flying. It is not unusual for an experienced hawk-watcher to age a redtail that is little more than a silhouette, just because the wings and tail look a bit long. Among Cooper's hawks, on the other hand, immatures have a longer tail but shorter wings, and are lighter in weight than their parents—a combination that makes them more maneuverable, giving them an edge in the kind of twist-and-dodge hunting they must learn.

The length of time required for an immature to acquire adult plumage varies from species to species, from a little more than a year for some of the smaller species like kestrels to up to five years for the largest raptors, such as bald eagles and California condors. A few raptors—bald eagles are again an example—go through several intermediate stages before reaching full adult plumage.

▸ *Bald eagles start as all-dark immatures, and over the course of four or five years molt into the white head and tail of adulthood.*

 ## PLUMAGE STAGES IN BALD EAGLES

NESTLING
Covered in gray down.

IMMATURE (FIRST WINTER)
All-brown body; extensive white mottling on underside of wing. Tail brown with white at base.

WHITE-BELLY I (SECOND WINTER)
Stomach white with dark streaking; dark hoodlike head and chest. Light triangle on back. More white mottling on tail.

WHITE-BELLY II (THIRD WINTER)
Even more extensive areas of white mottling on undersides.

TRANSITIONAL
Blend of immature and adult plumage; white head often speckled with dark feathers.

ADULT (BY FIFTH WINTER)
Trademark white head and tail; dark brown body.

▶ *Many raptors, like this bateleur, have colorful patches of facial skin, which may serve as visual displays in courtship and aggression. The skin changes from blue-green in young bateleurs to scarlet in adults.*

▸▸▸ SKIN COLORATION

In most birds the skin is completely hidden, but colored skin patches play an important display role among many raptors. The vultures, especially the king vulture of the New World tropics, have raised this color display to its highest form. In this bizarre and beautiful species, the head and neck are brilliant orange, and the head is covered with a fine coat of purplish, hairlike bristles; the red beak is surrounded by orange wattles, and the eyes are white.

While such flashy displays are rare, many raptors do have small areas of colorful skin on the face, especially around the eyes. The snail kite has a patch of scarlet skin between the fleshy cere at the base of the bill and the eyes, which are surrounded by red eyelids. Similar facial patches are found in bateleur eagles, serpent-eagles, African harrier-hawks, secretary-birds, caracaras, and forest-falcons, among others. Colorful eyelids are a hallmark of many falcons.

The color of skin patches often changes with age. On young peregrine falcons the cere, legs, and skin around the eyes are bluish, but they change to bright yellow with maturity. Other raptors, like harrier-hawks, can change or deepen the facial color in seconds by blushing. Crested caracaras can change the color of their facial skin from orange to yellow in moments. Such changes are usually the result of excitement, such as in courtship or territorial defense.

4

Řaptor Senses

Vision

"Eyes like a hawk" isn't an empty compliment. Raptors have some of the most highly developed visual capacities of any of the vertebrates, and they are well above the level enjoyed by humans. Some species of eagles have been shown to be able to detect the movements of prey animals more than a mile away.

That said, it is necessary to stress that science has very little hard information on exactly what, and how well, raptors see. The usual comparison—that raptors can see as well as humans with 8-power binoculars—is both misleading and exaggerated. Hawks do not possess highly magnified vision, although raptors do have small depressions on the retina that create a slight magnification. More importantly, they are apparently able to discriminate fine details at a much greater distance and in much less time than humans, thanks to an abundance of receptor cells in the retina. While some species, including Old World vultures, have up to eight times the receptor cells of a human eye, biologists have downgraded the degree of visual acuity in most raptors from eight times that of humans to about two and a half or three times—which is still very impressive.

A raptor's eye still shows much of its reptilian ancestry, including a bony ring that encases it within the eye socket. Perhaps the most remarkable aspect of a raptor's eye is its size, huge even by the relatively enormous standards of bird eyes. An eagle's eyes are larger than a grown man's, even though the eagle's body weight is roughly one-twentieth that of a human being. Because only a small portion of the eye is visible from the outside, the true size of a raptor's eyes is apparent only when you look at a skull. The eye sockets are cavernous, almost meeting in the middle of the skull, accommodating the relatively deep eyes. This greater distance from lens to retina is one of the reasons raptors have such marked visual acuity.

Encased in bone, a raptor's eyes can move only slightly, and the bird changes its viewpoint by moving its entire head. There are specialized muscles surrounding the eye, however, that permit the hawk to change the curvature of the lens, rapidly altering the focus—an essential mechanism for a creature that dives after fast-moving prey.

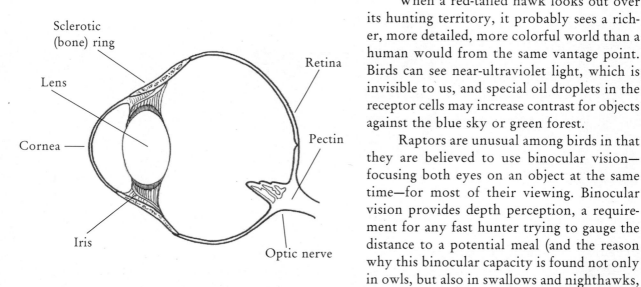

▲ A raptor eye is encased in a bony sclerotic ring, and is much larger, proportionately, than the eyes of mammals. (Credit: Scott Weidensaul)

When a red-tailed hawk looks out over its hunting territory, it probably sees a richer, more detailed, more colorful world than a human would from the same vantage point. Birds can see near-ultraviolet light, which is invisible to us, and special oil droplets in the receptor cells may increase contrast for objects against the blue sky or green forest.

Raptors are unusual among birds in that they are believed to use binocular vision—focusing both eyes on an object at the same time—for most of their viewing. Binocular vision provides depth perception, a requirement for any fast hunter trying to gauge the distance to a potential meal (and the reason why this binocular capacity is found not only in owls, but also in swallows and nighthawks, which must pinpoint small, moving insects). An exception to the binocular vision rule is found in some of the vultures, which lack both it and the ability to rapidly focus the eye.

▶▶▶ EYE COLOR

A characteristic of many raptor families is that eye color changes from youth to adulthood. This is especially common among accipiters, which often develop fiery red or orange irises when they reach adulthood.

While it is possible to accurately judge the age of many hawks by their plumage patterns, eye color is a much less reliable gauge; one three-year-old sharp-shinned hawk may have pale orange eyes, while another of the same age may already have the blood red eyes of an adult. Among Cooper's hawks, the eyes of the males deepen in color faster than those of females of the same age.

▲ *The color of a raptor's eyes often changes with age. This female Cooper's hawk, although wearing blue-gray adult plumage, has orange eyes between the yellow of youth and the blood-red of maturity.*

In female northern harriers, however, the change from the brown iris of an immature to the yellow iris of an adult occurs at a predictable rate, and researchers have used the percentage of brown flecking to judge the hawk's age up to age five, when the eye becomes completely yellow. This method doesn't work with males, whose eyes turn from dark gray to yellow within their first year.

Eye color probably plays an important role in courtship and dominance. Because full adult eye color isn't attained until well after the bird has reached breeding age, it may serve potential mates as a clue to the hawk's level of fitness and ability to survive. The pale eyes of an immature may also deflect some of the aggression of territorial adults, which may see the young bird as less of a threat.

While studying Cooper's hawks, biologists Noel and Helen Snyder noticed that chicks often mistook the red eye of the adult for a piece of meat and pecked at it with their sharp, hooked bills—a dangerous situation, and one that would seem to decrease the advantage of having a colorful eye. Yellow eyes, on the other hand, were ignored by feeding chicks. They believe that the long period of color change, from yellow to orange to red, gives the adults several seasons of experience in feeding chicks before they have to contend with the dangers of enthusiastic offspring.

OSPREY
Pale yellow to bright yellow.

HOOK-BILLED KITE
Black to white.

HONEY-BUZZARDS
Brown to yellow.

SCISSOR-TAILED KITE
White to red.

MISSISSIPPI KITE
Brown to red.

SEA-EAGLES
Variable; may remain brown (white-bellied sea-eagle), lighten from brown to amber (African fish-eagle), or turn from brown to yellow (bald eagle, Pallas' fish-eagle, Stellar's sea-eagle, white-tailed eagle).

OLD WORLD VULTURES
Brown to red or yellow (lammergeier, Eurasian griffon, Egyptian and red-headed vultures), or may remain brown (white-backed, white-rumped, cinereous vultures).

HARRIERS
Brown to yellow (may remain brown in a few).

CHANTING-GOSHAWKS
Whitish or yellow to red.

ACCIPITERS
Grayish (nestlings) or yellowish (immatures) to brilliant yellow, orange, or red.

BUTEOS
Variable; may remain brown (zone-tailed and red-backed hawks), yellow to brown (red-shouldered, red-tailed, and broad-winged hawks), or brownish to yellow (ferruginous hawk).

BOOTED EAGLES
Brown to yellow (lesser spotted eagle); may remain brown or lighten somewhat (golden, wedge-tailed, and steppe eagles).

HAWK-EAGLES
Variable; brown to yellow (Bonelli's, crowned, and martial eagles), yellow to orange (ornate hawk-eagle), or may remain brown (rufous-bellied eagle).

SECRETARY-BIRD
Gray to brown.

CARACARAS
Variable; may remain same or lighten.

FOREST-FALCONS
May remain brown (collared forest-falcons) or turn yellow (barred forest-falcons).

FALCONS
Remain dark brown; turn white in greater kestrel.

▸▸▸ EYE PROTECTION

One of the reasons raptors look so imperious is the presence of bony "brows" above the eye, which give the birds a glowering, serious look. Known as *supraorbital ridges,* these hard shields minimize glare on the protruding eye, and offer a degree of protection when the raptor is flying through dense cover.

▲ Bony ridges
project above
the eyes of most
raptors, like this
red-shouldered
hawk, protect-
ing and shading
the eye.

The eyeball is also protected by a translucent "third eyelid" known as the *nic-titating membrane*, which is drawn from front to back rather than vertically, like the true eyelids. The nictitating membrane is used regularly to moisten the eye, especially in flight, but it is also drawn across the eye at the moment of attack, when flying through brush, or even when feeding the young—anytime when there is a chance the eye might be scratched or damaged.

HEARING

A raptor's hearing, while quite sharp, is not nearly as highly developed as its visual ability. The ears are simple openings in the skull, behind and below the eye near the jaw hinge, and covered with sparse feathers known as *auriculars*. The muscles anchoring the auriculars form a shallow funnel, which presumably helps direct sound into the ear.

Stretched across the ear hole is an eardrum, or *tympanum,* covering the middle ear. This structure transmits sound waves into the fluid-filled inner ear, or *cochlea,* where hair cells in turn translate them into nerve impulses for transmission to the brain.

▸▸▸ HUNTING BY SOUND

Hawks, eagles, and other diurnal raptors are almost exclusively visual hunters—but there are some intriguing exceptions. A few groups have apparently developed an ability to hunt largely by sound, at least in some situations.

Harriers are the best examples. A dozen or so species are found over the Northern Hemisphere, and all exhibit a distinct facial ruff—a rim of short, dense feathers surrounding the face, which serves to funnel sound waves into the unusually large ear openings, just as with owls. Unlike with owls, however, harriers' ear openings are symmetrical, so sound waves sometimes reach both ears at the same instant, which may limit a bird's ability to locate sounds with pinpoint accuracy.

The northern harrier usually hunts by flying within a few feet of the ground, with its head cocked, using both sight and sound to locate small mammals and birds. Researchers have shown that harriers can find vole nests hidden in thick grass by listening for the squeaks of the rodents.

Most hawks have an excellent sense of hearing. Cooper's hawks have been known to hunt quail by zeroing in on the males' ringing calls, and it is likely that other raptors do much the same thing.

Besides harriers, a few other raptors also have facial ruffs. The forest-falcons of Central and South America, which hunt dense, shadowy rain forests and are at least partially nocturnal, have a truncated version of a ruff around the back edge of the face, and enlarged ear openings; and harpy eagles from the same region also have pronounced ruffs.

The bat hawk of Africa and the East Indies also has partially nocturnal habits, chasing bats in the gloom of dusk, although it does not hunt by sound. Hunting is done completely by sight, aided by the bat hawk's unusually large eyes. Several falcons— the Eurasian hobby, sooty falcon, Madagascar kestrel, and Dickinson's kestrel—are occasionally nocturnal or crepuscular, and Dickinson's kestrel has exceptionally large eyes for its head size. Hobbies, in fact, often hunt bats by moonlight.

▾▾▾ SMELL AND TASTE

Birds can smell and taste, although the tiny size and limited development of their brains' olfactory lobes make it unlikely that the senses are very important. The assumption has always been that birds, since they hunt by sight and bolt their food, rather than chew, have little use for either smell or taste.

▸ *The huge harpy eagle of Latin America has a pronounced facial disk, and may rely on its sense of hearing to help it locate prey in the forest canopy.*

▸ Inset *Unlike most raptors, turkey vultures have a keen sense of smell, which they use for locating hidden carcasses.*

*W*hile most birds have a poorly developed sense of smell, vultures are one of the exceptions—although the debate over whether or not they use smell to locate food goes back centuries.

John James Audubon conducted experiments in the 1820s that (to his mind) proved that turkey vultures use only sight, not smell, to find carrion. Other ornithologists of Audubon's day argued the opposite position just as heatedly.

Audubon, it turns out, was wrong. New World vultures tend to have larger olfactory lobes than those of other raptors. This trait is especially evident in turkey vultures (which have been known to gather near leaking natural gas pipelines, lured by a rotten-meat odor added to the gas) and their tropical cousins, the greater and lesser yellow-headed vultures.

Recent experiments with hidden chicken carcasses show that not only can turkey vultures find carrion by smell, they can also discriminate between the merely spoiled and the completely putrefied, avoiding meat that has become too rotten for even their strong stomachs. In experiments in Central America, biologist David Houston found that turkey vultures could not find a hidden carcass less than twelve hours old, presumably because it had not yet developed much odor; a day later, however, they were easily able to track down the food.

Another subject of ongoing debate is the sense of smell in the spectacular king vulture of Central and South America. The king has somewhat enlarged olfactory lobes, and some researchers believed it hunted mostly by smell, but more recent experiments with captives suggest it does not. Instead, it and the black vulture (which also seems to lack a sense of smell) watch for descending turkey and yellow-headed vultures to signal the location of a carcass. This arrangement seems to be mutually advantageous, because the much larger and more powerful king can open big carcasses with tough skin that would defeat the smaller birds.

Interestingly, New World condors and Old World vultures do not appear to have evolved a significant sense of smell, probably because most species live on open plains or in mountains, where carcasses can be easily found by sight.

OTHER SENSES

*S*cience is only beginning to explore the other possible senses that birds may possess. For example, pigeons and a few other birds have been shown to have crystals of a mineral known as magnetite in their heads, which allows them to sense—and navigate by—the earth's magnetic field; pigeons may also navigate by ultrasonic sound waves generated by winds, oceans, and other natural phenomena. There is no reason to believe raptors might not use these same senses. Just recently, researchers learned that Eurasian kestrels use ultraviolet light to locate active rodent pathways by looking for urine.

5

FLIGHT

TYPES OF FLIGHT

Almost all birds fly, but few other groups do so with the dazzle and flair of raptors. A Swainson's hawk wheeling across a prairie sky is a study in fluid grace, while a merlin, hurtling after a smaller bird in a blistering tail-chase, looks like a bullet given feathers.

Air pressure is what enables birds to fly. Air passing over the top of the curved wing must travel faster than air taking the shorter route beneath it; air pressure therefore decreases above the wing, generating lift. (You can demonstrate the same principle by holding a light piece of paper by the corners, with one edge just below your bottom lip, and blowing over the top surface. The paper rises.) Even the wing feathers have a curved airfoil design, adding to the bird's buoyancy.

A raptor's wings, unlike those of an airplane, are not static. There are dozens of muscles that control the position of the wing itself and the feathers covering it. A soaring ferruginous hawk may flex its wings into wide fans, reaching for every bit of lift in a rising bubble of warm air, then fold them seconds later as it dives for a rodent. In the dive, the hawk can control its direction, speed, and altitude with fractional adjustments of its wings, including the tiny "trim tabs" at the bend known as the *alulas*.

Raptors use several general forms of flight, depending on the circumstances:

••• SOARING FLIGHT   Although this is the hallmark of the buteos and vultures, virtually all raptors soar from time to time, including falcons. Soaring takes advantage of the fact that the sun warms the ground unevenly, producing bubbles of rising warm air known as *thermals*. Raptors often seek out thermals and ride them, wings and tails outstretched, as the current carries them effortlessly upward.

In mountains, where winds are often deflected upward, raptors may pursue a more dynamic form of soaring. If the bird stays on the upwind side of the ridge, the deflection currents provide a continuous source of lift. This is one reason the Appalachians are such an important raptor migration route in autumn—the prevailing northwest winds allow hawks to ride along the ridges for hundreds of miles with little effort.

Soaring birds, including most raptors, have emarginated primary feathers— that is, the outermost wing feathers taper sharply toward the tip, creating slots between the feathers, like splayed fingers, when the wings are outstretched. Air forced up through the slots expands and increases lift, and also reduces turbulence. Slotting is especially evident on large raptors like eagles and vultures.

AVIAN ADAPTATIONS FOR FLIGHT

*H*ollow bones with thin walls, internal struts.
• *Air sacs throughout body.*
• *Massive flight muscles supported by keeled breastbone.*
• *Fused pelvic and shoulder girdles, vertebrae.*
• *Rapid digestive system.*
• *High metabolic rate.*
• *Toothless; hollow, lightweight bill.*
• *Egg-laying rather than live birth.*

••• GLIDING FLIGHT Unlike soaring, which allows the raptor to rise, gliding is downhill all the way. With the wings partially withdrawn (even slightly so) the hawk glides down at a controlled angle—the less wing area, the steeper the glide. Migrating buteos like broad-winged hawks efficiently combine soaring and gliding, riding thermal columns until the lift falters, then gliding—sometimes many miles—until they find the next bubble of rising air.

••• ACTIVE FLIGHT   This is the most expensive for a raptor in terms of energy, so flapping flight is often mixed with soaring and gliding. Accipiters in particular are noted for their characteristic flap-flap-glide pattern, which allows hawk-watchers to identify them at extreme distances.

••• HOVERING   Being fairly large, few raptors are accomplished at hovering. For one thing, the maneuver is extremely wasteful of energy, because the lift usually generated by forward momentum is missing, and must be compensated for by sheer muscle power.

Still, some raptors make a practice of hovering, using it to scan ground when no perches are available. The small falcons and kites do it best—the American kestrel so often that it has acquired the nickname "windhover." Some large raptors also hover; ospreys and rough-legged hawks do so routinely, although without the grace of a kestrel.

▶ With its shorter wings and tail, the black vulture may require stronger thermal lift to soar than the turkey vulture—perhaps one reason the black vulture does not range as far north as its larger relative.

GETTING A LIFT

𝒜lthough turkey vultures and black vultures are both expanding their ranges northward, the turkey vultures are found hundreds of miles farther north than their smaller cousins. The reason, some theorize, is lift. Although heavier, turkey vultures have more wing and tail area per pound than the stubbier black vultures, giving the former greater lift. This means turkey vultures may be able to use weak northern thermals more efficiently than black vultures.

Red-tailed and ferruginous hawks employ a different technique, when hunting, to achieve the same end. Known as *kiting*, it is essentially flying in place, facing into the wind with partially folded wings. A kiting redtail hangs perfectly motionless in the sky, but through binoculars you can see the constant flicks of its wings and tail, needed to hold its position.

▼ Turkey vultures fly with a distinct, upward tilt to their wings, and teeter from side to side—a technique that allows them to fly at relatively slow speeds, and one used by several other raptors, including harriers and zone-tailed hawks.

▶ Active flapping burns up a great deal of energy, so many hawks, like this red-tailed hawk, use less strenuous forms of flight like soaring and gliding whenever possible.

Speed of Flight

Raptors are fast—in fact, they probably number among them the fastest animals on Earth. Many species are thought to exceed 100 miles per hour in dives, and speeds of more than 175 mph have been credited to the peregrine falcon. In contrast, a cheetah (the fastest mammal) can muster 50 to 70 mph in very short bursts.

Even the fastest raptor, however, probably cannot match the fastest swifts in level, flapping flight, and falconers know that a fit racing pigeon will outfly a peregrine falcon on the level. It is only by using gravity in the steep, headfirst dive known as a *stoop* that falcons can achieve their breathtaking speeds.

Unfortunately, there is remarkably little reliable information about flight speeds. Most measurements come from pacing free-flying hawks from vehicles or airplanes, an imprecise technique that does not take into account such factors as tail- or headwinds. Nor is there any way to measure effort. Raptors have been timed flying over measured courses, for instance, but there is no way to know if the birds being clocked were loafing or flying flat-out.

In 1942, ornithologist Maurice Broun tried timing hawks migrating along the Kittatinny Ridge in Pennsylvania, using a jury-rigged telephone link between two lookouts two-thirds of a mile apart. When a hawk would pass the first station, a helper would ring Broun with the species and time, and he would watch for it to pass his post at the second station. Because migrating hawks rarely fly in an absolutely straight line, the results are fairly crude estimates, but it is interesting to note that most of the 152 hawks traveled about 30 mph, regardless of species.

More sophisticated studies, some involving radar, have borne out Broun's initial findings. Although most raptors can fly quite fast when they need to, mostly they take their time. For hawks in migration, 20–40 mph seems to be normal.

The most spirited debate has always been over the question of greatest flight speed among raptors. The winner is generally acknowledged to be the peregrine falcon, with dive speeds of 175–200 mph frequently quoted. Higher speeds have been claimed, including an astonishing 273 mph based on a British naval analysis of film footage in the 1940s. More recent research, however, indicates that 175 mph may be the peregrine's true upper limit. In unhurried level flight, observation and radio-telemetry both show that the peregrine is no faster than most raptors, averaging about 40–50 mph.

Other raptor specialists believe the gyrfalcon, rather than the peregrine, deserves credit as the fastest living thing on the planet. They note that the gyr is heavier and more powerfully built than the peregrine, perhaps giving it a speed edge in a dive, although it only rarely stoops on its prey. More often the gyrfalcon simply overtakes the hapless duck or ptarmigan in level flight—a feat few peregrines can match.

MEASURED FLIGHT SPEEDS OF NORTH AMERICAN RAPTORS

SPECIES	SPEED (MPH)
Bald eagle	36–44 (migrating)
Golden eagle	28–32 (migrating) 120 (diving to escape peregrine falcon)
Northern harrier	14–38, average 24 (migrating)
Sharp-shinned hawk	28 (level flight) 16–60, average 30 (migrating)
Cooper's hawk	21–55, average 29 (migrating)
Northern goshawk	38 (flapping/gliding flight)
Broad-winged hawk	20–40, average 32 (migrating)
Red-shouldered hawk	18–34 (migrating)
Red-tailed hawk	20–40, average 29 (migrating) 120 (dive—estimate)
American kestrel	16–36, average 24 (migrating)
Merlin	30–45 (flapping)
Peregrine falcon	28–32 (flapping/gliding flight) 62 (level flapping flight) 175–200 (dive) 273 (dive—estimate based on analysis of motion picture)

(Sources: Broun and Goodwin 1943; also Terres 1980, Kerlinger 1989, Tennesen 1992)

FLIGHT MIMICRY

The animal world is full of mimics, but while many birds imitate the songs of other species, few mimic their appearance. One tropical American hawk appears to be an exception, though.

The zone-tailed hawk of the American Southwest and tropics is a buteo that looks and flies like a turkey vulture. Its plumage is sooty gray, with faint light bars on the tail and under the wings, and in flight it apes the strongly uptilted wings and rocking motion of a vulture; the light markings on the undersides of the primary feathers even match the silvery sheen on the vulture's wings.

Zonetails feed on small mammals, lizards, and amphibians, all prey with well-developed vision. It seems likely that by imitating turkey vultures, zone-tailed hawks can more easily approach their quarry; in fact, the hawks often fly with turkey vultures, making the deception even harder to detect. Some scientists dispute the notion of flight mimicry by zonetails, noting that long wings and a strong dihedral (V-shape) are the most stable flight profile for a bird that must soar at low speed and altitude. However the resemblance evolved, it is of obvious benefit to the hawk.

A few bird-eating raptors also exhibit what appears to be flight mimicry. Sharp-shinned hawks and merlins both occasionally switch from their usual direct, level flight to an undulating series of shallow rises and stalls, quite similar to the rolling flight pattern of woodpeckers and blue jays, presumably to trick their prey.

While not an example of flight mimicry, the astonishing resemblance of the immature gray-bellied goshawk and the adult ornate hawk-eagle is worth noting—although what if any survival advantage this might convey has not been established. Both inhabit lowland rain forests in South America, and except for lacking the hawk-eagle's crest, the young goshawk is a dead ringer—the same black cap, chestnut cheeks and neck, black-barred under parts, and banded tail. In fact, the immature goshawk is so unlike the adult, which is black above and white below, that until the 1960s it was considered a separate species.

◄ *A resident of the American Southwest and tropics, the zone-tailed hawk looks remarkably like a turkey vulture, even down to its flight posture, leading many scientists to believe the hawk mimics harmless vultures in order to fool its prey.*

2

ECOLOGY

AND

NATURAL

HISTORY

▼

6

Behavior

Daily Routine

For most raptors, the daily cycle begins at daybreak. Newly wakened hawks seem to have much in common with newly wakened humans as they rouse themselves from sleep. The hawks may stretch luxuriantly—fanning the tail and first one wing, then the other, extending their legs, yawning. They defecate, preen, and may regurgitate a pellet of indigestible food remains.

Some raptors bathe early in the morning, although bathing is not usually among their first activities, while others almost never take water baths. Some raptors, even those normally silent the rest of the day, will vocalize early in the morning, often calling back and forth with their mate in the breeding season.

Smaller raptors generally start the day earliest, especially those that hunt songbirds, which are most active in the hour before and after sunrise. Others often seem to be in no hurry to start their day, especially the larger buteos, eagles, and falcons. Red-tailed hawks may stay on or near their nighttime roost until the sun has been up for an hour or more before finally heading off to hunt. Accipiters, which normally stay in thick cover, routinely engage in morning soaring sessions, thermaling high into the air; the reason for this activity is unclear.

The most important daily activity is hunting. Except for a bird that has just finished gorging, a raptor is always on the lookout for a meal. There are exceptions, however: Birders occasionally see hawks with distended crops making kills. This is not blood-thirsty behavior, but reflects the fact that a predator must seize opportunities whenever they arise.

How active a raptor will be during the day depends on many factors—time of year, habitat, abundance of prey. A hawk will have to forage more actively during the depths of winter to find enough to eat than it will in August, when there is an abundance of young, inexperienced prey. Activity levels vary as well by species; buteos tend to be more sedentary than accipiters, but a red-tailed hawk that spends two hours scanning a hayfield for voles is hunting just as intensively as the harrier that spends an equivalent amount of time ceaselessly quartering the same field.

A good deal of a raptor's day may be spent doing almost nothing, as this study of wintering bald eagles on the lower Connecticut River shows. Note that immature eagles, because of their less polished hunting skills, must spend more time looking for food.

Percentage of time	Adults	Immatures
Perching	*93.2*	*76.5*
Passive flight	*3.2*	*5.2*
Active flight	*2.2*	*11.3*
Feeding	*1.2*	*3.7*
Waiting	*.2*	*3.3*

Preening and Grooming

Much of a raptor's day is devoted to caring for its feathers, which must be carefully preened to stay in peak condition. The bird delicately pulls its feathers through its partly closed bill, smoothing and rejoining the separated barbs, or gently nibbling along each feather in turn to remove dirt.

In addition to grooming disheveled feathers, preening helps reduce the number of parasites like feather lice and feather flies, and helps waterproof the raptor's plumage by spreading oil from a gland at the base of the tail.

Bathing

Raptors seem to take great delight in bathing—at least judging by the gusto with which many go about it. Because they do not swim, raptors require shallow water with firm footing, and usually pick a spot where they can watch for danger, since bathing puts them in a vulnerable position. Peregrine falcons wintering in England bathe daily, despite the chill, choosing running water a few inches deep. British writer J. A. Baker, who spent several winters observing peregrines, found that they often chose places where the stream bottom matched the the color of their plumage.

▲ *An adult California condor sunbathes in a captive breeding facility.*

The bathing raptor may squat belly-deep in the water, shaking vigorously to soak itself, or it may repeatedly dip its head and shoulders, shrugging the water over its back. The bath may last only a few moments or up to half an hour, and is usually followed by an extended preening session.

▸▸ DUST-BATHING AND SUNBATHING

Odd as it may sound, many birds, including some raptors, will "bathe" in dust or light soil, going through much the same set of motions as when bathing in water—squatting low and rapidly churning their wings. This performance showers the body with a heavy, uniform coating of dust.

More common in gamebirds and songbirds than raptors, dust-bathing is still a bit of a puzzle. The most logical explanation is that the dust chokes and kills skin and feather parasites, and experiments on captive quail have shown that dusting promotes good feather condition.

Many raptors sunbathe while perching, holding their wings and tail open and aligning themselves with the sun for maximum effect. This practice is similar

▶ Raptors bathe with gusto, wading into shallow water and energetically splashing water over their head and back, as this peregrine falcon is about to do.

to the wing-drying behavior of vultures, which stand hunched like gargoyles in the morning, waiting for the sun to dry the dew from their feathers. Bateleurs have an especially dramatic sunbathing posture, with the wings completely outstretched and cupped upward toward the sun.

A unique form of preening known as *anting,* in which birds rub ants, beetles, and other chemical-producing insects through their feathers (or use man-made items like mothballs and cigarette butts), has not been recorded in raptors.

▸▸▸ ROOSTING

As the day winds down, a raptor heads for its nighttime shelter—"going to roost." A hawk may also go to roost in exceptionally bad weather, or stay there longer than normal in the morning when there is heavy rain or snow.

Roost sites should offer security from wind, weather, and predators, so they tend to be used repeatedly. Poor roost selection can be fatal; even large raptors like red-tailed hawks, and, especially, immature birds that perch in the open, are at risk from nocturnal hunters such as raccoons and great horned owls.

As a rule of thumb, raptors choose roost sites that mirror their hunting perches and breeding sites—sheltered cliff ledges for peregrines and prairie falcons, dense conifers for sharp-shinned hawks and goshawks. Harriers often roost on the ground in marsh or meadow vegetation, sometimes forming large groups in winter. Many vultures in both the Old World and New roost communally, and it is a common

▶ *Sunbathing is a common raptor activity, especially among turkey vultures wet with heavy dew.*

sight in much of North America to see a flock of turkey vultures in the dim light of dawn, sitting like figureheads on a dead tree. A mated raptor pair often roosts together, even outside of the breeding season, and recently fledged siblings may roost close to one another for a period of time after leaving the nest.

PERSONALITY

"Personality" is a slippery word when applied to animals, but different species—and individuals—do have different temperaments. Some, like ospreys, American swallow-tailed kites, broad-winged hawks, and rough-legged hawks, are notoriously tame around humans, tolerating a close approach, while others like golden eagles are much more skittish. American kestrels, though they often nest around human dwellings (frequently in barns and house eaves) are nevertheless difficult to approach.

Northern or arctic species, including northern goshawks and gyrfalcons, tend to be tolerant of humans, probably in large part because they come from regions where people are scarce. Even these birds can learn to be wary of humans, though, after they've had startling encounters with traffic, pet dogs, and overly enthusiastic birders.

Falconers have known for centuries that personalities vary among groups of raptors. As a whole, buteos tend to be mellow, rather easy-going birds, while accipiters are nervous and high-strung. Among falcons, prairie falcons have a reputation for unpredictability and foul temper, while peregrines and gyrfalcons are generally easier to handle.

FEARLESSNESS

Anecdotes about the fearlessness and single-mindedness of accipiters are legion, particularly hawks that are chasing food. But the most determined of all may be the northern goshawk.

Edward Forbush, an early-twentieth-century ornithologist, recounted the story of a goshawk in Connecticut that "followed a hen into a kitchen and seized her on the kitchen floor in the very presence of an old man and his daughter. The father beat off the hawk with a cane, while the daughter closed the door and finally killed the bold bird." Forbush went on to tell of another goshawk that chased a chicken under a woman's skirt.

Modern banders have experienced much the same determination. Most hawks, having been lured by a captive pigeon, netted, weighed, banded, and measured, depart immediately. Goshawks, however, frequently return to the nets within minutes, still trying to get the harnessed pigeon inside.

The smaller accipiters can be no less bold. Cooper's hawks and sharp-shinned hawks often hunt backyard bird feeders, and the presence of nearby people and household pets may be completely ignored. I have had juncos and house finches snatched mere feet from me as I was filling my feeders.

▲ Screaming
with fury, a
female goshawk
attacks a pho-
tographer that
has approached
too closely to
her nest.

Some of the most remarkable instances of fearlessness, as in Forbush's goshawk tales, may arise from a condition known as "hunger panic," involving raptors that are starving.

INTELLIGENCE

Intelligence is another difficult attribute to measure. Biologists agree that much of a bird's behavior is based on instinctive reactions, although recent experiments with parrots, ravens, and other species suggest that they may be able to reason to at least a limited extent.

Reasoning and intelligence are not the same thing, however, and birds have proven in laboratory experiments that they are the mental equals of many mammals—even monkeys—at solving some problems. Birds are especially good at situations that require counting, or remembering the location of multiple objects in space.

Unfortunately, there has been little research done on the question of raptor intelligence (in part because they are difficult to work with in captivity), so we are left to guess based on their behavior. Certainly raptors can learn, both by observation and from trial and error. The young of many species spend weeks or months with their parents, learning by watching. But some lessons, it seems, come only with time. After an inexperienced juvenile hawk has made enough unsuccessful head-on attacks, it will learn to use the terrain and vegetation to its advantage—or it will die of starvation.

Adult raptors use strategy and concealment to an amazing degree when hunting. Accipiters often use hedgerows, buildings, and other cover to hide their approach to places where they know there will be prey, such as bird feeders; and high-flying buteos and falcons often attack from such an angle that, to their prey, they are lost in the sun's glare.

Raptors have also shown an ability to make use of humans and their inventions. American kestrels learned that trains scare other animals, and began following them in Mexico, snatching up prey. Red-tailed hawks may do the same with tractors, flying from perch to perch, watching for small mammals flushed by the machines. Peregrine falcons avoid attacking ducks sitting on water, and along the south Florida coast and elsewhere, they have learned to follow boats, which flush the ducks into the air where they can be captured.

PLAY

Play, as human behaviorists have long known, is an important tool for learning. Among raptors, individual and group play is common among nestlings and immatures, and while it becomes less common among adults, the urge to play appears to last through the bird's life.

Young raptors often play with objects in the nest, grabbing them repeatedly with the same lunge-and-squeeze movements they will use later in life on real prey. Once on the wing, siblings will perform mock fights—stooping on each other or grappling talons in midair—as a way of honing their flying skills.

Adults may do many of the same things, although it is more difficult to tell if a red-tailed hawk diving at his mate is engaging in play or a courtship display. Like cats with mice, raptors often toy with their prey, dropping them and recapturing them over and over again. While unpleasant for the quarry, this is not meaningless cruelty, since the raptor is able to practice essential skills. By the same token, adult raptors may spend long periods of time playing with inanimate objects like pine cones, corncobs, sticks, or (in the reported case of one prairie falcon) a dried chunk of cow manure.

But is it fun? That's a question only the birds can answer.

TOOL USE

Once considered the exclusive realm of humans, tool use is actually more common among animals than previously realized. Among raptors, however, only one species has been proven to use tools—the Egyptian vulture.

When it comes across an unprotected ostrich egg, the vulture carefully selects a fist-size, heavy rock, which it throws repeatedly against the shell until the egg breaks. With eggs from smaller species of birds, the vulture may dispense with the tool and hurl the egg against the ground. Similar stone-dropping behavior of the black-breasted kites of Australia with the heavy eggs of emus has recently been proven.

7

SOCIAL STRUCTURE

Raptors are generally considered solitary except in the breeding season, but a wide variety of hawks, eagles, vultures, and falcons are social during all or part of the year.

THE FLOCK

A few species are truly gregarious—they forage, roost, and breed in flocks. Several Old World vultures fit this description, as do lesser kestrels and red-footed falcons. More species are partially social, perhaps roosting in flocks but breeding in single pairs, or forming flocks only during migration. Others, like some harriers, are solitary or paired in summer, but form communal roosts in winter.

Among smaller birds, flocking may be a form of protection, but among raptors the most likely reason for the behavior is to gain information about where to find food. This is especially valuable for raptors that depend on patchy, unpredictable food sources, like carrion or insect swarms—and in fact, insectivorous raptors like kites and small falcons are more likely to hunt in flocks than are bird- or mammal-eating species.

▶ *Many vulture species are social in their roosting and feeding habits, as evidenced by this communal black vulture roost.*

Perhaps the most fascinating example of social structure among raptors is the cooperative hunting of the Harris' hawk of the American Southwest, in which family groups of adults and immatures work closely together to flush and kill large prey like jackrabbits. This remarkable social system, almost perfectly analogous to a wolf pack, is covered in more detail in chapter 10, in the section on cooperative hunting.

Foraging flocks may be made up of a single species, or of several. Vulture flocks are excellent examples of multispecies gatherings, which often include tawny-eagles and a variety of nonraptors, such as crows.

A relative handful of raptor species—about fifteen percent—are colonial nesters, breeding in close association with other raptors, almost always of their own species.

Another exception are raptors that are usually solitary but that migrate in large, cohesive flocks, such as broad-winged and Swainson's hawks in the Americas, and honey-buzzards and Amur falcons in the Old World. It is important to distinguish between species that will occasionally form small flocks, like red-tailed hawks, and those that do so regularly, or that form especially huge aggregations. Biologists have coined the terms "faculative flockers" for the former and "obligate flockers" for the latter. Of the 133 migratory raptors in the world, about half will form flocks, but fewer than two dozen do so on a regular basis.

Even if they do not necessarily travel in large flocks, raptors may gather in large social staging areas prior to migration, usually in places where food is abundant. Spectacular concentrations of American swallow-tailed kites form each year in late summer in Florida, where more than thirteen hundred kites have been seen roosting in an area of just a few acres.

BLACK VULTURE
(semicolonial)

CALIFORNIA CONDOR
(occasional; prior to extinction in the wild)

ANDEAN CONDOR
(occasional)

OSPREY

AMERICAN SWALLOW-TAILED KITE
(occasional)

WHITE-TAILED KITE
(semicolonial)

SNAIL KITE

MISSISSIPPI KITE

LETTER-WINGED KITE

SCISSOR-TAILED KITE

RED KITE
(occasional; sometimes with black kites)

BLACK KITE
(some races; occasionally with red kites)

WHITE-BACKED VULTURE

WHITE-RUMPED VULTURE

LONG-BILLED VULTURE

RUEPPELL'S GRIFFON

HIMALAYAN GRIFFON

EURASIAN GRIFFON

CAPE GRIFFON

RED-HEADED VULTURE
(occasional; with other vulture species only)

WESTERN MARSH-HARRIER
(occasional; small, loose colonies)

NORTHERN HARRIER
(occasional; loose colonies)

MONTAGU'S HARRIER

CHIMANGO CARACARA

LESSER KESTREL

RED-FOOTED FALCON

ELEONORA'S FALCON

SOOTY FALCON

RAPTORS THAT ROOST SOCIALLY

NEW WORLD

Vultures and condors (all species)
American swallow-tailed kite
White-tailed kite (somewhat social)
Snail kite
Plumbeous kite
Mississippi kite
Northern harrier
Rough-legged hawk (in winter)
Chimango caracara

OLD WORLD

Black-shouldered kite (outside breeding season)
Scissor-tailed kite (small flocks, nonbreeding season)
Red kite (somewhat social)
Black kite
Brahminy kite
Vultures (most species)
Western marsh-harrier (in migration)
Pallid harrier (in migration)
Montagu's harrier (outside breeding season)
Rough-legged buzzard (in winter)
Lesser kestrel
Red-footed falcon

RAPTORS THAT USUALLY MIGRATE IN LARGE FLOCKS (MORE THAN TEN BIRDS)

NEW WORLD

Turkey vulture
Mississippi kite
Plumbeous kite
Broad-winged hawk
Swainson's hawk

OLD WORLD

European honey-
  buzzard
Black kite
White-rumped vulture
Pallid harrier
Montagu's harrier
Levant sparrowhawk
Lesser spotted eagle
Greater spotted eagle

Tawny-eagle
Lesser kestrel
Eurasian kestrel
Australian kestrel
Red-footed falcon
Amur falcon
Eleonora's falcon
Sooty falcon
Eurasian hobby

Gregarious roosting is fairly common behavior among some raptors, especially outside of the breeding season. Again, it occurs most often among species like vultures, which feed on patchy, widely scattered food sources; sharp-shinned hawks, which feed on small birds that are evenly distributed, would gain little from a communal roost. Food concentrations may also force normally solitary species to gather in large numbers, a situation common among sea-eagles, for example. A salmon run on Alaska's Chilkat River attracts between four and five thousand eagles each winter, and open water below hydroelectric dams and warm-water discharges in the East concentrate lesser numbers of eagles. Winter salmon runs also concentrate the rare Stellar's sea-eagles in northeastern Asia.

Broad-winged hawks, which gather in vast flocks for their flight south each autumn, scatter once they reach the tropics and resume a solitary lifestyle. Swainson's hawks, on the other hand, sometimes stay in large flocks on their Argentine wintering grounds, hunting grasshoppers.

RAPTORS THAT FLOCK IN NONBREEDING SEASON

NEW WORLD

Black vulture
Turkey vulture
California condor
Andean condor
White-tailed kite (small
  flocks)
Snail kite
Plumbeous kite
Mississippi kite
Bald eagle (immatures
  in breeding season; all
  ages in winter near
  food concentrations)
Swainson's hawk (in
  some locales)

OLD WORLD

Black-shouldered kite
Scissor-tailed kite (small
  flocks)
Black kite
Whistling kite
White-bellied sea-eagle
  (small groups)
African fish-eagle (at
  food concentrations)
White-tailed eagle (especially immatures)
Stellar's sea-eagle (along
  winter salmon rivers)

Pallid harrier
Lesser spotted eagle
Greater spotted eagle
Tawny-eagle
Amur falcon
Red-footed falcon
Lesser kestrel
Eurasian kestrel
Eurasian hobby
Sooty falcon
Eleonora's falcon

INTERACTIONS WITH NONRAPTORS

A raptor's most common interaction with nonraptors occurs, of course, during hunting—but there are other, less predatory interplays through the course of each day.

For example, raptors are routinely harassed by other birds, including birds much smaller than themselves. Novice bird-watchers are often amazed to see a large buteo or an accipiter being routed by a mob of tiny songbirds—birds that are no match for the hawk's power or armament. The small birds only rarely strike the raptor, yet the hawk almost always turns tail and flees rather than go on the attack.

Such mobbing behavior is most common in the breeding season, when a songbird's hormonal urge to defend its territory and nest is highest. But why expose itself to danger? Biologists have several theories: that songbirds in a mob can chase a predator from their neighborhood while minimizing the risk to themselves individually; that they alert other birds to the hawk's presence; or that they condition the raptor to avoid the area.

Raptors carrying food are much more likely to be mobbed, and the smaller birds can tell the difference between aimless soaring flight, which is ignored, and more direct, purposeful hunting behavior. Experiments with tame, tethered hawks show that songbirds can even tell when a hawk is hungry or sated.

Generally the mob is content to just drive the raptor away, but there have been recorded cases of raptors being killed by mobbing birds, including an osprey killed by frigatebirds. Red-winged blackbirds were seen to force a kestrel down into water by the persistence of their attacks.

▲ *Particularly during the breeding season, smaller birds often mob and chase raptors with impunity. In this case, an eastern kingbird routs an osprey.*

Raptors are also mobbed as a matter of course by larger birds. Crows are notorious for their dislike of larger hawks and owls, which prey on them, and some species even have a specific call used to muster the troops when a perched raptor is found. It is not unusual to find a red-tailed hawk sitting stoically in the midst of three or four dozen enraged, raucous crows, or for the crows to follow the hawk from perch to perch through half the morning.

One of the abiding mysteries of mobbing is why the raptor does not usually retaliate. In the case of a large buteo mobbed by songbirds, it may be simple agility; the small birds would be able to avoid the attack, so why bother? For a hawk mobbed by crows, attacking one might invite a blind-side assault from the rear; again, patience and a quick retreat may be the simplest solution.

Smaller birds will mob raptors in self-defense as well. Flocking birds like starlings and robins will often form a tight, swirling ball a few yards over a falcon or an accipiter, matching its every move while always staying overhead. If the hawk tries to attack, it must fly up, and the songbirds will have the advantage of height and speed.

INTERACTIONS WITH OTHER RAPTORS

Raptors also are harassed by other raptors. A Cooper's hawk hunting in a kestrel's territory may find itself coming under blistering aerial assault from the small falcon, which benefits by driving the larger and potentially dangerous competitor from its area. But even in migration, when territory and hunting competition aren't issues, raptors can be a testy lot. Smaller hawks especially—sharp-shinned hawks, kestrels, merlins—will harass their larger cousins, swooping and diving on them repeatedly.

The game is not without its dangers; at Hawk Mountain in Pennsylvania many years ago, a golden eagle being harassed by a red-shouldered hawk grabbed and killed it, and more recently both a bald eagle and a peregrine falcon being pestered by sharpshins killed and partially ate the smaller hawks.

In social situations, dominance hierarchies may develop among raptors, either within a species or between different species. On the African savanna, for example, a particularly large carcass may attract a half-dozen or so species of vultures, from small

▶ *Wings spread to make itself look larger and feet ready to attack, a young red-tailed hawk prepares to fight off an intruder.*

Egyptian vultures to huge Rueppell's griffons and lappet-faced vultures. The smaller species are opportunists, snatching what they can in the melee, but the larger, more aggressive birds like the lappet-faced or the white-backed vulture usually dominate the meal, while Rueppell's griffon may unseat even these big birds. This is not without advantages for the smaller species, however, because the tough skin on some large mammals can be opened only by the biggest vultures.

Intraspecies pecking orders are established based on age, sex, or even how hungry a bird may be. Within a group of Rueppell's griffons, dominance may shift and change through the feeding process, as first one individual and then another asserts itself, only to lose preeminence to other, hungrier vultures a short time later.

Piracy of food is a common interaction between raptors, and is covered in more detail in chapter 10, in the section on hunting.

COMMUNICATION

Raptors appear to communicate only by visual and vocal means; scent and scent-marking, which play such an important role among many mammals, would be of no use to birds with little sense of smell.

▸▸▸ VISUAL DISPLAYS

Much of what a hawk needs to communicate is transmitted visually, as befits an animal with superb vision.

Raptors have fairly rigid faces—they can't raise their eyebrows, purse their lips, or break into a grin. Yet by controlling the feathers on its head, a hawk can convey a surprising range of messages. Resting quietly, a Cooper's hawk's head feathers are smoothed and flattened, but should an intruding raptor enter its territory, the feathers flare, making the head bigger and forming a short, bristly crest on the nape of the neck.

A hawk's threat display is intended to make the bird look as big as possible. If caught on the ground and unable to fly, a raptor almost invariably opens its wings, flares its head and body feathers, fans its tail—and suddenly appears to almost double its size. This behavior is especially typical of nestlings. If the intruder comes closer, the bird may sit back on its tail, holding both feet extended and ready for instant action.

A hawk at rest will have a relaxed, slightly fluffed look to its body feathers, but in many species the feathers clamp down tightly against the body as the hawk prepares to fly, or when it becomes excited—a visual signal that prey species monitor closely. Birds feeding near a perched, relaxed hawk will suddenly show signs of nervousness if the hawk's profile slims and becomes more horizontal.

Young raptors often have particular postures that, combined with food-begging calls, are communicated to the adults when they return to the nest with prey. The most common is a low squat, wings drooping, with the head and tail held level with each other. In the courtship season, females may display in a similar fashion—a trait common in many families of birds, from tiny passerines up to eagles.

A number of raptors, mostly tropical species, have elaborate crests or head plumes, which can be raised or lowered at will. While the crests are often raised in an obvious threat, at other times the feathers may stand half-erect; and other meanings are unclear.

The most spectacular displays are generally those associated with courtship and are covered in chapter 8.

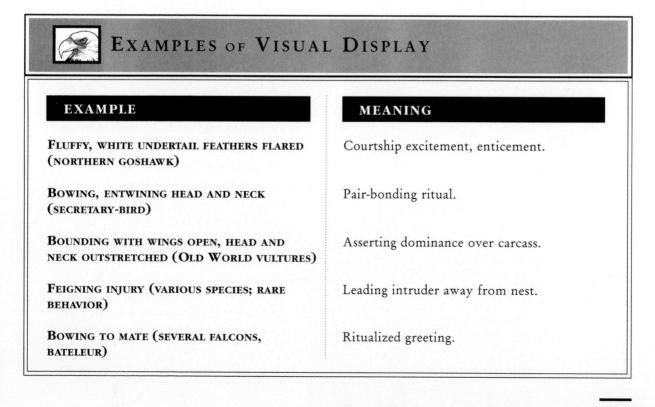

EXAMPLES OF VISUAL DISPLAY

EXAMPLE	MEANING
FLUFFY, WHITE UNDERTAIL FEATHERS FLARED (NORTHERN GOSHAWK)	Courtship excitement, enticement.
BOWING, ENTWINING HEAD AND NECK (SECRETARY-BIRD)	Pair-bonding ritual.
BOUNDING WITH WINGS OPEN, HEAD AND NECK OUTSTRETCHED (OLD WORLD VULTURES)	Asserting dominance over carcass.
FEIGNING INJURY (VARIOUS SPECIES; RARE BEHAVIOR)	Leading intruder away from nest.
BOWING TO MATE (SEVERAL FALCONS, BATELEUR)	Ritualized greeting.

▸▸▸ VOCALIZATIONS

Raptors are generally a silent group when compared to songbirds, but every species makes some sort of vocalization, from the piercing whistles of red-shouldered hawks to the hisses and grunts of New World vultures.

A single species may have many calls (biologist Heinz Meng catalogued forty different vocalizations for the Cooper's hawk alone), but most have only a few that are used often enough or loudly enough for humans to notice. In fact, people usually hear only those calls signifying alarm or anger. As one walks through the spring woods, the sudden, ringing *kak-kak-kak-kak* of an enraged female goshawk is an unmistakable warning. Much rarer is the opportunity to hear the dawn duet between the male and female near the nest.

Not every raptor makes the sound one might expect. Bald eagles in particular have a creaky, undignified cackle—so moviemakers and the producers of TV commercials usually dub in the more inspiring scream of a red-tailed hawk instead.

TYPICAL CALLS OF NORTH AMERICAN RAPTORS

BLACK VULTURE
Essentially silent; hisses, snarls, croaks.

TURKEY VULTURE
Essentially silent; may hiss or grunt.

OSPREY
Musical *chewp-chewp-chewp;* alarm call high-pitched *kip-kip-kip-kiweek-kiweek.*

BALD EAGLE
Creaky *kar-kar-kar-kar.*

MISSISSIPPI KITE
Normal adult call a two-noted, rising whistle. Juveniles give food-begging squeal.

NORTHERN HARRIER
Rapid *kek-kek-kek* (adult) or down-slurred *eeyah* (juvenile).

SHARP-SHINNED HAWK
Shrill *kiuk-kiuk-kiuk.*

COOPER'S HAWK
Harsh *kack-kack-kack.*

NORTHERN GOSHAWK
Clear, high-pitched *kak-kak-kak.*

GRAY HAWK
Loud *creee-ee-ee.*

RED-SHOULDERED HAWK
Descending *keer-yar,* clear and piercing, repeated several times. Imitated by blue jays.

BROAD-WINGED HAWK
Very high, piercing, descending whistle, *su-heeeeee.*

SWAINSON'S HAWK
Whistled *keee-yeer;* also short whistles.

RED-TAILED HAWK
Sharp, descending *see-yeeeer.*

GOLDEN EAGLE
Usually silent; may give musical *weee-hyo-hyo-hyo.*

AMERICAN KESTREL
High-pitched *killy-killy-killy.*

PEREGRINE FALCON
Unusually vocal near nest. Alarm call *hek-hek-hek;* also various screams and wails.

▶ *(Left) Head thrown back, a bald eagles gives its thin, creaky call.*

▶ *(Right) New World vultures, like their stork relatives, lack a syrinx, and can only hiss and grunt.*

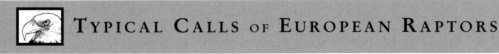

TYPICAL CALLS OF EUROPEAN RAPTORS

OSPREY
Musical *chewp-chewp-chewp;* alarm call high-pitched *kip-kip-kip-kiweek-kiweek.*

WHITE-TAILED EAGLE
Soft *kri-kri-kri,* lower in females.

EUROPEAN HONEY-BUZZARD
High, clear *pee-eer.*

BLACK KITE
Shrill *kwil-leeer;* displays a rapid chatter.

RED KITE
Whistled *hee-oo-ee-oo.* Display call similar to black kite, but shriller.

LAMMERGEIER
Usually silent; descending *quee-eer.*

EURASIAN GRIFFON
Grunts, hisses; whistles when disturbed.

WESTERN MARSH-HARRIER
High *kwee-yah,* similar to lapwing.

NORTHERN (HEN) HARRIER
Rapid *kek-kek-kek* (adult) or down-slurred *eeyah* (juvenile).

EURASIAN SPARROWHAWK
Normal call *kek-kek-kek-kek-kek.*

COMMON BUZZARD
Clear, down-slurred *peeee-ooo* (sometimes three syllables).

GREATER SPOTTED EAGLE
Doglike bark, *kyak-kyak-kyak.*

IMPERIAL EAGLE
Resonant *owk-owk-owk.*

EURASIAN KESTREL
Piercing *kee-kee-kee* or *keelee-keelee-keelee.*

EURASIAN HOBBY
Rapid *kew-kew-kew-kew.*

PEREGRINE FALCON
Unusually vocal near nest. Alarm call *hek-hek-hek;* also various screams and wails.

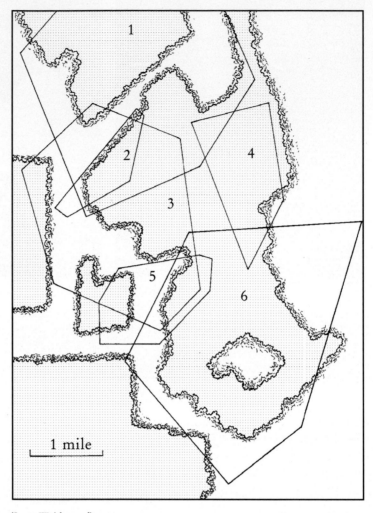

▶ Generalized home ranges in an area of field (shaded) and forest show how territories of different species may overlap, but ranges of the same species rarely do. Red-tailed hawk (1, 6), American kestrel (2, 4), red-shouldered hawk (3), Cooper's hawk (5).

(Scott Weidensaul)

▸▸▸ TERRITORY AND HOME RANGE

Biologists make a distinction between *breeding territories* (areas around the nest that are actively defended against intruders, usually of the same species) and a raptor's *home range* (all the land a bird uses, including areas that may overlap with the home ranges of other individuals).

Not surprisingly, breeding territories are usually (although not always) a great deal smaller than home ranges. The overall size of a raptor's home range is generally tied to its body size; a golden eagle has a considerably bigger home range than, say, a kestrel, because an eagle requires much more food. Species that prey most heavily on birds tend to have larger ranges, as do raptors living in prey-poor environments like the Arctic or a desert. The gyrfalcon, a large, bird-eating species living in the Arctic, has perhaps the biggest average range size of any North American raptor—up to four hundred square miles per pair.

AVERAGE BREEDING TERRITORY SIZE (SQUARE MILES)

SPECIES	TERRITORY SIZE

BALD EAGLE
10.4 (Kenai Peninsula, Alaska)

NORTHERN HARRIER
1 (Minnesota)
.5–2.0 (Michigan)
.6 (North Dakota)
1.5 (Orkney Islands, Scotland)

SHARP-SHINNED HAWK
1.7 (Oregon)
3 (Ontario)
.26–.50 (Wyoming)

COOPER'S HAWK
.12-2.0 (Michigan)
.8 (Wyoming)

RED-SHOULDERED HAWK
.03–.42 (Michigan)
.75 (Maryland)

RED-TAILED HAWK
1.65–1.79 (Michigan)
.3–1.2 (Wyoming)
.5 (California)

SPECIES	TERRITORY SIZE

SWAINSON'S HAWK
.5–1.6 (Wyoming)

HARRIS' HAWK
1–2 (Arizona)

GOLDEN EAGLE
19–59 (California)
6.8–12.4 (Utah)
10–28 (Scottish Highlands)

AMERICAN KESTREL
.8 (Michigan)
.43-.70 (Wyoming)

PRAIRIE FALCON
10 (Wyoming)

PEREGRINE FALCON
1 (Queen Charlotte Islands, British Columbia)

(Sources: Brown and Amadon, 1968; Craighead and Craighead 1956; Johnsgard 1990)

AVERAGE HUNTING TERRITORY SIZE (SQUARE MILES)

SPECIES	TERRITORY SIZE

BALD EAGLE
25 (Arizona)

RED-TAILED HAWK
1.5–3.8 (wintering in Michigan)
.5 (California)

FERRUGINOUS HAWK
2.0–2.6 (Utah)

GOLDEN EAGLE
37 (southern California)
52–104 (wintering in Appalachians)
19–59 (California)
25–35 (Utah)
22 (Scotland)

AMERICAN KESTREL
1.0–2.2 (wintering in Michigan)

SPECIES	TERRITORY SIZE

MERLIN
5.2–11.2 (Montana)

PRAIRIE FALCON
10 (Wyoming)

PEREGRINE FALCON
40 (Scottish moors)
17–25 (Britain)

GYRFALCON
28–400 (Arctic)

(Sources: Brown and Amadon, 1968; Craighead and Craighead 1956; Johnsgard 1990)

▸▸▸ Territorial Defense

In most species, the core breeding range around the nest is actively defended against other raptors, often including other raptor species. A few are nonterritorial or only mildly so; California condors would often allow intruding adults to land on the nest ledge, and ospreys are at best weakly territorial. Mississippi kites, which often breed in colonies, do not appear to defend their nest area at all against other kites.

Accipiters defend the immediate zone around the nest, and will not hunt within it. Among buteos, territoriality is more confusing. Virtually all species will defend their breeding territory against others of the same species, as well as those raptors that either compete for nest sites or food, or pose a threat to the chicks. Red-tailed and Swainson's hawks, for instance, compete directly for nest sites in parts of the West, and will attack intruders of the other species. In the East, the same situation applies to red-tailed and red-shouldered hawks. Interestingly, in many areas Swainson's hawks and ferruginous hawks seem to tolerate each other's presence, even when nesting close to one another, and may cooperate to drive predators from the area.

Golden eagles are highly territorial against other golden eagles, while in the Arctic, the eagles themselves come under fierce assault from rough-legged hawks, peregrine falcons, and gyrfalcons, especially the last. Because of their size and speed, gyrs are a definite threat to any intruding raptor, and they have been known to kill rough-legged hawks, ravens, and other large predatory birds.

American kestrels, on the other hand, rarely make territorial attacks against other kestrels, even when their hunting ranges overlap. And prairie falcons, which chase peregrines away at every opportunity, seem remarkably tolerant of ravens, which feed on birds' eggs and presumably are a threat to the falcon's nest.

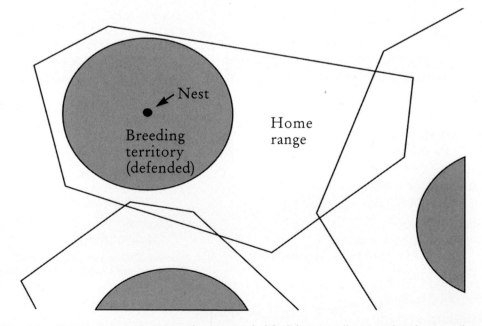

▲ *Home ranges in many raptor species consist of an aggressively defended core, usually surrounding the nest, and a much larger hunting territory that may or may not be defended, and which may overlap with others of the same species.*

8

Courtship and Breeding

Breeding Habitat Requirements

Every species of raptor has its own preferred habitat, a mix of terrain, vegetation, and climate that best suits its needs.

Some species are extremely flexible in their habitat preferences, such as peregrine falcons, which may be found nesting along a river on the arctic coast, on the fortieth-story window ledge of a city skyscraper, or on a cliff overlooking a New England hardwood forest. But on second glance, it is apparent that the same requirements are being met in each case—a high, inaccessible nesting site, wide open skies, and lots of birds to hunt.

Other raptors, conversely, have very rigid habitat requirements. In North America, the snail kite may be the most exacting. It demands freshwater marshes with fairly low vegetation, and it feeds only on apple snails captured from areas of open water within the marsh. Areas with tall vegetation, or covered by floating mats of water plants, are useless to snail kites.

Most raptors fall somewhere between these two extremes, and individuals within a species show a certain degree of flexibility, sometimes using habitats that are unusual for the species as a whole. The same thing may happen for a regional population, like the merlins of Saskatoon, Saskatchewan, which have adapted to city life, nesting in old magpie and crow nests, and hunting over city streets for house sparrows. Red-shouldered hawks inhabit lowland river-bottom forests in most of their eastern range, but prefer pine woods and oak forests in Florida, and are fairly common there around homes.

PREFERRED BREEDING HABITATS

SPECIES	HABITATS

NORTH AMERICAN RAPTORS

BLACK VULTURE
Open country, often near human habitation.

TURKEY VULTURE
Open country, agricultural land, woodlands.

CALIFORNIA CONDOR
Arid mountains.

OSPREY
Near large bodies of fresh or salt water.

AMERICAN SWALLOW-TAILED KITE
Lowland forests, cypress swamps near open marshes.

WHITE-TAILED KITE
Grasslands with stands of trees.

SNAIL KITE
Freshwater marshes containing apple snails.

MISSISSIPPI KITE
Open country with scattered trees.

BALD EAGLE
Near large bodies of fresh or salt water.

NORTHERN HARRIER
Open country, including marshes, cropland.

SHARP-SHINNED HAWK
Mixed hardwoods/conifers.

COOPER'S HAWK
Deciduous or mixed woodlands.

NORTHERN GOSHAWK
Coniferous or mature hardwoods.

COMMON BLACK-HAWK
Riparian woodlands.

HARRIS' HAWK
Upland desert, mesquite woodlands.

GRAY HAWK
Riparian woodlands.

RED-SHOULDERED HAWK
Moist woodlands (hardwood or mixed hardwood-conifer).

BROAD-WINGED HAWK
Deciduous woodlands.

SHORT-TAILED HAWK
Marshes or grasslands near mature hardwoods.

SWAINSON'S HAWK
Grasslands with scattered trees.

WHITE-TAILED HAWK
Gulf Coast grasslands, inland brush.

ZONE-TAILED HAWK
Rugged terrain near waterways.

RED-TAILED HAWK
Varied; generally open country with wooded areas.

FERRUGINOUS HAWK
Semiarid grassland.

ROUGH-LEGGED HAWK
Arctic tundra, boreal forest.

GOLDEN EAGLE
Varied; open country in West, wetlands, tundra in East.

CRESTED CARACARA
Open grasslands with scattered palmettos.

AMERICAN KESTREL
Variety of open habitats, including gras lands, agricultural lands, deserts.

MERLIN
Variable; conifer forests with openings in North, grasslands with groves of trees in northern Plains.

PEREGRINE FALCON
Varied; always near cliffs or other tall nesting sites.

GYRFALCON
Tundra.

PRAIRIE FALCON
Open country; arid grassland to desert.

EUROPEAN RAPTORS

OSPREY
Near large lakes or coast.

EUROPEAN HONEY-BUZZARD
Open deciduous or mixed woodlands.

BLACK-SHOULDERED KITE
Open country with groves of trees.

RED KITE
Hilly woodlands with openings.

BLACK KITE
Flexible; generally mix of woodland and cultivated ground.

WHITE-TAILED EAGLE
Rocky coastline, rivers, or large lakes.

LAMMERGEIER
High, remote mountains.

EGYPTIAN VULTURE
Flexible; mountains to lowlands.

EURASIAN GRIFFON
Mountains with nesting ledges.

CINEREOUS VULTURE
Remote mountains.

SHORT-TOED EAGLE
Varies, but usually fairly open terrain.

WESTERN MARSH-HARRIER
Wetlands with abundant reeds.

NORTHERN (HEN) HARRIER
Open ground, from wetlands to croplands.

PALLID HARRIER
Open ground including wetlands, croplands, and grasslands.

MONTAGU'S HARRIER
Open country, often near shrubs or trees.

LEVANT SPARROWHAWK
Woodlands.

EURASIAN SPARROWHAWK
Deciduous or mixed forest.

NORTHERN GOSHAWK
Deciduous or coniferous forest.

COMMON BUZZARD
Variety of open habitats.

LONG-LEGGED BUZZARD
Dry grasslands and steppes.

ROUGH-LEGGED BUZZARD
Arctic tundra.

LESSER SPOTTED EAGLE
Wooded mountains mixed with open country.

GREATER SPOTTED EAGLE
Forested land near lakes or rivers.

SPANISH EAGLE
Dry grasslands with scattered trees.

IMPERIAL EAGLE
Open country with scattered trees or small groves.

GOLDEN EAGLE
Primarily in mountains.

BOOTED EAGLE
Mountain forests (hardwoods and conifers) with clearings for hunting.

continued

SPECIES	HABITATS
BONELLI'S EAGLE	Wooded mountains.
LESSER KESTREL	Open ground, agricultural land.
EURASIAN KESTREL	Variety of open habitats, including fields, moors, even cities.
RED-FOOTED FALCON	Open ground with small groves of trees.
ELEONORA'S FALCON	Sea cliffs and rocky islands.
MERLIN	Moors, coastline, and other open ground.

SPECIES	HABITATS
EURASIAN HOBBY	Moist lowlands with groves and small woods.
LANNER	Dry, open country.
SAKER	Arid plains.
GYRFALCON	Arctic tundra and coastline.
PEREGRINE FALCON	Sea cliffs, mountains.

COURTSHIP BEHAVIOR

Most vertebrates have elaborate courtship displays designed to attract the opposite sex, and raptors are no exception. Courtship behavior probably serves several purposes—besides catching the eye of a prospective mate, it may also showcase an individual's skills, making mate selection easier. A poor hunter unable to present his intended with food in ritualized courtship feeding activity, for instance, has a poor chance of getting a mate. Many displays involve complex aerobatics, which may also be a way for one raptor to quickly judge the fitness of another.

Courtship behavior may occur at almost any time of the year among pairs that spend the nonbreeding season together, but it grows in frequency and intensity as the birds come into breeding condition. The most common forms of display are aerial maneuvers, which biologists have lumped into a number of broad, descriptively named categories—"high-circling," "tumbling," "sky-dancing," "power-flying," "flutter-gliding," and so forth. A single species may use many different displays during courtship, and some of the displays are also used for other purposes, such as warning off intruding rivals.

The delivery of food by the male to the female is often an integral part of the courtship process. Once seen as largely symbolic, food delivery may in fact have a more concrete purpose—to give the female the nourishment she needs to get through the long, draining process of egg-laying, incubation, and chick care.

Sometimes the male delivers the food without preamble, but most species have special calls or flight displays that go along with it. American kestrel males may circle the female on bowed, fluttering wings, then deliver a vole or mouse to her perch; she will often flutter her wings and call in much the same way a young bird will beg for food—a common courtship display among birds of all kinds. Females may urge the male to hunt by giving the food-begging calls and display.

"Courtship" behavior continues in some form through the breeding season, when it serves to strengthen the pair bond between the male and female. Sharp-shinned hawks, Cooper's hawks, and northern goshawks have a morning duet during nest-building, a long series of shrill *kee-kee-kee* notes that may go on and off for an hour, that concludes in mating.

 ## COURTSHIP BEHAVIOR: NORTH AMERICAN RAPTORS

BLACK VULTURE

Courtship dives, spirals, chases; males may strut on ground.

CALIFORNIA CONDOR

Male displays open wings, bowed head.

OSPREY

Rapid-pursuit flight.

WHITE-TAILED KITE

Pair circles in flight, locks talons.

BALD EAGLE

Varied flight displays, including talon-locking by pair, which spins downward together.

NORTHERN HARRIER

Male performs dives, barrel-rolling "sky dance," transfers prey to female in midair.

NORTHERN GOSHAWK

Varied flight displays, including slow flapping of wings, undulations, dives. Undertail feathers ("pantaloons") may be flared.

RED-SHOULDERED HAWK

Mutual soaring and diving near nest.

RED-TAILED HAWK

Mutual soaring and diving; mock combat in which pair may lock talons.

FERRUGINOUS HAWK

Parachuting down with cupped wings; diving and locking talons.

GOLDEN EAGLE

Undulating flight; high spiral ending in dive.

CRESTED CARACARA

Fighting among males may serve as display.

AMERICAN KESTREL

Male makes power dives; may fly with quivering wingtips while calling.

PRAIRIE FALCON

Male performs aerobatics, power dives for female.

PEREGRINE FALCON

Pair performs swoops and dives while calling; male presents food while bowing.

(Sources: Ehrlich, Dobkin and Wheye, 1988; Brown and Amadon, 1968)

OSPREY

Series of dives and swoops by male, sometimes carrying fish; mutual soaring.

EUROPEAN HONEY-BUZZARD

Mutual soaring; male swoops up and hovers with distinctive "shaking" flaps of wings held high above the back.

BLACK KITE

Aerial pursuit, mutual soaring, talon-grappling.

WHITE-TAILED EAGLE

Mutual soaring, talon-grappling, and tumbling.

LAMMERGEIER

Spectacular swooping display while calling; eaglelike talon-grappling.

EGYPTIAN VULTURE

Swooping displays and talon-grappling.

EURASIAN GRIFFON

Mutual soaring.

WESTERN MARSH-HARRIER

Male performs spectacular aerial loops, spirals, and dives; mutual soaring.

MONTAGU'S HARRIER

"Sky dance" similar to northern harrier's.

EURASIAN SPARROWHAWK

Mutual soaring, undulating flight.

COMMON BUZZARD

Mutual soaring; steep dives and swoops.

LESSER SPOTTED EAGLE

Mutual soaring; male may make undulating dives.

IMPERIAL EAGLE

Mutual soaring and calling, mock combat, and talon-grappling.

BOOTED EAGLE

Steep, rapid dives and swoops; mock combat.

BONELLI'S EAGLE

Repeated dives and ascents; mutual soaring.

EURASIAN KESTREL

Male stoops repeatedly at female, calling.

RED-FOOTED FALCON

Minimal diving display by male.

ELEONORA'S FALCON

Mutual or small-group aerial displays, including rapid pursuit and dives.

EURASIAN HOBBY

Both birds perform rapid, agile maneuvers on the wing.

LANNER

Aerial pursuit, dives, and mutual soaring.

SAKER

Mutual soaring with dives.

(Source: Brown and Amadon, 1968)

▸▸▸ Unusual Pair Bonds

Raptors have traditionally been seen as symbols of fidelity, mating for life (presumably) or at least for a very long time.

Not all raptors follow this monogamous lifestyle, however. Northern harriers will often form single-mate pairs, but they rarely remate with the same bird the following season. However, when their favorite prey—meadow voles—are at a population peak, male harriers may mate with two or more females at the same time. In fact, a male may mate with as many as seven females, all nesting within his defended territory. There is usually a preferred female (or females), however, whose chicks get the largest share of the male's attention or his food-gathering talents.

Virtually every pair bond imaginable has been recorded among the Harris' hawks of the Southwest. Most pairs are monogamous, but polygyny is common, and polyandry—one female mated with two or more males, which help care for the nest—may occur in as many as half the nests in some areas. A nest may be tended by two males and two females, all of which mate; other nests may have a monogamous pair of adults and a number of "nest helpers," which may be immature young from previous nestings, or completely unrelated birds.

The variations are bewildering, and seem to be tied, at least to some extent, to the region. Simple monogamy is most common among Harris' hawks in Texas, nest helpers with monogamous adults in New Mexico, and polygamous pair bonds in Arizona.

Polyandry is rare in birds as a whole, but there are several other raptors in which it is known or suspected. Galapagos hawks engage in polyandry, and bateleurs have been known to have a second male (often an immature) helping out at the nest.

Recent studies of songbirds, once considered monogamous, revealed that females of many species sought mates other than the males with whom they were paired, and biologists believe such liaisons may be far more common among all birds than previously suspected, although the reasons for such philandering are open to debate.

▸▸▸ Types of Mating Systems

▸▸▸ **MONOGAMY**   An extended, exclusive pair bond between a male and female. It is the most common mating system among raptors, although the extent to which otherwise monogamous birds engage in liaisons outside the pair is unclear

▸▸▸ **POLYGAMY**   Any mating system in which a bird of one gender forms pair bonds with more than one bird of the opposite sex.

▸▸▸ **POLYGYNY**   A system in which one male forms pair bonds with several females. (This differs from promiscuity, which involves mating without the formation of any lasting pair bond.) Polygyny is sometimes tied to food abundance, since high prey numbers make it easier for one male to provide for several nests of chicks. It is common among harriers and bateleurs, and rare in ospreys, accipiters (Eurasian sparrowhawk), buteos (red-tailed hawk and common buzzard), and falcons (peregrine, Eurasian kestrel, and merlin).

▸▸▸ **POLYANDRY**   A system in which one female mates with several males. Among raptors, it is recorded only in Harris' hawks and Galapagos hawks.

▲ *A pair of red-tailed hawks engages in a courtship display flight, soaring near one another with their legs hanging.*

▶ *Among some species of raptors, pair bonds may last for several years, perhaps for life. Here, a pair of red-shouldered hawks perches together.*

▶ *Some of the most common aerial displays by courting raptors: (A) shallow undulating flight; (B) deep undulating flight; (C) dives and swoops; (D) mutual soaring, diving and foot-touching; (E) parachuting; (F) talon-grappling; (G) whirling or cartwheeling.*

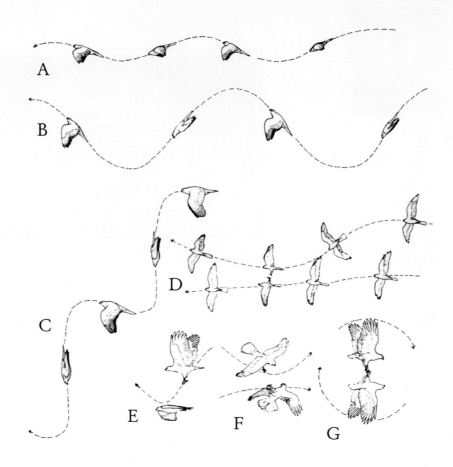

A

B

C

D

E

F

G

(Adapted from Hawks, Eagles & Falcons of North America, *Johnsgard 1990; after Brown and Amadon, 1968, and Cramp and Simmons, 1980)*

▶ *The spectacular "sky dance" of a male northern harrier, as seen from several perspectives to show the huge barrel-rolls during high-intensity display. Males may perform a low-intensity display that lacks the rolls.*

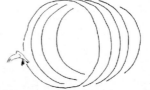

Side View—High Intensity

Front View—High Intensity

Side View—Low Intensity

(Adapted from Harrier: Hawk of the Marshes, *Hamerstrom, 1986)*

9

NESTING
AND
NESTLINGS

⋮ NESTS

Songbirds build new nests almost every year, but most raptor nests are constructed for the long haul, and nest sites—sometimes the nest itself, refurbished each spring—may pass from generation to generation. Bald eagles are known to have used the same nest for thirty-five years, and several osprey nests are known to have been in use for forty to forty-five years.

Perhaps because suitable sites are rare, the cliff eyries (as raptor nests are sometimes known) of peregrine falcons often have continuous tenancy stretching back decades. Until DDT use wiped out the eastern population of the peregrine, some falcon eyries were known to have been used continuously for between fifty and eighty years, while some modern sites in England were used as far back as the thirteenth century.

Raptor nests tend to be simple platforms or masses of sticks placed in inaccessible locations. Many species (including all falcons except caracaras) build no nest at all, using cliff ledges, ground scrapes, or the abandoned nests of other species. Only a few, such as harriers, habitually nest on the ground, although species that ordinarily nest in trees, such as merlins, may ground-nest in treeless regions.

▶ Eurasian kestrels may still use traditional nest sites such as tree cavities or rock ledges, but this adaptable species now uses many man–made structures for breeding, including bridges, church towers, and other buildings.

▸▸▸ NEST SITE SELECTION

As a rule, raptors tend to nest in the same kind of habitat and site in which they themselves were raised. This preference can lead to specialized local populations, like the peregrine falcons that once bred in open tree nests in the central Mississippi valley. That population became extinct during the DDT era following World War II, and the habit of tree-nesting was lost.

On the island of Mauritius, the critically endangered Mauritius kestrel may have inadvertently saved itself from extinction when a single pair switched from nesting in tree cavities, where introduced monkeys were able to snatch the eggs, to an unclimbable cliff. Their offspring, thereafter, showed a clear preference for cliff nests.

On the whole, females make the final choice about where the nest will go, although there are indications that in some species males make the site selection, at least part of the time.

Raptors may show clear preferences for certain kinds of trees, although the criteria may differ from region to region. One study showed that in Maryland, broad-winged hawks most often picked white oaks, while in western New York they chose larches, and in Wisconsin white birches were picked more often. In the same study, red-shouldered hawks chose red or white oaks most frequently, but the researchers believed the tree species was less important than its form—a large tree with a main crotch splitting into three or four branches, sturdy enough to support the nest and easily accessible from the air.

The three accipiters in North America have distinct tree preferences for their nests. Sharp-shinned hawks most often pick dense stands of young conifers, usually close to openings or hardwood forests where songbirds are abundant. Cooper's hawks may choose deciduous trees or (less often) conifers, but the trees tend to be larger and growing in mature woods. Goshawks in the East most often pick hardwoods, and those in the West seem to like conifers; but the most important criterion seems to be that the tree be large with a sizable crotch.

NEST TREE PREFERENCES

A study of broad-winged hawks and red-shouldered hawks in western New York shows the variety of trees that may be used for nesting, as well as each species' preferences in that area:

TREE SPECIES	BROAD-WINGED NESTS	RED-SHOULDERED NESTS
Scotch pine	1	0
European larch	6	1
Quaking aspen	1	1
Yellow birch	1	2
American beech	0	7
Northern red oak	2	0
Sweet crab apple	1	0
Black cherry	3	1
Sugar maple	2	0
Red maple	0	2
Maple species	0	2
American basswood	1	0
White ash	0	2
Total	**18**	**18**

(Source: Crocoll and Parker, 1989)

SPECIES	NEST SITES
▼ **NORMAL**	
Black vulture	Inside hollow logs and trees, caves, dense thickets.
Turkey vulture	Cliffs, caves, hollow logs, or tree stumps.
Osprey	Dead trees, man-made structures (nesting platforms, buoys, utility poles, etc.).
Mississippi kite	Tops of tallest trees in hardwood groves.
Bald eagle	Large trees with commanding view of surroundings.
Northern harrier	On or near ground in marsh or grassland; may use muskrat lodges as foundation.
Sharp-shinned hawk	Near trunks of conifers.
Cooper's hawk	Deciduous or coniferous trees.
Northern goshawk	Tall conifers or hardwoods.
Red-shouldered hawk	Near trunks of hardwoods or conifers.
Broad-winged hawk	Mature hardwoods or conifers; sometimes in old bird or squirrel nests.
Red-tailed hawk	Mature trees; occasionally cliffs.
Swainson's hawk	Trees or large shrubs; occasionally cliffs.
Ferruginous hawk	Live or dead trees; on ground or cliffs.
Crested caracara	Tops of palmettos, or trees.
American kestrel	Natural or artificial cavities.
Merlin	Natural tree cavities, old bird nests, or rock ledges; occasionally on ground.
Prairie falcon	Cliffs or rock ledges.
Peregrine falcon	Cliffs; man-made structures including skyscraper ledges, bridges.

SPECIES	NEST SITES
▼ **UNUSUAL**	
Turkey vulture	Inside barns, abandoned buildings; tree cavities.
Osprey	On ground, on duck blinds, old windmills.
Bald eagle	On ground (coastal Alaska).
Sharp-shinned hawk	Abandoned blue jay nests; hollow branches; inside small caves.
Swainson's hawk	Utility poles.
American kestrel	Rafters of steel plant.
Peregrine falcon	Tree cavities, open tree nests (central Mississippi basin only).

(Sources: Harrison, 1975, 1979; Terres, 1980; Palmer, 1988)

NEST SITES—EUROPEAN RAPTORS

SPECIES	NEST SITES
▼ **NORMAL**	
European honey-buzzard	Large trees, usually deciduous (often over old hawk or crow nests).
Red kite	Large trees, generally over abandoned bird nests.
Black kite	Crotches of trees, usually on foundations of old bird nests.
White-tailed eagle	Large conifers (usually), on rocky ledges or cliffs.
Lammergeier	Rock ledges or caves.
Egyptian vulture	Rock ledges or caves.

SPECIES	NEST SITES
Eurasian griffon	Cliffs.
Cinereous vulture	Large trees, usually conifers.
Short-toed eagle	Low, dense trees.
Western marsh-harrier	On ground in marshy vegetation.
Levant sparrowhawk	Deciduous trees along river.
Eurasian sparrowhawk	In conifer (less often deciduous) trees.
Common buzzard	Large trees; less often on cliffs.
Long-legged buzzard	Variable; usually cliffs or steep banks.
Rough-legged buzzard	Cliffs (trees in southern portions of range).
Lesser spotted eagle	Large trees near forest opening.
Greater spotted eagle	Large trees.
Imperial eagle	Large trees, often isolated from forest.
Bonelli's eagle	Cliffs and trees.
Lesser kestrel	Tall buildings, cliffs.
Eurasian kestrel	Rock ledges, tree cavities, old bird nests.
Red-footed falcon	Old bird nests, especially rook nests.
Eleonora's falcon	Cliff ledges.
Merlin	Old bird nests; on ground in treeless areas.
Eurasian hobby	Abandoned or appropriated bird nests.
Lanner	Cliff ledges, abandoned bird nests.
Saker	Abandoned bird nests, cliff ledges.
Gyrfalcon	Cliff ledges, ground scrapes, or old hawk nests.
Peregrine falcon	Cliff ledges or tall buildings; abandoned bird nests in trees (rare).

continued

SPECIES	NEST SITES
▼	
UNUSUAL	
Black kite	Inside old buildings.
Egyptian vulture	Old buildings, trees.
Common buzzard	Haystacks; deserted huts.
Golden eagle	Abandoned buildings.
Lesser kestrel	Old walls; tree with many cavities.
Eurasian kestrel	Bridge superstructures; cranes; buildings.
Lanner	Utility poles, city buildings.
Peregrine falcon	Ground nests in bogs.

(Sources: Newton, 1979; Brown and Amadon, 1968; Cade, 1982)

NEST SIZES

Normal nest sizes for some North American raptors that build their own nests:

SPECIES	OUTSIDE DIAMETER
▼	
Snail kite	15 inches
Mississippi kite	10–25 inches
Bald eagle	5 feet (new nests) 8–10 feet (old nests) 9.5 feet wide, 20 feet deep (largest bald eagle nest on record)
Northern harrier	15–30 inches
Sharp-shinned hawk	24–26 inches
Cooper's hawk	24–28 inches
Northern goshawk	36–48 inches
Red-shouldered hawk	18–24 inches
Broad-winged hawk	15–17 inches
Red-tailed hawk	28–30 inches
Swainson's hawk	48 inches (approximate)
Ferruginous hawk	24–42 inches
Golden eagle	5–6 feet

(Sources: Harrison, 1975, 1979; Palmer, 1988)

▸▸▸ Nest Construction and Materials

Among raptors that build their own nests, twigs, sticks, and branches are the material of choice for the bulk of the structure. While the best supply of dead branches
would seem to be on the ground, most raptors collect their material on the wing.
Swallow-tailed kites are noted for their aerobatic approach, breaking off twigs with
their feet while zooming past at high speed, but many others—accipiters, buteos, and
even eagles—do the same maneuver with varying degrees of grace. Cooper's hawks
and sharp-shinned hawks, which line the nest cup with bark flakes, collect the flakes
in the same manner, grabbing them like prey.

Both sexes often work together to build the nest, although one (usually the
female) takes the larger role. In a study of northern harriers, males always started
building the nest, but the females always finished the job. Once the foundation of
the nest is finished, the female raptor forms the cup, generally about the same size
as her body, and may line it with soft material like grasses, rootlets, or pieces of
inner bark. Feathers may occasionally be used, but not to the extent as in many
other groups of birds, such as waterfowl.

The length of time needed to build the nest varies, depending on the size of the
structure and the tenacity of the builders. Golden eagle nests may take from five
days to two months to build (and like bald eagle nests, will be added to for years to
come), while ospreys can have a new nest ready in two or three weeks, and a white-
tailed kite in seven to ten days. For cliff-nesters like many falcons, preparing the nest
site may require little more than scraping a shallow depression in the soil of a high
ledge.

▶ *A single egg rests in the huge stick platform of a golden eagle cliff nest in Montana. Such eyries may be used by generations of raptors.*

CHARACTERISTIC ADDITIONS TO NEST

SPECIES	ITEMS
Osprey	Junk, litter.
European honey-buzzard	Pieces of old wasp nests.
American swallow-tailed kite	Spanish moss.
Black kite	Variety of junk and litter.
Red kite	Pieces of rags.
Egyptian vulture	Pieces of rags, fur.
Sharp-shinned hawk	Bark flake lining.
Cooper's hawk	Bark flake lining.
Northern goshawk	Bark flake lining.
Red-shouldered hawk	Bits of junk (corncobs, paper, old bird and tent caterpillar nests, etc.).

The nests of eagles, especially sea-eagles, grow in size with each new year and layer of material. The bald eagle makes what are probably the largest nests built by single pairs of birds (some colonial weavers build large nests as a group effort), and eagle nests are far and away the heaviest. One famous nest in Vermilion, Ohio, occupied for thirty-five years, weighed more than two tons when its tree gave way at last in 1925. Another bald eagle nest, this one in Florida, holds the record for the greatest size of any raptor nest—nine and a half feet across and twenty feet deep; its weight was not recorded. Nests of those proportions represent the work of generations of eagles; newer nests are more commonly five to seven feet wide and about as deep.

While not comparable to the huge mass of eagle nests, those of ospreys are also added to annually, and attain great size. Four hundred pounds has been given as an average weight for osprey nests in some areas.

Ospreys are among the most flexible species when it comes to adding man-made objects to the nest. In fact, osprey nests provide a telling barometer of how life has changed in America. Consider the two lists on page 127 of items retrieved from osprey nests—one from the nineteenth century, one from the twentieth. Both lists are quoted by Alan Poole in his book *Ospreys: A Natural and Unnatural History.*

ITEMS RETRIEVED FROM OSPREY NESTS

19TH CENTURY	20TH CENTURY
Barrel staves and hoops	Dolls
Feather duster	Styrofoam cups
Lathes and shingles	Pieces of TV antennas
Blacking brush and bootjack	Buoys
Parts of oars and a small rudder	Hula hoops
Part of oilskin "sou'wester"	Broken hoe
Cork and cedar net floats	Pieces of fish nets
Rag doll	Plastic hamburger cartons
20 feet of hemp rope	Old flannel shirts
Small doormat	Bicycle tires
Toy sailboat, with sail attached	Rubber boots
Bleached sheep skulls, cattle bones	

Golden eagles and a number of other raptors are noted for building and maintaining alternate nests—one golden eagle pair had twelve, while another had eight. These nests may provide a fallback if the main nest is destroyed early in the breeding cycle; and in the event of a nesting failure, the pair often moves to one of its backup nests the following season. Northern harrier males in Europe frequently build unused nests known as "dummy" or "cock" nests, but their function seems to be courtship rather than actual nesting.

▸▸▸ NEST DEFENSE AND ABANDONMENT

Raptors vary widely in how vigorously they defend their nests. Red-tailed hawks, despite their size, are often retiring and shy—either sinking low into the nest to hide from view, or fleeing entirely if a human should begin to climb its nest tree. Bald eagles are equally wary.

Accipiters, on the other hand, can be as fiery in nest defense as they are in most other aspects of their lives. Biologists studying Cooper's hawks in Arizona had to resort to wearing hard hats with faces painted on the backs to keep their scalps intact. Northern goshawks are even more fierce, frequently slicing the scalps of people who just happen to be passing through the vicinity of the nest. (Interestingly, goshawks in Europe are very retiring around the nest, perhaps reflecting many more centuries of persecution.)

Even among accipiters, though, individual temperaments vary. Some goshawks slip away from the nest without a peep of protest when a human arrives, while others

◂ Bald eagles build the largest nests of any individual bird, with the biggest weighing as much as two tons.

stay nearby, screaming alarms but never actually striking. Eastern Cooper's hawks are less likely to attack intruders than some western populations, a trait seen in other species as well—again, perhaps because eastern raptors have been persecuted by humans for a considerably longer period of time.

If a raptor pair is disturbed badly enough (or repeatedly enough) while nesting, it may abandon the nest completely. Abandonment is more likely before the eggs hatch, however, and only rarely occurs once the chicks have hatched. The likelihood of desertion seems tied to the amount of time the parents have invested in the nesting attempt.

With chicks in the nest, adults will sometimes tolerate an astonishing degree of disturbance, including humans climbing into the nest to band the young. At times, people have moved entire nests out of harm's way without the adults deserting.

Nest Pest Control

Early ornithologists were puzzled by the habit, practiced by many raptors, of decorating the nest with bits of fresh greenery or other plant matter. Unlike structural material used to build the nest, this greenery is often replaced on a regular basis.

While the greenery may help advertise the nest's availability to potential mates, a more significant reason may be pest control. Hawks show a clear preference for plants whose leaves contain insecticidal chemicals, like cherry, which contains hydrocyanic acid that is released as the leaves wilt. Besides killing or discouraging parasites like feather lice and biting flies, the chemicals may also curtail bacterial growth.

More than half of all North American raptor species apparently use this natural method of pest control, including most of the buteonines. Interestingly, though, pest-control methods are not always consistent within a genus; while northern goshawks use large amounts of greenery, sharp-shinned hawks rarely, if ever, do so. Cooper's hawks are somewhere between the two extremes. Vultures, whose rank nests would presumably benefit most from the help, do not collect greenery.

SPECIES THAT USE GREENERY (NORTH AMERICA)

AMERICAN SWALLOW-TAILED KITE (SPANISH MOSS)	HARRIS' HAWK (LEAVES, CACTUS)	ZONE-TAILED HAWK
MISSISSIPPI KITE*	RED-SHOULDERED HAWK	RED-TAILED HAWK
NORTHERN HARRIER	BROAD-WINGED HAWK*	FERRUGINOUS HAWK
COOPER'S HAWK	SHORT-TAILED HAWK	GOLDEN EAGLE
NORTHERN GOSHAWK*	SWAINSON'S HAWK*	CRESTED CARACARA (OCCASIONAL)
COMMON BLACK-HAWK	WHITE-TAILED HAWK	MERLIN
		Frequently or in large quantities

▶ *Gawky and homely, a three-week-old black vulture chick stands in its nest cave.*

▸▸▸ NEST ASSOCIATES

A raptor's nest would hardly seem to be the safest place for a smaller bird to raise its own young, yet birds have frequently been observed nesting inside the bulky mass of a large hawk or eagle nest. In the American West, kestrels and western king-birds have nested in the walls of golden eagle nests; orioles, kingbirds, and house sparrows may use the nests of Swainson's hawks; and black-billed magpies may use the nests of ferruginous hawks. Along the East Coast, osprey nests have provided shelter for house sparrows, house wrens, common grackles, and black-crowned night-herons; and finchlike weavers often use the stick nests of African raptors as a foundation for their woven nests.

For smaller birds, having a raptor nest nearby has advantages, too. Many accip-iters, despite their bird-eating habits, will not hunt in the immediate vicinity of their nests, so songbirds living close by may be safe from that threat, as well as from other predators like crows that the hawks will drive away.

Old raptor nests may be reused by other species, like the Cooper's hawk nest in New England that was subsequently used by red-tailed hawks, and great horned and barred owls. Great horned owls, which begin breeding as early as February in northern states, often usurp hawk nests, forcing the raptors to rebuild elsewhere.

Perhaps the strangest recorded example of sharing a nest was a great horned owl in Florida that laid its eggs in the wide nest of a bald eagle. Remarkably, the two species incubated a short distance from each other in the same nest. Great horned owls have also nested in openings in the sides of eagle nests, and bald eagles have been found actually incubating owl eggs, which may have been laid in the eagles' absence.

Biologists banding bald eagle chicks in Michigan in 1990 discovered a live, uninjured red-tailed hawk chick in a nest with two eaglets. The hawk was only three and a half weeks old and unable to have flown to the nest. Three nestling redtails have also been found in eagle nests along Puget Sound. Because the hawks were younger than the eaglets, they could not have hatched from eggs laid prior to the eagles' moving in, and the most likely explanation is that one of the adults brought the hawks to the nest for food but did not kill them. Under the right conditions, an adult may treat a small nestling making a food-begging call as just another mouth to be fed. Although the Michigan redtail was moved to another redtail nest, two of the Puget Sound hawks successfully fledged.

AVERAGE EGG-LAYING DATES

SPECIES	DATES
NEW ENGLAND & NEW YORK	
Turkey vulture	April 15–May 5
Osprey	May 6–18
Bald eagle	April 1–21
Northern harrier	May 23–June 4

Average Egg-Laying Dates

SPECIES	DATES
Sharp-shinned hawk	May 22–June 3
Cooper's hawk	May 10–20
Northern goshawk	April 17–30
Red-shouldered hawk	April 18–29
Broad-winged hawk	May 16–31
Red-tailed hawk	April 4–May 17
Peregrine falcon	April 12–26
American kestrel	May 12–24

Western States (primarily Washington, Oregon, California)

Osprey	April 2–May 3
White-tailed kite	April 2–29
Bald eagle	March 2–11
Sharp-shinned hawk	May 22–June 11
Cooper's hawk	April 19–May 17
Red-tailed hawk	March 19–April 1
Swainson's hawk	April 24–May 11
Ferruginous hawk	April 16–May 10
Golden eagle	Feb. 26–March 4
Prairie falcon	April 5–15
Peregrine falcon	April 8–23

(Sources: Bent, 1937, 1938)

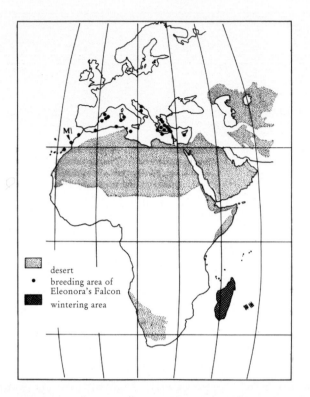

▶ *Breeding range of Eleonora's falcon, which travels to Madagascar to winter.*

desert

• breeding area of Eleonora's Falcon

wintering area

ELEONORA'S FALCON

*A*cross the Mediterranean basin each autumn, hundreds of millions of songbirds make the long, exhausting flight over the inland sea from Europe to northern Africa. Waiting for them—and depending on them—are thousands of Eleonora's falcons, which have altered their breeding cycle to make the most of this influx of food.

For most of the year, Eleonora's falcon is insectivorous, but in late summer its diet shifts more and more to small birds. Weeks, even months after other raptors have completed their nesting seasons, this species is just beginning to nest on the rugged sea cliffs of Mediterranean islands like Cyprus, Sicily, Sardinia, and the Balearics; it is also found on the Canary

Islands off the northwestern African coast, another pathway for migrant songbirds.

Just as the falcon eggs hatch in early September, the exodus of small birds reaches its peak. The adult falcons fly out over the ocean, soaring or holding stationary in the wind as they watch for incoming prey. The small birds, tired from the long flight, have nowhere to hide, and can only attempt desperate evasive maneuvers. Some are forced down into the water to drown.

The chicks develop rapidly and leave the nest area within two weeks of fledging—just as the songbird migration is ending. Not long after, the falcons depart the Mediterranean for their wintering grounds in Madagascar, where they resume their diet of flying insects.

▶ *A male Swainson's hawk mounts the back of his mate for copulation, which lasts only a few moments. Mating may take place several times a day throughout the breeding season.*

Mating, Egg-laying, and Incubation

▸▸▸ Mating

Raptors, like most birds, do not have external genitalia; the reproductive tract ends at the *cloaca*, the opening beneath the tail that is controlled by a muscular sphincter, and that also serves as vent for the large intestine.

The male's paired testes produce sperm, which is stored in the seminal vesicles just above the cloaca. Through most of the year the testes are small and nonfunctional, an adaptation that reduces unnecessary weight, but just prior to the mating season they may grow several hundred times in size. The female's ovaries likewise undergo rapid growth prior to breeding.

To mate, the male balances on the perched female's back, twisting his tail down and to one side as she raises hers. This brings the openings of their cloacas together for the so-called "cloacal kiss," during which sperm is transferred by a muscular ejaculation. For creatures as dangerously armed as raptors, the close physical contact required for mating can be hazardous, and the male sometimes balls up his feet to avoid harming the female with his talons.

Copulation is usually a brief act, and the male often slips off the female's back before cloacal contact occurs. Repeated copulations over a period of weeks or months is common in raptors, and biologists believe many of the mountings are actually a ritualized stage of courtship, rather than actual attempts to mate. At the peak of the breeding season, a pair may copulate a dozen or more times a day.

Most scientists are skeptical of reports of raptors, especially falcons, Old World vultures, and bateleurs, mating in midair. Swifts do mate in flight, but it seems more likely that tales of aerial copulation in raptors stem from a misinterpretation of courtship displays such as talon-grappling.

▸▸▸ EGG-LAYING AND INCUBATION

While most female birds have but a single ovary, female raptors have two, usually containing several thousand minute ova, the unfertilized eggs. In preparation for mating, an ovum swells enormously with nourishing yolk and is released from one of the clustered ovarian follicles into the oviduct; here it is fertilized by the male's sperm. Over the next twenty-four hours or so, the fertilized ovum travels down the long, tubular oviduct, where the albumen ("white") is added, then the shell membranes, and finally the hard, brittle shell.

Many raptor eggs are white, but those that are marked with color receive it from patches of pigment-secreting cells in the wall of the lower oviduct. The egg's twisting movements as it descends the oviduct are responsible for the characteristic splotches, scrawls, or spots found in many species. If the egg moves slowly, the pigment will be concentrated in large blotches, as is the case with many North

▶ *The markings on raptor eggs (black vulture shown here) are the result of pigment glands in the oviduct.*

American raptors; rapid movements create a pattern of streaks and smears. The eggs of falcons and caracaras often have a buff or reddish ground color, sometimes completely covered with an overlay of fine, rusty speckles. The last eggs in a clutch may have less pigment.

An egg is ordinarily laid every two or three days, usually first thing in the morning, until the clutch is complete. With the exception of some falcons, most raptors begin incubating as soon as the first egg is laid—which leads to staggered rates of development in the clutch, and the first-laid egg hatching before subsequent eggs. Known as *asynchronous hatching*, it was long thought to be a way of providing a buffer in case food supplies were poor, since the chicks that hatch later would be more likely to starve, leaving more food for the older chicks. One of the results of asynchronous hatching is the so-called Cain and Abel syndrome, discussed in more detail below.

Biologists (and bird breeders) have traditionally split birds into two groups—*determinate layers*, which lay a fixed number of eggs, and *indeterminate layers*, which will continue to lay replacement eggs should something happen to the first. The larger raptors seem to be determinate, while at least some of the smaller species are indeterminate, like the Eurasian sparrowhawk that was forced to lay twenty-three eggs by scientists who plucked each new egg from her nest. But even this prodigious output falls far short of the record set by a northern flicker, a woodpecker, which laid seventy-one eggs in seventy-three days to replace those taken in the name of science.

▸▸▸ THE COST OF LAYING EGGS

For a female raptor, laying an egg is an expensive proposition, requiring the outlay of considerable energy. Smaller raptors tend to lay larger eggs in proportion to their body size than do larger raptors, thus increasing the burden. Smaller raptors also tend to lay larger clutches, so their overall output is also much greater. A female American kestrel, for instance, lays eggs that average more than eleven percent of her body weight—and because she may lay six or more eggs, over the course of a week she may produce more than half her body weight in eggs.

EGG WEIGHTS

SPECIES	EGG WEIGHT AS PERCENTAGE OF FEMALE'S BODY WEIGHT	NORMAL CLUTCH
Turkey vulture	5.6	2
California condor	2.5	1
European honey-buzzard	5.6	2
American swallow-tailed kite	7.9	2
Mississippi kite	8.7	1–2
Black kite	6.3	2–3
Red kite	6.1	2–3
White-tailed eagle	2.7	1–3
Bald eagle	2.3	2–3
Egyptian vulture	4.9	2
Eurasian griffon	3.6	1
Northern harrier	5.8	4–5
Montagu's harrier	7.1	4–5
Sharp-shinned hawk	10.7	4–5
Eurasian sparrowhawk	7.5	4–6
Cooper's hawk	7.1	4–5

SPECIES	EGG WEIGHT AS PERCENTAGE OF FEMALE'S BODY WEIGHT	NORMAL CLUTCH
Northern goshawk	5.3	3–4
Red-shouldered hawk	8.1	2–4
Broad-winged hawk	8.6	2–3
Red-tailed hawk	5.2	2–4
Common buzzard	6.4	2–4
Lesser spotted eagle	5.9	2
Golden eagle	3	2
American kestrel	11.4	4–6
Eurasian kestrel	9.5	4–6
Eurasian hobby	10.4	2–3
Peregrine falcon	5.3	3–4

▶ *A clutch of five eggs—typical for the species—occupy the center of a northern harrier's ground nest.*

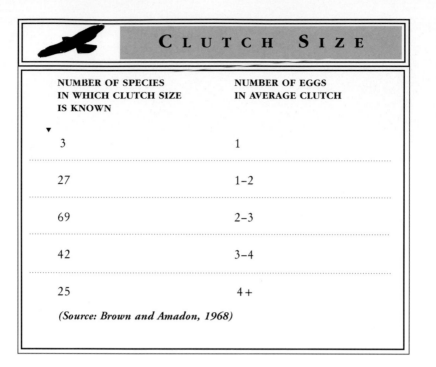

CLUTCH SIZE

NUMBER OF SPECIES IN WHICH CLUTCH SIZE IS KNOWN	NUMBER OF EGGS IN AVERAGE CLUTCH
3	1
27	1–2
69	2–3
42	3–4
25	4+

(Source: Brown and Amadon, 1968)

▸▸ FREQUENCY OF REPRODUCTION

While small birds often raise more than one brood of chicks each year (mourning doves may raise as many as six families), raptors typically lay just one set of eggs each breeding season.

Because their young have a prolonged period of development, and require care weeks or months after they leave the nest, there may not be time enough to raise more than a single brood in one year. Also, because raptors are at or near the pinnacle of the food chain, a pair needs to raise only a small number of chicks over their lifetime in order to keep the population stable—unlike songbirds or gamebirds, which lose most of their offspring to predators.

Although in North America single broods are the norm, a few of the smaller species of raptors, including Mississippi and white-tailed kites, may have two broods, while the California condor normally reproduces only every other year, as a result of the extraordinarily long period of time the chick is dependent on the adults. Harris' hawks, which are oddballs in most reproductive matters, are also unusual among buteonines in often rearing two broods. Kestrels in the North raise just one brood, while those in the South, or in areas with high rodent populations, on rare occasions may raise two.

Should something happen to the eggs prior to hatching—should a raccoon raid the clutch, or the nest blow down in a storm—the female will often lay a replacement set of eggs. This phenomenon is known as *double-clutching* or *recycling,* and it is most common in tropical and temperate-zone species; arctic raptors rarely do so, because the summer breeding season is so short. Likewise, it is common in falcons and accipiters, less so among buteos, and rare among eagles. The interval between failure and relaying varies—harriers need about eight days, while peregrine falcons take nearly two weeks to remate and lay.

Double-clutching can be used by biologists trying to increase the numbers of certain endangered raptors. The first set of eggs can be stolen and reared in captivity, allowing the adults to reclutch, thus doubling their production; sometimes the second clutch is taken as well, in which case the female dutifully lays a third. By double-clutching captive California condors, biologists have dramatically increased the population of this critically endangered species.

REPRODUCTIVE INFORMATION

SPECIES	CLUTCH SIZE (Normal/Range)	INCUBATION PERIOD (Days)	NESTLING PERIOD (Days)
NORTH AMERICA			
Turkey vulture	2 (1–3)	38–41	66–88
Black vulture	2 (1–3)	37–48	80–94
California condor	1 (1)	42–50	180
Osprey	3 (2–4)	32–43	44–59
Mississippi kite	1–2 (1–3)	30–32	34
Bald eagle	2 (1–3)	34–37	70–98
Northern harrier	5 (4–9)	31–38	30–35
Sharp-shinned hawk	4–5 (3–8)	30–35	24–27
Cooper's hawk	4–5 (3–6)	32–36	27–34
Northern goshawk	3–4 (2–5)	35–38	35–42
Harris' hawk	2–4 (1–5)	33–36	43–49
Red-shouldered hawk	3 (2–4)	28–33	39–45
Broad-winged hawk	2–3 (1–4)	28–32	35–42
Swainson's hawk	2–3 (2–4)	28–36	36–46

continued

SPECIES	CLUTCH SIZE (Normal/Range)	INCUBATION PERIOD (Days)	NESTLING PERIOD (Days)
Red-tailed hawk	2–3 (1–5)	30–35	43–48
Ferruginous hawk	3–5 (2–6)	28–33	44–48
Rough-legged hawk	3–6 (2–7)	28–31	39–43
Golden eagle	2 (1–4)	43–45	65–77
American kestrel	4–5 (3–7)	27–31	28–31
Merlin	4–5 (3–7)	28–32	30–35
Peregrine falcon	3–4 (2–6)	32–34	35–40
Prairie falcon	4–5 (2–7)	29–33	35–42

(Sources: Johnsgard, 1990; Ehrlich, Dobkin and Wheye, 1988)

EUROPE

SPECIES	CLUTCH SIZE	INCUBATION PERIOD	NESTLING PERIOD
▾ Osprey	3 (2–4)	32–43	44–59
European honey-buzzard	2 (1–3)	37	40–44
Red kite	2–3 (1–5)	31–32	50–60
Black kite	2–3 (1–5)	31–37	42–50
White-tailed eagle	2 (1–4)	38	70–84
Lammergeier	1–2	53–60	107–117
Egyptian vulture	2 (1–3)	40–42	95
Eurasian griffon	1	52–59	110–115
Cinereous vulture	1	52–55	90–120
Short-toed eagle	1	47	70–75
Western marsh-harrier	4–5 (3–8)	32–38	42
Northern (hen) harrier	4–6 (1–12)	29–33	35–38
Montagu's harrier	4–5 (3–10)	28–30	35–40

SPECIES	CLUTCH SIZE (Normal/range)	INCUBATION PERIOD (Days)	NESTLING PERIOD (Days)
Eurasian sparrowhawk	4–5 (2–7)	32–35	26–30
Northern goshawk	3 (1–5)	35–38	40–43
Common buzzard	2–4 (2–6)	33–35	42–49
Long-legged buzzard	2–3 (2–5)	32–34	45–48
Lesser spotted eagle	2 (1–3)	42–43	58
Greater spotted eagle	2 (1–3)	42–44	60–65
Imperial eagle	2 (2–3)	43	65
Eurasian kestrel	4–5 (4–9)	28	28–32
Red-footed falcon	3–4 (2–6)	25–28	26–28
Eurasian hobby	2–3	28	28–32
Lanner	3 (3–4)	32–35	44–46
Gyrfalcon	3–5 (2–7)	34–35	46–49

(Sources: Primarily Newton, 1979; also Brown and Amadon, 1968)

▸▸▸ CARE OF THE EGGS

The eggs must be kept constantly warm during their development, so the adults incubate them almost around the clock, settling down in the nest so the eggs are brought into contact with their bare skin. The brood patch, a temporary gap in the feathers of the belly that facilitates incubation, is found on the females and, in some species like the American kestrel, on the males as well. The skin of the brood patch is heavily supplied with blood vessels, increasing its heating abilities, and allowing the adults to keep the eggs at an optimum temperature of about 100 degrees Fahrenheit.

The male is usually the primary food provider, even when he helps with incubation duties. While he may deliver prey directly to the nest, many species have ritualized behavior for passing food. The male northern harrier flies toward the nest, calling, and as the female rises to meet him he drops the prey. She flips over onto her back or pulls up sharply, neatly grabbing the falling animal from midair.

Especially early in the incubation period, the female carefully turns the eggs at least once a day, keeping the embryo from sticking to the inside of the shell; in large clutches she also brings the outermost eggs to the center for even heating. Aside from that, the roughly month-long incubation is uneventful as the adults provide a warm, living shield for their eggs.

▸▸▸ HATCHING AND BROODING

Inside the egg, the fertilized ovum develops rapidly into an embryo. As the incubation period draws to an end, the egg has lightened markedly, as a result of water loss through the permeable shell; and the shell itself has thinned quite a bit as the growing chick has removed calcium for its new bones. Inside the egg a large air space has formed, and as the chick begins to struggle against the shell, it begins to breathe for the first time. It will also start to call, and its mother will answer from outside, encouraging it.

Like all birds, raptor chicks have an "egg tooth"—a misnomer, since the small protrusion on the tip of the bill is not a tooth at all. Coupled with special enlarged neck muscles, the egg tooth allows the chick to file and chip its way free of the shell. It may take a day or more of strenuous effort to first break the shell, then hours longer to open a hole big enough to come through.

At hatching, a raptor chick is helpless, completely dependent on its parents for survival. The youngster is covered with a layer of down feathers, but is unable to regulate its body temperature, and must be brooded—a continuation, in a sense, of incubation. Young vultures, accipiters, and buteos hatch with their eyes open, while falcons are born with closed eyes. The chicks can move their heads, raising them with difficulty when a parent offers food, but at first they are incapable of any real mobility.

A newborn raptor chick looks oddly proportioned. The head and especially the feet are outsized—in fact, a nestling's legs and feet reach nearly their adult size long before the birds leave the nest, permitting scientists to band them well before they fledge.

▸▸▸ IMPRINTING

Odd as it may seem, birds do not instinctively recognize others of their species as being the same as themselves. Instead, as chicks they "imprint" on whatever large, moving, vocalizing object cares for them. In the wild, of course, this is invariably their parents, and the nestlings develop the correct self-image for their species. It is this image that will eventually determine their choice of a mate.

Raptors raised by humans, however, may be looking for something entirely different. Imprinted raptors will shun their own species—they may even be frightened of other raptors, since they "see" themselves as human. Such birds cannot be released to the wild without tragic consequences.

▶ *After hours of exhausting work, a red-tailed hawk chick has succeeded in opening a hole in its eggshell.*

▶ *The small, white bump near the tip of this American kestrel chick's bill is the egg "tooth," which helps the youngster chip through the eggshell, then falls off shortly after hatching.*

Fortunately for biologists working with endangered species, raptors can safely be fed by hand for their first few days without imprinting. Peregrine falcon caretakers in captive breeding facilities routinely feed newborn chicks, for example, before placing them with foster parents.

Scientists now believe that imprinting is the mechanism by which birds develop many traits once considered instinctive. For instance, they appear to imprint on the same kind of nest sites in which they were raised, and in a larger sense may imprint on their parents' habitat.

Imprinting is of more than academic concern to biologists raising endangered raptors in captivity. In order to prevent the chicks of peregrine falcons, California condors, and others from imprinting on humans, their handlers must be careful not to let them see people, feeding them using elaborate hand puppets that duplicate the head and neck of an adult of their species. The puppets used to feed California condors are especially realistic, made from leather and plastic.

Human-imprinted raptors recognize humans, not other hawks, as potential mates; and this trait also comes into play in breeding endangered species. Imprinted male peregrine falcons will attempt to copulate with humans, mounting a special hat with a rubber brim that catches the sperm, which is then used to artificially inseminate captive females.

Nestlings

At first, a nestling's days are filled with just two activities—eating and sleeping, the latter under the protective, warming feathers of the brooding female. When the male delivers food, he may stop at a favorite "butcher block," a tree or stump some distance from the nest where he will partially pluck and decapitate the quarry; at other times he will transfer the food to his mate as soon as he returns.

A female raptor is surprisingly delicate when it comes to feeding. Newly hatched nestlings have little muscle control, and their raised heads wobble dizzily as they gape, begging food. The female will pluck part of the prey, holding it down firmly beneath her feet, then tear off tiny bits of meat, which she offers to the chicks. As they grow and their eyes open (something that can happen within hours of hatching), the chicks become more energetic and aggressive in fighting for each morsel.

The chicks receive no water during their weeks in the nest, so their moisture requirements are filled by the prey their parents bring them. This water demand, coupled with the benefits of bringing in fewer and larger packets of food, may explain why many otherwise insectivorous raptors feed their nestlings on small mammals, birds, or reptiles; the calcium provided by vertebrate bones may also be a major benefit.

The nestling period lasts anywhere from about three and a half weeks for sharp-shinned hawks to six months for California condors, but the average for medium-size raptors like broad-winged or red-tailed hawks is about five and a half to six and a half weeks. The grayish down that covers most newly hatched raptors gives way to flight and contour feathers, a process that begins in red-tailed hawk chicks in about two weeks. The flight feathers erupt from the wings first, along with the tips of the tail feathers, and by four weeks of age the down has been replaced on the wings, back, and most of the underside. The last areas to retain down are the head and neck.

▸ *Fluffed to capacity, a female northern goshawk in Wyoming broods her newly hatched chicks to protect them from the elements. Note the fresh pine boughs decorating the nest.*

3-5 days

13-15 days

25-27 days

30-33 days

▶ *Development of a red-tailed hawk chick from shortly after hatching until 30–33 days old; chicks usually leave the nest at 42–46 days of age. Note how wing and tail feathers develop most rapidly.*

(From Handbook of North American Birds, *Vol. 5, Palmer, 1988)*

Once redtail chicks reach the age of three weeks, they have become quite mobile, scampering around the nest's limited space. As their flight feathers grow, they spend more and more time exercising their wings, sometimes lifting off for a moment—then bumping back down again with what could be called a surprised expression.

▸▸▸ CAIN AND ABEL SYNDROME

As mentioned earlier, because incubation usually begins as soon as the first egg is laid, the first chick may be several days older—and markedly bigger—than its youngest siblings. The result is squabbling that can escalate to death.

The Cain and Abel syndrome, or cainism, is most dramatic in eagles, especially large, booted *Aquila* eagles, such as the tawny-eagle. Two or three eggs are usually laid, but in the vast majority of cases only the oldest survives—among Verreaux's eagles of Africa, in fact, no nest with two surviving young has been found, although two eggs are usually laid. Sometimes the younger chick dies of starvation, but frequently the elder simply kills it, although it rarely eats its younger sibling. Lesser spotted eagles and crowned hawk-eagles also almost always kill smaller chicks. The phenomenon is much rarer in medium-size raptors like buteos, and almost unknown in small species.

This behavior would seem to make little sense, eggs being so energetically expensive for a female raptor to produce.

But the extra eggs may be a form of insurance. If something happens to the older egg (or, later, to the older chick), the younger sibling will survive. Likewise, in a year with abundant food the smaller chicks may get enough to eat and survive. The frequency, for example, of cainism among bald and golden eagle chicks goes down dramatically when food is abundant. (Siblicide is also more likely if the older chick is a female and the younger a male—since an older female sibling will be even larger and more dangerous than an older male sibling would be.)

As with double-clutching, cainism can provide biologists with a way to help endangered species. By removing the youngest eaglet, rearing it in captivity, and then releasing it, rare populations might be bolstered.

▸▸▸ FLEDGING

Fledging marks the chick's departure from the nest and the beginning of its independence—although that independence may be quite limited at first. Leaving the nest may not even require flight; many raptor chicks first become "branchers," working their way out among the limbs of the nest tree, but returning to the nest at night.

The initial flight usually has a desperate, careening quality to it, as the chick battles gravity and clumsiness to stay aloft. Crash landings are common, but the fledglings master the art of flying within a few days or weeks. Mastering the art of feeding themselves takes much longer, and the parents supply almost all the chicks' food at first. The fledglings have a certain degree of hunting instinct (some young hawks begin to hunt small, easily captured prey as soon as they leave the nest), but tackling larger or more elusive prey takes practice and education. Play—mock attacks, pouncing, and the like—is an important part of the learning process.

Whether the parents make an intentional effort to instruct their young is hard to say, but the fledglings certainly learn by observation. The adults may also assist the chicks in their hunting; adult red-tailed hawks have been seen to point out voles for their circling offspring.

Observers have watched many species bring live prey back to their fledged chicks, but it is unclear whether this is a deliberate attempt to teach the youngsters how to hunt, or whether the prey simply was not killed. With peregrine falcons, at least, the teaching seems intentional, since the adults will catch and release the same prey animal several times if the youngsters don't respond immediately. The endangered Mauritius kestrel also brings prey to its young, starting with insects brought to the nest.

Gradually the family breaks up, as the chicks roam farther and farther from the nest area and become more proficient hunters. The adults may actively chase them away, although most of the time the parents simply cease providing food. The period from fledging to dispersal varies not only from species to species, but within a single brood. Kestrels may be gone in as little as two weeks, while young bald eagles may stay with their parents until well into autumn—or they may leave in a month.

▲ *Two red-tailed hawk chicks crouch in a nest with the remains of their last meal, a large gopher snake.*

▶ *Fledgling American kestrels, their tails not yet grown to full length, already show the distinctive plumage differences between the sexes—females on the left, male on the right.*

AVERAGE LENGTH OF DEPENDENCE ON PARENTS
(EGG-LAYING TO DISPERSAL)

SPECIES	TIME
▼	
American kestrel	80 days
Red-tailed hawk	140 days
Golden eagle	200 days
California condor	1 year or more

Hunting
and
Diet

Hunting—and the physical adaptations that allow it—define a raptor. Almost everything humans find attractive or repugnant about birds of prey stems from their predatory lifestyle: the shielded eyes and hooked beak, the taloned feet, the swift and dashing attack.

What Raptors Eat

Raptors are almost entirely carnivorous, although a few habitually eat vegetable matter, especially the oil-rich husks of palm nuts. Many species, even those capable of killing their own food, will eat carrion, but the vast majority specialize in catching and killing their own prey.

There is almost no creature between the size of a grasshopper and a small antelope that isn't prey to at least one raptor species. Small mammals like rodents,

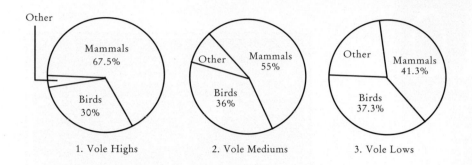

Other

Mammals
67.5%

Birds
30%

1. Vole Highs

Other

Mammals
55%

Birds
36%

2. Vole Mediums

Other

Mammals
41.3%

Birds
37.3%

3. Vole Lows

shrews, and rabbits are the overwhelming favorites, with birds and large insects also near the top of the list. But raptors show some remarkably specialized tastes. Several kinds, including Old World honey-buzzards and the New World's red-throated caracara, habitually eat wasp and bee larvae. The white-bellied sea-eagle of southern Asia regularly feeds on sea snakes, among the most venomous of reptiles, a feat matched by the laughing falcon of Central and South America, which preys on

PREY SAMPLES FROM A RED-TAILED HAWK NEST IN MICHIGAN (OVER THREE MONTHS)

SPECIES	NUMBER
Rabbit	4
Fox squirrel	7
Muskrat	11
Raccoon	1
Ground squirrel	3
Meadow vole	32
Ring-necked pheasant	3
Small and medium-size birds	12*

*Included starling, flicker, red-winged blackbird, domestic pigeon, bluebird, wood thrush, and several species of sparrows)

(Source: Craighead and Craighead, 1956)

▲ *Raptors like this red-tailed hawk are opportunists, taking whatever prey is abundant and most easily captured. In this case, it was a small rodent.*

snakes, including the deadly fer-de-lance. Snail kites and slender-billed kites are extremely specialized, feeding only on a particular kind of freshwater snail.

The list of potential prey is seemingly endless, in part because most raptors are opportunists, taking whatever happens to be abundant and easy to catch. That fact is often reflected in analysis of food pellets and prey remains at nests.

The red-tailed hawk is an example of a species that has a very general diet, taking a wide variety of prey. Mammals the size of voles, mice, and young rabbits are caught most frequently, with birds of various sorts ranking second in importance— but redtails will also catch snakes, frogs, lizards, toads, large salamanders, insects, crustaceans, and spiders. I have seen an immature redtail on a country road after a rain apparently picking up large earthworms driven onto the road by the flooding. But while the species as a whole is generalist, individual redtails, like most raptors, often develop specialties based on their own hunting experience, what their local territory offers, and the season.

In eastern farm country, redtails may prey heavily on meadow voles, cottontails, and squirrels, but they take mostly jackrabbits in arid western areas, and snowshoe hares and arctic ground squirrels in Alaska. Golden eagles in the American West feed heavily on mammals like ground squirrels and jackrabbits, while the tiny eastern population in subarctic Canada are mostly bird hunters, taking ducks, geese, herons, and bitterns along waterways.

RAPTOR FOODS

Raptors eat a remarkable variety of foods, and most raptors are opportunistic, taking whatever fortune brings their way. Some, however, have dietary specialties, as shown in this sample of species from around the world (even these species may take other foods as well):

SPECIES	DISTRIBUTION	PRIMARY PREY
King vulture	New World tropics	Carrion
Osprey	Worldwide	Live fish
Hook-billed kite	Rio Grande valley through New World tropics	Land snails
American swallow-tailed kite	SE U.S., New World tropics	Treefrogs? (U.S.)
European honey-buzzard	Eurasia	Wasps and bees
Snail kite	SE U.S., New World tropics	Aquatic snails
Mississippi kite	SE U.S., Mexico, Central America	Flying insects
White-bellied sea-eagle	India, southern Asia, Australia	Sea snakes, fish
Palm-nut vulture	Southern Africa	Oil palm nut husks
Lammergeier	Southern Europe, SW Asia, Middle East, parts of Africa	Carrion including large bones and marrow
Crested serpent-eagle	Tropical Asia, Philippines	Tree snakes
Northern harrier	North America, Europe, northern Asia	Small mammals, insects, birds
Sharp-shinned hawk	North, Central, South America	Songbirds

SPECIES	DISTRIBUTION	PRIMARY PREY
Chinese goshawk (gray frog hawk)	SE Asia	Frogs
Common black-hawk	SW U.S., New World tropics	Crabs (in tropics); fish, amphibians, reptiles (U.S.)
Black-collared hawk	Central, South America	Fish
Swainson's hawk	Western U.S.	Small mammals
Galapagos hawk	Galapagos Islands	Lava lizards, giant centipedes
Rough-legged hawk	Circumpolar in Arctic	Lemmings, other small rodents
Short-tailed hawk	SE U.S., New World tropics	Small birds
Harpy eagle	New World rain forests	Sloths, monkeys, large birds
Philippine eagle	Philippines	Monkeys, flying lemurs
Black eagle	India, southern Asia, Malaysia	Bird eggs, chicks
Verreaux's eagle	Sub-Saharan Africa	Rock hyraxes
Crowned hawk-eagle	Sub-Saharan Africa	Monkeys, small antelope
Secretary-bird	Africa	Ground mammals, large insects
Red-throated caracara	Central, South America	Wasp larvae
Laughing falcon	Mexico, Central and South America	Snakes, including venomous species

continued

SPECIES	DISTRIBUTION	PRIMARY PREY
Pygmy falcon	Eastern, southern Africa	Insects
Philippine falconet	Philippines	Butterflies, moths
Eurasian kestrel	Eurasia, Africa	Small mammals
Seychelles kestrel	Seychelles Islands	Lizards
Barred kestrel	Madagascar	Chameleons (?)
Peregrine falcon	Worldwide	Small, medium-size birds
Gyrfalcon	Circumpolar in Arctic	Ptarmigan

(Primary sources: Brown and Amadon, 1968; Cade, 1982; Snyder and Snyder, 1991)

▸▸ FEEDING ADAPTATIONS

Predictably, the long list of feeding specializations has also brought about a number of unusual adaptations among raptors. In fact, as has been noted in previous chapters, much of their physiology has been shaped by the hunt, including eyesight, foot and beak structure, and flying ability.

But even within those broad areas there are adaptive refinements, based on the demands of a particular diet. Ospreys, which feed almost exclusively on live fish, have a laundry list of adaptations absent in hawks that feed on terrestrial prey. The soles of an osprey's feet are covered with tiny, sharp tubercules that create a nonslip surface for gripping the fish, and their outermost toes can swing back with the rear toe, providing a two-front-two-back foot position that makes it easy to handle a wriggling fish. The talons are quite long and strongly curved, for the same purpose, and the osprey's oil gland is unusually big for a raptor, providing an abundance of waterproofing oil for preening.

Beaks are among the most "plastic"—that is, the most easily adapted—parts of a bird's body; there is an incredible variety of bill lengths and shapes among shorebirds, for instance. Raptor beaks, on the other hand, are more uniform, but there are some interesting exceptions. The snail kite, found from Florida through South America, has an astonishingly long, curved, slender beak, which it uses to pry freshwater snails out of their shells. The closely related slender-billed kite of South America feeds on the same kind of snails, and has a beak that is even longer and thinner.

The hook-billed kite, which just crosses the southern U.S. border from Mexico, also feeds on snails—but these are land snails, and instead of deftly twisting the animal from its shell, the hook-billed kite crunches through the shell to get to the meat inside. It, too, has a strongly curved bill, but the upper mandible is grotesquely deep, providing the greater strength needed to crush snail shells. (Hook-billed kites are also unusual in the variation of beak size among local populations—some birds have much more massive beaks than others. The reason for these adaptations isn't clear, but it may allow birds with heavier bills to tackle larger, thicker-shelled snails.)

FEEDING ADAPTATIONS

SPECIES	PREY	ADAPTATIONS
Osprey	Fish	Nonslip tubercules on feet; unusually thick, dense, oily body feathering; long legs; long small intestine for digesting scales and bones.
Honey-buzzards	Wasps	Densely feathered head to protect against stings.
Cuckoo-falcons	Stinging caterpillars	Dense facial feathers.
Hook-billed and snail kites	Large snails	Huge, curved bill for removing snails or crushing shells.
Crane hawk, harrier-hawks	Small vertebrates	Double-jointed leg for reaching inside tree cavities.
Lammergeier	Bones (in part)	Stiff, specialized tongue for scooping marrow from broken bones.
Black-collared hawk	Fish	Soles of feet spiny.
Secretary-bird	Small mammals, Large insects	Long legs for rapid running, good visibility in grasslands.

▸▸▸ VEGETARIAN RAPTORS?

One of the universals about birds of prey is that they feed on meat. A few, like swallow-tailed kites and some caracaras and vultures, may eat plant material occasionally (and sometimes inadvertently), but only one species makes a livelihood of it.

That bird is the palm-nut vulture, a raptor also known as the vulturine fish-eagle. Traditionally classified as a link between the sea-eagles and the Old World vultures, the palm-nut vulture is a stunning creature—white except for its black back, secondary wing feathers, and tail, with bright orange skin around the eyes and mouth. It inhabits much of sub-Saharan Africa, wherever the oil palm grows.

Palm-nut vultures eat a variety of meats, including carrion, but they show a strong preference for the fat-rich husk of the palm nut. The nuts also attract African harrier-hawks (a genus unrelated to true harriers) and black kites, but neither relies on the nuts to the degree the palm-nut vulture does.

HUNTING

▸▸▸ HUNTING TECHNIQUES

The list of hunting techniques is long, but most raptors use variations on a few basic themes: ambush, perch hunting, soaring, aerial pursuit, or diving.

⋯ **AMBUSH** Accipiters are masters of the sneak attack, weaving and dodging through dense cover, skimming low along fencerows and flushing startled songbirds, rocketing out of nowhere at backyard bird feeders. Harriers use the element of surprise in their hunting, quartering back and forth across a field or along a weedy ditch, rarely rising more than a few feet above the ground. Masked by tall grass, the hawk surprises rodents and small birds when it pivots and lashes down with its long legs.

⋯ **PERCH HUNTING** Hunting from a perch is perhaps the most common technique, since it offers the advantage of using the least amount of energy. Virtually all raptors perch hunt, waiting patiently for an unwary animal to show itself; and thanks to its excellent eyesight, a raptor sitting on a high, unobstructed perch can keep watch over a huge area. Once the prey is sighted, the raptor takes off in pursuit, often using intervening cover to mask its approach.

⋯ **SOARING** Hunting from the wing is used most often by open-country species, especially buteos and eagles, although falcons and accipiters will soar if air conditions permit it. A soaring hawk, wheeling a thousand or more feet above the ground, is scarcely noticeable to its prey, but the hawk's vision again allows it to closely monitor what is happening on the ground. The disadvantage, of course, is that diving from such a great height takes many seconds, and few prey animals expose themselves for such a dangerously long period of time. High-altitude soaring

▶ *A golden eagle methodically plucks a jackrabbit it has killed. Eagles often hunt by soaring at low and mid-altitudes, scanning the ground for prey.*

is therefore rarely used for hunting, although soaring at low altitude—a few hundred feet or less—is a common practice.

··· HOVERING   Only a relatively few raptors use a hovering approach while hunting, a technique that ornithologists have likened to perch hunting without a perch. In North America the species most often seen hovering are the American kestrel and white-tailed kite, which use the technique to catch small mammals, insects, and birds. Red-tailed, white-tailed, and ferruginous hawks also hover, using a specialized method known as *kiting,* in which they face into the wind and match their forward speed to the wind's velocity, so that they hang motionless over the ground. A kiting buteo may spot prey, then drop a few hundred feet, pull up into a kite again, relocate the animal, then slide forward into a killing dive.

··· AERIAL PURSUIT   Chasing down other birds in midair is the realm of the falcons, although accipiters, buteos, and others will do so on occasion. The peregrine falcon may circle high above the ground ("waiting on" in the jargon of falconers), then drop into a steep, incredibly fast dive when it spots prey. Not all falcons use this approach, however; prairie falcons take a large percentage of their prey on the ground after a long, shallow dive; and gyrfalcons and merlins often pursue birds in nearly level flight.

··· PLUNGE-DIVING   Plunge-diving is a specialized hunting method used almost exclusively by ospreys. The osprey soars and wheels several hundred feet above the water, periodically stopping to hover with a deep, labored wing-

▼ *Gyrfalcons are one of the few raptors capable of overtaking fast, agile prey like ducks in level flight. Most other falcons, like the peregrine, depend on a high-speed dive.*

beat. When it spots a fish swimming near the surface, the osprey tucks its wings and dives, at the last moment throwing its wings back and plunging in feet first.

The bird disappears in the splash, completely submerging for an instant, then flaps heavily into the air with the fish in its talons, struggling under the weight of its waterlogged feathers. Bald eagles and most other raptors that prey heavily on fish have a less dramatic approach, skimming low over the water and snatching fish without wetting themselves, although black-collared hawks may plunge-dive on occasion.

••• GROUND PURSUIT   Accipiters can be effective predators on the ground. Cooper's hawks and northern goshawks have been known to chase rabbits and birds on foot through thick brush, and I have seen a sharp-shinned hawk go into a tangle of wild roses on foot, flushing the sparrows and juncos hidden inside. I also know of a Cooper's hawk, found with a badly broken wing and incapable of flight, that was nevertheless plump and well fed. Because the wing had healed (although improperly), the hawk must have been taking all its food on foot for many weeks.

Many other raptors occasionally hunt on foot, especially inexperienced immatures—Swainson's hawks for grasshoppers, red-tailed hawks and harriers for voles, and bald eagles for dying salmon. But ground-hunting is not the preferred hunting technique for raptors—with the exception of the secretary-bird of Africa, and to a lesser extent several of the caracaras.

••• WILDFIRES   Many grassland raptors make use of the wildfires that are common in open country. White-tailed hawks, Swainson's hawks, and aplomado falcons in North America; greater spotted eagles and lanner falcons in Africa; and Australian kites are all attracted to the smoke of distant fires, and hunt the leading edge of the flames for creatures running in panic. White-tailed hawks will hunt right through the smoke for insects blown up by the rising air, and a large fire may attract two or three dozen of the hawks, which come from miles around.

Regardless of how they are found, prey animals are always taken in the feet, not the beak, and the talons usually do the killing as well (the lone exception is the secretary-bird, which often uses the beak for grabbing prey). As long as the quarry continues to move, the hawk may hold it away from its body with both feet, repeatedly squeezing it to drive the talons deep into vital organs. Falcons, however, often administer a final, fatal bite through the neck, using their specially notched bill to fit between the cervical vertebrae.

►► COOPERATIVE HUNTING

In keeping with their generally solitary nature, most raptors are also solitary hunters. A pair will sometimes hunt together; red-tailed hawks are known for their cooperative tactics on gray squirrels, for instance. The squirrel's usual defense when it sees a predator is to scurry to the far side of the tree, and this can be very effective against a single hawk. But an experienced pair of redtails will come in from opposite directions, leaving the squirrel with nowhere to hide.

Other species may use similar ploys—peregrine falcons against swifts, and crowned hawk-eagles against monkeys. Golden eagles have, on very rare occasions, been seen hunting in twos and threes against large prey like pronghorn fawns. True social hunting, however, of the sort employed by wolves or humans, is known in only one raptor, the beautiful Harris' hawk of the Southwest and Latin America. As noted earlier (on page 113), this buteonine is also quite unusual in its breeding biology.

Dr. James C. Bednarz of Arkansas State University, the biologist who uncovered the cooperative hunting of Harris' hawks in New Mexico, found that the hawks almost always hunt in family groups, usually numbering about five individuals including the adults and their offspring. Their tactics are sophisticated—a leapfrog maneuver to flush prey, or a "relay attack" in which hawks take turns chasing a cottontail or jackrabbit to exhaustion. If the prey holes up in thick brush, the hawks will surround it and send one or two in on foot to flush it out. Bednarz has pointed out that in terms of hunting strategy and social structure, Harris' hawks are very similar to wolves.

Having made a kill, the hawks share it— and because by hunting cooperatively they can kill prey larger than a single hawk can tackle, there is more food for all the pack members than if they were hunting alone. (Even more remarkably, Bednarz and his crew discovered that the adults always waited until the juveniles in the hunting party finished before they ate.)

It seems likely that the birds' cooperative hunting and cooperative breeding reinforce each other—perhaps giving this intriguing desert hawk an evolutionary advantage.

◄ *A banded peregrine falcon looks up from its prey, a pigeon killed on a deserted beach parking lot.*

▸▸▸ Prey Selection and Hunting Success

Given a raptor's sophisticated armament and refined hunting abilities, it is surprising that in almost every study ever conducted, failed attacks far outnumber successful ones.

Mammalian predators like wolves and the big cats often "test" their prey, making preliminary attacks when they encounter huntable animals, but breaking off if the quarry shows no sign of weakness. Such testing is less obvious among raptors, but judging from the high rate of unsuccessful attacks, it seems likely that they, too, can't always judge the fitness and condition of their prey without trying an attack.

An animal in obvious distress attracts a raptor's attention quickly, however. A peregrine falcon perched along a tidal marsh may see thousands of shorebirds in the course of a day without ever stirring from its post—but if it spots one sandpiper with a limp, that flies more slowly than its flock-mates, has erratic wingbeats, or some other visual signal that sets it apart from its companions, the falcon may be aloft and on the attack in an instant.

▲ *The Harris' hawk is unique among raptors for its highly cooperative hunting behavior, although the pack-like technique has only been recorded in a few locations.*

Predators are often credited with policing the health of the animals on which they prey, and while they certainly do weed out the sick and infirm, it is not a conscious effort on their part. The less fit are simply easier to catch.

Raptors also develop preferences based on the most commonly seen and captured prey species in their area, and learn to specialize in particular prey—developing a "set," in falconry jargon. This can become a self-reinforcing process, for the more often a bird finds a particular food, the better it becomes at finding it—developing what biologists call a "specific search image" that allows them to pick out prey against the confusion of their surroundings. Like many birds, raptors may not immediately recognize unusual prey as food until they have seen it for a period of time—which is one reason biologists trapping hawks for banding sometimes avoid using white lab mice as bait for their cage traps, preferring brown mice since they are more similar to wild species.

Experienced adults usually have markedly higher success at hunting than clumsy young birds. Some individuals also develop especially sharp skills. One of the most remarkable displays of hunting prowess ever witnessed came, ironically, from a raptor born in captivity. In the late 1970s, a male peregrine falcon nicknamed "Red Baron" was released as a chick in coastal New Jersey as part of the major reintroduction campaign for that endangered species. Because he hunted open country, researchers were able to closely monitor the Red Baron's hunting attempts later when he reached adulthood.

In 1978, he successfully captured prey (songbirds and shorebirds, primarily) seventy-three percent of the times he attacked. The next year his average was even better, with a success rate of ninety-three percent for 102 attempts. In the process, he managed an amazing streak of sixty-eight hunts without a miss over forty-four consecutive days.

Raptor expert Tom Cade, who recounts the Red Baron's exploits in his book *The Falcons of the World,* lists the success rates for several species (see chart opposite), hunting different prey in different situations.

Raptors that are extremely hungry may go into what is known as hunger panic, causing them to attack prey far beyond their ability. Again, these are often immature birds. This is the likely explanation for golden eagles attacking deer and pronghorn, or goshawks attacking domestic dogs.

▸▸▸ HUNTING FOR BATS

Bats, with their nocturnal habits, acrobatic flight, and radarlike echolocation abilities, would seem to be safe from diurnal raptors. However, a few hawks and falcons have learned to specialize in bats as prey, and in a number of locations—especially near caves with huge bat colonies—individual raptors of many species have discovered how to hunt these flying mammals. Bat predation by raptors is an illuminating example of the adaptations both predators and prey must develop to survive.

The bat falcon of the lowland forests of Central and South America is named for its taste in bats, although bats do not comprise all, or even most, of its diet; small birds and large insects are taken more often. Bats can be a very important food

SUCCESS RATES OF FALCONS

SPECIES	NUMBER OF CASES	PREY/SITUATION	PERCENTAGE SUCCESS
Peregrine falcon	252	Autumn migration	7.5
	113	Racing pigeons	16
	55	Pigeons	62
	32	Australian lakeshore	31
Aplomado falcon	174	Hunting insects	82.2
	37	Hunting birds	18.9
	68	Pair hunting birds	44.1
New Zealand falcon	20	Hunting birds	55
Merlin	139	Autumn migration	5
	343	Birds on winter shore	12.8
American kestrel	246	Insects, reptiles in Costa Rica	39.4
	403	Perch hunting	52
	93	Hovering	23
	199	Insects, invertebrates	85.4
	34	Vertebrates	23
	47	Still hunting	36.2
	7	Hovering	14.3

(Source: Cade, 1982)

source, however, and for that reason bat falcons hunt most actively at or beyond dusk.

The Old World bat hawk, found from Africa to New Guinea, shows the same specialization in catching bats and small, fast-flying birds like swifts and swallows. Unlike the bat falcon, the bat hawk is often active only for a short time at dawn and dusk, and focuses its attention on areas with large concentrations of bats.

A bat is a fairly spare meal—the wings are bone and skin, and there is little more meat on the body than on a small mouse. Bat hawks compensate by eating rapidly, swallowing the bat whole while still in flight, to allow more time to catch others. A bat hawk's physiology reflects its diet; although its bill is small, the mouth gape is unusually wide (for easy swallowing of a cumbersome meal) and the eyes are especially large.

SPECIES	PERCENTAGE OF SUCCESSFUL ATTACKS
Falcons	90–100
Accipiters	90
Buteos	20–50
Owls	30

RAPTOR SUCCESS RATES HUNTING BATS AT CARLSBAD CAVERNS, NEW MEXICO

Even individuals of species that ordinarily do not hunt bats may turn to this food source if bats are abundant. The millions of bats pouring each night from Carlsbad Caverns, New Mexico, provide food for a variety of local raptors, although a study in the 1960s found varying degrees of efficiency among aerial predators.

In Africa, Eurasian hobbies, African goshawks, and Wahlberg's eagles all target bats (in daylight or dusk), making a kill just about half the time. At some African caves, up to ten species of hawks have been recorded preying on bats emerging from underground. Eurasian hobbies wintering in India may specialize in the tiny bats known as pipistrelles, and other falcons like the sooty falcon and Madagascar kestrel will hunt bats near or after dark.

Bats are not defenseless, however. In Puerto Rico, for example, after merlins began hunting bats leaving a cave entrance, the bats altered their usual flight path, staying low in a gully hidden by vegetation.

▸▸▸ MANTLING AND EATING

Once a raptor has made a kill, it may spread both wings and its tail, hunching over the prey and hiding it from view. This action is known as *mantling*, and it may prevent other raptors from seeing the kill, and possibly trying to steal it.

The raptor may feed on the ground, especially if the animal killed is fairly heavy, but more often it carries its prey to a perch in order to eat, where it is safe from attack by ground predators. Small animals like mice may be swallowed whole by larger raptors, but bigger animals are eaten more methodically. The prey may be partially plucked, especially if it is a bird. Accipiters are exceptionally thorough at this, often leaving behind a circle of feathers on the ground, known among birders as "feather doughnuts" or "feather puddles." Such plucking posts may be used habitually by resident hawks.

▶ *Raptors often "mantle" their prey, using their wings and tail to shield it from view, as this immature sharp-shinned hawk is mantling the Steller's jay it has killed.*

There is usually very little left when a raptor finishes—the feathers, beak, and legs from a bird; pieces of fur and the larger bones from a rabbit or other medium-size mammal. Entrails, especially the intestines, are often discarded uneaten.

When it is finished eating, a raptor will carefully clean its beak by stropping it gently against a branch. The talons, however, are not cleaned, and a captured hawk's feet may provide a hint of its recent meals, with mammal hairs and bird feathers clinging to the dried blood until they are washed off by rain or the next bath.

▸▸▸ FOOD CACHING

Hunting is a chancy way to make a living; sometimes prey is abundant, and sometimes it is all but nonexistent. A few raptors have learned to safeguard against starvation by caching extra food.

Food caching is most common in falcons, and all six species found north of Mexico (excluding the crested caracara) have been observed stashing and retrieving food. The behavior is much less common among other raptors, although in North America northern goshawks regularly cache food, and ferruginous hawks do so on rare occasions. A number of African birds, including the secretary-bird, cache food when conditions are right. Caching may be found in one species but not in its closest relatives—while goshawks hoard food, for example, sharp-shinned and Cooper's hawks are not known to do so.

CACHE SITES USED BY AMERICAN KESTRELS

HOLLOW TREES

HOLLOW RAILROAD TIES

UTILITY-POLE SWITCHBOXES

GRASS CLUMPS

EMPTY NEST BOXES

RAIN GUTTERS

HOLES BENEATH TREE ROOTS

HOLLOW FENCEPOSTS

TOPS OF UTILITY POLES

Caching food occurs most often in the breeding season, especially when the chicks are still too small to eat everything the male brings to the nest. Male goshawks will hide prey items near the nest, usually fetching them a few hours later, but sometimes returning for them three or four days after they are killed.

Falcons of many species make a habit of caching food, and will defend the area near the cache against intruders. Peregrines store excess food during the breeding season, beginning with incubation, when the female won't leave the nest except to take food from her mate. Should she ignore his cries telling her that he has food—if, for example, she has just fed the chicks—he may stash the prey, usually somewhere on the nest cliff. In the Queen Charlotte Islands off British Columbia, where peregrines feed on the abundant marbled murrelets, the falcons hunt at dawn when the small seabirds are leaving their burrows, and cache enough to feed on all day. At a peregrine nest in Australia, prey was stored in the morning, then retrieved later in the day to feed the chicks.

Gyrfalcons and aplomado falcons hoard food only during the breeding season, and merlins do so most often during that period; but American kestrels cache prey year-round. One kestrel may maintain a number of storage sites, and the locations may range from hollow trees to utility-pole switchboxes. The food is usually retrieved anywhere from a few hours to a few days after it is deposited, although if the kestrel is given a windfall—such as live mice supplied one after another by curious scientists—it may hide more than it can use before spoilage sets in. One female killed and stashed twenty mice in quick succession.

Natural windfalls may also come along. A male peregrine in New York, in the days before DDT wiped out the eastern population, discovered a stream of migrating blue jays crossing a wide river, where they were easy to catch. The peregrine killed so many, the biologist observing him reported, that eventually the bird ran out of cache sites.

Owls routinely hoard food in winter when spoilage is minimal and recover most of the prey they cache. Among diurnal raptors the recovery rate varies widely, depending on the time of the year. In one study of American kestrels, food was recovered nearly sixty percent of the time in cold weather, but less than ten percent of the time in the warmer months, when it would presumably spoil quickly.

▸▸▸ PIRACY

Although rare in most orders of birds, piracy—stealing food from another animal—is common in raptors. Piracy happens most frequently between different species, as when rough-legged hawks steal food from prairie falcons, but may occur within a species, as when Eleonora's falcons pirate freshly captured songbirds from other falcons returning to the breeding colonies, or when lesser kestrels steal food brought to the nests of their neighbors.

Bald eagles are famous for their piratical attacks on ospreys, but this is far from standard behavior. Such attacks are rare in many regions and virtually unknown in some coastal areas where the two species are common. It may be that robbery from an osprey is simply noticed more often because both birds are large and obvious, for bald eagles routinely steal from other birds—not just raptors, but also waterbirds like loons, diving ducks, gulls, and even river otters. Bald eagles along the Platte River have been seen taking food—usually dead ducks or jackrabbits—from a variety of other raptors, including ferruginous, red-tailed, and rough-legged hawks; golden eagles; and other bald eagles.

In fact, at many places where bald eagles gather for the winter, like the upper Delaware River in New York and along the eastern shore of the Chesapeake Bay, free-for-alls may break out among eagles trying to rob one another. The degree of piracy seems to depend on the abundance of food, for in areas like the Chilkat River in Alaska, where salmon spawn in immense numbers, thousands of eagles congregate in relative harmony.

As noted, piracy is not always directed against other raptors. An aplomado falcon in eastern Mexico was observed stealing crayfish from little blue herons, and an American kestrel forced a grackle to drop a trout fingerling it had taken from a hatchery raceway, even though kestrels do not ordinarily eat fish. Turkey vultures have been known to harass great blue heron nestlings, forcing them to regurgitate fish, which the vultures then eat.

▸ *Rueppell's griffon is one of many raptor species worldwide that have been recorded pirating food from other raptors.*

RAPTORS THAT PRACTICE PIRACY

NEW WORLD

Turkey vulture

Northern harrier

Bald eagle

Savanna hawk

Red-tailed hawk

Rough-legged hawk

Golden eagle

Crested caracara

American kestrel

Aplomado falcon

Merlin

Prairie falcon

Peregrine falcon

OLD WORLD

European honey-buzzard

Black kite

African fish-eagle

White-bellied sea-eagle

White-tailed eagle

Hooded vulture

White-backed vulture

Rueppell's griffon

Lappet-faced vulture

Northern (hen) harrier

Montagu's harrier

Western marsh-harrier

Brown snake-eagle

Bateleur

Eurasian sparrowhawk

Rough-legged buzzard

Tawny-eagle

Verreaux's eagle

Eurasian kestrel

Lesser kestrel

Red-footed falcon

Eleonora's falcon

Merlin

Eurasian hobby

Lanner falcon

Peregrine falcon

WHO ROBS WHOM?

RAPTORS ROBBED BY NONRAPTORS

Black kite (carrion crow)

Bald eagle (glaucous-winged gull)

Northern harrier (common crow, snowy owl, short-eared owl)

Golden eagle (black-billed magpie, raven common crow)

Eurasian kestrel (hooded crow, carrion crow, short eared owl)

Merlin (hooded crow)

MAMMALS ROBBED BY RAPTORS

Stoat (common buzzard)

Weasel (Eurasian kestrel)

Jackal (lappet-faced vulture)

(Sources: Primarily Brockmann and Barnard, 1979; also Palmer, 1988)

►►► CARRION

An animal need not be freshly killed to become food for a raptor. Although the vast majority of species kill live prey most of the time, few will turn down fresh carrion, especially when food is scarce.

Vultures are the only carrion specialists, however, and both Old and New World clans have become extremely efficient at finding and using carcasses. Contrary to popular belief, most vultures do not prefer rotten meat—in fact, infestations of insects like maggots can render meat inedible to many vultures, and captives always select fresh meat if given a choice.

Vultures do have a much greater tolerance for pathogens than most animals, however. Turkey vultures are highly resistant to botulism, and hog cholera viruses are killed by passage through their digestive systems. Thus, the scavenging activities of vultures may actually help stem the spread of diseases, especially in tropical climates.

All vultures share several physical adaptations geared to their lifestyle, including the trademark naked head. Among African vultures, however, how far the bare skin extends down the neck depends on where the species feeds on a carcass. White-backed vultures routinely plunge their heads deep inside the body cavity, and consequently their necks are bare almost to the shoulder; smaller Egyptian vultures pick scraps from the outside, and have heads that are bare only to the back of the skull. Lammergeiers, which have fully feathered heads, feed on carcasses only when other vultures are finished.

► *While most raptors will consume carrion on occasion, vultures—like this turkey vulture with an egg-laden turtle hit by a car—make a career out of it.*

Almost all raptors will probably take fresh carrion on occasion, even species with specialized diets like osprey, which have been seen to eat dead fish. In North America bald and golden eagles feed regularly (at times even heavily) on carrion, as do crested caracaras. Rough-legged hawks scavenge, especially in winter, and carrion can be an important food for red-tailed hawks—as evidenced by one study that showed remains of cows, horses, sheep, and bobcats in redtail pellets.

ALMOST EXCLUSIVELY
- Black vulture
- Turkey vulture
- California condor
- Lammergeier
- Egyptian vulture (also eggs, invertebrates)
- Eurasian griffon
- Cinereous vulture

REGULARLY OR OCCASIONALLY
- Mississippi kite
- Black kite
- Red kite (primarily cold weather)
- White-tailed eagle
- Bald eagle
- Red-tailed hawk
- Common buzzard
- Rough-legged hawk
- Greater spotted eagle
- Imperial eagle
- Golden eagle
- Crested caracara
- Gyrfalcon

RARELY
- Osprey
- Short-toed eagle
- Western marsh-harrier
- Northern harrier
- Pallid harrier
- Montagu's harrier
- Eurasian sparrowhawk
- Sharp-shinned hawk
- Cooper's hawk
- Northern goshawk
- Common black-hawk
- Harris' hawk (questionable)
- Broad-winged hawk
- Red-shouldered hawk
- Swainson's hawk
- Lesser spotted eagle
- Booted eagle
- Bonelli's eagle
- Eurasian kestrel
- American kestrel
- Red-footed falcon
- Merlin
- Eurasian hobby
- Prairie falcon
- Lanner
- Saker
- Peregrine falcon

··· EATING BONES   The lammergeier, or bearded vulture, is one of the most majestic of all diurnal raptors, with a wingspan of nearly nine feet, a long wedge-shaped tail, and a peculiar, drooping "mustache" of dark bristles framing its mouth. Although the lammergeier feeds mostly on carrion, it has the unusual sideline of eating bone marrow—and a dramatic way of obtaining it.

Lammergeiers have a wide range, from Portugal and northern Africa to the mountains of central Asia and down the African Rift Valley. In some areas lammergeiers have developed the taste for marrow, which they satisfy by carrying large, heavy bones aloft in their feet, then dropping them to the rocks below; the vulture may go into a steep dive before releasing the bone, increasing its velocity. When the bone smashes, the lammergeier lands and uses its specialized stiff, scoop-shaped tongue to remove the marrow.

Apparently, suitable bone-smashing sites are hard to find, because lammergeiers use the same spots repeatedly, leaving deposits of smashed bones littering the grounds. Such traditional locations are known as *ossuaries.*

By developing this habit of smashing bones, the lammergeier is able to exploit a food supply unavailable to other raptors, one that is unusually high in fat. Not all bones are smashed, and smaller ones are simply swallowed whole and digested—a process that takes about two days, in the case of a cow's vertebrae.

Lammergeiers are reputed also to smash turtles in the same way they smash bones. According to the Roman naturalist Pliny the Elder, the Greek poet Aeschylus was killed in 456 B.C. when a lammergeier mistook his bald head for a rock—and dropped a tortoise on him.

◄ *The spectacular lammergeier, found in Eurasia and Africa, is unique among raptors in its diet, which may be comprised of 85 percent animal bone, along with lesser amounts of carrion.*

Seasonal Changes in Diet

While most raptors feed year-round on basically the same kinds of prey, some species undergo marked seasonal shifts in their diets. This phenomenon may be weather-related—a red-shouldered hawk in Ohio will find few frogs in December—or it may be tied to other causes. In almost every case, however, the shift reflects a change to the most abundant and nutritious prey available.

One category of seasonal dietary change applies to raptors that migrate to different habitats in summer and winter. Broad-winged hawks travel from the eastern hardwood forests of North America to the tropical forests of Central and South America, and their diet shifts from a variety of vertebrates to one made up largely of insects.

The list on page 175 contains some generalizations; a particular raptor's diet depends on habitat, prey availability, and individual preferences. For example, while some researchers have found that harriers switch heavily to young birds during the breeding season, others found an equal dependence on meadow voles, birds, and young rabbits.

▶ *A prairie falcon feeds on a gray partridge, flushed from the ground and killed in midair.*

▸▸▸ Sample Diets

Much of what we know about raptor diets comes from a check of prey remains at nest sites, or direct observation from blinds. The lists on pages 176–177 are typical results from studies of nests of fourteen pairs of Cooper's hawks in Missouri and a single broad-winged hawk pair in Wisconsin. Along with other information, the charts show the percentage of total diet by weight, known as *biomass,* that each species represents. Biomass gives a more accurate picture of the hawk's diet, since bigger prey provides more food in fewer kills.

SEASONAL VARIATIONS IN DIET

SPECIES	SUMMER DIET	WINTER DIET
	(Most important prey items listed first)	
Northern harrier	Young birds, small mammals	Small mammals (mostly meadow voles)
Red-shouldered hawk	Variety of vertebrates, including snakes, frogs, toads; invertebrates	Small rodents
Broad-winged hawk	Small mammals, birds, snakes, amphibians	Insects, lizards, frogs
Common buzzard	Young rabbits, ocellated lizards (northeastern Spain)	Insects, small mammals
Swainson's hawk	Small and medium-size mammals	Insects
Harris' hawk	Variety of vertebrates	Rabbits hunted cooperatively
Greater spotted eagle	Small mammals, birds, amphibians, reptiles	Insects
American kestrel	Large insects, small mammals	Small mammals, small birds in North; insects and lizards in South
Prairie falcon	Small mammals (esp. ground squirrels), birds	Birds, small mammals
Bat falcon	Mostly birds (breeding season)	Mostly insects (rainy season)
Sooty falcon	Small and medium-size birds (breeding season in Arabia)	Insects, bats (migration, Africa)
Eleonora's falcon	Migrant landbirds (autumn breeding season)	Insects (remainder of year)
Red-footed falcon	Insects (adult diet)	Small vertebrates (nestling diet)

PREY SPECIES	NUMBER DELIVERED TO NEST IN BREEDING SEASON	PERCENTAGE OF TOTAL DIET BY WEIGHT (BIOMASS)
BIRDS	**225**	**64.8**
Blue jay	33	10.1
Northern bobwhite	14	8.3
Common grackle	20	7.7
European starling	25	6.8
Northern flicker	10	4.5
Mourning dove	9	4.2
American robin	16	4.1
American crow	2	3.6
Unidentified birds	26	3.6
Rock dove	2	2.8
Yellow-billed cuckoo	10	1.7
Pileated woodpecker	1	1.3
Eastern meadowlark	3	1.0

(Bird species comprising less than 1% each of biomass: red-headed woodpecker, hairy woodpecker, downy woodpecker, gray catbird, brown thrasher, red-winged blackbird, brown-headed cowbird, northern oriole, scarlet tanager, northern cardinal, rufous-sided towhee, indigo bunting, American goldfinch, tufted titmouse, house sparrow, chuck-will's-widow, whip-poor-will.)

MAMMALS	**31**	**33.8**
Eastern cottontail (immature)	7	14.5
Gray squirrel	7	10.9
Eastern fox squirrel (immature)	3	4.7
Eastern chipmunk	6	2.1

(Mammal species comprising less than 1% each of biomass: eastern woodrat, cotton rat, unidentified small rodents, unidentified bat.)

REPTILES	**3**	**1.4**
Black rat snake	1	0.7
Unidentified snake	1	0.67
Five-lined skink	1	0.07

(Source: Prescott, 1985)

PREY SPECIES	NUMBER EATEN IN 19 DAYS	PERCENTAGE OF TOTAL DIET BY WEIGHT (BIOMASS)
BIRDS	**30**	**21.5**
Unidentified small birds	23	7.2
Ruffed grouse	1	6.6
Northern flicker	2	5.2
Blue jay	1	1.6

(Other bird species: Nashville warbler, yellow-billed cuckoo, ovenbird.)

PREY SPECIES	NUMBER EATEN IN 19 DAYS	PERCENTAGE OF TOTAL DIET BY WEIGHT (BIOMASS)
MAMMALS	**43**	**62.5**
Eastern chipmunk	12	36.7
Unidentified small mammals	9	6.2
Flying squirrel	1	4.9
Star-nosed mole	3	4.4
Short-tailed shrew	7	3.9
Southern red-backed vole	6	3.6
Unidentified voles	4	2.8
Water shrew	1	trace
AMPHIBIANS	**26**	**12.7**
American toad	16	9.3
Wood frog	7	1.2
Unidentified frog or toad	3	1.2
REPTILES	**8**	**2.2**
Eastern garter snake	5	1.6
Northern ringneck snake	2	0.6
Smooth green snake	1	trace

(Source: Rosenfield and Gratson, 1984)

11

▼

Migration

Raptors are highly mobile animals, able to cover great distances in a remarkably short period of time. Not surprisingly, therefore, large-scale movements like migration play a major role in the life cycle and ecology of many species.

Not all movements are migratory, however. A raptor moves freely about its territory on a daily basis, and may shift from one part of a large hunting range to another from one week to the next. Outside the breeding season, some raptors like harriers are noted for their nomadic behavior, drifting from one locale to another in search of food.

One of the most important forms of nonmigratory movement is postbreeding dispersal. At the end of the nesting season, immature raptors leave their parents' territory—sometimes on their own, and sometimes chased by the increasingly hostile adults. They scatter in every direction, a movement that increases the genetic mix of the species by reducing the chances for inbreeding.

Dispersing individuals usually stay within the species' normal geographic range, but if the population is growing, dispersal may force them into new breeding territory. This is most likely how the rapid northward expansion of turkey vultures and black vultures has occurred, and may explain the rapid spread of white-tailed kites in this century.

Migratory Movement

Migration is a regular shift from a breeding range to a nonbreeding range. The distance involved may be relatively short or span thousands of miles, but it accomplishes the same purpose—to give the raptor the benefit of the best possible conditions year-round.

The Swainson's hawk, for example, nests in the grasslands of the United States and the Canadian West, where it feeds heavily on insects—a food that disappears with the onset of cold weather. Some insectivorous raptors shift to other foods, as American kestrels do in winter, but the Swainson's hawk takes a different approach. By migrating south to the pampas of Argentina—a one-way journey of up to seven thousand miles that takes two or three months—it is able to arrive just in time for the austral summer, and live in grassland habitat with abundant insects.

 ## TYPES OF MOVEMENT

LOCAL
Short-term movements in or near a raptor's normal home range.

DISPERSAL
An outward spread of individuals, usually involving young, newly independent birds after the breeding season ends.

NOMADIC MOVEMENTS
Irregular movements by adults or immatures, usually in response to sporadic changes in food supply.

LOCAL SEASONAL MOVEMENTS
Short-distance movements in response to changing seasons, such as golden eagles dropping to lower elevations for the winter (altitudinal migration).

MIGRATION
Long-distance movements, usually between breeding and nonbreeding areas.

IRRUPTIONS
Unpredictable movements by a normally resident raptor, usually in response to low food supplies. Occurs mainly in arctic species.

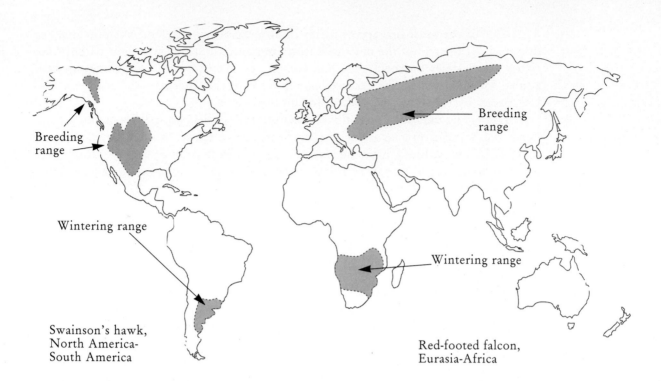

Breeding range

Breeding range

Wintering range

Wintering range

Swainson's hawk,
North America-
South America

Red-footed falcon,
Eurasia-Africa

If it seems puzzling that a northern hawk would fly so far south, it is. The epic migration of the Swainson's hawk makes more sense, though, if you think of it as a *southern* bird that flies north to breed. During the ice ages, most raptors (in fact, most birds in general) would have been restricted to the temperate and tropical zones far south of the glaciers. After the ice melted, some presumably began to expand their range farther and farther north, returning to their ancestral home in the south each winter. Over time, as the glaciers retreated completely, the distance the migrants covered would have grown to its current scale.

Swainson's hawks are not alone in their expansive migration. Broad-winged hawks travel nearly as far, from the northeastern United States and southern Canada to as far south as Peru, a journey of more than four thousand miles, although not all broadwings travel this far. Tundra peregrines from the Arctic migrate far down into South America as well, as do ospreys. Rough-legged hawks leave the arctic coastal plain where they breed, but their migration takes them no farther south than the northern United States, where the winters are also quite cold. As long as a bird completely vacates its breeding range, it is considered a *complete migrant,* regardless of the distance—or the climate of its winter home.

Other raptors hardly migrate at all. Many species in the southern and southwestern United States are year-round residents, while other species, known as *partial migrants,* may retreat from portions of their range but remain resident in others. The three different North American subspecies of merlins are examples of strikingly different migratory habits. The black merlins of the northern Pacific Coast are generally year-round residents, while the taiga merlins, which breed in the boreal forest across Canada, migrate as far south as Ecuador. Last, the pale prairie merlins of the northern Plains mostly migrate south into the southern United States and northern Mexico, but some stay put through the winter.

▶ *Not all migratory raptors travel to balmy climates. The rough-legged hawk, a complete migrant, moves south only to southern Canada and the northern United States.*

Equally complicated migratory patterns are found in red-tailed hawks, harriers, Cooper's hawks, kestrels, and others, including a phenomenon known as *leapfrogging*, where northern birds migrate over and beyond resident populations. One of the best examples is the peregrine falcon, the arctic subspecies of which migrates to Central and South America, leapfrogging over the less migratory race in temperate

▲ Although some of the pale prairie subspecies of the merlin are year-round residents of their breeding range, other individuals are migratory.

North America. In fact, as the chart shows, partial migrants far outnumber complete migrants and resident species.

Migratory habits are not completely cast in stone. As hydroelectric dams and warm-water discharges from power plants have increased in number, keeping large stretches of rivers ice-free, bald eagles have begun to winter much farther north than in decades past. Garbage dumps in some areas have permitted turkey vultures to stay farther north than they once did, and in Europe red kites enjoy a similar situation.

MIGRATORY HABITS OF NORTH AMERICAN RAPTORS

RESIDENT (NON-MIGRATORY)	PARTIAL MIGRANTS	COMPLETE MIGRANTS
California condor (formerly)	Black vulture • Turkey vulture	Osprey
White-tailed kite*	Bald eagle • Northern harrier	American swallow-tailed kite*
Snail kite*	Sharp-shinned hawk • Cooper's hawk	Mississippi kite
White-tailed hawk* (possibly migrant)	Northern goshawk • Common black-hawk	Broad-winged hawk
Crested caracara	Harris' hawk • Gray hawk	Swainson's hawk
	Red-shouldered hawk • Short-tailed hawk*	Rough-legged hawk
	Zone-tailed hawk • Red-tailed hawk	
	Ferruginous hawk • Golden eagle	
	American kestrel • Merlin	
	Prairie falcon • Peregrine falcon	*U.S. or North American population*
	Gyrfalcon	

MIGRATORY HABITS OF NORTH EURASIAN RAPTORS

RESIDENT (NON-MIGRATORY)	PARTIAL MIGRANTS	COMPLETE MIGRANTS
Black-shouldered kite Spanish eagle	Red kite • Black kite White-tailed eagle • Lammergeier Egyptian vulture • Eurasian griffon Cinereous vulture Western marsh-harrier Northern (hen) harrier Pallid harrier • Levant sparrowhawk Eurasian sparrowhawk Northern goshawk • Common buzzard Long-legged buzzard Rough-legged buzzard Imperial eagle • Golden eagle Booted eagle • Bonelli's eagle Eurasian kestrel • Merlin • Lanner Saker • Gyrfalcon • Peregrine falcon	European honey-buzzard Short-toed eagle Montagu's harrier Lesser spotted eagle Greater spotted eagle Lesser kestrel Red-footed falcon Eleonora's falcon Eurasian hobby

Year-round

Resident (White-tailed kite)

▶ *The white-tailed kite is a nonmigratory, year-round resident.*

Partial migrant (Cooper's hawk)

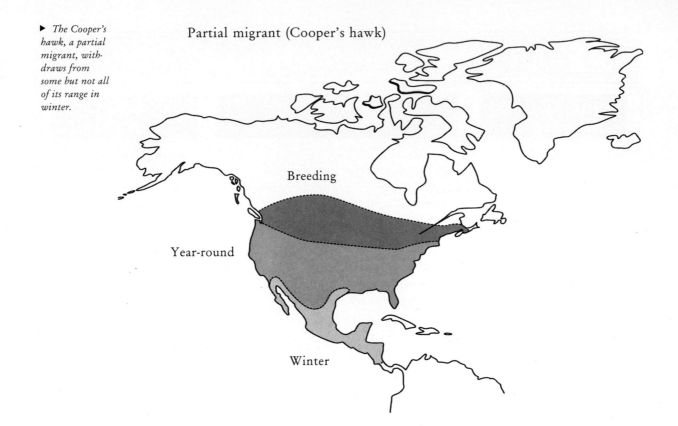

The Cooper's hawk, a partial migrant, withdraws from some but not all of its range in winter.

Breeding

Year-round

Winter

Complete migrant (Rough-legged hawk)

Breeding

Wintering

The rough-legged hawk, a complete migrant, vacates its entire breeding range.

1886	1926	1962
1896	1935	1972
1906	1945	
?	1954	*(Source: Newton, 1979)*

IRRUPTIONS

Not all raptors fit neatly into migratory/nonmigratory categories. Populations of many arctic or boreal species like northern goshawks are ordinarily nonmigratory but wander south in years when food supplies on their breeding grounds are scarce. These birds are known as *irruptive* species, and their incursions south are usually referred to as invasions.

Migration counts and other records show that goshawk invasions are tied to the ten-year population cycles of northern grouse and snowshoe hares, with major southward irruptions when one or both of the cycles hits bottom.

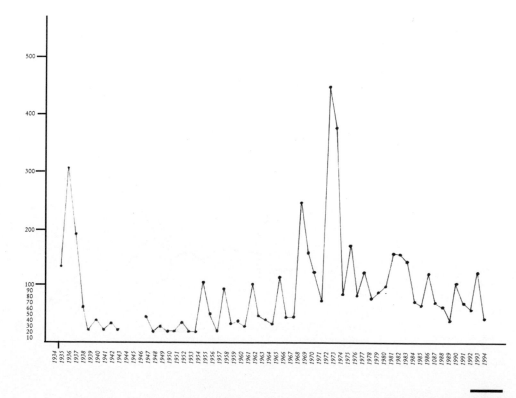

▶ *Annual migration counts of northern goshawks at Hawk Mountain Sanctuary, Pennsylvania, showing the cyclical nature of the migration, and major "invasions" in 1935, 1968 and 1972. (No counts were conducted 1943–45 due to World War II).*

▸▸▸ Major Migration Routes

A migrating raptor does not wander aimlessly—it has a genetically encoded sense of where to fly and at what time of the year, a sense that seems to be triggered (among other things) by the changing ratio of daylight to darkness.

A young sharp-shinned hawk on its first migration may leave eastern Canada in mid-September, heading south. It flies alone, and does not benefit from adult guidance. Like the young of many other raptor species, a young sharpshin tends to migrate earlier than an adult. It drifts due south across New England, turning only when it hits Long Island Sound, then bends to the southwest to follow the coast.

By the first week of October it reaches New Jersey, funneled—along with tens of thousands of other sharpshins, most of them juveniles—down the peninsula at Cape May. Here the hawks face a choice: Risk the thirteen-mile overwater crossing of Delaware Bay, or hook north across the mouth of the bay. A similar choice faces them on the Delmarva Peninsula, before they get back to the main body of the southeastern United States, where most will winter.

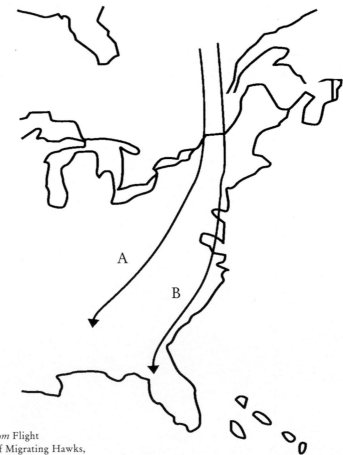

▸ *Generalized fall migration routes for adult sharp-shinned hawks (A) and immature sharp-shinned hawks (B) traveling south from eastern Canada. A majority of adults follow the Appalachian ridges, while most immatures drift south along the coast.*

(Adapted from Flight Strategies of Migrating Hawks, *Kerlinger, 1989)*

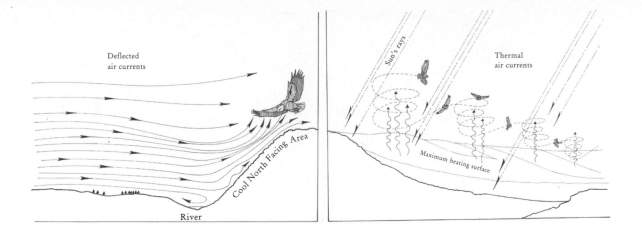

Deflected
air currents

Cool North Facing Area

River

Sun's rays

Thermal
air currents

Maximum heating surface

An adult sharp-shinned hawk, on the other hand, is much more likely to avoid the coastal route taken by its offspring. It, too, may drop straight south across New England, but when it strikes the Appalachians it may well veer southwest, following the parallel ridges deep into the South, shaving many days and much exertion from its trip.

Mountains and bodies of water, in fact, are among the greatest influences on the migratory paths of raptors. Mountain chains, especially long, continuous ranges like the Appalachians, provide deflection currents—updrafts caused by prevailing winds that hit the mountainsides and deflect upward. And because few raptors willingly cross large expanses of water, their routes often bend around such obstructions as lakes, bays, and oceans, concentrating the migration along the shore. South-pointing peninsulas like Cape May in New Jersey, Cape Charles in Virginia, and the Marin Headlands in California funnel raptors in autumn, while north-pointing sites like the Keweenaw Peninsula in Michigan do the same in spring.

Migratory "bottlenecks" occur all over the world and result in spectacular concentrations of raptors. In the Eastern Hemisphere, the largest so far discovered is Eilat in Israel, where vast numbers of migrating raptors streaming out of Africa are concentrated by the Gulf of Aqabah. Major concentrations also occur at the Straits of Gibraltar, Bosporus in Turkey, and other locations.

In the Americas, the largest raptor bottleneck—indeed, the heaviest migration point recorded anywhere in the world—is the narrow coastal plain in Veracruz State, Mexico. Here, enormous flocks of broad-winged and Swainson's hawks, Mississippi kites, and turkey vultures, all species dependent on thermals, are funneled between the Gulf of Mexico and the inland volcanic mountain range. In Veracruz, this strip, where the hot climate produces powerful thermals, pinches down to a belt just a few dozen miles wide.

The numbers of birds seen in Veracruz are astounding. In 1992, the first time the fall migration was properly censused, more than 2.5 million raptors were counted. Nearly half a million, mostly broad-winged hawks, were recorded in a single day. Even that was eclipsed two years later, when 3.2 million raptors were tallied, including more than 900,000 broadwings, Swainson's hawks, and turkey vultures in one day at just one site in the town of Cardel.

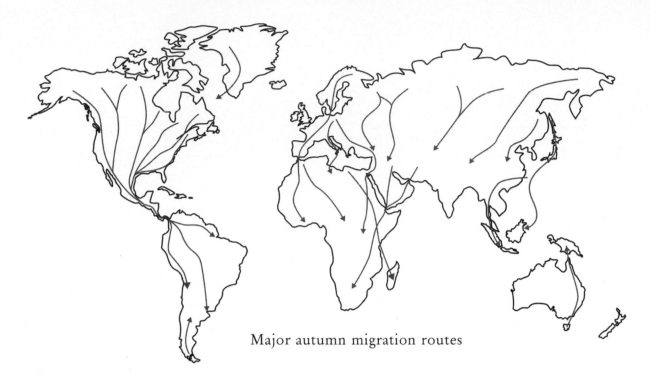

Major autumn migration routes

▲ *Major autumn migration routes followed by raptors worldwide, showing an avoidance of long-distance water crossings.*

What is even more remarkable is that the Veracruz bottleneck was essentially unknown to science until very recently. In fact, scientists believe, other and potentially even larger concentration points may well exist, especially in Asia, where relatively little fieldwork has been done. At least one Chinese bottleneck, at Beidaihe, has recently been discovered.

▶ *Falcons, like this immature peregrine falcon, tend to be coastal migrants, while buteos tend to travel most often on inland routes.*

 ▸ *Thousands of broad-winged hawks form a sheet across the sky in Veracruz, Mexico, where nearly a million hawks may pass in a single day.*

Not every species follows the same route south. Falcons tend to be coastal migrants, while buteos stay along inland ridges, for the most part. Regional populations, even from neighboring areas, may take different paths in migration. Ospreys are common migrants along both the Atlantic Coast and the Appalachian ridges, but when coastal populations crashed in the 1960s as a result of pesticide contamination, the number of ospreys migrating along the Appalachians stayed stable or actually rose. It seems likely that the ridge-migrant ospreys are mostly birds from inland lakes in New England and Canada, where DDT's effects were much less severe.

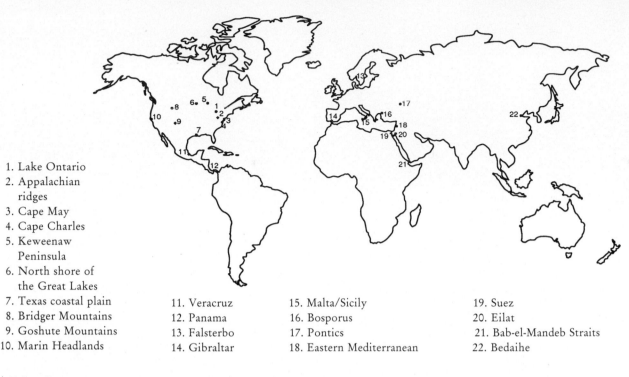

1. Lake Ontario
2. Appalachian ridges
3. Cape May
4. Cape Charles
5. Keweenaw Peninsula
6. North shore of the Great Lakes
7. Texas coastal plain
8. Bridger Mountains
9. Goshute Mountains
10. Marin Headlands
11. Veracruz
12. Panama
13. Falsterbo
14. Gibraltar
15. Malta/Sicily
16. Bosporus
17. Pontics
18. Eastern Mediterranean
19. Suez
20. Eilat
21. Bab-el-Mandeb Straits
22. Bedaihe

▲ *Major migratory bottlenecks around the world. The concentration of known sites in Europe, the Middle East and North America probably reflects greater interest by researchers, and other sites undoubtedly exist in South America, Africa and Asia.*

Nor does a species always take the same path from year to year. Broad-winged hawks are legendary for their fickle migrations in the East. One year a hawkwatch may tally forty thousand broadwings, and the next year—the main flight path having shifted a hundred miles to the east or west—observers will only see a trickle. This is because broadwings, unlike most other migrating hawks, rely more on thermals than wind currents along mountain ridges or the coast. In recent years, researchers have tried creating a "picket line" of counters, strung across more than fifty miles during the peak broadwing migration, in an attempt to locate the biggest flocks.

▸▸▸ MIGRATION TIMING

Like all migrant birds, raptors are surprisingly punctual in their travels. Each species has a peak migration period. It may be compressed as with broad-winged hawks, which pass through New England and the mid-Atlantic states in roughly three weeks, or it may encompass several months, as does the migration of northern harriers in the East.

There may also be differences between the sexes, and between adults and immatures. Hawk-watchers have long known that the migration of young accipiters and red-tailed hawks will peak each year before the majority of the adults begin to pass through. Female accipiters (which, because of the large size difference, are easy to tell from males) tend to migrate earlier, but one study of red-tailed hawks noted that larger redtails tend to migrate later than smaller redtails. Because red-tailed hawks aren't strongly dimorphic, and can't be sexed in the hand like accipiters, it remains only speculation that females migrate later than males.

▶ *Depending on the species, raptor migration may be compressed into just a few weeks, or last for several months, as is the case with northern harriers in the East.*

 ## MAJOR KNOWN MIGRATORY BOTTLENECKS

This listing of major migratory routes and bottlenecks is far from complete, and many more—particularly in Asia—no doubt remain to be discovered by science.

NEW WORLD

CENTRAL APPALACHIAN RIDGES (HAWK MOUNTAIN, ETC.) (FALL)

CAPE MAY, NEW JERSEY (FALL)

CAPE CHARLES, VIRGINIA (FALL)

SOUTHERN SHORE GREAT LAKES, ESPECIALLY LAKE ONTARIO (SPRING)

NORTHERN SHORE GREAT LAKES (FALL)

KEWEENAW PENINSULA, MICHIGAN (SPRING)

TEXAS COASTAL PLAIN (FALL)

GOSHUTE MOUNTAINS, NEVADA (FALL)

BRIDGER MOUNTAINS, MONTANA (GOLDEN EAGLES—SPRING/FALL)

MARIN HEADLANDS, CALIFORNIA (FALL)

VERACRUZ COASTAL PLAIN, MEXICO (SPRING/FALL)

PANAMA ISTHMUS (SPRING/FALL)

OLD WORLD

EILAT, ISRAEL (SPRING)

MALTA/SICILY (SPRING)

PONTICS, TURKEY (EASTERN BLACK SEA) (FALL)

EASTERN MEDITERRANEAN COAST, ISRAEL/LEBANON/SYRIA (FALL)

BOSPORUS, TURKEY (FALL)

GIBRALTAR/SOUTHERN SPAIN (FALL)

SUEZ, EGYPT (FALL)

BAB-EL-MANDEB STRAITS, YEMEN/ETHIOPIA (FALL)

FALSTERBO, SWEDEN (FALL)

BEIDAIHE, HEBEI PROVINCE, CHINA (FALL)

The following charts show the peak migration periods for several species of raptors at four well-known locations in the United States

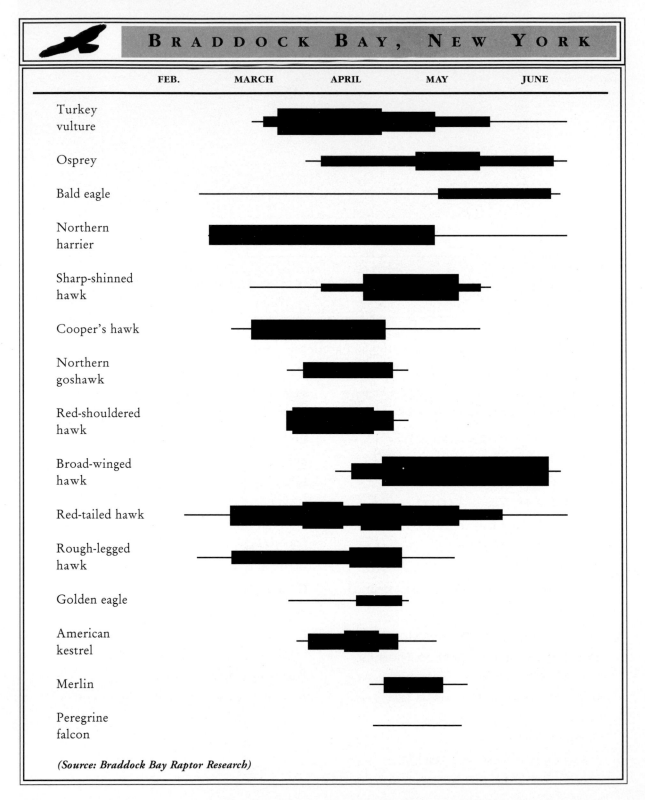

			BRADDOCK BAY, NEW YORK		
	FEB.	MARCH	APRIL	MAY	JUNE
Turkey vulture					
Osprey					
Bald eagle					
Northern harrier					
Sharp-shinned hawk					
Cooper's hawk					
Northern goshawk					
Red-shouldered hawk					
Broad-winged hawk					
Red-tailed hawk					
Rough-legged hawk					
Golden eagle					
American kestrel					
Merlin					
Peregrine falcon					

(Source: Braddock Bay Raptor Research)

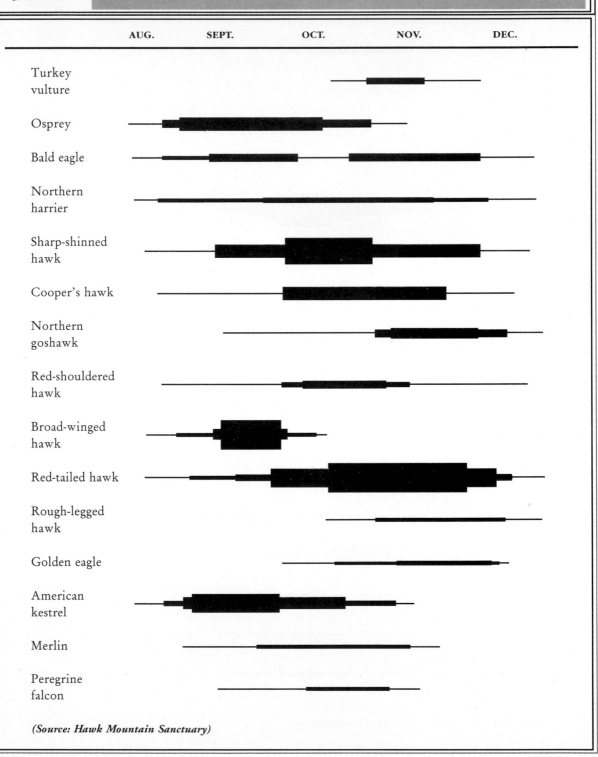

	AUG.	SEPT.	OCT.	NOV.	DEC.
Turkey vulture					
Osprey					
Bald eagle					
Northern harrier					
Sharp-shinned hawk					
Cooper's hawk					
Northern goshawk					
Red-shouldered hawk					
Broad-winged hawk					
Red-tailed hawk					
Rough-legged hawk					
Golden eagle					
American kestrel					
Merlin					
Peregrine falcon					

(Source: Hawk Mountain Sanctuary)

Goshute Mountains, Nevada

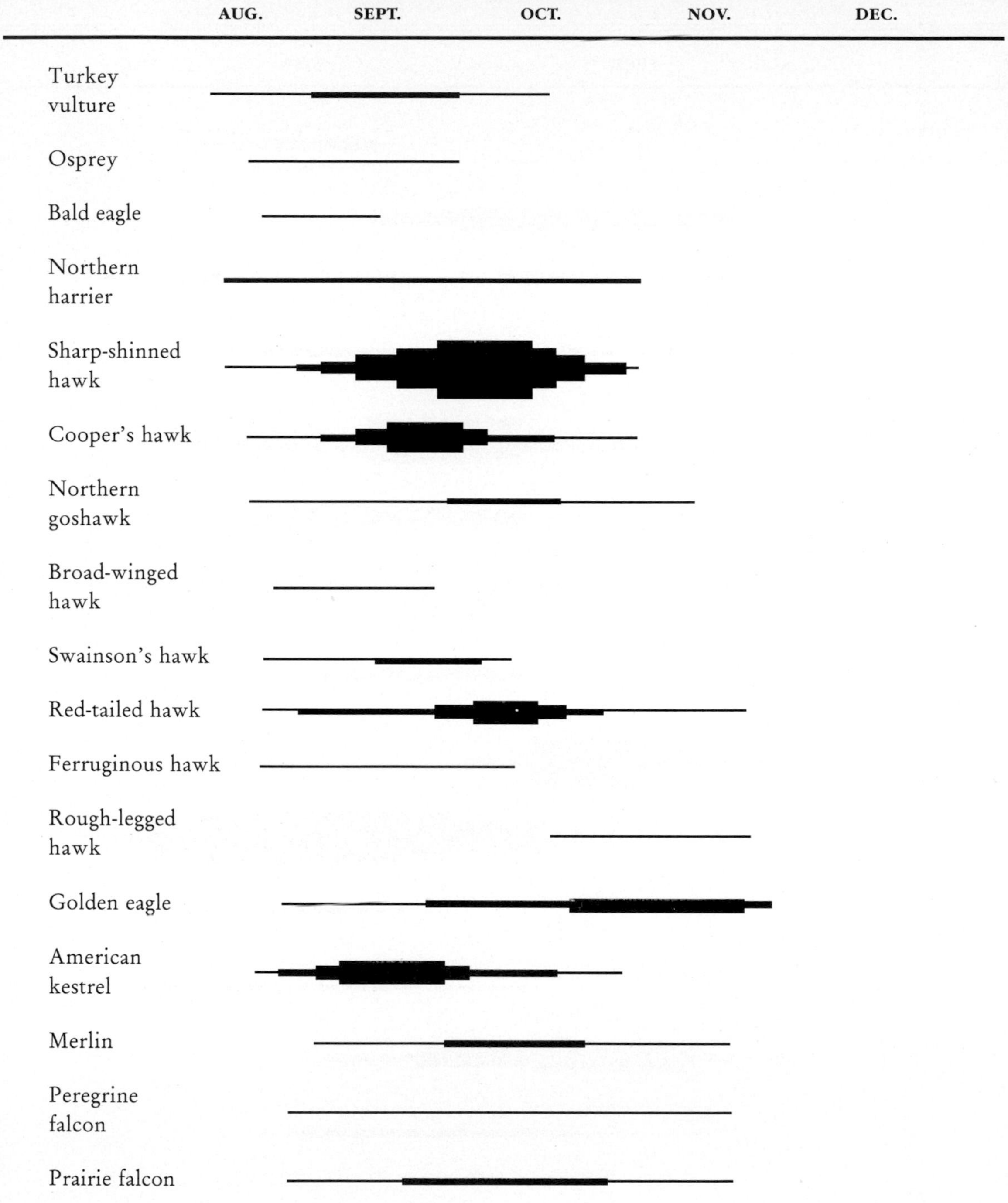
AUG.
SEPT.
OCT.
NOV.
DEC.
Turkey vulture
Osprey
Bald eagle
Northern harrier
Sharp-shinned hawk
Cooper's hawk
Northern goshawk
Broad-winged hawk
Swainson's hawk
Red-tailed hawk
Ferruginous hawk
Rough-legged hawk
Golden eagle
American kestrel
Merlin
Peregrine falcon
Prairie falcon

(Source: Hawk Migration Association of North America)

	AUG.	SEPT.	OCT.	NOV.	DEC.
Turkey vulture					
Osprey					
White-tailed kite					
Bald eagle					
Northern harrier					
Sharp-shinned hawk					
Cooper's hawk					
Red-shouldered hawk					
Broad-winged hawk					
Red-tailed hawk					
Ferruginous hawk					
Rough-legged hawk					
Golden eagle					
American kestrel					
Merlin					
Peregrine falcon					
Prairie falcon					

(Source: Hawk Migration Association of North America)

DIFFERENCE IN AUTUMN MIGRATION TIMING

IMMATURES BEFORE ADULTS
Northern harrier
Sharp-shinned hawk
Cooper's hawk
Northern goshawk
Red-tailed hawk
American kestrel
(possible)

ADULTS BEFORE IMMATURES
Osprey
Golden eagle (possible)
Peregrine falcon

MALES BEFORE FEMALES
Red-tailed hawk
(possible)
Peregrine falcon (imma-
tures only)

FEMALES BEFORE MALES
Northern harrier
Sharp-shinned hawk
Cooper's hawk
Merlin

(Source: Primarily Kerlinger, 1989)

▸▸▸ NAVIGATION AND ORIENTATION

Exactly how birds find their way across thousands of miles during migration has been one of the abiding mysteries of the natural world. It is not enough to merely put it down to instinct; a migrating raptor may be born with a genetic "map" telling it what heading to follow, but it first must know where it is, and must be able to determine its directional heading along the way.

Migration, therefore, has two main components—a raptor must orient itself with the world, and navigate to its destination. Research (mostly with pigeons, which are easier to work with than wild birds) has shown that landmarks are important for short-distance travel in, say, a hawk's hunting territory. But what about a young raptor making its first trip south? Then landmarks are of little help in unknown terrain, although large landscape features like shorelines and mountains—known as "leading lines"—may affect its course. Wind is also a major factor, sometimes blowing the raptor off course if it comes from the wrong quarter.

▲ *Migration involves the bird's ability to know where it is (orientation) as well as where it is going (navigation). Science is just beginning to understand the ways in which raptors like this red-tailed hawk migrate.*

Birds appear to use a variety of clues to help them orient and navigate on migration. Diurnal migrants like hawks, eagles, and falcons use the sun for orientation, and compensate instinctively as it moves across the sky. (Nocturnal migrants like most songbirds do the same with the moon and stars.)

Other guideposts are beyond human senses. Some birds, at least, are sensitive to the Earth's magnetic field, allowing them to navigate on both short- and long-distance travels. Birds also seem to be able to sense extremely low frequency sounds of the sort generated by wind and waves; these sound waves carry for hundreds, even thousands of miles, and may provide markers along the way. Researchers are also examining the role of barometric pressure, wind direction, and even ultraviolet light in bird navigation.

▸▸▸ Fasting on Migration

One of the more intriguing questions about raptor migration is whether certain long-distance migrants like broad-winged and Swainson's hawks feed during their trip.

Both species migrate in enormous flocks from North America down to the tropics, the broadwings stopping in Central America and northern South America, the Swainson's hawks continuing all the way to the Argentine pampas, a trip of

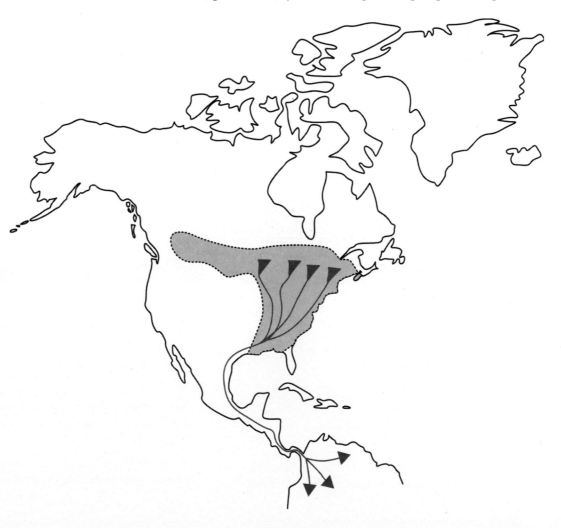

▸ Primary autumn migration routes of broad-winged hawks, which merge along the Gulf Coast into a single, narrow stream through Mexico and Central America. This concentrated migration, some biologists believe, may have led broad-winged and Swainson's hawks to evolve fasting as a way to avoid competition for food.

nearly seven thousand miles. Both species feed on migration in North America—broadwings are often seen snatching insects from midair, or hunting along roads—but some raptor experts contend that they stop feeding as they move south into Mexico, joining flocks that may number in the tens of thousands, and fasting during the bulk of their passage.

The evidence is mostly circumstantial. Despite the hundreds of thousands of these hawks passing through bottlenecks like eastern Mexico and Central America at any given time, few have been seen to feed, and areas where thousands roost at night show no droppings or pellets. Those migrant hawks that have been dissected usually have empty crops, and weakened, starving hawks are often picked up beneath the roosts.

Theoretically, a Swainson's hawk should be able to store up enough fat to tide it over on its journey, and fasting would both speed the long trip (since no time would be lost to hunting) as well as eliminate competition for scarce resources among the tremendous concentration of hawks. Fasting would also be an advantage to Swainson's hawks, a grassland species that must traverse long stretches of lowland forest. And because Swainson's and broadwings use thermals during migration, their energy demands would be fairly low.

Many ornithologists dismiss the fasting theory, however, pointing to evidence that the hawks do indeed hunt while traveling through the tropics; they also question whether raptors are capable of storing enough body fat to last them through the journey. Only future research is likely to settle the question once and for all.

ARGUMENTS FOR AND AGAINST FASTING

FOR

- Few accounts of migrant hawks seen feeding in tropics.
- Weakened, starving hawks picked up in roosting areas.
- Absence of pellets and feces below nighttime roosts.
- Low energy requirements for thermal flight.
- Presumed difficulty of finding enough food for flocks of tens of thousands of hawks.

AGAINST

- Lack of evidence that hawks can fast for such long periods.
- Weakened, starving birds indicate hawks cannot go long periods without food.
- Raptors may not be able to store enough fat to provide energy during a long fast.
- Abundance of food (i.e., insects) in tropics makes fasting unnecessary.

▸▸▸ NIGHT MIGRATION

No hawk, eagle, or falcon is primarily nocturnal, although a few, such as the northern harrier and forest-falcons, do hunt in the murky twilight of dawn and dusk. However, there are hints that some raptors migrate at night at least on occasion.

For instance, researchers counting migrating owls at Cape May, New Jersey, by watching the revolving beam of a lighthouse have reported seeing northern harriers heading out across Delaware Bay well after midnight. Along the coast and on inland mountain ridges, ospreys are often the last migrants of the day, still traveling at dusk when hawk-watchers have a hard time distinguishing them against the sky.

Nocturnal migration has been proven for only one North American raptor, however—the peregrine falcon. Along the Texas coast, where the arrival of migrant peregrines is carefully noted, many seem to appear overnight, and observers along the Atlantic Coast have seen the falcons heading to sea at dusk. Most conclusively, radio-telemetry studies show that some peregrines routinely spend the night at sea,

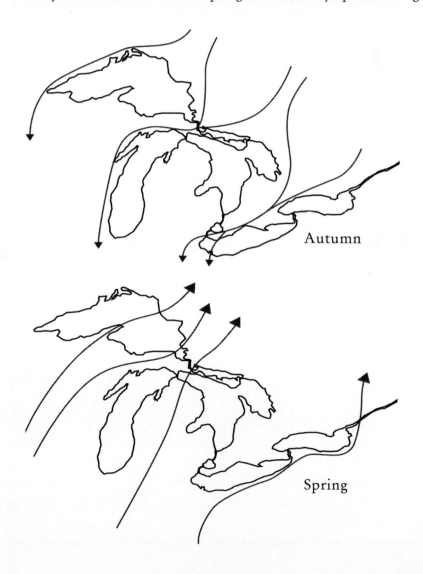

Autumn

Spring

▸ *Differences between routes taken in spring and autumn by raptors migrating around the Great Lakes, showing how the birds generally avoid major water crossings.*

▲ *Although most raptors migrate only by day, a few, such as ospreys, may travel at night, and a number of species that make long over-water crossings have no choice but to fly in darkness.*

LONG-DISTANCE
OVER-WATER MIGRANTS

SPECIES	DISTANCE (MILES)	ROUTE AND BODY OF WATER
Japanese sparrowhawk, Chinese goshawk	1,280	Japan–East Indies (Philippine Sea)
Amur falcon, lesser kestrel	1,200	India–Africa (Arabian Sea)
Merlin	280–500	Iceland–Great Britain (Atlantic Ocean)
Peregrine falcon	280	Aleutians–Alaskan mainland (island-hopping)

SPECIES	DISTANCE (MILES)	ROUTE AND BODY OF WATER
Gyrfalcon, peregrine falcon	220–430	Greenland–Labrador (Labrador Sea)
Gray-faced buzzard, Japanese sparrowhawk	372	Japan–Philippines (Philippine Sea)
Red-footed falcon, Eurasian hobby	196	Canary Islands–Africa (Atlantic Ocean)
Eurasian kestrel, peregrine falcon, black kite	181	Cape Verde Islands–Africa (Atlantic Ocean)
Peregrine falcon	176	Norway–Scotland (North Sea)
European honey-buzzard, osprey, black kite, red-footed falcon, hobby	125	Italy–Tunisia/Libya (Mediterranean Sea)
Chinese goshawk	125	China–Philippines (South China Sea)
Eleonora's falcon	125	Mediterranean islands–Africa (Mediterranean Sea)
Amur falcon, sooty falcon	125	Arabian Peninsula–Africa (Red Sea crossings)
Northern harrier, osprey, broad-winged hawk, merlin, peregrine falcon	77	Florida Keys–Cuba (Straits of Florida)
Osprey, merlin, peregrine falcon	75	Newfoundland-Nova Scotia (Cabot Strait)
Goshawk, Cooper's hawk, sharp-shinned hawk, red-shouldered hawk, red-tailed hawk, rough-legged hawk, other species	50	Michigan–Ontario (Lake Superior)
Osprey, sharp-shinned hawk, American kestrel, merlin, northern harrier, other species	38	New York–Ontario (Lake Ontario)

(Sources: McRae, 1985; Kerlinger, 1989)

soaring on thermals. Because adult male peregrines are quite rare in migration even along the coast, some authorities believe they may in fact be pelagic migrants, only occasionally coming to shore to perch.

Raptors that must cross expanses of water too wide to cover in a single day may be forced to fly at night. The following is a list of these long-distance over-water migrants; some distances vary, depending on which of several routes the birds would take:

▸▸▸ NONBREEDING RANGES

Birders in the Northern Hemisphere talk blithely about "winter" ranges and "summer" ranges for migrant birds, but biologists are more and more likely to use the terms "breeding" and "nonbreeding"—and for good reasons. For one thing, many raptors migrate to the tropics, where the seasons are wet and dry, not hot and cold; others migrate into the Southern Hemisphere, where the seasons are the reverse of the north. Such birds never "winter" at all.

Another concern is the assumption, noted previously, that the migrants are northern birds that go south for a brief interlude. The opposite is probably closer to the truth, as the calendar shows. Broad-winged hawks, for example, spend less than five months in their northern breeding grounds, and the other seven months either migrating or on their nonbreeding range in South America.

Of all the facets of a raptor's life, science knows the least about about the nonbreeding period. This is partly because many species spend this time in remote tropical regions that have been little studied, and partly because the birds themselves are generally quieter, more solitary, and less conspicuous then. It is clear that most raptors have as strong a fidelity to their nonbreeding range as to their breeding territory. One study of ospreys in Senegal, for instance, showed that six out of nine marked birds returned to the same place the following winter.

That's not surprising, because a raptor's nonbreeding needs are just as essential as those during the nesting season. It must find a place with good cover, abundant food, and an absence of dangers. Once the spot is found, it makes sense for the bird to return there year after year.

Exceptions are always intriguing, though, partly because they cast light on the general rule. The great majority of broad-winged hawks, for example, travel to Central and South America, but a small number—almost always immatures—winter in the southern half of Florida. In the past forty years, a handful of young Swainson's hawks have begun to do the same thing. It is thought that these inexperienced birds were blown off course on their first migration, and became trapped on the Florida peninsula, unwilling to make the long water crossing over the Caribbean. Some, at least, learn from their mistakes, for broadwings banded in Florida one year have been found the following winter in Central America. Because there are few adults among the Florida hawks, it seems likely most learn to correct for wind drift the following autumn.

A raptor's "winter" range may cover a huge area, but the majority of individuals will be found in the core, or primary, range. Again using broad-winged hawks

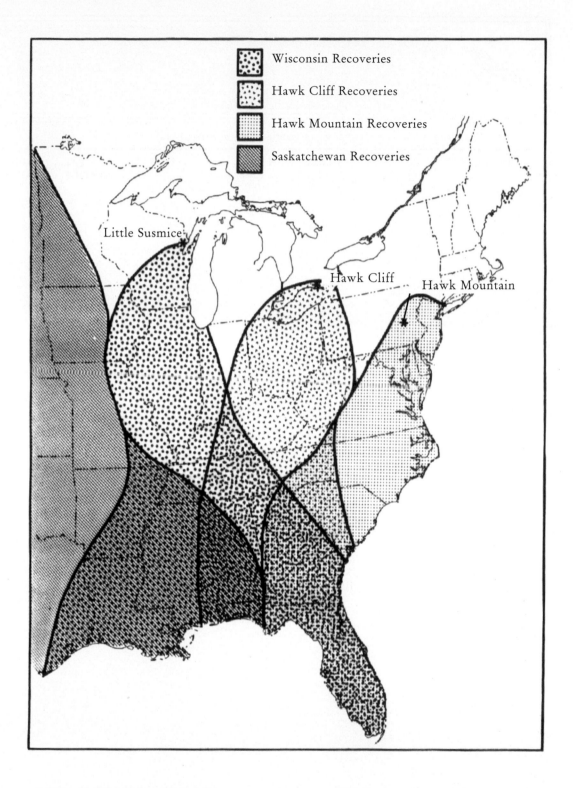

Legend:
- Wisconsin Recoveries
- Hawk Cliff Recoveries
- Hawk Mountain Recoveries
- Saskatchewan Recoveries

Little Susmice

Hawk Cliff

Hawk Mountain

▲ *Winter distribution of red-tailed hawks in eastern North America. Redtails banded in four different regions showed distinct, but overlapping, wintering areas.*
(Adapted from Brinker and Erdman, 1985)

"WINTERING" AREAS OF RAPTORS THAT BREED IN NORTH AMERICA

Nonbreeding areas (+ primary; − secondary; ? unknown)

SPECIES	CANADA	U.S.	MEXICO	CENTRAL AMERICA	SOUTH AMERICA
Black vulture*		+			
Turkey vulture*		+	+	+	?
Osprey		−	−	+	+
American swallow-tailed kite					+
White-tailed kite**		+			
Snail kite**		+			
Mississippi kite					+
Bald eagle*	+	+			
Northern harrier*		+	+	−	−
Sharp-shinned hawk*	−	+	+	+	
Cooper's hawk*		+	+	+	
Northern goshawk*	+	+ (partial migrant)			
Common black-hawk	+				
Harris' hawk**		+			
Gray hawk			+	+	
Red-shouldered hawk*	+				
Broad-winged hawk			−	+	+
Short-tailed hawk*		+			

Nonbreeding areas (+ primary; – secondary; ? unknown)

SPECIES	CANADA	U.S.	MEXICO	CENTRAL AMERICA	SOUTH AMERICA
▼ Swainson's hawk					+
White-tailed hawk**		+			
Zone-tailed hawk*		+	+		
Red-tailed hawk*	–	+	+	–	
Ferruginous hawk*		+	+		
Rough-legged hawk	+	+			
Golden eagle*		+	+		
Crested caracara**		+			
American kestrel*		+	+	–	
Merlin*		+	+	+	–
Prairie falcon*		+	+		
Gyrfalcon*	+	–			
Peregrine falcon*		+	+	+	+

*some populations resident on breeding range
**essentially nonmigratory

"WINTERING" AREAS OF RAPTORS THAT BREED IN EUROPE

Nonbreeding areas (+ primary; – secondary)

SPECIES	NORTH EUROPE	SOUTH EUROPE	MEDITER./ MIDDLE EAST	SUB-SAHARAN
▼ Osprey*			–	+
European honey-buzzard				+
Black-shouldered kite**			+	
Black kite				+

continued

Nonbreeding areas (+ primary; − secondary)

SPECIES	NORTH EUROPE	SOUTH EUROPE	MEDITER./ MIDDLE EAST	SUB- SAHARAN
Red kite*	−	+	+	
White-tailed eagle*	+	+	−	
Lammergeier*		+	+	
Egyptian vulture*		+	+	+
Eurasian griffon*		−	+	+
Cinereous vulture*		+	+	
Short-toed eagle				+
Western marsh-harrier*	−	+	+	−
Northern (hen) harrier*	+	+	+	
Pallid harrier			+	+
Montagu's harrier			−	+
Levant sparrowhawk			−	+
Eurasian sparrowhawk*		+	+	+
Northern goshawk*	+	+	−	
Common buzzard*	+	+	+	+
Long-legged buzzard*			+	−
Rough-legged buzzard	+	+		
Lesser spotted eagle				+
Greater spotted eagle			+	−
Imperial eagle*			+	−
Spanish eagle**		+		
Golden eagle*	+	+	+	
Booted eagle				+
Bonelli's eagle*		+	+	−

Nonbreeding areas (+ primary; – secondary)				
SPECIES	**NORTH EUROPE**	**SOUTH EUROPE**	**MEDITER./ MIDDLE EAST**	**SUB-SAHARAN**
Lesser kestrel				+
Eurasian kestrel*	+	+	+	+
Red-footed falcon				+
Eleonora's falcon				+
Merlin*	–	+	+	
Eurasian hobby				+
Lanner**			+	+
Saker*			+	–
Gyrfalcon**	+	–		
Peregrine falcon*	+	+	+	+

some populations resident on breeding range
essentially nonmigratory

as an example, their total winter range stretches from southern Mexico to Peru and Brazil, but most of them winter from southern Central America to Colombia and Venezuela.

▸▸▸ NONBREEDING HABITAT REQUIREMENTS

There can be dramatic differences between the habitat a raptor chooses for nesting and the area in which it spends the nonbreeding season. The greater spotted eagle of Eurasia, for example, is found in the nesting season in wooded river valleys, but it travels to the African savanna in autumn.

But for most raptors, the change of locale does not mean a fundamental change of habits. Broad-winged hawks inhabit deciduous forests in the East in summer and lowland rain forests in the tropics in winter, but both environments provide the bird with a high, unbroken canopy and an abundance of small vertebrates. Likewise, Swainson's hawks travel each year from the North American prairies to the pampas of Argentina—but at both ends of the journey, they hunt in open grasslands.

The quality of wintering habitat can mean the difference between survival and death, especially for immature raptors in their first year. It also greatly affects the following breeding season, especially for females; a meager winter may reduce her overall condition, cutting into the number of eggs she can produce come spring.

Among many raptors, the populations in nonbreeding ranges seem to be divided by age and sex. In most cases where the question has been studied, adults tend to winter farther north than immatures—perhaps giving the older birds an advantage in spring, when they have less distance to cover returning to the breeding

grounds. Even in the same winter range, the two sexes may prefer different habitats. Female American kestrels, several studies have found, are more likely to hunt wide-open, treeless grassland, while wintering males take the brushier areas or fields with taller vegetation.

The difference is even more marked between male and female northern harriers. Males tend to hunt brushier terrain, weedy fencerows, and corn stubble, looking for small birds, while the rodent-hunting females stick mostly to open grasslands. One study, in fact, found that there is more overlap between the diet and habitat preferences of female harriers and rough-legged hawks than there is between male and female harriers.

GEOGRAPHIC DIFFERENCES IN WINTER RANGE

ADULTS NORTH OF IMMATURES

Bald eagle (?)	Eurasian sparrowhawk
Northern goshawk	Red-tailed hawk
Steppe eagle	Gyrfalcon

MALES NORTH OF FEMALES

Pallid harrier	Sharp-shinned hawk
American kestrel	

FEMALES NORTH OF MALES

Eurasian sparrowhawk	Sharp-shinned hawk
Northern goshawk	Prairie falcon

NO DIFFERENCE BETWEEN ADULTS AND IMMATURES

Osprey

(Source: Kerlinger, 1989)

12

Life Span and Mortality

In order to survive, a juvenile raptor must master the complexities of flight, hunting, and attack strategies within the first months of life. Even with protection and coaching by parents, the average mortality rate for all young raptors is probably in the neighborhood of sixty-five to seventy-five percent. Banding and other studies have shown that in some cases, as many as ninety percent of young raptors perish in their first year.

For those skillful (or lucky) enough to survive to their first or second birthday, the chances of growing old steadily increase. According to one study, nearly three-quarters of all young red-tailed hawks die in their first year, but the mortality rate for the survivors decreases through each of the next four years, down to an annual rate of about thirteen percent.

▶ *Red-tailed hawks are among the most long-lived of raptors, with one banded bird surviving more than 23 years in the wild.*

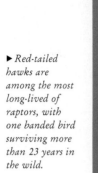 **JUVENILE MORTALITY RATES**

SPECIES	MORTALITY RATE (percentage)
Osprey	53.4 (North America)
	59.7 (Europe)
Black kite	30.9
Bald eagle	78.5
Eurasian sparrowhawk	49.6
Cooper's hawk	77.5
Red-shouldered hawk	62.6
Red-tailed hawk	73.4
Common buzzard	63.5
Eurasian kestrel	52.2
American kestrel	68.8
Peregrine falcon	57.4 (North America and Europe)

(Source: Brown and Amadon, 1968)

As a rule of thumb, the larger a raptor is, the longer it will live. The average life span for small falcons like kestrels is barely more than a year, and one study of American kestrels found that only fifteen out of more than five hundred lived to more than age four. Even in captivity, kestrels usually only live two or three years, although a few remarkable captives lived more than fourteen. Sharp-shinned hawks rarely live past five years of age, while eagles, on the other hand, have survived forty or fifty years in captivity, and California condors and turkey and black vultures may likewise live for very long periods.

The maximum life span for most raptors in the wild is still largely a mystery, although banding studies give an indication. The trouble is that so few banded raptors are ever recovered and reported; the oldest *banded* raptor may not, in fact, be the oldest in the population.

For raptors like sharp-shinned hawks and American kestrels, which are banded each year by the thousands, longevity information is probably fairly accurate. For species like Harris' hawks, of which less than two thousand have been banded and fewer than fifty ever recovered, the results are much less reliable.

LONGEVITY RECORDS— BANDED WILD RAPTORS

SPECIES	OLDEST AGE RECORDED (Years/Months)	WHERE BANDED
Turkey vulture	16.10	Ohio
Black vulture	25.06	Louisiana
Osprey	23.00	Maryland
Bald eagle	21.11	Alaska
Snail kite	7.00	Florida
Black-shouldered kite	5.11	California
Mississippi kite	8.00	Louisiana
Northern harrier	16.05	Ohio
Sharp-shinned hawk	9.10	Ontario
Cooper's hawk	10.06	Pennsylvania
Northern goshawk	13.00	Minnesota
Red-shouldered hawk	19.11	Maryland
Broad-winged hawk	18.04	Florida
Red-tailed hawk	23.05	Pennsylvania

SPECIES	OLDEST AGE RECORDED (Years/Months)	WHERE BANDED
Swainson's hawk	15.11	Saskatchewan
Rough-legged hawk	17.09	Illinois (wintering)
Ferruginous hawk	15.11	Alberta
Harris' hawk	12.07	Texas
Golden eagle	17.01	Saskatchewan
Crested caracara	8.11	Florida
American kestrel	11.07	New York
Merlin	7.10	New Jersey
Prairie falcon	10.07	Alberta
Peregrine falcon	12.03	Pennsylvania

(Source: Clapp, Klimkiewicz, and Kennard, 1982; Klimkiewicz and Futcher, 1989)

AGES OF CAPTIVE RAPTORS

As with wild banding records, these are only the maximum recorded ages—not the maximum possible ages.

SPECIES	MAXIMUM AGE RECORDED (Years)
Turkey vulture	20
California condor	45
Bald eagle	48
Northern goshawk	19
Red-tailed hawk	29
Golden eagle	46
Crested caracara	13
American kestrel	17
Prairie falcon	10

(Source: Terres, 1980)

Natural Mortality Factors

▶▶ Diseases And Parasites

Like any living organisms, raptors are susceptible to a wide variety of diseases and parasites. Because of their solitary nature, however, raptors are usually spared major epidemics.

··· BACTERIA
Bacterial diseases like avian tuberculosis, avian cholera, and botulism may be spread by prey, and bald eagles—which frequently scavenge waterfowl weakened by botulism outbreaks—suffer from that sometimes fatal disease rather commonly. Turkey vultures, on the other hand, have nearly 100,000 times the resistance to botulism as found in pigeons.

Bumblefoot, a bacterial staph infection that causes severe swelling and tissue death in the feet, is much more common in captive birds with improper perches than in wild raptors. Falconers and wildlife rehabilitators prevent its occurrence by avoiding smooth perches, which create worn spots on the foot pads; rope, wrapped tightly around the perch, is the most common preventive measure.

▲ *Hippoboscid flies are a common external parasite on raptors, living between the feathers and feeding on the bird's blood.*

··· VIRUSES AND FUNGAL INFECTIONS
Among the most important viral diseases that afflict raptors is avian pox (fowl pox), which causes lesions and growths on the bird's head, eyes, tongue, and feet. Severe cases can interfere with the birds' vision and respiration, and can be fatal. Fungal infections include aspergillosis, an often fatal respiratory disease commonly found in raptors; infected birds often cough and breathe open-mouthed.

··· PARASITES
A parasitic disease infamous among falconers is trichomoniasis, more commonly known as frounce. Caused by a protozoan common in the upper gastrointestinal tracts of pigeons and doves—especially domestic pigeons—the disease leads to lesions inside the mouth and throat of infected raptors, and can kill quickly by suffocation or starvation.

A variety of external parasites make their living on the skin and among the feathers of raptors; some of them, like a kind of louse found only on California condors, are probably specific to individual species of raptors. The most noticeable are the hippoboscid flies, also known as flat flies or louse flies, biting insects that crawl, crablike, among the body feathers. Slow-flying and nearly indestructible (researchers who handle raptors sometimes use needlenosed pliers to kill

RAPTOR DISEASES AND PARASITES

BACTERIAL DISEASES
    Tuberculosis
    Botulism
    Avian cholera
    Salmonellosis
    Coccidiosis
    Bumblefoot
    Psittacosis (chlamydiosis)*

VIRAL DISEASES
    Avian pox
    Newcastle disease (Old World)*

FUNGAL DISEASES
    Aspergillosis

INTERNAL PARASITES
    Trichomoniasis
    Roundworm infections (*Capillaria, Ascariasis*)
    Flukes
    Tapeworms

EXTERNAL PARASITES
    Hippoboscid (flat) flies
    Sucking (mallophagan) lice
    Feather mites and red mites
    Bird fleas
    Ticks*

rare in raptors

them) hippoboscids may transmit blood parasites, but will not bite humans. Female flat flies give birth to fully formed young, with no intermediate stage.

Other common external parasites include biting lice and feather mites, which are present on most birds, but usually not at levels that cause serious health problems. A sick bird, however, which is listless and doesn' t preen or bathe, may suddenly find itself also fending off a heavy infestation of lice or mites. Sucking lice and red mites feed on blood, while feather mites feed on the raptor's plumage, and may cause weakening of the feathers at unusually high levels.

In rainy summers, or in damp nest locations, tachnid fly larvae may infect the ear openings of raptors. Extremely common in some areas, the maggots usually do no permanent damage, although hearing loss and some deaths of nestlings have been reported.

▸▸▸ ACCIDENTS

Young animals can find an infinite number of ways to get into trouble, and immature raptors are no different. Accidents account for a large percentage of annual deaths, and inexperienced young account for most of the victims.

Many raptors are killed or injured simply by flying into objects. This may seem odd, given a raptor's eyesight, but it is difficult to notice a utility line or a barbed-wire fence against a cluttered background while diving at seventy or eighty miles per hour. Nor are the hazards all man-made; wildlife rehabilitators treat many raptors that have been injured in collisions with branches, sticks, tree trunks—even cliffs.

Human objects do present special problems for raptors, however. Automobiles kill untold thousands each year, especially species like kestrels and

red-tailed hawks that routinely hunt rodents along the grassy verges of highways. High-voltage lines have been death traps for large raptors, especially in the West, where utility poles are often the only suitable nesting sites for miles around. A bird can perch on a single power line with impunity, but should its wing touch a neighboring line, the result is electrocution. Golden eagles in particular, with their seven- or eight-foot wingspans, are at risk, and many power companies have redesigned their transmission towers to minimize the danger to raptors.

In years past, shooting was a significant cause of raptor mortality, but the incidence of illegal shooting has dropped dramatically in North America, although it remains a serious threat in developing countries, as well as in the Mediterranean basin. Chemical contamination and other environmental hazards have been, and continue to be, significant causes of mortality; they are discussed in more detail in the section on conservation.

CONSERVATION

13

Conservation Challenges

▸▸▸ Habitat Destruction

No animal can survive without a home. Unfortunately, wildlife habitat is disappearing at a frightening rate, pushing many species of raptors toward the brink.

The situation is gravest in the tropics, where wild habitats—not only rain forest, but a host of ecosystems—are being altered or destroyed. Tropical island species, inhabiting small, restricted ranges to begin with, are especially at risk, and many of the most threatened species of raptors are those like the Philippine eagle and Javan hawk-eagle, Gundlach's hawk in Cuba, and Ridgway's hawk in Hispaniola, whose woodland homes have been decimated by deforestation.

If habitat loss is pervasive enough, it can endanger even wide range raptors. The horrific losses of lowland forest in Central America and highland forest in South America have placed more than a dozen species of raptors at risk, including the harpy eagle. Many of the largest species are especially vulnerable because they require enormous territories and are unable to adjust to human disturbance.

In North America, the conversion of virgin forest in the Northeast to a mix of woodlots and fields in the nineteenth century was devastating to northern goshawks,

▶ *As hardwood forests in the Northeast have matured, northern goshawks have returned to much of their former range.*

although as the forests have matured in recent decades, goshawks have been able to reclaim some of their former range. In New England, habitat changes tilted the balance away from red-shouldered hawks, once the most common species of large buteo in the region, to red-tailed hawks, which are more common today.

In the Pacific Northwest, controversy over the logging of old-growth forests has centered on spotted owls, but other species, including diurnal raptors, are also at risk. The Queen Charlotte goshawk, a small, dark subspecies of the northern goshawk found only in coastal British Columbia and southeastern Alaska, is thought to be declining as a result of logging, and is being considered for protection under the federal Endangered Species Act. The total population is unknown, but biologists have found fewer than twenty nests in the Alaskan portion of its range.

▸▸▸ DESTRUCTION OF MIGRATION CORRIDORS

Habitat conservation efforts have traditionally focused on the breeding habitat of species—a dangerously narrow view for migrant birds. In recent years, more attention has been given to saving wintering grounds, especially in the tropics, but experts point out that the weakest link in the chain of protection may be migration corridors, the travel lanes used twice each year.

Although used only for a few weeks in spring and fall, migratory corridors are vital to migrant raptors. Unfortunately, relatively little is known about where the hawks travel, or what habitat features are important along the way. In the Appalachians, for instance, conservation efforts have often focused on the ridges themselves, which are used during the day as hawks follow deflection wind currents for lift. But that may not be sufficient.

One recent radio-telemetry study in Pennsylvania suggests that migrating red-tailed hawks often leave the ridges in evening to roost in the valleys, where they hunt shortly after dawn before resuming their migration. These valley farmlands, however, are being rapidly developed, raising the possibility that we may preserve the ridges but lose the equally important feeding and resting habitat on either side.

The situation is especially critical at the major continental "bottlenecks" like Veracruz in Mexico and Eilat in Israel, where millions of raptors squeeze through narrow passages. Only since 1992 have scientists been censusing the migration through Veracruz, for instance, but it is clear that virtually all the broad-winged hawks in the world, as well as a large percentage of the global population of Swainson's hawks and many other species, pass through this thin stretch of coastal plain.

The landscape in Veracruz has been radically altered, however. Much of the native dry tropical forest has been leveled for grazing and sugarcane, forcing the hawks to roost in smaller and more vulnerable patches of forest. Pesticide use is rampant, and despite nominal legal protection, hawks are still shot in untold numbers for sport, for food, or out of a basic ignorance of the value of predators. Even though migrant hawks pass through this part of Mexico for only a few months each year, preserving at least a remnant of the natural landscape is absolutely essential for the hawks' survival.

It may already be too late in some parts of the world. Recent surveys of historical migration bottlenecks in Taiwan showed that several are no longer used by

▼ *Once covered in tropical dry forest, most of central Veracruz has been converted to pasture and sugar cane fields, leaving little woodland for migrating raptors.*

raptors traveling from Korea and Japan to the Philippines, as a result of massive habitat changes.

To address the problem of preserving migratory corridors—as well as the direct persecution raptors still suffer in many parts of the globe—internationally respected Hawk Mountain Sanctuary has launched an initiative known as Hawks Aloft Worldwide.

The project has two objectives—to create a global atlas identifying all known migratory watch sites for birds of prey, and to provide training to local organizations around the world for generating effective land conservation programs. Initial efforts are already underway in Veracruz and other Latin American locations.

▸▸ SHOOTING, TRAPPING, AND DIRECT PERSECUTION

At one time, the only good hawk was a dead hawk. It was considered a civic responsibility to shoot game-killing, chicken-stealing vermin like hawks.

Times have changed, and most people now recognize the importance of wild predators. But not everyone. Even though raptors are fully protected in many countries, illegal shooting continues, sometimes on such a scale as to threaten the survival of some species.

The situation is worst in developing countries, where an influx of modern weapons has made it easy for what were once subsistence hunters to slaughter wildlife indiscriminately. In Colombia each spring, for example, *campesinos* use lanterns and guns to kill roosting Swainson's and broad-winged hawks, using some for food and rendering the fat for folk medicine; hawk-shooting is also tied to folk beliefs about Lent. Such situations are repeated all along the birds' migration route through Latin America.

Some of the most disturbing examples of large-scale shooting, however, come not from tropical countries but from Mediterranean Europe. Shooting migrating raptors for sport is a grave problem in Malta, and in Sicily and the toe of mainland Italy, where gunners occupy concrete bunkers in the hills, killing for sport thousands of honey-buzzards and other species exhausted after the long ocean crossing.

In Malta alone, as many as sixteen thousand gunners kill more than ten thousand raptors each year during the spring and autumn migration. The dead include marsh-harriers, honey-buzzards, Eurasian hobbies, Eurasian kestrels, endangered lesser kestrels, and at least eight other species. Across the Mediterranean, the annual toll has been placed at 100,000 raptors.

In Portugal, illegal shooting during the fall dove-hunting season—often to acquire stuffed taxidermy specimens—is considered the leading cause of death in raptors. Similar situations occur in portions of many other Mediterranean basin countries, including Spain, France, and Greece. Legal protection for raptors, which is on the books in all these countries, is obviously useless without vigorous enforcement.

While large-scale shooting of raptors is generally a thing of the past in North America, it does continue in some areas. As recently as the 1970s, ranchers in the

▲ *Legal and illegal trade in live raptors flourishes in many regions, particularly for prized falconry species like the saker falcon of Eurasia.*

▶ *Large-scale shooting of raptors continues in many parts of the world, including the killing of migrating Swainson's hawks in Colombia.*

West were hiring helicopter-borne gunners to kill golden and bald eagles, and shooting continues to be the leading cause of death for young bald eagles. In the late 1980s, gamekeepers on a huge private estate in central Virginia were convicted of killing a variety of hawks, with some reports placing the toll in the hundreds.

While shooting is the most common way of killing raptors, there are other methods. In ranching regions like the American West and Australia, poisoned carcasses were (and in some areas still are) placed out for scavenging eagles and hawks, a technique also once commonly used in northern Europe by gamekeepers. Pole-trapping—placing a leg-hold trap on a high post, where raptors are likely to perch—is a simple, cheap way to kill birds of prey, and one that is still used in some regions despite its illegality.

In North America, a lucrative black market for raptor feathers and body parts —especially those of eagles—is fueled by Indian lore enthusiasts. While Native Americans can be issued permits to possess eagle parts, which are supplied by the U.S. Fish and Wildlife Service from salvaged birds, non-Indians often pay exorbitant prices for feathers, feet, and skulls. Ironically, several of the largest eagle-poaching rings to be broken have involved Native Americans.

International trade in raptors, taking live birds for pets or falconry, or for feathers and body parts, is a continuing threat in many areas of the world. With its abundance of oil money and long tradition of falconry, the Middle East provides the strongest market for wild-caught raptors, even though many species can be easily bred in captivity. Thousands of lagger, saker, and peregrine falcons, as well as other raptors, are taken each year in Asia both legally and illegally; and peregrine falcons, illegally trapped in Mexico, have been intercepted in transit to the Middle East.

▸▸▸ PESTICIDES AND OTHER CHEMICALS

One of the most insidious threats to raptor survival continues to be chemical contamination. In the decades following World War II, pesticides almost wiped out bald eagles and ospreys in North America and peregrine falcons in several regions of the world, and had a serious impact on many other raptor populations.

While the use of many notorious toxins like DDT has been largely banned in the United States, they are still widely used in much of the developing world. Besides threatening resident species in developing countries, the pesticides are an ongoing danger to migratory species that ingest them on their wintering grounds.

▲ *Thinned by DDT contamination, this peregrine falcon egg cracked under the weight of the incubating female.*

Chemical contamination rarely kills a raptor outright; instead, the substances often cripple reproduction. The most famous examples are the organochlorines like DDT (and DDE, its metabolite that forms in a bird's body), which alter the amount of magnesium and phosphate in newly formed eggshells. As magnesium and phosphate levels rise, the shell becomes thin and brittle, so that the eggs simply collapse under the weight of the incubating female. Contaminated females also lay a high percentage of infertile eggs, and high phosphate levels may even kill the embryo outright.

The role of eggshell thinning in the disappearance of peregrine falcons came to light in the 1960s, and an examination of old egg collections, many dating back to the nineteenth century, proved that falcon eggshells began to decrease in thickness rather suddenly in 1947—the year that DDT was introduced into widespread use as an agricultural chemical.

Raptors suffer so badly from pesticide effects as the result of a process known as *bioaccumulation*, or *biomagnification*. Herbivores like grasshoppers consume relatively low levels of a pesticide, storing it in their body tissues. These, in turn, are eaten by insectivorous birds, which accumulate each small dose in the grasshoppers' bodies within their own, greatly magnifying the effect of the pesticide. The songbirds are then eaten by raptors, which over the years can build dangerously high levels of the chemical within their fatty tissues.

Those species at the end of long food chains, or food chains that involve many carnivorous links, are especially at risk. During the peak of DDT use, bird-eating raptors like peregrine falcons, merlins, Cooper's hawks, and sharp-shinned hawks showed much higher levels of DDE than did mammal hunters like golden eagles and Swainson's hawks—birds that eat at the end of very short food chains.

▶ Chemical contamination from long-lived pesticides like DDT has presented an enduring problem for raptors like ospreys, which accumulate dangerous doses of the toxins from the food they eat.

Raptors that feed on aquatic prey, like ospreys and bald eagles, also suffered very badly. Aquatic food chains are especially long and complex, and involve many intermediate links of carnivores eating small carnivores, climbing from predatory insects through tiny minnows to large fish, and ultimately to the birds of prey. These two groups of raptors—bird eaters and fish eaters—suffered the worst declines from organochlorines.

Although DDT, lindane, dieldrin, and other so-called "hard" pesticides were banned from general use in the United States decades ago, their legacy remains. Such chemicals are extremely resistant to breakdown in the environment, and continue to plague some raptor populations, notably peregrine falcons in California; migrants also still pick up the substances on their tropical wintering grounds.

▶ Steep declines in sharp-shinned hawk counts at eastern migration sites suggests the small accipiters may be suffering from environmental toxins.

Nor are tropical species escaping the dangers of organochlorines and other, more modern substances. Biologists working with tropical raptors are seeing many of the same danger signs—faltering reproduction, thinning eggshells—that foretold the collapse of temperate-zone raptors like the peregrine.

Other chemicals still in common use in North America pose serious risks for wildlife, including raptors. Bald eagles have been only the most famous victims of carbofuran, a carbamate pesticide that has been heavily used on corn and other crops. The federal Environmental Protection Agency estimated that in the late 1980s, up to 2.4 million birds were being killed annually by carbofuran, a fast-acting toxin that causes severe damage to the nervous system.

Besides pesticides, raptors are adversely affected by a wide spectrum of synthetic chemicals, including polychlorinated biphenyls (PCBs) and such heavy metals as methyl-mercury, cadmium, lead, and aluminum. Most have multiple effects on a raptor's body, including nervous-system disorders and eggshell thinning. Little research has been done on the dangers posed to raptors by these substances, however.

DDT DÉJÀ VU?

Most conservationists consider DDT a past danger, given the modern recovery of bald eagles, ospreys, and peregrine falcons. But in the past decade hawk-watchers in the East have seen drastic decreases in the number of migrating sharp-shinned hawks —and some researchers are beginning to think that DDT is again to blame.

"Sharpies," as they're called, are among the most common hawks in North America. Through the 1970s and early 1980s, annual counts at Cape May, New Jersey, ran as high as 75,000 sharpshins, making it one of the most important migration points for this species.

Since the mid-1980s, however, sharpshin counts have plummeted by sixty to seventy percent at Cape May, falling from 35,000 in 1985 to 14,000 in 1991. Because of the many variables—weather, observer effort, and so forth—migration counts are not always an accurate measure of populations, but the fact that the downward trend has continued for nearly a decade suggests the decline is real.

So, too, does a more recent sharpshin decline at Hawk Mountain and other inland count stations. The reason for the time lag may be behavioral. Cape May's sharpshin migration is made up mostly of immatures, while the adults generally follow the inland ridges in subsequent years. If something is reducing sharpie populations, biologists would expect to see decreases in immatures first—which is exactly what has occurred in sharpies, and what happened years ago in bald eagles.

There could be many reasons for the sharpshin declines, including fragmentation of the hawk's forest habitat, decreases in the populations of songbirds on which they feed, changes in weather that have altered migration routes, and even acid rain. But blood samples from sharp-shinned hawks nesting in Canada showed high levels of DDT and other chemicals. Even though DDT is banned for most use in North America, it is commonly used in Latin America, where many of the songbirds on which sharpshins feed spend the winter. And because DDT is an extremely stable chemical, it continues to lurk in the environment decades after it was sprayed, working its way up the food chain to raptors.

14

LEGAL PROTECTION

While many game animals enjoyed a measure of legal protection as far back as the Middle Ages, protection for raptors has been slow to take hold—although some of the same medieval codes also prevented peasants from capturing raptors, which were reserved for falconry by the nobility.

Given that raptors were often seen as competitors for wild game and domestic livestock, the lack of protection for predators is not surprising; but even today, long after science has demonstrated their value, raptors still suffer from persecution in many parts of the world. Even in countries where protective laws are on the books, enforcement is often sparse or completely lacking.

(*Photo by Richard Pough and Henry Collins, courtesy Hawk Mountain Sanctuary*)

Modern raptor protection in the United States had its genesis in the Appalachians of eastern Pennsylvania, where in the late nineteenth and early twentieth centuries, thousands of hawks were shot each year during the autumn migration. The best-known gunning spot was along the Kittatinny Ridge north of Reading, at an overlook that became known as Hawk Mountain. "SPORTSMEN SHOOT MIGRATING HAWKS," trumpeted one local newspaper headline in 1929. "Pottsville Hunters Knock Down Pests from Point of Vantage in Blue Mountains. Kill 300 in a single day," the headline read.

Efforts to curtail the slaughter began at the turn of the century, but by 1932 it was still legal to shoot virtually any hawk in Pennsylvania, and a bounty of five dollars was being offered on goshawks—in effect an incentive to shoot all raptors, since few gunners could identify them on the wing. That year, however, conservationist Richard H. Pough and a friend visited the site and photographed the carnage, laying out rows and piles of dead hawks.

Those images caught the attention of a small group of conservationists led by Rosalie Edge, a firebrand New Yorker. The group purchased the 1,400-acre mountaintop in 1934 for $3,500, creating Hawk Mountain Sanctuary—the world's first refute for birds of prey. For decades thereafter, Hawk Mountain led the fight to extend legal protection to all raptors.

Protection came slowly—first to species like kestrels and ospreys that were seen as neutral, or to "beneficial" hawks like redtails, which feed on rodents. Bald and golden eagles were granted protection by Congress with the Bald Eagle Protection Act of 1940, although Alaska, where hundreds of eagles were shot for bounty, was excluded. Raptor protection was largely a state issue, however, and the three accipiters (sharp-shinned hawk, Cooper's hawk, and goshawk) were generally denied legal protection for years since they were reputed to be game- and poultry-killers. It was not until 1972 that the federal government extended the umbrella of complete protection to all migratory birds, including all raptors.

Today there are serious penalties—fines and imprisonment—under federal law for killing, injuring, or harassing any raptor, as well as its nest or eggs. In addition, certain species may be granted even more stringent protection under the federal Endangered Species Act (discussed below).

▶ *Through the 1950s and '60s, many states exempted accipiters like sharp-shinned and Cooper's hawks from legal protection. This led to the indiscriminate killing of many other species of raptors. (Courtesy Hawk Mountain Sanctuary)*

NATIONAL AND INTERNATIONAL LAWS PROTECTING RAPTORS

The year 1973 was a watershed for conservation of rare plants and animals around the world. In the United States, the Endangered Species Act (ESA) was approved by Congress, greatly strengthening federal protection of threatened and endangered species in the United States, while that same year, nations from around the globe signed the treaty known as CITES, the Convention on International Trade in Endangered Species of Wild Flora and Fauna.

▸▸▸ ENDANGERED SPECIES ACT

The federal ESA lists species of animals and plants that are found worldwide, and that the U.S. Fish and Wildlife Service has determined are endangered or threatened with extinction. The law severely restricts the possession or importation to the United States of listed species, and covers all federally sponsored projects including those overseas, providing important protection for rare creatures around the world.

According to the ESA, an *endangered* species is one at risk of extinction in all, or a significant part, of its range. A *threatened* species is one that is likely to become endangered within the foreseeable future in all, or a significant part, of its range.

There are many differences, and many similarities, between the ESA and CITES lists. Generally speaking, CITES Appendix I (a list of threatened species) is analogous to the ESA list.

▶ *Red-tailed hawks were among the species frequently shot by gunners in the early years of the 20th century.*

RAPTORS LISTED UNDER THE ENDANGERED SPECIES ACT

(Status: E = endangered, T = threatened)

SPECIES	STATUS	POPULATION WHERE THREATENED OR ENDANGERED
California condor	E	U.S. (CA)
Andean condor	E	Colombia to Chile, Argentina
Cuban hook-billed kite (subspecies of hook-billed kite)	E	Cuba
Grenada hook-billed kite (subspecies of hook-billed kite)	E	Grenada
Everglades snail kite (subspecies of snail kite)	E	U.S. (FL)
Bald eagle	E*	Conterminous U.S., except MI, MN, OR, WA, WI
Bald eagle	T	U.S. (MI, MN, OR, WA, WI)
Greenland white-tailed eagle	E	Greenland, adjacent islands
Christmas Island goshawk (subspecies of brown goshawk)	E	Christmas Island
Anjouan Island sparrowhawk (subspecies of Frances' goshawk)	E	Comoros Islands
Galapagos hawk	E	Galapagos Islands
Hawaiian hawk	E	U.S. (HI)
Harpy eagle	E	Mexico to Argentina
Philippine eagle	E	Philippines
Imperial eagle (formerly Spanish imperial eagle)	E	Spain, Morocco, Algeria

Proposed for reclassification to threatened, 1994.

continued

SPECIES	STATUS	POPULATION WHERE THREATENED OR ENDANGERED
Audubon's crested caracara (subspecies of crested caracara)	T	U.S. (FL)
Mauritius kestrel	E	Mauritius
Seychelles kestrel	E	Seychelles Islands
Northern aplomado falcon	E	U.S. (AZ, NM, TX), Mexico, Guatemala
American peregrine falcon (*F.p. anatum*)	E	North America, winters to South America
Eurasian peregrine falcon (*F.p. peregrinus*)	E	Europe, Eurasia, Africa, Middle East

*(Source: **Endangered and Threatened Wildlife and Plants**, U.S. Fish and Wildlife Service, Aug. 20, 1994)*

▸▸▸ CITES

The Convention on International Trade in Endangered Species of Wild Flora and Fauna—known by its acronym, CITES, pronounced "sigh-tees"—is one of the most comprehensive wildlife conservation agreements ever created. Drawn up in 1973, CITES now includes more than 120 signatory countries, which have agreed to abide by its three-tiered system of protection.

CITES consists of three lists, or appendices, each of which includes animals and plants at a different level of risk, and at a different level of protection against international trade.

Appendix I includes species that are critically endangered or at significant risk from trade—currently about seven hundred plants and animals. Virtually no legal trade is permitted involving these species.

Appendix II covers nearly three thousand animal and twenty-one thousand plant species. Those organisms listed can be traded under certain circumstances, but would be threatened by uncontrolled trade.

Appendix III contains species already protected by laws passed by the signatory countries, but not included in Appendices I and II.

When a country agrees to abide by CITES, it must also pledge to set up scientific management and enforcement programs.

SPECIES	YEAR LISTED

APPENDIX I

California condor	1975
Andean condor	1975
Cuban hook-billed kite	1977
White-tailed eagle (except the following subspecies)	1977
Greenland white-tailed eagle	1975
Bald eagle (except the following subspecies)	1977
Southern bald eagle	1975
Harpy eagle	1975
Philippine eagle (monkey-eating eagle)	1975
Imperial eagle	1977
Aldabra kestrel (subspecies of Newton's kestrel)	1975
Mauritius kestrel	1975
Seychelles kestrel	1975
Lagger falcon	1975
Gyrfalcon	1975
Peregrine falcon	1975

continued

As of 1979, all hawks, eagles, and falcons, except for New World vultures and those species listed in Appendices I or III, were listed under Appendix II. Species listed under Appendix II prior to 1979 were:

SPECIES	YEAR LISTED

▼
APPENDIX II

Osprey	1977
Red kite	1977
Sea-eagles and fish eagles (Genus *Haliaeetus*)	1977
Lammergeier	1977
Eurasian griffon (griffon vulture)	1977
Cinereous vulture	1977
Snake-eagles (Genus *Circaetus*)	1977
Harriers (Genus *Circus*)	1977
Eurasian (European) sparrowhawk	1977
Gundlach's hawk	1977
Northern goshawk	1977
New Guinea eagle (New Guinea harpy eagle)	1977
Golden eagle	1975
Secretary-bird	1976
All falcons and caracaras, except those listed in Appendix I	1975

▼
APPENDIX III

King vulture (Honduras)	1987

(Sources: Appendices I, II and III to the Convention on International Trade in Endangered Species of Wild Fauna and Flora, Sept. 30, 1992)

THREATENED AND ENDANGERED RAPTORS OF THE WORLD

BirdLife International (formerly International Council for Bird Preservation), founded in 1922 and based in Britain, closely monitors the status of rare birds around the world. These raptors are among the species identified by the group as being at risk.

THREATENED AND ENDANGERED RAPTORS OF THE WORLD

SPECIES	DISTRIBUTION	THREATS/CAUSES FOR DECLINE
Black honey-buzzard	New Britain Island	Deforestation.
Red kite	Eurasia	Unclear; probably multiple reasons including habitat loss.
Solomon sea-eagle	Solomon Islands	Loss of coastal forests.
Madagascar sea-eagle	Madagascar	Wetlands loss.
Pallas' fish-eagle	Asia	Chemical contamination (possible).
White-tailed eagle	northern Eurasia	Persecution, habitat destruction, pollution.
Stellar's sea-eagle	northeastern Asia	Small population, restricted range.
Cape griffon	southern Africa	Poor reproduction due to decline in food quantity and quality; persecution.
Cinereous vulture	Eurasia	Disappeared over much of former range.
Mountain serpent-eagle	Borneo	Habitat loss.

continued

SPECIES	DISTRIBUTION	THREATS/CAUSES FOR DECLINE
Andaman serpent-eagle	Andaman Islands	Habitat loss.
Madagascar serpent-eagle	Madagascar	Persecution; defor-estation.
Red goshawk	Australia	Forest fires set to improve grazing.
Small sparrowhawk	Sulawesi	Deforestation.
New Britain sparrowhawk	New Britain Island	Deforestation.
Imitator sparrowhawk	New Guinea region	Deforestation.
Semicollared hawk	western South America	Rare; localized range.
Gundlach's hawk	Cuba	Deforestation, shooting.
Gray-bellied goshawk	South America	Habitat loss.
Plumbeous hawk	northern South America	Habitat loss.
White-necked hawk	Brazilian coastal forest	Deforestation.
Gray-backed hawk	Ecuador/Peru	Deforestation.
Mantled hawk	South America	Deforestation.
Solitary eagle	Central, South America	Deforestation.
Crowned eagle	southern South America	Habitat loss, shooting.
Ridgway's hawk	Haiti/Dominican Republic	Deforestation.
Galapagos hawk	Galapagos Islands	Shooting; competi-tion from intro-duced predators.
Hawaiian hawk	Island of Hawaii	Habitat alteration.

SPECIES	DISTRIBUTION	THREATS/CAUSES FOR DECLINE
Rufous-tailed hawk	Andes	May be more common than once thought.
Crested eagle	Central, South America	Deforestation.
Harpy eagle	Central, South America	Deforestation.
New Guinea eagle	New Guinea	Shooting, habitat loss.
Philippine eagle	Philippines	Shooting, trapping, deforestation.
Spanish eagle	Iberian Peninsula	Habitat loss/alteration; chemical contamination; persecution; prey loss.
Javan hawk-eagle	Java	Habitat loss.
Wallace's hawk-eagle	Malaysia, Borneo, Sumatra	Deforestation.
Plumbeous forest-falcon	Colombia/Ecuador	Deforestation.
Buckley's forest-falcon	western Amazonia	Deforestation.
Lesser kestrel	Eurasia	Pesticides, agriculture, climatic changes.
Mauritius kestrel	Mauritius	Deforestation.
Gray falcon	Australia	Agriculture.
Orange-breasted falcon	Central, South America	Habitat loss, pesticides.

Not included: Seychelles kestrel (considered out of danger)
Peregrine falcon (global population never endangered)

(*Sources:* **Birds to Watch: ICBP World Checklist of Threatened Birds,** *1988;* **Rare Birds of the World,** *1988;* **Threatened Birds of the Americas,** *1992;* **Threatened Birds of Africa and Related Islands,** *1985.)*

▲ *The cinereous vulture, the largest raptor in Europe, has suffered major declines in this century from habitat loss, lack of food, and direct persecution.*

▲ *The Guadalupe caracara, a Mexican island subspecies of the crested caracara shown here, became extinct around 1900.*

EXTINCT RAPTORS

Remarkably, even though many species of raptors around the world are at risk—some critically—of extinction, only one species is known to have vanished in the past three hundred years, the period of European expansion.

It was the Guadalupe caracara, found only on tiny Guadalupe Island off the coast of Baja California. In general shape and size the Guadalupe caracara was very similar to its close relative, the crested caracara of the mainland—in fact, some experts consider it merely a subspecies.

However, the island race was barred evenly with brown, and had an orange, rather than red, face. They exhibited behavioral differences as well; while mainland caracaras nest in the tops of trees, palms, or cacti, desert-like Guadalupe Island offered few such opportunities, and the island birds generally nested on cliffs and ledges.

Trouble started when people introduced Angora goats to Guadalupe Island. The adults were too large to be attacked by caracaras, but the goats kids were killed, and herders fought back by methodically shooting the raptors, especially when they came to drink at the island's few water holes. The caracaras became extinct at around 1900—not long before the goat-herding ceased, too.

15

Management Techniques

Captive Breeding

Unlike gamebirds and waterfowl, raptors are difficult to breed in captivity—their courtship displays often involve dizzying aerial maneuvers, for instance, that are impossible in even the roomiest cage. Although falconers bred small numbers of hawks over the years, it was always easier to take birds from the wild. Peregrine falcons, for instance, had been bred in Germany prior to and during World War II, but it wasn't until peregrine populations began to collapse in the 1960s that the question of captive propagation became urgent, and North American biologists began working on the problem.

The private Peregrine Fund, first based at Cornell University, took the lead in rearing falcons, mingling traditional falconry methods with modern biology. What was once an inexact art became a precise science, and the Peregrine Fund eventually created a virtual assembly line of falcon production, rearing thousands of chicks for return to the wild.

Captive breeding often involves sophisticated manipulation of reproductive biology to get the greatest production, using techniques like multiple-clutching to

Many species have been bred in captivity for research, falconry, or zoo purposes. Listed are species that have been captively bred on a large scale for conservation or management reasons.

CALIFORNIA CONDOR   APLOMADO FALCON   PEREGRINE FALCON

quickly increase egg output. It also gives biologists the ability to control parentage and prevent inbreeding, while making sure that certain genetic lines are preserved.

Artificial insemination is often a key to captive breeding of raptors. A biologist wearing a hat with a special rubber rim enters the cage of an imprinted male falcon and goes through courtship behavior—bowing, chirping, and passing food. The male bird flies to the hat, as though mounting a female; the rubber rim catches the semen, which is later used to inseminate selected females.

Today, the Peregrine Fund and others are attempting to breed a wide variety of endangered raptors in captivity, including Philippine and harpy eagles, taita falcons, and Mauritius kestrels.

HACKING

Hacking, a method of releasing raptors into the wild adapted from an ancient falconry technique, has proven to be one of the most effective ways to restore wild raptor populations. Its use as a conservation technique was pioneered in the 1970s in the restoration of peregrine falcons in North America, and has since been used on a host of raptor species worldwide, from bald eagles in New York to lammergeiers in the Alps.

Originally, hacking was a way to partially train raptors for falconry. Chicks were taken from the nest and reared in an enclosure in a high place, such as a tower. The hawks were able to see their surroundings through slits in the enclosure, and at fledging the birds were allowed to fly free from an opened cage. Food was provided to keep them returning to the hack tower, but with time the youngsters learned to hunt on their own. When they were proficient at hunting, the falconer retrapped them—"taking them up"—and trained them to the fist.

All that was needed to turn this falconry method into a conservation technique was the elimination of the final step. A "hack box" is placed in the appropriate habitat, usually on a cliff or high tower, and is set up in such a way that the birds can see the land around them but never the humans who watch over them and feed them. Once the birds reach fledging age, the front of the box is removed; but food is supplied for weeks (sometimes months) thereafter, while they hone their hunting abilities. Eventually the birds disperse on their own.

Hacking works very well, but it does have disadvantages. Mortality among the chicks is high in the weeks and months following fledging, because they have no

▶ *Three young peregrine falcons sit in their hack box, from which they will be released in a few days.*

adults to guide and protect them. Great horned owls decimated hacked peregrines in parts of the central Appalachians early in the reintroduction effort, forcing a change to urban and coastal locations. It is important to remember, however, that mortality rates among juvenile raptors may be more than seventy-five percent even *with* parental help.

The young birds that are hacked out can come from wild populations or captive breeding programs. Peregrine falcon hacking in the United States and Canada relies almost exclusively on captively bred chicks, while the many bald eagle and osprey hacking programs, to restore those species to areas from which they disap-

---

NORTH AMERICAN RAPTORS THAT HAVE BEEN HACKED

CALIFORNIA CONDOR	COOPER'S HAWK (LIMITED)
OSPREY	GOLDEN EAGLE (LIMITED)
MISSISSIPPI KITE (LIMITED)	APLOMADO FALCON
BALD EAGLE	PEREGRINE FALCON

peared, use chicks removed from wild nests—from western Canada and Alaska in the case of northern bald eagles, and from the Chesapeake Bay for ospreys. In both cases, the wild populations are large and stable enough that scientists consider the removal of relatively small numbers of young to be insignificant.

Although peregrine falcons, bald eagles, and ospreys have been the main subjects for hacking, other raptors have been hacked, sometimes on a very limited basis. Cooper's hawks were experimentally hacked in Iowa; and Mississippi kite chicks from Kansas were hacked in Tennessee to reintroduce the species into that state. In the 1980s, golden eagle chicks from Wyoming were hacked into the wild in northwestern Georgia, and several captive-bred chicks were released privately in Pennsylvania, despite an absence of firm evidence that the species ever bred naturally south of the Adirondacks. Generally, these experimental reintroductions have not been successful.

Double-clutching

As described in Chapter 9, most raptors will lay replacement eggs if predation or an accident destroys their original clutch, a habit biologists have used with great success in rapidly increasing endangered populations. Double-clutching, or multiple-clutching, as this technique is also known, requires that one or more eggs (usually the entire clutch) be taken from the nest before they hatch and placed in incubators. The wild adults, meanwhile, generally start the courtship and mating process again, often even moving to a new nest site before eventually producing a second set of eggs.

Most (perhaps all) raptors will lay replacement eggs; these are the species on which the technique has been used to increase populations:

CALIFORNIA CONDOR   **BALD EAGLE**   **PEREGRINE FALCON**

Double-clutching has been especially useful with species like condors that have a naturally slow reproductive pace. By double- and even triple-clutching captive condors, biologists can raise the number of chicks each pair produces from one every two years to two or three per year. Because replacement eggs may have lower concentrations of toxins, the technique can also be used to "flush" pesticides from a female's system, producing healthier eggs with a greater chance of survival.

There are disadvantages and potential dangers with double-clutching. Unless captive foster parents are available, the chicks must be hand-raised by humans, exposing them to possible imprinting—a hazard that is usually avoided by using realistic hand puppets, and later by minimizing contact between the captives and their keepers. Also, producing a clutch of eggs requires a great deal of energy and time on the part of the adults, especially the female, and scientists must be careful to weigh the physiological stress. Generally, however, double-clutching has proven to be a safe and extremely effective management technique.

FOSTERING AND CROSS-FOSTERING

Fostering and cross-fostering are variations on the same theme—placing a chick in a nest with parents that are not its own, either of the same species (fostering) or of a different species (cross-fostering).

While both methods would seem to have great promise for raptor management, a number of problems limit their usefulness. Fostering is generally used to increase a locally threatened population, especially when the adults carry heavy pesticide loads and are producing infertile eggs. Ordinarily, the contaminated eggs are removed from the nest and replaced with either healthy, fertile eggs (taken from wild nests or captive pairs) or with dummy eggs that hold the female's attention through incubation.

If dummy eggs are used, chicks are substituted at the end of the normal incubation period—although scientists have found that chicks already partially grown have a better chance of survival than newly hatched nestlings. If the adults are taken aback by the sudden appearance of an active, hungry chick, they rarely show it, and usually begin caring for the chick immediately.

NORTH AMERICAN RAPTORS THAT HAVE BEEN FOSTERED

OSPREY	**FERRUGINOUS HAWK**
BALD EAGLE	**GOLDEN EAGLE**
RED-SHOULDERED HAWK	**PRAIRIE FALCON**
RED-TAILED HAWK	**PEREGRINE FALCON**

◀ *Fostering—placing eggs or chicks in an existing nest—has been successful with bald eagles, especially with pairs whose eggs had been poisoned by pesticide contamination.*

The advantage of fostering is that it maintains the "culture" of wild populations, since the chicks—regardless of their origin—learn the hunting techniques, habitat, and nesting preferences of their foster parents. This method may also serve as a bridge between an aging, contaminated population and a brighter future. Fostering has been used, for example, with bald eagles in parts of the East. Even though environmental levels of contaminants like DDT had fallen over the years, older breeding birds still carried high levels, but the fostered chicks they raised were much healthier.

Fostering has its limitations, however. Because many raptor chicks are aggressive to each other and because adults are limited in how much food they can catch, only one or two chicks can usually be added to a nest. And because fostering requires at least one wild breeding pair, it cannot be used to restore a species that has disappeared from an area.

That last disadvantage is the reason that cross-fostering—placing a chick or egg in the nest of another species—has been tried with a number of raptors. Cross-fostering poses a tricky problem, however, for the fostered chick may imprint on the species that raises it, rather than its own, and choose the wrong species for a mate. For that reason, this management technique is little used today.

NORTH AMERICAN RAPTORS THAT HAVE BEEN CROSS-FOSTERED

AMERICAN SWALLOW-TAILED KITE (WITH MISSISSIPPI KITE)

HARRIS' HAWK (WITH RED-TAILED HAWK)

PRAIRIE FALCON (WITH PEREGRINE FALCON, SWAINSON'S, RED-TAILED, AND FERRUGINOUS HAWKS)

PEREGRINE FALCON (WITH PRAIRIE FALCON)

▸▸ "Saving Abel"

Because raptor eggs hatch asynchronously, the oldest chick may be considerably bigger and stronger than its younger siblings. Especially in eagles, this often leads to the death of the youngest chick, a phenomenon known as the Cain and Abel syndrome, or cainism, discussed in Chapter 9.

One management technique, nicknamed "saving Abel," involves removing the younger chick from the nest, rearing it in captivity until it is big enough to fend off attacks, and returning it to its nest. Alternately, the chick may be fostered to a nest with infertile eggs. While the method has not been used widely in North America, it has been used with considerable success on the critically endangered Spanish eagle, and more recently on the Madagascar fish-eagle.

▸▸ Releasing Adults

Perhaps the least successful method of reintroducing or augmenting populations is releasing adult raptors either moved from another area or raised in captivity. Birds transplanted from one area to another have strong homing tendencies and the ability to cover vast distances easily, while those raised in captivity show little fear of humans and lack properly developed hunting skills.

Artificial Nest Sites

The number of safe, appropriate nest sites is often a major limiting factor for raptor populations. But unlike cavity-nesting songbirds like bluebirds, which readily accept artificial boxes, most raptors either build their own nests, take over the abandoned nests of other birds, or choose cliff ledges—none of which is easy to duplicate.

In North America, only the American kestrel will use nest boxes, although several other species, particularly ospreys and bald eagles, will build their own nests on specially designed platforms. In fact, there is a long history on the East Coast of erecting nesting sites for ospreys, often near homes and towns. In the nineteenth century, wagon wheels mounted on tall poles were common, and although the modern wooden platforms are somewhat more sophisticated, they accomplish the same ends.

In the West, where red-tailed hawks, ferruginous hawks, golden eagles, and other raptors often nest on high-tension electrical towers, specially designed platforms have been used to lure them into parts of the tower where they are less likely to be electrocuted. And in south Florida, where snail kite nests often collapse into the water before the chicks fledge, biologists have moved sagging nests built in cattails to baskets with success.

Because kestrels respond so well to nest boxes, a number of management plans have focused on erecting these boxes in suitable habitats. One of the most imagina-

▶ *Ospreys quickly adopt artificial nest platforms, allowing managers to easily bolster local populations.*

tive—and successful—projects occurred in the Midwest, where kestrel boxes were attached to the backs of interstate highway signs. Because highway borders are prime rodent habitat but offer few nesting opportunities for kestrels, the boxes were quickly occupied. In Iowa, where the idea originated, hundreds of young kestrels fledged in just the first few years, and some stretches of highway enjoyed a one hundred percent occupancy rate.

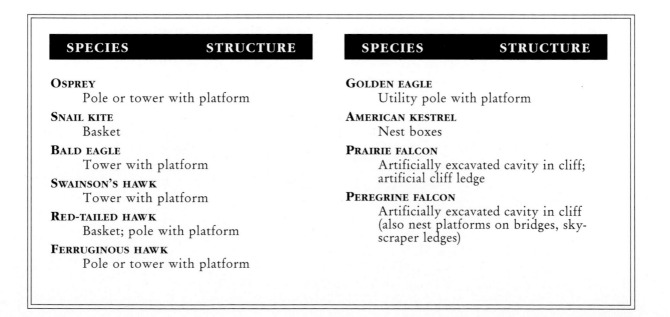

SPECIES	STRUCTURE
OSPREY	Pole or tower with platform
SNAIL KITE	Basket
BALD EAGLE	Tower with platform
SWAINSON'S HAWK	Tower with platform
RED-TAILED HAWK	Basket; pole with platform
FERRUGINOUS HAWK	Pole or tower with platform

SPECIES	STRUCTURE
GOLDEN EAGLE	Utility pole with platform
AMERICAN KESTREL	Nest boxes
PRAIRIE FALCON	Artificially excavated cavity in cliff; artificial cliff ledge
PEREGRINE FALCON	Artificially excavated cavity in cliff (also nest platforms on bridges, skyscraper ledges)

Supplemental Feeding

Providing food to wild raptors has several conservation applications. There may simply not be enough natural food to support the raptors, in which case supplemental food may allow the population to increase. And if the natural food supply is contaminated, a source of clean, healthy food may allow the birds to survive and reproduce while steps are taken to remedy the contamination.

California condors were the focus of a feeding program starting in the 1970s, in which biologists put out frozen road-killed deer, nicknamed "deersicles." The deer, it was hoped, would both provide a reliable food source and lure the condors away from carcasses that might contain toxins like lead bullets. The condors continued to eat contaminated meat, however, and toxins were implicated in the deaths of many of the last free-flying condors.

Additional information on the use of supplemental feeding for California condors appears in the next chapter.

"Vulture restaurants," as they've become known, have been used with success in Spain for threatened cinereous vultures, and in South Africa for lammergeiers and endangered Cape griffons. With the griffons, artificial feeding stations may help correct an unusual threat—a lack of calcium in the diet of chicks. Once, the huge vultures were dependent on large carnivores such as lions and hyenas to crack the bones of their prey; the resulting bone flakes were fed to the nestlings, providing calcium critical to bone development. As wild game has been replaced by cattle, and with fewer large predators existing to make kills, the griffons have lost their source of bone, and many chicks experience severe bone damage.

As useful as supplemental feeding may be, it must be remembered that it is a poor substitute for natural food supplies, and will never replace large, healthy herds of wild grazing animals.

16

ĊONSERVATION CASE HISTORIES

CALIFORNIA CONDOR

Classification: Endangered (U.S. ESA).

The largest raptor in North America, the California condor is also the most endangered—and the most expensive. Millions of dollars have been spent in an intensive effort to save it from extinction.

The condor has been on the wane since the end of the last ice age, judging from the fossil record. During the Pleistocene it was found from the Pacific Northwest south into Mexico and east to Florida, and at least one set of fossils has turned up in western New York, suggesting it roamed even farther than once believed. But the close of the last ice age was marked by a mass extinction of giant mammals—mammoths, mastodons, long-horned bison, and other once-abundant creatures that would have provided carcasses for condors.

By the arrival of Europeans, condors were found along the Pacific from Baja to the Columbia River, feeding on the carrion of elk, bighorns, pronghorns, and deer, and marine mammals washed up on the shore. A Spanish priest in Baja California was the first westerner to record sighting the species, in 1602; the first scientific specimen was collected in Monterey in 1792.

The Lewis and Clark expedition, which wintered at the mouth of the Columbia in 1805–1806, mentioned the presence of "a large kind of buzzard with white wings" several times in their journals. "The buzzard is, we believe, the largest bird of North America," they wrote. "One which was taken by our hunters was not in good condition, and yet the weight was 25 pounds. . . . This bird was not seen by any of the party until we had descended the Columbia River, below the great falls. . . ."

Condors are big, inviting targets, and because they breed at such a glacial pace, producing on average two chicks every three years, the losses from poisoning and shooting (for sport, scientific collecting, and sale of the feathers) took an immediate toll. The population shrank rapidly during the nineteenth century, so that by the beginning of the twentieth the condors were restricted to the rugged mountains of southern California and northern Baja. They disappeared from Mexico sometime prior to 1940, and the only remaining population was centered in the Los Padres National Forest north of Los Angeles.

The condor was acknowledged to be a rare and declining species for decades, and by 1965 the population stood at about sixty—a figure that continued to drop steadily, despite tightened protection and intense study. By 1981 there were fewer than twenty-five condors, and the following year a long-debated captive breeding program was finally instituted, using birds and eggs removed from the wild and creative management techniques like double-clutching to increase production. The policy change may have come just in time, because the remaining wild birds vanished at a shocking rate, some succumbing to lead poisoning and other environmental contaminants. Between 1984 and 1985, four of the five remaining breeding pairs disappeared, and only nine wild birds survived. The decision was made to bring the survivors into captivity, and the last free-flying condor, a male designated AC-9, was captured in 1987.

Most wildlife-management decisions are made on the basis of science, but the condor is such a famous, high-profile species that almost every step of the protection and recovery project has been dogged by controversy. The debate over captive breeding, for instance, dates to at least 1952, when an outcry from the National Audubon Society stopped a plan to take eggs and adults from the wild to start a zoo flock.

Arguments for and against captive breeding grew in volume—and rhetoric—through the 1980s, when some preservationist groups argued that condors would be better off extinct than maintained in captivity. Even the recovery project itself, jointly managed by several government agencies and private conservation organizations, was plagued by crippling internal politics and infighting.

Policy battles aside, condors proved surprisingly easy to breed in captivity, and in 1988 the first chick conceived and hatched in a zoo was born. Thereafter, the captive flock grew at a robust pace. The total number of condors rose from twenty-seven in 1987 to eighty-eight in 1994, and after an experimental release of Andean condors in order to test procedures, a total of eight young California condors were released in the species' old range in 1992, with additional releases in 1993.

The reintroduction has not gone smoothly, however. Lacking adult guidance, the young condors have gravitated toward human activity—approaching workers at oil-drilling sites in the mountains, even landing among swimmers on a crowded lake beach. Two birds were found chewing at the weatherstripping on a sliding glass door of a Santa Barbara house.

▶ The California condor is one of the most critically endangered raptors in the world, with a total population of less than 100. A few have been reintroduced to the wild, with little success.

Worse, the condors often choose electrical towers as perches, and several have been electrocuted or killed in collisions with wires; one even died after apparently ingesting antifreeze. Several of the least cautious survivors were later recaptured.

Another factor is that nothing has changed fundamentally in the southern California environment. If, as suspected, environmental toxins like lead were the cause of the swift collapse of the last wild breeding population, there is little reason to believe the situation has improved in the intervening decade. The condor-recovery team hopes to avert this problem by training the birds to feed on toxin-free stillborn calves, hauled by llamas to remote feeding stations in the mountains.

Another option—and one that is highly controversial, given the charged political atmosphere surrounding the condors—is introducing the species outside its historic range. Many experts believe southern California is too crowded and too polluted to ever support a wild, self-sustaining condor population, and plans have been drawn up for possible introductions in the Grand Canyon (where condors lived during the Pleistocene), Baja California (part of their historic range), or New Mexico.

The alternative sites have a similar drawback, however—a limited supply of natural food, in the form of large ungulates. Some kind of supplemental feeding would no doubt be required, but the alternate locations might provide a way to establish breeding flocks from which truly wild birds could be removed for eventual release in California.

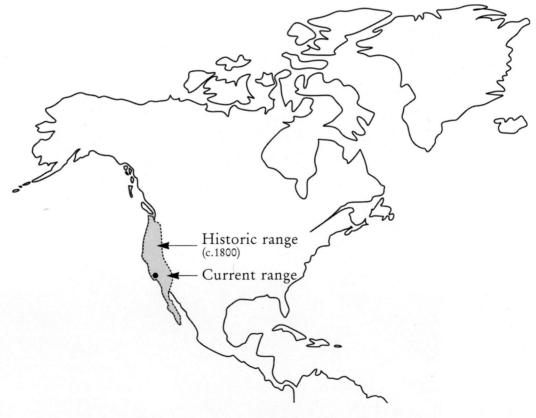

Historic range
(c.1800)

Current range

▶ *Historic and current (reintroduced) range of California condor.*

The condor recovery plan calls for the eventual establishment of more than two hundred birds in two separate wild populations—insurance against a single calamity wiping out the species. For that same reason, the captive flock has been divided between the Los Angeles Zoo and the San Diego Wild Animal Park in California and the World Center for Birds of Prey in Idaho.

▶ *The striking orange and red head of an adult California condor requires five or six years to develop; chicks and immature condors have drab brown heads.*

▶ *To avoid imprinting young California condors on humans, caretakers feed the captive-reared chicks using a hand puppet in the shape of an adult condor's head.*

CALIFORNIA CONDOR POPULATION

YEAR (All figures are for year's end)	WILD	CAPTIVE	TOTAL POPULATION
1890	less than 200	0	less than 200
1939	60–100	0	60–100
1965	about 60	0	about 60
1967	about 60	1*	about 60
1978	25–35	1	26–36
1982	21–24	3	22–25
1983	16	9	25
1984	11	16	27
1985	6	21	27
1986	2	25	27
1987	0**	27	27
1988	0	28***	28
1989	0	32	32
1990	0	40	40
1991	0	52	52
1992	7	56	63
1993	9	66	75
1994 (midyear)	3	85	88

* Sick male condor, "Topa Topa," captured 1967; remains in captivity.

** Last wild condor captured April 19, 1987.

*** First captive-born chick, "Molloko," hatched April 29, 1988.

(Source: U.S. Fish and Wildlife Service, 1994)

CAPTIVE CONDOR CHICK PRODUCTION

YEAR	CHICKS PRODUCED
1988	1
1989	4
1990	8
1991	12
1992	12
1993	15
1994	15

(Source: U.S. Fish and Wildlife Service, 1994)

OSPREY

Classification: No listing U.S. ESA; classified as threatened or endangered in several states

With its dependence on clean water and abundant fish, the osprey has always been in a vulnerable position, given mankind's shameful treatment of waterways over the years. Pollution took its toll on ospreys in many parts of the industrialized world, as did shooting—for ospreys were sometimes seen as competitors by fishermen, even though they tend to take slower roughfish like suckers, rather than game species. In parts of Europe and North America, ospreys disappeared by the turn of the century due to a combination of these threats.

Because it sits at the end of a long aquatic food chain, the osprey also suffered badly from pesticide poisoning following World War II. Consequently, populations that had come through the first half of the twentieth century largely intact, like those in the Chesapeake Bay and on the New England coast, experienced drastic declines as well.

In North America, ospreys have responded well to the banning of the worst pesticides, such as DDT, and eastern coastal populations have rebounded strongly. Hacking programs have restored a limited but growing number of breeding pairs to

WORLD OSPREY POPULATIONS

Figures show breeding pairs as of 1985; single question mark (?) indicates figure based on limited survey, double question mark (??) indicates estimate based on subjective description of abundance.

AREAS	NUMBERS
Britain	45
Scandinavia	2,850–3,200
Central Europe	130–140
Mediterranean, Spanish and Portugal	45–55
USSR(former) *(Includes Russia and all other republics)*	2,000–6,000 ??
Canary Islands	10–15
Cape Verdes	50 ?
Red Sea, Arabian Peninsula	40 ??
Sinai	45
Japan	20–55 ??
Australia	200–400 ??
Contiguous U.S.	7,500–8,000
Canada and Alaska	10,000–12,000

(Source: Adapted from Alan Poole, Ospreys: A Natural and Unnatural History, 1989)

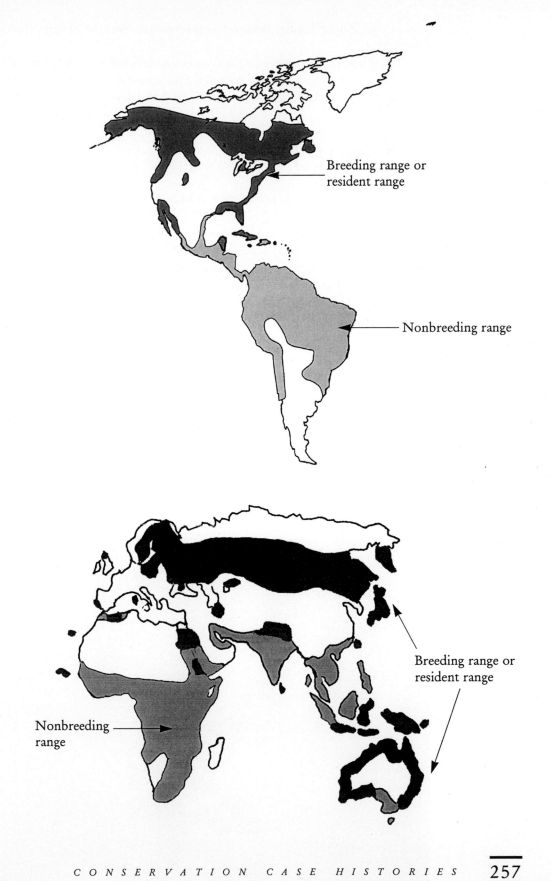

▶ *Worldwide range of the osprey.*

Breeding range or resident range

Nonbreeding range

Breeding range or resident range

Nonbreeding range

places like Pennsylvania, where the species had become extinct by the turn of the century.

Worldwide, the outlook for ospreys is decidedly mixed. Chemical contamination continues to be a danger, especially on tropical wintering grounds, as is the loss of prey from overfishing and pollution, and the destruction of coastal nesting areas.

Snail Kite

Classification: Endangered (U.S. ESA).

It is likely that snail kites (formerly known as Everglades kites) have always had a tiny range in the United States, restricted to the lakes and wide sawgrass marshes of central and southern Florida where their only food, the apple snail, is found. Although the snail kite is found over most of South and Central America, those in Florida and Cuba are a distinct subspecies, *Rostrhamus sociabilis plumbeus,* and the tiny U.S. population is the most northerly in the world.

Before Florida became a retirement, tourism, and agriculture mecca, snail kites were apparently locally common, with reports prior to the 1930s of flocks numbering one hundred or more. Wholesale drainage of south Florida, however, primarily for farming and sugarcane production, sent the kites into a downward spiral by the first decades of the twentieth century, robbing them of the wetlands that both they and the apple snail require. The population bottomed out at around forty kites in the 1960s, although the first complete census in 1972 showed about sixty-five birds.

More so than with any other critically endangered U.S. raptor, habitat preservation has been the key to saving the snail kite. Unlike slow-breeding condors, kites lay two or three eggs in each nesting, and may raise more than one brood each year—remarkable for a North American raptor, and unusual for an endangered species.

▶ *The fortunes of the snail kite are closely linked with its only food, the aquatic apple snail.*

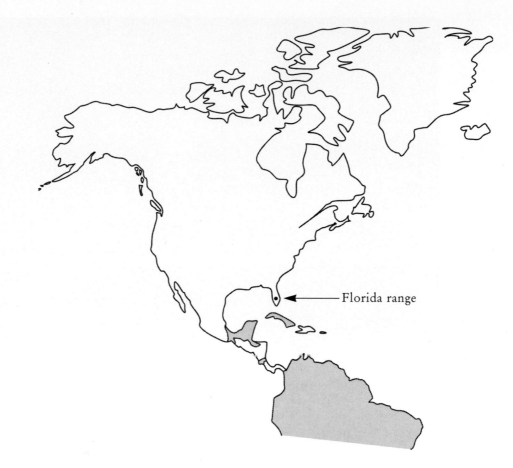

Florida range

▶ Range of the snail kite, showing wide distribution in Latin America. Although resident, during periods of drought and outside the breeding season, the Florida population ranges more widely in the state.

But kites are at the mercy of their environment. In good conditions their numbers can build quickly, but if water levels drop—during a prolonged drought, or as a result of human drainage projects—the kites lose their only source of food, and are forced to wander widely across Florida, looking for open water and snails. During such nomadic periods mortality is quite high, and starvation is common. By way of example, the kite population had grown to more than 650 in 1980, dropped by roughly half in a drought the next year, then rebounded to 668 by 1984. The chart shows how kite numbers fluctuated during the twelve years from 1969 to 1980.

Kite nests built in cattail beds frequently collapse, but by transferring flimsy nests to special baskets, biologists were able to increase chick production. The most important management consideration, however, is the water level. South Florida's natural flow of water, once a sixty-mile-wide sheet flowing through the marshes from Lake Okeechobee south through the Everglades, has been radically altered with ditches, impoundments, and dikes. Water managers can control the flow to mimic natural rhythms, but pressures from agricultural and residential users make doing so difficult.

There are even conflicts between those dedicated to saving rare species. Snail kites are caught in the middle of a struggle between land managers who are trying to restore the natural flow of water to Everglades National Park, and biologists who designated the man-made impoundments where many kites nest as "critical habitat" for the species—habitat that would be destroyed if the natural flow were restored.

▶ *A male snail kite drops into shallow water for a snail in Everglades National Park in Florida.*

Apple snails—and therefore snail kites—do best with fairly constant water levels, while many wading birds, including the endangered wood stork, breed only in dry spells that concentrate fish in small pools where they are easy to catch. Under natural conditions the Everglades would seesaw between these two poles, benefiting first one, then the other. Today both kites and storks are on the brink, however, and such tinkering with the water level could push one or both over the edge.

S N A I L   K I T E   P O P U L A T I O N S   I N   F L O R I D A

YEAR	NUMBER	YEAR	NUMBER
1969	98	1975	110
1970	120	1976	142
1971	72	1977	152
1972	65	1978	267
1973	95	1979	431
1974	81	1980	651

(Source: Sykes, 1983)

BALD EAGLE

Classification: Southern bald eagle (Lower 48 except Washington, Oregon, Minnesota, Wisconsin, Michigan)—endangered (U.S. ESA; proposed for downlisting to threatened).

Northern bald eagle (Washington, Oregon, Minnesota, Wisconsin, Michigan)—threatened (U.S. ESA).

Northern bald eagle—Alaska (not listed).

The bald eagle may be the most instantly recognizable raptor in the world, with its shining white head and tail—and its place as national symbol of the United

▲ *Even though Congress named the bald eagle the national symbol in 1782, the bird was subjected to legalized persecution for nearly two more centuries.*

States. Despite its symbolism, however, the bald eagle has suffered from both direct persecution like shooting, poisoning, and egg collecting, as well as habitat loss and, most serious of all, chemical contamination.

Originally, bald eagles occupied almost every corner of North America, from south Texas and the northern Baja to the edge of the arctic coastal plain, breeding most frequently along the coasts, large lakes, and river systems. Modern estimates put the bald eagle population prior to 1800 at about 250,000.

That range began to shrink almost as soon as Europeans began to settle the continent, although in some areas—Florida in particular—eagles and humans were able to coexist to a surprising degree until the twentieth century. In other regions, especially ranching areas of the West, bald and golden eagles were shot as threats to livestock, particularly in winter when large numbers of migrants moved south from Canada and Alaska.

Legal protection was slow in coming. The Bald Eagle Protection Act of 1940 made it a federal offense to kill the birds everywhere except in Alaska, where state bounties were being paid on bald eagles as late as 1953. The bird was finally listed as endangered in 1967 under the Endangered Species Preservation Act, a forerunner of the current federal Endangered Species Act.

Like the osprey, the bald eagle sits at the end of a long, mostly aquatic food chain, just the situation that can result in the buildup of toxins in the tissue of its prey—toxins that eventually accumulate in the eagle's body as well. And like the osprey, brown pelican, peregrine falcon, and other predatory birds, the eagle's already reduced numbers went into serious decline during the height of pesticide use in the 1950s and 1960s, as a result of impaired reproduction caused by this chemical contamination.

Bald eagles vanished completely from some areas, and were reduced to a shadow of their former abundance in others. The low ebb came in the early 1970s, just as DDT and its related toxins were being banned for most use in the United States. Even though the environment began to cleanse itself thereafter, older eagles still carried heavy enough loads of pesticides to affect reproduction; the adults would pair up and nest, but the eggs were infertile, or their shells so thin that they crushed under the female's weight.

Exact numbers are difficult to find, but by about 1970, the southern bald eagle was reduced to perhaps five hundred pairs, most in Florida, with lesser numbers in the Chesapeake Bay region, the Southeast coast, California, and the Southwest. Northern bald eagles in the Great Lakes, Pacific Northwest, and northern New England were more common, although they, too, suffered serious reproductive problems.

Using techniques pioneered with peregrine falcons, biologists in the Northeast began hacking bald eagles, starting with New York in 1976. But where falcon chicks had to be raised in captivity at a cost of more than a thousand dollars each, eaglets could be taken from wild nests in western Canada and Alaska, where the species remained common through the pesticide era. (Hacking projects in the southern Plains, including Oklahoma, used southern subspecies eagles from Florida.)

Hacking projects became popular in many parts of the United States in the 1980s, pumping hundreds of young eagles into the wild. New York, for example, hacked 198 eagles between 1976 and 1989. As is usually the case with young raptors, the eagles wandered widely during their four or five years prior to maturity, and when they eventually settled down, it was often hundreds of miles from their release site. This meant that eagle recovery was a regional, rather than a state, phenomenon.

Along with habitat protection and techniques such as fostering chicks into the nests of contaminated adults, hacking set the stage for a dramatic resurgence in bald eagle populations, especially in the latter half of the 1980s, when nesting and winter counts climbed to record post-DDT levels. According to the U.S. Fish and Wildlife Service, the number of territorial pairs of bald eagles in the Lower 48 states rose from 1,757 in 1984 to 4,016 in 1993. Winter counts tell an even more dramatic tale, increasing from 2,772 in 1968 to 13,807 in 1983.

By 1994, bald eagles had recovered sufficiently for the U.S. Fish and Wildlife Service to propose "downlisting" the species, changing its classification under the federal Endangered Species Act from endangered to threatened—an acknowledgment that even though eagles were not out of danger, they were at considerably less risk than twenty years before.

Not everyone is convinced that downlisting is appropriate. Bald eagles in the Southwest continue to concern conservationists, who note that there were only about thirty occupied territories in 1992, with markedly lower chick production and higher adult mortality compared to other regions. There is also worry that as the hacked eagles mature, they may accumulate troublesome levels of toxins and experience a downturn in reproduction.

Finally, habitat protection remains a key issue in the long-term survival of the bald eagle. Human use of waterfront property continues to rise, putting increasing pressure on eagles both in winter and during the nesting season. The James River in Virginia, for instance, has become a major summering ground for nonbreeding eagles, which number as high as two hundred. Major riverside development has been proposed for land adjacent to the James River National Wildlife Refuge, however, raising the possibility of serious disturbance for the eagles. Some conservationists worry that downlisting will indicate to the public that the need for eagle habitat protection has passed.

▶ Ten bald eagles crowd a tree along Alaska's Chilkat River, where a winter salmon run attracts thousands of the great raptors each year.

BALD EAGLE POPULATIONS

This chart shows the steady improvement in bald eagle populations in the Lower 48 states from 1976 through 1993. The figures represent occupied territories, not necessarily breeding pairs, and do not include juvenile eagles.

STATE	1976	1981	1984	1989	1993
Alabama	—	—	1	1	10
Arizona	5	10	17	25	27
Arkansas	—	—	3	1	20
California	—	50	64	83	103
Colorado*	—	3	4	10	19
Connecticut	0	0	0	0	1
Delaware*	—	4	3	5	7
Florida	—	—	375	439	667
Georgia	—	—	3	9	17
Idaho	—	13	20	49	70
Illinois	0	2	2	9	12
Indiana	0	0	0	2	13
Iowa	0	0	1	7	31
Kansas	—	0	0	1	5
Kentucky	—	—	1	2	10
Louisiana	—	—	19	45	103
Maine	41	63	66	109	150
Maryland	—	53	60	97	152
Massachusetts	0	0	0	4	9

STATE	1976	1981	1984	1989	1993
▼ Michigan	84	101	107	165	246
Minnesota	122	190	245	390	565
Mississippi	—	—	1	1	8
Missouri*	0	1	1	6	14
Montana	—	24	51	78	144
Nebraska	—	0	0	0	2
Nevada	0	0	0	0	0
New Hampshire	0	0	0	1	1
New Jersey	1	1	1	4	6
New Mexico	—	—	—	—	2
New York	0	2	2	9	20
North Carolina	—	—	1	4	8
North Dakota	—	0	0	1	1
Ohio	5	6	7	12	24
Oklahoma	—	1	3	0	10
Oregon	—	97	114	166	221
Pennsylvania	—	4	4	10	17
Rhode Island	—	0	0	0	0
South Carolina	—	—	33	53	88
South Dakota	—	0	0	0	2
Tennessee	—	—	2	14	22
Texas	—	—	15	25	37
Utah	—	0	1	2	3

continued

STATE	1976	1981	1984	1989	1993
Vermont	—	0	0	0	0
Virginia*	—	39	60	92	151
Washington	—	121	207	367	469
West Virginia	0	1	1	1	5
Wisconsin	149	188	239	336	465
Wyoming	—	26	23	45	59
Totals	**407** **	**1,000** **	**1,757**	**2,680**	**4,016**

Active nests rather than occupied territories.
** *Incomplete surveys 1976–1981.*

(Source: U.S. Fish and Wildlife Service, 1994)

BALD EAGLE CONCENTRATIONS

FALL/WINTER

Blackwater National Wildlife Refuge, MD

Cedar Glen Eagle Roost, IL

Cedar Valley, UT

Chilkat River, AK

Eagle Valley, WI

Ferry Bluff Eagle Sanctuary, WI

Glacier National Park, MT

Karl Mundt National Wildlife Refuge, SD

Lower Susquehanna River, PA-MD

Oak Valley Eagle Refuge, IL

Pere Marquette Eagle Roost, IL

Prairie State Eagle Refuge, IL

Reelfoot Lake National Wildlife Refuge, TN

Rocky Mountain Arsenal, CO

Rush Valley, UT

San Luis Valley, CO

Swan Lake National Wildlife Refuge, MI

Upper Delaware River, NY-PA-NJ

SUMMER (NONBREEDING)

James River National Wildlife Refuge, VA

▶ *So large and powerful it could be considered an eagle, the ferruginous hawk of the American West has declined significantly in some areas, probably as a result of habitat alteration.*

▼ *The ferruginous hawk feeds primarily on small and medium-sized mammals like rabbits and ground squirrels.*

Ferruginous Hawk

Classification: Petitions pending for ESA listing; endangered or threatened in several states.

Largest and most eaglelike of the North American buteos, the ferruginous hawk is a creature of the Plains, found in summer from the southern Canadian prairies to New Mexico and northwest to central Washington. Its size and pale plumage, including the trademark rusty "leggings," make the ferruginous a striking bird, whether perched on a rocky bluff or sailing against a blue western sky. Little wonder its Latin name is *regalis*.

Ferruginous hawks have concerned conservationists for years. While some states, such as Wyoming, have robust populations, the species has all but disappeared from other parts of its historic range, including eastern North Dakota, and parts of Oregon and Arizona. Still other regions have experienced drastic declines in ferruginous hawk numbers, especially Saskatchewan, Alberta, and Manitoba.

The ferruginous hawk seems to be little affected by pesticide contamination, probably because its diet of ground squirrels, jackrabbits, and other medium-size mammals doesn't accumulate chemicals to the same degree a long aquatic or avian food chain does. Instead, the trouble appears to be largely a result of habitat alteration. Ferruginous hawks do best on unaltered grasslands—and there are few such areas left.

Large parts of the bird's range, especially in Canada, have become choked with aspen saplings as a result of fire suppression, while cultivation has rendered other former grasslands unsuitable for the hawk's prey, and thus for the hawk. Grazing, on the other hand, has a less harmful effect on the ferruginous hawk, although the bird is much more sensitive to human disturbance than are many buteos, and the trampling feet of cattle often kill the scattered large trees in which the hawks nest.

Biologist Richard Olendorff, reviewing the status of the ferruginous hawk for the federal Bureau of Land Management, made twenty-seven specific recommendations to increase ferruginous hawk numbers. His suggestions include:

—Manage habitat to provide prey species.

—Provide a variety of nest-site choices.

—Consolidate collapsing nests in the off-season, and reinforce nest trees. Protect active nest trees from cattle, which trample roots and strip bark.

—Erect artificial nests, nesting baskets, and nest platforms.

—If tree-shrub habitat is converted to grassland, leave scattered trees for nest sites.

—Manage land to create a mosaic of grassland and sagebrush steppe.

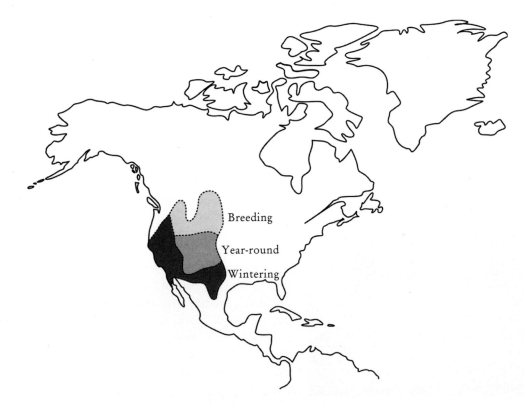

▶ *Breeding and winter ranges of the ferruginous hawk.*

FERRUGINOUS HAWK POPULATIONS

STATE/PROVINCE	NUMBER OF PAIRS Estimated number of breeding pairs in 1992
Arizona	5–10
California	1
Colorado	150–175
Idaho	200–250
Kansas	25–50
Montana	175–200
Nebraska	25
Nevada	250–300
New Mexico	26
North Dakota	350–400
Oklahoma	25
Oregon	250
South Dakota	350–375
Texas	5–10
Utah	200–225
Washington	30–40
Wyoming	800+
Alberta	1,181–2,223
Saskatchewan	170
Manitoba	50

(*Source:* **Status, Biology and Management of Ferruginous Hawks: A Review,** *Olendorff, 1993*)

Northern Aplomado Falcon

Classification: Endangered (U.S. ESA).

As with the ferruginous hawk, the loss of grassland habitat is also at the root of the aplomado falcon's problems. Remarkably beautiful, with dark gray upper parts, a light eyeline, a black "cummerbund," and cinnamon-colored thighs, the aplomado originally ranged north from South and Central America and Mexico into the American Southwest, hunting grasslands with a scattering of mesquite and yucca.

Its U.S. range stretched from the southern Gulf coast of Texas west to southeastern Arizona—a region that was heavily altered by agriculture. Land that wasn't lost to farming often became choked with mesquite, which was no longer held in check by periodic wildfires. Aplomado falcons also suffered from egg collecting for scientific and private collections and, later, from pesticide contamination. They began to decline in the nineteenth century, and their numbers dropped dramatically in the 1940s. The species stopped nesting in Arizona in the 1880s, while the last Texas nest was found in 1941, and the last U.S. nest was found in 1952 in New Mexico.

Eggs taken from Mexico between 1977 and 1988 formed the core of a captive breeding program, and releases began in southern Texas in the mid-1980s. After a hiatus, the reintroduction began again in the early 1990s at Laguna Atascosa National Wildlife Refuge, and plans call for the eventual release of four hundred falcons in the southwestern states and northern Mexico.

While none of the released aplomado falcons has yet nested, biologists believe success is only a matter of time. Brush-control efforts throughout the region should provide suitable habitat, although the threat of chemical contamination remains. The released birds are being periodically retrapped and blood samples taken for toxin analysis.

▶ *Aplomado falcons, which vanished from the grasslands of the Southwest earlier this century, are being raised in captivity and reintroduced to Texas.*

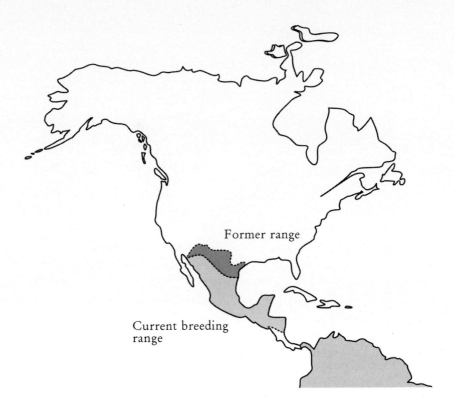

PEREGRINE FALCON

Classification: Continental anatum *and Eurasian* peregrinus *subspecies—endangered (U.S. ESA). Arctic* tundrius *subspecies—formerly listed as threatened; removed from U.S. ESA December 1994.*

It is ironic that the peregrine falcon, perhaps the most widespread raptor in the world and described as the most successful wild bird in existence, has become a symbol of endangered species protection. Found on every continent except Antarctica, from arctic tundra to Australian desert, the peregrine's future would have seemed secure. But in North America and parts of Europe and Asia, that security unraveled with frightening speed.

Peregrines were originally found over most of North America, although even in precolonial days they were probably never very common. The biggest limiting factor was most likely their nest sites, because peregrines require high, remote cliffs, and, with the exception of small populations in the Mississippi basin that adapted to nesting in cavities in huge old-growth timber, peregrines were absent in flat country like the Great Plains, the South, and the Midwest. At any given time, the total North American population was probably just five thousand peregrines, only half of which would be breeding adults.

Shooting, egg collecting, human development, and the extinction of the pas-
senger pigeon certainly reduced peregrine numbers somewhat, but on the whole the
falcons adapted well to civilization. In 1942, a survey by Joseph J. Hickey showed
408 known eyries in the eastern United States and Canada (including Labrador)
and Greenland. Of those, 275 were in the eastern United States, and about 210
were active. Based on his findings, Hickey estimated the population in the eastern
states at about 350 pairs.

But following World War II, organochlorine pesticides like DDT were introduced into wide use, and toxins began to seep into the environment. Raptors like
peregrine falcons, which sit at the end of long, complex food chains, ingested dangerously high concentrations of these contaminants.

Unbeknownst to anyone, eastern peregrines suffered an almost total reproductive collapse. By the 1960s, just as ornithologists were becoming aware of the crisis,
the damage was complete. A frantic search in 1964 revealed not a single nesting
pair—not even a lone adult peregrine—east of the Mississippi, where twenty years
before there had been two hundred active eyries.

The news was equally grim in other regions. California's one hundred pairs
had dropped to just ten or twenty, and only two or three pairs remained out of the
forty once found in Utah. Even the Arctic, where the bulk of North America's peregrines breed, was hard hit, with some populations cut in half. The story was the
same in much of Europe, where some northern populations declined by as much as
ninety-five percent.

The peregrine falcon, as a species, however, was never in danger of global extinction. Populations such as those in Asia, Africa, Australia, and South America suffered little or no decline. But on a subspecies level, the chemical contamination was catastrophic. The *anatum* subspecies, for example, which once occupied most of temperate North America, was decimated, taking with it its unique genetic heritage.

Peregrine recovery required human intervention. The most important step was the virtual banning of DDT and related chemicals in the United States in the early 1970s. But how to restock the empty eyries? Although some experts recommended letting nature take its course, most agreed that it would take decades, perhaps centuries, for peregrines to filter back into the East from surviving populations.

Instead, biologists led by Dr. Tom J. Cade of the Peregrine Fund, founded in 1974 at Cornell University, plotted an ambitious plan for reintroducing the peregrine falcon. Using captive falcons, they produced hundreds of nestlings that were hacked out at release sites in the East—coastal salt marshes and urban areas, where the chicks, lacking the protection of adult falcons, could be free from threats by great horned owls. Along the coast, at places like Forsythe National Wildlife Refuge in New Jersey, chicks were hacked from high towers, while in many cities—Albany, Philadelphia, Toronto—the birds were released on high rooftops.

The choices were not without controversy; although a few peregrines had nested in cities prior to the population crash, urban areas were never a common environment for them, and they were completely absent as nesting birds along the mid-Atlantic coast, where there were no natural eyries. Nor was the choice of hack sites the only sticking point. The native subspecies in the East was *P.f. anatum*, but the breeding project at Cornell used tundra peregrines from the Arctic, Peale's falcons from the Pacific Northwest, and even peregrine subspecies from Spain, Scotland, and Chile. Critics charged that captive breeders were releasing mongrels. The Peregrine Fund and its supporters countered that there simply weren't enough *anatum* peregrines in captivity to produce the number of purebred chicks required, and none at all from the eastern race. Any peregrine, they said, was better than no peregrine.

Criticisms aside, the reintroduction was a stunning success. More than twelve hundred captive-bred chicks were released in the East over roughly a ten-year period, starting in 1974. Although many of the released birds perished before reaching maturity, the survivors fulfilled biologists' hopes by setting territories and breeding. By 1993 there were ninety-eight pairs in the eastern states, including twenty-one pairs in New York, thirteen in Virginia, and twelve in Vermont. In other regions of the continent where the damage from DDT was not as severe, a mixture of protection from chemicals and captive reintroductions sent populations back toward historic levels. In all, the number of pairs in the Lower 48 probably neared one thousand for the first time in decades.

But if the peregrine has been returned to the skies of the East, it is a somewhat different bird from the falcons that originally lived there. While New England peregrines have reoccupied many historic eyries (lower numbers of owls made wilderness hacking possible), in some other areas the peregrine is an urban species. Pennsylvania, which once had dozens of eyries along the Susquehanna and Delaware Rivers, now has six pairs, all urban. Most nest under bridges in Philadelphia, where they are exposed to heavy chemical contamination; one nest is directly over

▶ Biologists at the privately founded Peregrine Fund pioneered techniques for raising large numbers of captive-bred peregrine chicks for release into the wild.

▶ An attendant checks a captive-reared peregrine chick before placing it in a hack box.

a federal Superfund cleanup site. Their fledging rates are so poor that for several years, Philadelphia eggs have been taken from their nests, reared in captivity with a foster mother, then hacked out elsewhere.

Falcon recovery has been so strong that many people, including the Peregrine Fund, have urged that the western U.S. population be downlisted under the federal Endangered Species Act from endangered to threatened; and the arctic race has been removed from the list entirely, since it seems to have recovered to natural levels.

Even these organizations recognize, however, that the peregrine isn't completely safe. While DDT and similar pesticides are banned in the United States, they are still made and used in developing countries, where migrating falcons risk contamination; the birds on which they prey may also pick up a toxic load while in the tropics.

HISTORIC PEREGRINE ABUNDANCE

These figures are estimates of the number of peregrine falcon nesting territories prior to European settlement of North America, based on known eyries. Biologists believe the normal peregrine population was somewhere around eighty or ninety percent of these figures, since some territories will always be vacant.

REGION	NUMBER OF TERRITORIES
Eastern United States, southeastern Canada	400
Rocky Mountains, Great Basin, central Mexico	400
Pacific Coast	500
Baja California, coastal mainland Mexico	125
Southeastern Alaska, Aleutians, Queen Charlotte Islands	850
Arctic and subarctic Alaska and Canada	5,000–8,000
Total	**7,275–10,275**

(Source: L. Kiff in Peregrine Falcon Populations, 1988)

NUMBER OF CAPTIVE-BRED PEREGRINE FALCONS RELEASED

LOCATION	NUMBER
Eastern U.S.	1,229
Midwest and south central Canada	698
Western U.S.	2,598

(Source: The Peregrine Fund. Figures through 1993.)

NESTING PAIRS OF PEREGRINE FALCONS—LOWER 48

LOCATION	1989	1993
Arizona	135+	250+
California	90+	123+
Colorado	37	62
Connecticut	0	1
Delaware	2	1
District of Columbia	—	1
Georgia	0	1
Idaho	3	14
Illinois	3	1
Indiana	1	4
Iowa	0	4
Kansas	0	1
Maine	5	5
Maryland	8	9

LOCATION	1989	1993
Michigan	2	5
Minnesota	7	16
Missouri	0	4
Montana	5	10
Nebraska	0	2
Nevada	2	4
New Hampshire	8	8
New Jersey	11	11
New Mexico	29+	25
New York	16	21
North Carolina	8	6
Ohio	1	6
Oregon	10	27
Pennsylvania	3	6
South Carolina	0	1
Texas	10	10+
Utah	88+	115+
Vermont	7	12
Virginia	13	13
Washington	12	24
Wisconsin	2	6
Wyoming	11	29
Total	**531**	**840**

(Source: The Peregrine Fund, 1993)

One of the Peregrine Fund's "hawk barns," where peregrines and other endangered raptors are bred.

Madagascar Serpent-eagle

Classification: No listing U.S. ESA; CITES Appendix II.

The Madagascar serpent-eagle might be the least-known raptor in the world. This long-tailed bird of prey, about the size and shape of a goshawk, is found only in the coastal rain forest of the island of Madagascar. The serpent-eagle is considered one of the six rarest birds in the world, known from a handful of museum specimens.

Virtually nothing is known about the serpent-eagle's habits or lifestyle. The only foods it has been reported to eat are chameleons, lemurs, and poultry, although that may be a result of limited knowledge, rather than a limited diet.

Despite a number of intensive, well-organized searches, no Madagascar serpent-eagle was found after the last specimen was collected in 1930s. That caused many ornithologists to conclude that the hawk was either extinct or nearly so, given the appalling rate of destruction of the island's rain forests.

In 1993, however, biologists working with the Peregrine Fund sighted what they were certain were serpent-eagles in an untouched area of forest. When they returned a few weeks later with equipment to catch and radio-track the birds, however, farmers had moved in and cleared much of the land.

In January 1994, Malagasy biologists trained by the Peregrine Fund managed finally to catch the rare raptor in a different fragment of rain forest. The discovery was an accident (the hawk flew into a mist net set up to capture songbirds), but the researchers photographed and measured the hawk and attached a small radio transmitter so its movements could be followed.

Peregrine Fund officials hope that confirmation of the presence of the endangered serpent-eagle will spur conservation efforts to save the small amount of Madagascar forest still remaining.

GIANT FOREST EAGLES

Classification: CITES Appendix I; U.S. ESA—endangered.

Although they live half a world apart, the Philippine eagle and the harpy eagle of the New World tropics have much in common. They are the largest of the world's eagles, and the most powerful birds of prey on the planet. Both inhabit mature tropical rain forest, hunting high in the canopy for prey too large for other raptors. Both have ornate head plumes—a shaggy crown in the Philippine eagle, and a double crest in the harpy. And both are in danger of extinction.

The Philippine eagle, in fact, is one of the most critically endangered birds in the world, with a total population of about forty-five in the wild (some estimates run as high as two hundred) and another eighteen in captivity. Formerly known as the monkey-eating eagle, this truly awesome creature has a wingspan of seven feet (smaller than many eagles), but its body is heavy and powerful, and the talons are as thick and long as grizzly bear claws. The beak has the meat-cleaver appearance of a sea-eagle's.

▶ *The harpy eagle of the New World tropics, the largest and most powerful raptor in the world, is the focus of growing concern among conservationists as its forest home is destroyed.*

▲ *The destruction of the Latin American tropics endangers not only harpy eagles, but dozens of other raptors, including the spectacular ornate hawk-eagle.*

As recently as the 1930s, an estimated ten thousand eagles were found on the larger islands in the Philippine archipelago, but the species now exists only on Luzon and Mindanao, where rapid destruction of the remaining forest, coupled with illegal shooting and the capture of chicks for the illegal wild bird trade, has decimated its numbers. Conservationists have mounted last-ditch public education campaigns, and a few Philippine eagles have been bred in captivity. Most observers believe the population continues to fall, however.

Harpy eagles are the even larger New World equivalent of the Philippine eagle; massive hunters that can weigh nearly twenty pounds (almost twice a bald eagle's weight), they handle prey as heavy as sloths, monkeys, and prehensile-tailed porcupines. In the words of raptor expert Leslie Brown, the harpy eagle "is unquestionably the world's most powerful raptor, and accordingly the world's most formidable bird."

The harpy eagle once ranged from southern Mexico through Central America and the northern two-thirds of South America—wherever mature rain forest was found. While large areas of suitable harpy eagle habitat remain in the Amazon Basin, the destruction of Latin American rain forest has driven the harpy from many areas.

Biologist Jack Clinton-Eitniear, reviewing what was known of the status of the harpy eagle in 1987, reported it was restricted to isolated fragments of virgin forest in southern Mexico and Central America, and had apparently vanished from El Salvador; the total Costa Rican population, he concluded, "may not exceed several mature pairs." The situation was almost as grave in some South American countries such as Argentina.

The World Center for Birds of Prey in Boise, Idaho, is working with both Philippine eagles and harpies, and is building a small captive population of the latter; the Philippine Eagle Foundation has also successfully bred two Philippine eagles. The survival of both species in the wild, however, requires preservation of large tracts of mature forest—enough to provide each pair with the enormous hunting range it requires.

Conservationists are also concerned about several other species of forest eagles, including the crested eagle and ornate hawk-eagle in the New World tropics, and the New Guinea eagles in the mountains of New Guinea. As do their larger cousins, these spectacular raptors require undisturbed forest in which to nest and hunt.

SPANISH EAGLE

Classification: CITES Appendix I; U.S. ESA—endangered.

With its white shoulder epaulets against the dark brown of its body, the handsome Spanish eagle was for years considered a subspecies of the more widespread imperial eagle. Found today only in parts of the Iberian Peninsula, the eagle once ranged as far south as the Atlas Mountains of Morocco and Algeria, but vanished there as a breeding species after the 1920s.

Today, the Spanish eagle is all but extinct in Portugal, and survives in Spain only in such protected pockets as the Coto de Doñana and the Montes de Toledo. Recent estimates place the world population at about 110 pairs.

During the nineteenth century, bird collectors shot adults and took eggs, forcing the species into decline not long after it was described for science in the 1860s. Illegal shooting, poisoning (often unintentional, resulting from predator-control efforts), chemical contamination, and loss of a major prey base to rabbit epidemics have since further eroded Spanish eagle numbers.

The proliferation of high-voltage electrical transmission lines has also had a profound impact on Spanish eagles, and the leading cause of death is now electrocution. Perhaps most damaging, however, has been habitat loss and alteration, as native plant communities have been replaced by government-sanctioned artificial plantings of exotic species.

As with many large raptors, Spanish eagle nestlings practice siblicide, with the oldest chick or chicks often killing the youngest. Starting in the 1970s, biologists began transferring the youngest siblings to nests with infertile eggs, where the foster parents successfully raised them. Also helpful is the fact that siblicide, while likely in the early nestling phase, becomes rarer as the chicks age. Scientists have removed the smallest chicks and kept them in captivity through the critical period, then returned them successfully to their own nests.

GOLDEN EAGLES IN EUROPE

The golden eagle, a close relative of the Spanish eagle, is one of the most widespread raptors in the world, found across almost all of the Northern Hemisphere. While its population is quite large in the United States and Canada, it has fared considerably less well in parts of Europe and the Mediterranean, where the species has been reduced to a remnant in many countries.

COUNTRY	ESTIMATED BREEDING PAIRS	COUNTRY	ESTIMATED BREEDING PAIRS
SPAIN	1,192–1,265	CORSICA	29–35
NORWAY	700–1,000	ROMANIA	28–30
SWEDEN	600	GERMANY	25–30
SCOTLAND	420–425	ESTONIA	25–30
RUSSIA (PART)	300–700	PORTUGAL	15–20
ITALY	250–339	POLAND	15
FRANCE	250	SICILY	13
GREECE	210	CRETE	10
FINLAND	220	LATVIA	10
SWITZERLAND	200–250	UKRAINE	5–6
BULGARIA	130–140	CYPRUS	2
YUGOSLAVIA (FORMER)	100	ENGLAND	1–2
AUSTRIA	60–250	HUNGARY	1
CZECHOSLOVAKIA (FORMER)	60–70	LITHUANIA	unknown; few
ALBANIA	40–50		
BELARUS	30–40	TOTAL	4,971-6,151
SARDINIA	30–38		

(Source: "Status of the Golden Eagle, Aquila chrysaetos," J. Watson, 1992)

MAURITIUS KESTREL

Classification: CITES Appendix I; U.S. ESA—endangered.

The island of Mauritius has a bleak place in the history of conservation. It was home to the dodo, a large, flightless pigeon that was eradicated within fifty years of its discovery by European sailors. But the lush, volcanic island east of Madagascar, and its neighbors in the Mascarene group, were home to other wonders—dodolike birds called solitaires, as well as pink pigeons, beautiful parakeets, and an endemic species of kestrel. Similar to the Eurasian kestrel, from which it no doubt evolved, the Mauritius species, *Falco punctatus,* is unique in that males and females look the same, with rusty, barred upper parts and a streaked breast.

Unfortunately for its wildlife, Mauritius turned out to be ideal for growing sugarcane, and much of the island was converted to huge plantations. Another hazard—the macaque monkey—was imported to the island, where it decimated tree-nesting birds, including the falcons. The number of kestrels plummeted, prompting biologists Leslie Brown and Dean Amadon to write in 1968: "It seems probable that this little falcon will pass into extinction without anything significant being known about its breeding habits."

There was little hope of a happy ending. By the time anyone got around to censusing the Mauritius kestrel in 1973, the total population was just eight or nine birds, and that dropped to six a year later. A mated pair was taken into captivity for breeding, however, and one of the two remaining wild pairs made what might have been a crucial change in their behavior. Instead of nesting in a tree hole, where the macaques could plunder the eggs, they chose a tiny cavity in the face of a cliff. Their chicks survived, and in turn began choosing cliff sites for their own nesting attempts.

Meanwhile, the captive breeding program was not going well. At first the captive pair would not breed, and additional wild birds that were brought in as captives died—all of them by 1980, when the wild population stood at fifteen. The captive flock had to be laboriously rebuilt with wild eggs and chicks.

This time, remarkably, captive breeding was successful, and over the years more than three hundred chicks were released to the wild. In a break with tradition, however, some of the birds were released not in the almost vanished native forest, but in the greatly altered habitat that covers most of Mauritius today. The kestrels adapted easily to the new environment, feeding on the abundant small vertebrates and nesting in artificial boxes erected for them. By 1992 the wild population was estimated at between 150 and 200 birds, with a high rate of breeding success, hatching up to 50 chicks each year.

4

RAPTORS

IN THE

HUMAN

WORLD

17

Ṙaptors
as
Ṡymbols

⋮ Birds of Paradox

⋮ The relationship between humans and raptors has been a long, decidedly uneasy one. For thousands of years people have trained hawks to hunt for them, and raptors have been objects of religious veneration and totemic power probably for as long as humans have had the intelligence to worship.

At the same time, however, people have persecuted raptors down through the centuries with zeal, exterminating them whenever possible—accusing them of destroying livestock and wild game, and even of carrying off children. Even our name for this group of hunting birds comes from the same root as words like "rapacious" and "rapine."

The most cursory review of cultural history shows the central place raptors have occupied in human mythology and symbolism. While most modern cultures no longer view hawks as religious deities, their power as symbols remains strong—just ask the fans of the Philadelphia Eagles, the Seattle Seahawks, the Atlanta Falcons, and a host of other sports teams. Dig a quarter out of your pocket or look at a dollar bill, both of which carry the stylized image of the bald eagle, America's national bird. Mexican flags bear the image of an eagle with a snake, part of the founding legend of Mexico City.

Legends and Myths

With their mesmerizing speed, keen eyesight, sharp talons, and ability to drift so high they disappear to the human eye, it is easy to see why raptors have been cast in the role of mythological symbols. In the legends of the Ata people of Mindanao, in the Philippines, an eagle rescues a man and woman from a great flood that kills everyone else, and carries them to safety.

In classical mythology, eagles recur frequently—as omens of war or companions and messengers of the gods, like the eagle that carried Ganymede to the heavens. Only eagles lived with the gods on the summit of Mount Olympus; because of their association with Zeus, for whom they carried thunderbolts, eagles were believed to be immune to lightning, and eagle wings were sometimes buried in fields by the Greeks to ward off storms. Vultures appear in Greek mythology as well, particularly the two that punished Tityus by ripping out his liver, which regrew each month only to be torn out again. (Prometheus, another mythological figure, was condemned to the same fate for the sin of giving fire to humans, although in some versions the bird is an eagle.)

Raptors were also seen as portents by ordinary humans in Greek and Roman days. The height, direction, and speed of an eagle's flight could all be construed as good or bad omens, in a practice known as *ornithromancy*—predicting the future by watching the movements of birds. An *auspex* was such an observer of birds—hence the modern words "auspices" and "auspicious."

Just as the ancient Greeks believed the calm weather that comes near the winter solstice—the halcyon days—was tied to the nesting of kingfishers, they also believed that bad weather and violent winds were controlled by ospreys. In North America, coastal fishermen once watched ospreys to get a sense of the coming weather—high, soaring flight was considered an omen of a brewing storm.

The Harpies of ancient Greek mythology were predatory monsters with the heads of women and the bodies of huge raptors, so dirty that they defiled everything they touched. Two of the most notable mythological "raptors," though, were the griffin and Roc. References to the griffin (also spelled *griffon* or *gryphon*)—a huge, fierce creature with the head and wings of an eagle and the body of a lion—date to at least the time of the ancient Mesopotamians, and continued through the Middle Ages.

The Greeks believed the griffin lived in mountains far to the east, where it built its nest of gold and laid a single egg of agate. Unlike the vile Harpies, the griffin was seen as a protective entity, and its image was often used on household items.

The Roc sprang from the mythology of the Middle East and Persia; Sinbad the Sailor encountered it on his second voyage, a bird as large as a cloud, capable of carrying off elephants. Sinbad was taken to the Roc's nest, where he saw an egg fifty feet long, and later escaped by holding onto the bird's legs, each the size of a tree trunk. Although the Roc was commonly depicted as a huge eagle, some experts believe the legend may have arisen from Arab traders who visited Madagascar, home of the eight-foot-tall, one-thousand-pound—though flightless—elephant bird.

Eagles play both noble and villainous roles in Native American mythology. In a story found among some tribes in the northern Rockies, Eagle helped Dove

Vultures, with their unsavory feeding habits and naked heads, are the subject of legends and folklore wherever they are found. In the ancient Maya civilization of Central America, representations of king vultures were even incorporated into the sophisticated glyphic writing system, including the glyph for the rank of ahau, or king.

In the rural South in generations past, being touched by a vulture's shadow portended sickness, misfortune, or even death. Children were told that if they were bad, a vulture would catch them and peck out their eyes—something easy for a farm child to believe, since the eyes of a carcass are among the first things to be eaten by vultures.

There are dozens of old American folk beliefs about vultures—that if you make a wish before a vulture flaps its wings it will come true, for instance. Some of the folklore is completely contradictory, however; in one region the sight of a vulture over a house meant death, in another, good news.

In Native American cultures, vultures were frequently seen as more benign, even beneficial, although some tribes, including the Mandan, considered them unclean. Among many tribes, vulture blood or feathers were used in curing ceremonies or to ward off disease—a practice followed by English colonists in Virginia, who used the fat to treat arthritis. In the Old World, bile from Egyptian vultures was thought to have a number of medicinal uses, and some African cultures still believe that eating vulture brains gives people the power to predict the future.

In Eurasia, vultures were often linked to war, since they were a constant presence on the battlefield, squabbling over the bodies of the dead. Vultures feasting on slain enemies is a common theme in Mediterranean art dating back nearly five thousand years.

---

rescue her children from an ogre, then with the additional aid of other animals helped them to make their escape.

In a story told by the Jicarilla Apache, however, great eagles are among the dangerous beasts fought by the hero Jonaya'iyan. First he kills a huge elk that has been terrorizing the tribe, and he wraps himself in its magical skin. The female eagle, I-tsa, carries him to her nest, where he is left for her two chicks to consume. But when the female returns, Jonaya'iyan kills her with an antler from the elk, then does the same to her mate with the other antler. Finally, he hits the two chicks on the head, stunting them—which is the reason that eagles do not grow to monstrous proportions today.

A similar tale exists among the Tagish of western Canada. In this version the hero is Beaver Man, who destroys the giant animals that have terrorized humans. In this story, Beaver kills the adult eagles with a spear, then puts a louse in the surviving chick's ear so it never grows big enough to threaten people again.

Many aboriginal cultures have "animal bride" stories, in which humans and animals marry. The Inuit of Greenland and Baffin Island tell the tale of two girls who find the bones of an eagle and a whale along the beach. One is taken by an eagle for his mate, the other to the bottom of the sea by the whale. The whale bride's brothers come to rescue her in a boat, but the eagle bride engineers her own escape by saving the sinew from the small birds that the eagle brings her (on Baffin Island, they say she used caribou sinew). With this she makes a rope, climbs down from the high cliff, and is taken away by a passing hunter in his kayak.

Widespread among Natives of both North and South America was belief in Thunderers, often thought to be one or more giant birds—the "Thunderbird," as it is often simplistically called today. In some tribes these huge birds were said to carry lakes of water on their backs, which fell as rain, and as their name implies, they controlled thunder and lightning. Some experts have speculated that Thunderbird legends are a lingering cultural memory of the huge, vulturelike teratorns of the late Ice Age.

Eagles have inspired more folk beliefs and legends than any other diurnal raptors. The idea of eagles carrying away children is embedded in European and Mediterranean culture, appearing in Greek myths, medieval manuscripts, nursery fables, and religious teachings.

Ornithologists admit that when pressed by extreme hunger, raptors may attack unusual prey, and there may have been cases in the distant past when an eagle attacked an unattended infant. But such cases, if they have ever occurred, must be exceedingly rare, and none has ever been documented. The law of gravity argues against it as well; an eagle would be physically unable to lift any but the smallest of babies.

Old myths die hard, however. Supermarket tabloids periodically run spurious photographs purporting to show baby-snatching eagles in action. One recent sequence showed a stuffed golden eagle with a toddler, identifying it as a "harpie eagle" from Argentina.

⋮ Religious Significance

Few cultures placed raptors as squarely in the middle of their religious beliefs as did the ancient Egyptians. Horus, the falcon-headed god of the sky, was one of the most important of the animal-gods in the Egyptian pantheon. Sometimes depicted as a bird, Horus is more often shown as a human figure with the head of a falcon; tomb paintings and texts like the Book of the Dead often show Horus with distinctive "mustache" markings similar to those of the lanner, a common species in Egypt. Horus is also often shown with a disk representing the sun on his head, a symbol of his connection to the sky, and the "eye of Horus" was a popular amulet, thought to confer good health.

Devout Egyptians sought favor by visiting temples like the one at Saqqara, where archeologists have discovered the mummies of an astounding 800,000 falcons, most kestrels, along with millions of mummified ibis, baboons, and other animals personified by Egyptian deities. Each falcon was embalmed, wrapped in painted linen, and slipped into a long pottery tube before being stacked like cordwood in the underground chambers. It appears that the mummies were available for purchase by

EGYPTIAN RAPTOR DEITIES

HORUS

Son or brother of Isis, depicted as falcon-headed man.

MUT

Vulture goddess of Ascheru temple.

NEKHBET

Protective vulture goddess of city of Elkab; goddess of childbirth. Image part of crown of Isis.

▼ *Egyptian wall painting from Trebes Dynasty XVIII. The goddess of Nekhbet of Elkab, from Shrine of Anubis.*

pilgrims—and that the sellers weren't above fraud, since some of the "falcon" mummies were actually other, less desirable species.

Vultures were also significant in Egyptian religion and art. Two goddesses, Mut and Nekhbet, were depicted as vultures, and vultures (along with falcons) were used as hieroglyphic writing symbols. Especially dramatic are the gold or silver pectorals, or chest ornaments, showing vultures with outstretched wings, that have been found in many Egyptian tombs.

(Credit: The Metropolitan Museum of Art.)

▲ *Assyrian alabaster wall panel from the Palace of Ashur-nasir-apal II (885—860 B.C.)*
An eagle-headed winged being pollinating the sacred tree.

(Credit: The Metropolitan Museum of Art. Gift of John D. Rockefeller, Jr., 1913.)

▸▸▸ RAPTORS IN THE BIBLE

The Middle East sits squarely in the great migratory stream that links Eurasia and Africa, and dozens of species of raptors can be found in the Holy Land. Many of the resident and migrant species are eagles, and eagles appear frequently in the Bible—most often as symbols of freedom and wildness, although sometimes representing the haughtiness among humans, or viciousness in nature.

 MAJOR BIBLICAL RAPTOR REFERENCES

OLD TESTAMENT

EXODUS 19.4

You have seen what I did to the Egyptians, and how I bore you on eagles' wings and brought you to myself.

LEVITICUS 11.13–18 (DEUT. 14.12 SIMILAR)

And these you shall have in abomination among the birds, they shall not be eaten, they are an abomination: the eagle, the vulture, the osprey, the kite, the falcon according to its kind, the ostrich, the nighthawk, the seagull, the hawk according to its kind, the owl, the cormorant, the ibis, the water hen, the pelican, the carrion vulture.

DEUTERONOMY 32.11

Like an eagle that stirs up its nest, that flutters over its young, catching them, bearing them on its pinions, the Lord alone did lead him, and there was no foreign god in him.

2 SAMUEL 1.23

In life and death they were not divided; they were swifter than eagles, they were stronger than lions.

JOB 9.26

They go like the skiffs of reeds, like an eagle stooping on the prey.

JOB 28.7

That path no bird of prey knows, and the falcon's eye has not seen it.

JOB 39.26–30

Is it by your wisdom that the hawk soars, and spreads his wings toward the south? Is it at your command that the eagle mounts up, and makes his nest on high? On the rock he dwells and makes his home in the fastness of the rocky crag. Thence he spies out the prey; his eyes behold it afar off. His young ones suck up the blood; and where the slain are, there he is.

PSALMS 103.5

Who satisfies you with good as long as you live, so that your youth is renewed like the eagle's.

PROVERBS 23.5

When your eyes light upon it it is gone; for suddenly it takes to itself wings, flying like an eagle toward heaven.

PROVERBS 30.17

The eye that mocks a father and scorns to obey a mother will be picked out by the ravens of the valley and eaten by the vultures.

PROVERBS 30.18–19

Three things are too wonderful for me; four I do not understand: the way of an eagle in the sky, the way of a serpent on a rock, the way of a ship on the high seas, the way of a man with a maiden.

ISAIAH 34.15

Yea, there shall the kites be gathered, each one with her mate.

ISAIAH 40.31

But they who wait for the Lord shall renew their strength, they shall mount up with wings like eagles.

JEREMIAH 49.16

Though you make your nest as high as the eagle's, I will bring you down from there, says the Lord.

EZEKIEL 10.14

And every one had four faces: the first face was the face of a cherub, the second face was the face of a man, and the third the face of a lion, and the fourth the face of an eagle.

DANIEL 4.33

He was driven from among men, and his body was wet with the dew of heaven till his hair grew as long as eagle's feathers, and his nails were like birds' claws.

HOSEA 8.1

Set the trumpet to your lips, for a vulture is over the house of the Lord, because they have broken my covenant and transgressed my law.

HABAKKUK 1.8

Yea, their horsemen come from afar; they fly like an eagle swift to devour.

NEW TESTAMENT

MATTHEW 24.28 (LUKE 17.37 SIMILAR)

Wherever the body is, there the eagles will be gathered together.

REVELATION 4.7

On each side of the throne are four living creatures, full of eyes in front and behind: the first living creature like a lion, the second living creature like an ox, the third living creature with the face of a man, and the fourth living creature like a flying eagle.

REVELATION 12.14

But the woman was given two wings of the great eagle that she might fly from the serpent into the wilderness.

▶ *Japanese painting on silk. Tokugawa Period (1615—1868). Attributed to Kano Tsunenobu (1636—1713). (Credit: The Metropolitan Museum of Art, H.O. Havemeyer Collection, bequest of Mrs. H.O. Havemeyer, 1929.)*

Raptors and Native Americans

Raptors played a profound role in Indian life in both religion and art. The Plains-style war bonnet, a circle of carefully strung eagle tail feathers attached to a leather cap, is the most recognized of many Native uses of raptor feathers. Indians used hawk and eagle feathers for fans, shield and lance decorations, dance costumes, and a myriad of other functions, both mundane and ceremonial. While eagle feathers were probably used more widely than any other, the feathers of buteos—especially red-tailed hawks—were also prized.

Medicine bundles—collections of mystically significant items, which were suggested in dreams and carried by individuals throughout their lives—were collected by white anthropologists during the eighteenth and nineteenth centuries (frequently by less-than-ethical means). These bundles often included talons, feet, feathers, and skulls of raptors—sometimes whole, stuffed birds, like the stuffed kestrels and red-tailed hawks that have been found in some instances.

Raptor remains show up, as well, in archaeological excavations of Native sites. In the American Southwest, for instance, kestrel bones have been found in the ruins of pueblos, suggesting the birds were kept either as pets or for religious purposes.

Raptors appear in Indian art, especially on petroglyphs, or rock art, in the West and Southwest. The greatest use of raptors in Native art, however, was among the tribes of the Pacific Northwest. Eagles were (and are) among the most frequently depicted creatures, along with ravens, beavers, and orcas—all animals infused with great symbolic significance for these coastal peoples.

Although eagles appear in many kinds of Pacific Coast "formline" art, in which the bodies of the animals are abstracted to fill all of the available space on the object, their depiction on totem poles is best known. Used by many tribes to show rank or memorialize the dead, the poles were originally carved with stone adzes and beaver-tooth chisels, sanded smooth with sharkskin or horsetail stems. Raptors might be rendered realistically (although with wings and beaks usually turned down to fit the outlines of the pole), but more often the carvers took a whimsical degree of artistic license within the rather formal design rules of the art form.

▸▸▸ Golden Eagles in Native American Cultures

In North American Native cultures, the golden eagle eclipsed all other raptors as a symbol of spiritual power, a status in keeping with this enormous bird's size and hunting ability. Indians in virtually every corner of the continent had some form of eagle dance, usually centering on this species. Among the Papago, killing a golden eagle was as supernaturally charged as killing a human enemy.

Golden eagles were frequently taken from the nest as chicks, raised in the village, and eventually sacrificed; this ceremony is best documented among the Pueblo cultures of the Southwest. After a prolonged period of captivity, the young eagle was killed by smothering, its feathers taken for ceremonial use and its body prepared for burial like that of a human child. (In other areas, buteos or, as noted below, California condors were substituted. In parts of Latin America, harpy eagles or Andean condors filled the role.)

Golden eagle feathers were especially prized in many tribes, particularly the Plains and northern Rockies cultures that fashioned the black-and-white tail feathers of immature eagles into the famous headdress. (Feathers from young bald eagles, which are also mottled with dark pigment, were used to a lesser extent.) Individual eagle feathers were also commonly worn in the hair, and the position on the head or markings on the feather often conveyed information about the wearer's past deeds or social status. In other tribes, such as the southwestern cultures, golden eagle down was used for ceremonial adornment.

Catching a golden eagle was a difficult, sometimes dangerous job. Pit trapping was the only proper way among most tribes, and nineteenth-century naturalist George Bird Grinnell, an adopted member of the Blackfoot, quotes several accounts of how eagles were caught in his book *Blackfoot Lodge Tales*.

The pit, large enough to hide a man, was dug on a high point or ridge, and the dirt carried far away to avoid alerting the eagles. The top was roofed with long poles, then thatched with grass and twigs. A stuffed wolf or coyote skin was propped up as though alive, with a large piece of bloody buffalo meat for bait. The hunter would hide inside the pit, and when the eagle landed to take the meat from the wolf, he would reach up through the thatch and grab its legs.

Eagle trapping was surrounded by ritual. Among the Blackfoot, Grinnell reported, a hunter prayed, sang, and smoked before setting out in the predawn hours, and he carried with him a human skull, whose spirit would protect him from injury. While the hunter was in the pit, his wife back in camp could not use a leather awl, since to do so could make the eagle scratch her husband. Nor could the hunter eat rosehips, which would also make the eagle claw at him.

Once the eagle was captured and killed (by suffocation or by breaking its neck), a small piece of pemmican—a mix of dried meat, fat, and berries that was a mainstay of the Plains Indians' diet—was placed in its mouth as an offering. At the end of the day the eagles that had been caught were laid out by the lodge and again given pemmican.

In some tribes, eagle-trapping territories were passed down from generation to generation. And by some accounts, two to five eagle carcasses could buy an excellent horse.

▸▸ CONDORS AS RELIGIOUS SYMBOLS

For the Indians of the Pacific Coast, the California condor was a creature of great power and religious significance. Condors—living, dead, and in effigy—figured in many Native ceremonies, including ritual sacrifice and burial. Among some tribes, the death of important leaders was marked by the sacrifice of a captively reared condor chick. The feathers from these sacrificial condors were sometimes used, with golden eagle feathers, to decorate dance skirts, cloaks, and other ceremonial garments.

Archaeologists have uncovered the remains of condors from a number of Indian sites in California, including what appeared to be ritual burials of whole condors in shell mounds along San Francisco Bay. At another location, the grave of a man included condor mandibles, whose location in the grave suggested he may have been buried in a ceremonial condor-skin costume. Bone artifacts, most commonly whistles made from the long wing bones, have also turned up in several excavations. Prehistoric rock art along the California coast includes many raptorlike figures, among them a painting in Condor Cave in the San Rafael Mountains of a flying condor, the body done in white and the head in red.

Condor-feather costumes figured prominently in the ritual dances of California tribes like the Chumash, who revered the condor as a powerful and mystical being. Some of the more elaborate costumes included whole, tanned condor skins, which the dancer wore laced to his body.

The loss of wild condors, starting with the capture of AC-9 in 1987, was a blow to traditional Chumash beliefs. Since releases of captive-bred condors began in 1992, Chumash elders have been involved in some aspects of the planning, particularly in the use of a release site in remote Lion Canyon—the place where, in Chumash cosmology, the world began, and the condor spirit sprang to life.

Condor ceremonies were also once common throughout the extended range of the Andean condor, but unlike those involving California condors, some of the rituals involving Andeans have survived to modern times. Some involve little more than capturing a young condor, keeping it in captivity for a period of time, then ritually releasing it. The most infamous, however, is the gruesome *Condorachi,* or "tearing of the condor," in which a live condor is tethered upside down by its feet, while riders on horseback pummel it with their fists. Finally, the man whose blow succeeds in killing the bird is accorded the honor of biting out the condor's tongue— and of paying for the next festival.

A related ritual, which originated near Cuzco, involves sewing the feet of a live condor to straps, tying it to the back of a bull, then allowing both to race madly through the village. Unlike the victim of the *Condorachi,* the condor will be released if it survives until morning—a symbol of the victory of native Quechua culture over the Spanish bull.

▸▸ "Sky Burials"

Although the sanitation benefits of vultures have long been recognized by people, in only a few locations around the world has this been taken to its extreme—as a means of disposing of human corpses.

The most famous example is the "Towers of Silence" in Bombay, India, where Parsees place their dead for consumption by red-headed vultures. The practice apparently began in Persia, growing out of the Zoroastrian belief that burial or cremation of the dead defiles the sacred elements of earth and fire; the custom was carried east in the seventh and eighth centuries when the Zoroastrians were driven out of Persia by the rise of Islam.

These so-called "sky burials" are also practiced in parts of Tibet and Mongolia, and have lingered until recently in Iran, the original Zoroastrian homeland. Vultures were also apparently used in medieval Bulgaria to dispose of the bodies of executed criminals. In Tibet, a caste known as dissectors prepare the body for presentation to the vultures by dismembering and disemboweling it; the Himalayan griffons are then called to the site by a dissector swinging a long leather sling that hums through the air.

Paintings from Catal Hüyük in Turkey dating back some eight thousand years show clearly identifiable Eurasian griffons and cinereous vultures descending on headless corpses. Another shows a living human between the vultures, brandishing what may be a sling similar to those still used in Tibet.

▸▸▸ BALD EAGLES AS A NATIONAL SYMBOL

One of the first acts of the United States' Continental Congress in 1776, after severing its ties with Britain, was the creation of a national seal, an emblem of the new nation's ideals and goals. The choice of a seal, and the symbols to go on it, fell to Thomas Jefferson, Benjamin Franklin, and John Adams, all among the drafters of the Declaration of Independence.

The trio's first ideas were complex and full of biblical or classical references—Hercules, Moses and the Pharaoh, the Goddess of Justice—and weren't accepted by Congress. Later committees began considering eagles, although at first they toyed with the sort of double-headed eagles found on many European coats of arms. Finally, in 1782 the secretary of the Congress, Charles Thomson, got the task of taking the earlier proposals and creating a simple, effective seal.

His idea, after some alterations, was accepted by Congress June 20, 1782. It showed a bald eagle with a striped shield on its chest, holding the olive branch of peace in one foot and the arrows of war in the other. In its beak was a banner with Jefferson's motto *E Pluribus Unum* (From Many, One), and a constellation of thirteen stars is over its head. In the first versions the eagle was somewhat scrawny and chickenlike, but through the nineteenth and twentieth centuries it was revised several times, making the eagle appear more powerful and realistic.

Much has been made of Ben Franklin's dissent over the choice of the bald eagle. Franklin, in a letter to his daughter, claimed that the bald eagle was a poor national symbol—for, Franklin said, ". . . he is a bird of bad moral character; he does not get his living honestly," but steals fish from the osprey. Whatever Franklin's reservations about eagles may have been, some scholars believe his recommendation that

RAPTORS IN THE NIGHT SKY

Of the eighty-nine recognized constellations, only one is considered to have the shape of a raptor—Aquila, the Eagle, an easily seen, pitchfork-shaped arrangement near Hercules in the Northern Hemisphere. Aquila includes the bright star Altair, the upper point in the "Summer Triangle" with the stars Deneb and Vega. (Vega is in the constellation Lyra, the Harp, which was once known as Vultur, the Vulture.)

In Greek astronomy, Aquila may represent one of several mythological eagles, including the bird that carried Ganymede to heaven. Another legend says that the stars are the king Meropes, who was changed into an eagle by Hera to quiet his grieving.

SPORTS SYMBOLS AND MASCOTS

FOOTBALL

NATIONAL FOOTBALL LEAGUE
Atlanta Falcons
Philadelphia Eagles
Seattle Seahawks

HOCKEY

NATIONAL HOCKEY LEAGUE
Chicago Blackhawks

MINOR AND JUNIOR LEAGUES
Detroit Falcons
Louisville Icehawks
Moncton Hawks
Portland Winter Hawks
Salt Lake Golden Eagles
Seattle Thunderbirds
Thunder Bay Thunder Hawks
Wheeling Thunderbirds

BASKETBALL

NATIONAL BASKETBALL ASSOCIATION
Atlanta Hawks

BASEBALL

MAJOR LEAGUE BASEBALL
None

MINOR LEAGUES
Boise Hawks
South Bend Silver Hawks

COLLEGE TEAM NICKNAMES

Eagles (Boston College, Eastern Michigan University)
Falcons (Air Force Academy, Bowling Green University)
Golden Eagles (University of Southern Mississippi)
Hawkeyes (University of Iowa)
Jayhawks (University of Kansas)

the United States pick the wild turkey was meant as a joke.

In choosing an eagle for a national emblem, Congress was perpetuating a tradition that stretches back thousands of years. The Roman legions went to battle behind standards that bore the image of the imperial eagle, and across Europe and Asia, even earlier cultures like the Sumerians had chosen eagles (usually booted eagles like the golden, rather than sea-eagles like the bald) as their totemic or battle symbols. Closer to home, the eagle was a symbol of the Iroquois confederacy, perched at the top of the great Tree of Peace, watchful for enemies.

Few ancient cultures, however, made eagles such ubiquitous symbols as does modern America. Next to the U.S. flag, no other American symbol has such wide use in day-to-day life; bald eagles appear on coins, stamps, flagpoles, weather vanes, Boy Scout badges (the highest rank being Eagle), and in uncountable varieties of advertisements and logos.

Oddly, although the national symbol is a raptor, none of the states has chosen one as its official state bird. Most picked songbirds; a few, game species like grouse or pheasants; and several others, waterbirds like loons, pelicans, or gulls. Even Mississippi, long known as the Eagle State because of the bald eagle on its coat of arms, chose a mockingbird.

18

Falconry

"Man has emerged from the shadows of antiquity with a peregrine on his wrist," wrote noted bird artist Roger Tory Peterson. Falconry, one of the oldest partnerships between human and wild animal, dates back at least four thousand years to the Middle East, although other experts claim the sport had its inception in Asia even earlier.

In falconry, a raptor is trained to capture and kill wild game. Other animals have been trained for hunting, most notably dogs, but falconry is unique in that it relies on wild, rather than domesticated, animals; only the ancient use of trained cheetahs in Asia is analogous. Because raptors could not be bred in captivity until recently, hunting hawks have never been more than a single generation from the wild.

THE HISTORY OF FALCONRY

In the centuries before firearms, a trained falcon or hawk was the best way of catching flying birds. It was not, however, the easiest way of gathering food—nets, snares, and other traps worked more efficiently and required less time. For that reason, falconry was largely the sport of the idle rich, people who could afford to spend the time and money to keep, house, and train birds that brought little in the way of practical reward.

FALCONRY'S HIERARCHY

In the Middle Ages, falconry adherents followed a traditional social structure that laid out the species of hawks and falcons that each class was permitted to fly; punishment for violating the code was said to include the loss of a hand. Not all references to this hierarchy agree on who could fly what:

Emperor: Golden eagle (or gyrfalcon)
King: Gyrfalcon
Prince: Female peregrine
Earl or other high nobleman: Peregrine falcon
Baron: Tiercel peregrine
Knight: Saker falcon
Squire: Lanner falcon
Noblewoman: Merlin
Yeoman or landed gentry: Northern goshawk
Page or yeoman: Eurasian hobby
Priest: Female Eurasian sparrowhawk
Holywater clerk: "Musket" (male Eurasian sparrowhawk)
Knave, servant, or child: Eurasian kestrel

In fact, the nobility often made it illegal for the lower classes to fly hawks, at least those species that were capable of catching game worth eating. The fifteenth-century *Boke of St. Albans,* which sets out the hierarchy of falconry followed through much of the Middle Ages, notes that raptors such as gyrfalcons and peregrines could be flown by only the highest-ranking men. Servants, if they wished to participate in the sport of chivalry, could fly a kestrel, a falcon capable of killing little more than mice and sparrows. In many countries, there were harsh penalties for overstepping class bounds with hunting hawks; in some cultures, for a peasant to take a peregrine chick from its eyrie could result in death.

Falconry was not only a status symbol in medieval life. As a sport it was pursued with a fervor far exceeding that of any sport in the twentieth century—people even brought their hawks to church. The nobility spared no expense when it came to their falcons. One thirteenth-century ruler, Holy Roman Emperor Frederick II, built mews for housing his falcons that were as elaborate as castles; he also wrote the six-volume *The Art of Falconry,* which for centuries was the definitive work on the subject. Even the clergy took part with abandon; the *Boke of St. Albans,* for instance, was written by an English prioress, Dame Juliana Barnes.

Falconry was even more extravagant in Asia. Marco Polo reported in 1276 that when Kublai Khan went hunting (carried by elephants because his gout was acting up) his contingent included more than five hundred raptors ranging from gyrfalcons to golden eagles, tended by ten thousand falconers on horseback.

Falcons, especially gyrfalcons and peregrines, were the objects not only of sport but of diplomacy, and even war. No self-respecting noble went on campaign without his falcons and falconers in attendance. Treaties were sealed with the gift of

rare raptors, and captive princes were on occasion ransomed by payments of rare hawks. Especially prized were white-phase gyrfalcons from Greenland, a small but lucrative trade item for Viking colonists on that island.

Not all raptors are suitable for falconry. Some, such as honey-buzzards, are too sluggish and are, by nature, not inclined to chase the sort of quarry sought by falconers—gamebirds, rabbits, and the like. The smaller accipiters—sharp-shinned hawks in North America, Eurasian sparrowhawks in Europe—are also too small to be of much interest, and are too high-strung. In Tunisia and parts of the Middle East, however, sparrowhawks are captured during migration, trained quickly for use on songbirds, then released several weeks later.

Golden eagles have long been considered among the premier birds of the sport, but their size and strength make them daunting—even dangerous—to work with. Goldens are capable of taking prey well beyond the reach of other birds, however, and in Asia teams of eagles have for centuries been flown against deer, antelope, and even wolves.

Certain raptors were, by tradition, used for particular quarry that brought out the best in their abilities. Peregrines in Europe were flown against gray herons, an exceptionally large target, although grouse, wood pigeons, and rooks were common prey. Merlins, the favored hawk of medieval noblewomen, were especially exciting against skylarks. When attacked, the lark would try to escape by flying in a fast, upward spiral—"ringing," in falconry terms—as the larger, heavier merlin labored to match its ascent.

Modern Falconry

Falconry fell rapidly from favor with the invention of firearms, although it never completely died out. This was particularly true in the Middle East and parts of Asia, where falconry remains as much an obsession now as it was centuries ago. The Middle East, fueled by oil money, has for years been the primary market for wild-caught raptors—both legally and illegally taken. Operation Falcon, a controversial federal sting investigation into illegal trafficking in falcons, revealed that some Saudi falconers were willing to spend $100,000 for a prime wild-caught bird.

The sport of falconry enjoyed something of a renaissance in the early twentieth century in Europe, and interest in flying hawks has grown steadily in North America since World War II. Modern falconers must contend with strict government regulation, however. Novice falconers must apprentice with a master permit holder, and the number and species of birds taken from the wild, as well as their care in captivity, are carefully controlled.

Increasingly, falconers are turning to captive-bred raptors, although many purists still insist that the ultimate hunting hawk is a wild-caught "haggard" (adult) or "passager" (immature on its first

▲ *Hooded goshawks riding on their fists, two falconers wade through a frozen cattail marsh looking for game.*

migration). Nonetheless, captive breeding has given falconers a chance to experiment with unusual hybrids, and to use species like Harris' hawks that have a limited natural range in North America. Harris' hawks, in fact, with their agility and innate tendency to hunt cooperatively, are now one of the most popular species with North American falconers.

Once the language of chivalry and nobility, many of falconry's terms have found their way into modern English—although their original meaning may have been lost along the way.

The word "codger," for example, which today means an elderly person, comes from the falconry term "cadger," someone who carries a portable perch, or cadge. Because most cadgers were older falconers, the term came to be used for anyone getting on in years. By the same token, "callow" has come to mean someone young and untested—a use that arose from its original meaning, a raptor nestling with unhardened feather quills. Other everyday terms, "boozer" and "gorged," also stem from the language of falconry.

TERM	DEFINITION

AUSTRINGER:
Trainer of accipiters.

BEWITS:
Thin straps attaching bells to the jesses.

BOWSE:
To drink; a falcon that drinks heavily is a "boozer."

BRANCHER:
Prefledgling raptor that has scrambled out of the nest into the surrounding branches.

CADGE:
Portable perch.

CALL IN:
To lure to the fist with food.

CALLOW:
Nestling raptor whose feathers are still in the blood-quill stage.

CASTING:
Pellet of indigestible fur, feathers, and bones regurgitated by raptors several hours after a meal.

CAST OFF:
To release the hawk from the fist.

CREANCE:
Long leash used in training flights.

ENTERING:
Training a raptor to hunt a particular species or variety of game.

EYAS (EYASS, EYESS):
Bird originally removed from the eyrie as a nestling. It remains an eyas for its entire period of captivity.

EYRIE (AERIE):
Raptor nest (especially cliff ledge).

FALCON:
Strictly speaking, only the female of a falcon species; the male is a tiercel.

FALCONRY:
Strictly speaking, hunting with falcons rather than other raptors. In general practice, hunting with any raptor.

FEAK:
Hawk's act of wiping its beak after feeding.

FOOTED:
To be grabbed by a raptor's talons.

FURNITURE:
Jesses, bells, bewits, hoods, and other falconry paraphernalia.

GORGE:
The crop; a sated falcon is "gorged."

HACK:
Technique in which young raptors are placed in an outdoor location and fed until fledging, then recaptured for use in falconry. In recent years, a modification of this technique has been used to return captive-bred raptor chicks to the wild.

HAGGARD:
Bird trapped as an adult.

HAWKING:
Hunting with raptors other than falcons; used somewhat interchangeably with "falconry."

HAWK OF THE FIST:
Accipiters, buteos, and eagles, birds trained to return to the fist for food.

HAWK OF THE LURE:
Falcons, trained to come to a lure, rather than the fist, for food.

HOOD:
Leather device that covers the hawk's head (except the beak), blindfolding it and keeping it calm. Often intricately crafted, with feather topknots.

continued

TERM	DEFINITION

INTERMEWED:

Bird that has completed its first molt in captivity.

JACK:

Male merlin.

JESSES:

Leather straps affixed to the hawk's tarsus, and clipped to the leash. Traditional jesses are knotted, one-piece leather bands; modern almeryi jesses consist of a leather band attached with a grommet, and a knotted leather strap passing through the hole.

LONGWING:

Falcon.

LURE:

Leather object, usually vaguely bird-like in shape, to which meat is tied. Lure is whirled around the falconer's head on a cord to call in the falcon.

MANNING:

The process of taming a wild-caught raptor.

MEWS:

Enclosed area where hunting raptors are kept.

PASSAGER:

Immature captured during migration.

PITCH:

Maximum altitude of a falcon prior to stooping.

RINGING (RINGING UP):

To fly upward in a spiral, usually while chasing game.

ROUSE:

Action in which a raptor raises, shakes, and lowers its body feathers.

SHORTWING:

Accipiter.

STOOP:

Spectacular hunting dive of a falcon, especially a peregrine.

▲ *Hooded to keep it calm, a trained gyrfalcon waits on a falconer's gloved fist.*

TERM	DEFINITION

TIERCEL (TERCEL):

Male falcon; from Latin, *tertius*, a third, because males are often a third smaller than females.

WAIT ON:

To watch for prey while soaring high overhead.

WARBLE:

Stretching wings.

WEATHER:

To spend time on an outdoor perch.

YARAK:

Asian Indian term for a readiness to hunt, especially in accipiters.

19

Raptors and Economics

Impact on Livestock

Raptors obviously have an impact on the populations of the creatures that they hunt. But exactly what that impact is, and its magnitude, has been a continuing puzzle.

At one time, people assumed that raptors—indeed, all predators—were inherently "bad," because they killed animals that humans valued, such as livestock and poultry, songbirds and wild game. Kill the killers, so the reasoning went, and you'll increase the number of desirable animals.

Even many respected ornithologists of the nineteenth and early twentieth centuries split raptors into two camps—so-called "beneficial" or "neutral" species, which included rodent-eating birds like red-tailed hawks or insect-hunters like kestrels, and "injurious" species that preyed heavily on game or poultry.

Accipiters were most often lumped under the destructive heading; even the tiny sharp-shinned hawk was branded for its habit of killing songbirds. Arthur Cleveland Bent, whose *Life Histories* series on North American birds remains a classic of ornithology, called the sharpshin an "audacious murderer" and "blood-thirsty villain," and the Cooper's hawk a "larger edition of feathered ferocity." Of the

goshawk, Bent wrote: "He is cordially hated, and justly so, by the farmer and sports-man; and for his many sins he often pays the extreme penalty."

Much of the antipathy toward birds of prey came from farmers, who did lose many free-ranging chickens to hawks, particularly Cooper's hawks and goshawks. Unfortunately, few people could tell one hawk from another, or bothered to try. A redtail hunting mice in the pasture was as likely to be shot for chicken-stealing as an accipiter—more likely, in fact, because the Cooper's hawk would make a lightning attack and disappear, while the buteo would be soaring around in the open.

But as poultry farming became an indoor business rather than a backyard undertaking, and as biologists began to study the actual food habits of raptors, a dif-ferent picture emerged. Hawks, it was realized, provide many services critical to an ecosystem—controlling the population of the animals they hunt, and weeding out the sick and infirm. Gradually, the public accepted the fact that most hawks eat a

◀ *Because it often kills songbirds and game species, the Cooper's hawk (left) was usually labeled an undesirable raptor in the early 20th century.*
▶ *In contrast, the red-shouldered hawk (right), which eats mostly rodents, was considered beneficial.*

diet heavy in rodents and other small mammals, and light on game species. That understanding finally led to legal protection for all North American raptors.

In the West, the issue of eagle predation on calves and sheep continues to be a sore point between ranchers and conservationists, however. While legalized aerial shooting of bald and golden eagles is a thing of the past, some are still shot, poisoned, or trapped on the sly.

Although eagles may occasionally kill sheep (they feed far more often on the carcasses of sheep and calves that died of other causes), ornithologists point out that the impact on ranching as a whole is minor. Furthermore, any slight damage the eagles inflict is probably offset by predation on jackrabbits, ground squirrels, and other mammals that compete with livestock for grazing.

▸▸▸ BOUNTIES

The loss of livestock to raptors was long used as a justification for bounties—government payments to encourage the killing of predators. Not only are bounties environmentally foolhardy, they are far from cost-effective for the governments that pay them. As early as the 1880s, biologist C. Hart Merriam pointed out that

Pennsylvania was paying ninety thousand dollars a year in bounties to save about five thousand chickens. Add to that the cost of crop damage from rodents that would otherwise be killed by the predators, Merriam calculated, and the state was losing more than two thousand dollars for every dollar in poultry that it saved. Nevertheless, bounties on goshawks persisted in that state until the 1950s, and on owls and foxes through the 1960s.

RAPTORS AND GAME ANIMALS

Just as raptors have been blamed for taking poultry and livestock, they have also been blamed for killing wild game that would otherwise fall to human hunters. And as with livestock depredation, this belief led to bounty systems, some of which persisted until the 1950s or 1960s in some areas.

Game-management agencies, which once worried about raptors killing off small game, eventually realized that under natural conditions, a predator will not wipe out its prey. Because most raptors are opportunists that instinctively under-

---

"GOOD" AND "BAD" RAPTORS

The following is a list of raptors that were rated by ornithologists around the turn of the 19th century as beneficial or injurious to human interests, based on their food habits. Those that ate mostly rodents or insects were considered good, and given at least nominal legal protection; those feeding on songbirds, game, or poultry were thought bad, and subject to shooting, poisoning, or bounties. Such judgments are ill-conceived, and thankfully long out of fashion.

"BENEFICIAL"
Turkey vulture

Northern harrier

Bald eagle

Red-shouldered hawk

Red-tailed hawk

Broad-winged hawk

Rough-legged hawk

American kestrel

"INJURIOUS"
Sharp-shinned hawk

Cooper's hawk

Northern goshawk

Peregrine falcon

"NEUTRAL"
Osprey

(Source: Sutton, 1928)

---

stand the law of diminishing returns, they will switch to other, more easily hunted species if one becomes scarce.

That is not to say that raptors will not take game animals if the opportunity presents itself. In certain areas, under certain conditions, red-tailed hawks may eat sizable numbers of cottontails and ring-necked pheasants (especially if the latter are dimwitted, pen-reared birds stocked just prior to hunting season). Quail may be important in the diets of some Cooper's hawks, and in northern states and Canada, goshawks take substantial numbers of ruffed grouse, red squirrels, and snowshoe hares. But like human hunters, the raptors are only skimming the excess—the large majority of individuals that are fated to die each year to keep the population from ballooning uncontrollably.

It is generally only under unnatural conditions that predation can have a serious impact on prey animals. One such situation occurs in the northern Plains, a region dotted with small wetlands known as potholes, the most important breeding areas for North America's waterfowl. So many of the potholes have been drained, however—and so much of the surrounding grassland plowed under for crops—that nesting ducks are squeezed into the tiny areas that remain, where cover is scarce. Predators like foxes, raccoons, skunks, coyotes, and raptors learn to hunt these areas, and nest predation is high enough to have an impact on waterfowl numbers. But the predation is a symptom, not the disease—and the cure is better land management, not predator control.

▼ *Researchers have found that the breeding success of northern harriers is tied closely to the abundance of their major prey species, the meadow vole, rising and falling in lockstep with the rodent's population cycles.*

In recent years, our understanding of how hawks function as predators has changed. It was always assumed that predators controlled the populations of the species they hunted, but the reverse now seems true—they are themselves controlled by their prey.

After twenty-five years of study in Wisconsin, biologist Frances Hamerstrom calls the northern harrier "the hawk that is ruled by a mouse." Harriers, she found, thrive or fail based on cycles in meadow vole populations—raising many chicks in years when vole numbers are high, and few in years when food is scarce. Contrary to long-accepted wisdom about hawks controlling the numbers of rodents, the harriers seem to have almost no effect on the voles. The voles, however, have an enormous effect on the hawks. Other studies are showing that much the same principle holds for other raptors, and for predators in general. Raptors, like all wild creatures, are neither good nor bad—those are human distinctions that simply do not apply to nature. Instead, raptors fulfill the role for which evolution has shaped them, cogs in an almost infinitely diverse machine.

THE ECONOMICS OF HAWK-WATCHING—A CASE STUDY

It has been known for decades that "consumptive" wildlife recreation, such as hunting and fishing, pumps millions of dollars into local and national economies every year in the form of equipment purchases, lodging, and travel. Only recently, however, have researchers begun to look at the impact of such "nonconsumptive" sports as hawk-watching. The results have been astounding.

In 1990–1991, Dr. Paul Kerlinger of the Cape May Bird Observatory, a pioneer in the subject of birding economics, conducted a survey of visitors to Hawk Mountain Sanctuary in eastern Pennsylvania, the oldest and best-known refuge for migrating raptors in the world. Annual visitation at Hawk Mountain that year was 53,000, and while Kerlinger and sanctuary curator Jim Brett found that nearly seventy percent were Pennsylvania residents, the sanctuary drew people from thirty-two states and eight foreign countries.

A majority of visitors were male, averaging thirty-eight years old, and with above-average education and income. Their disposable income was liberally shared through the community. The study found that visitors patronized at least 150 local restaurants and food stores; forty-three motels, hotels, and bed-and-breakfasts; and twenty-three campgrounds—more than two hundred local businesses in all.

Their expenditures, along with Hawk Mountain's annual budget of $800,000 (supported privately, largely through its fifteen thousand members), pumped about $1.5 million directly into the local economy. The total economic impact, however, is considerably greater, thanks to "multiplier" effects, which ripple through the economy. The researchers estimated Hawk Mountain's overall economic impact at between $42.5 and $3.7 million each year. Even that, Kerlinger and Brett said, was conservative, given that Hawk Mountain's visitation continues to climb—to seventy thousand people in 1992.

Nor did the study address the larger question of travel, beyond asking whether or not visitors purchased gasoline locally. Other research has shown that roughly half of the $1,850 the average birder spends on the hobby each year is for travel.

Kerlinger and others have studied similar birding hot spots around the United States and Canada. At Cape May, New Jersey, in 1993 (where the attractions extend beyond hawks to shorebirds, waterfowl, and songbirds), visitation exceeded 100,000 birders, and spending topped $1,000,000.

Conservation is often cast as a barrier to economic growth, but the studies at Hawk Mountain and elsewhere clearly show that such "nonconsumptive" wildlife activities as hawk-watching can have a tremendous, positive impact on local economies. This information can be especially valuable for conservationists, who increasingly are being forced to justify habitat preservation and species protection in terms of their impact on economic growth. Conservationists in developing countries are also paying close attention to such studies, which indicate the potential for ecotourism, a form of development that can both benefit local residents and preserve natural ecosystems.

20

Hawk-Watching

Each spring and autumn, as the twice-yearly spectacle of bird migration plays itself out across the North American continent, hundreds of thousands of people make a migration of their own. They congregate on windy mountaintops and lonely beaches, on grassy hills near suburban shopping malls, in rickety fire towers and on bluffs overlooking the Great Lakes or Pacific Ocean.

They are hawk-watchers, and their ranks are growing every year. Just as birding is enjoying an unprecedented boom in interest, so this variant on the sport is experiencing a groundswell, as more and more people discover the excitement of watching raptors in the wild.

Traditionally, hawk-watching is an autumn activity, although a number of spectacular spring migration points have been found. Though it has also traditionally been an eastern sport, hawk-watching in the West is gaining popularity, with several important sites—the Marin Headlands by the Golden Gate Bridge in San Francisco, for instance, or the Grand Canyon in Arizona—as standouts.

Hawk-watching takes advantage of the fact that hawks follow the path of least resistance on their long flights north and south. That often means following mountain ranges, which provide steady updrafts as prevailing winds are deflected. In the West, mountain ranges can also provide a passage around inhospitable deserts, as happens in the Goshute Mountains of Nevada. Many raptor species tend to follow the ocean rather than ridges; for these birds, like sharp-shinned hawks and falcons, bottlenecks along the coast are the places to watch. At Cape May, New Jersey, tens of thousands of hawks are funneled to the end of the peninsula that juts far out into Delaware Bay.

In spring, hawks catch southerly winds and migrate north across a broad front, avoiding the coast and inland ridges. Consequently, most of the autumn locations produce few hawks in spring. Those birds traveling east of the Mississippi, however, must contend with the Great Lakes, which form an enormous east-west barrier. To avoid crossing large bodies of water, many hawks turn along the lake shores, piling up in astounding numbers. Hawkwatches like Braddock Bay and Derby Hill in New York, on the shores of Lake Ontario, may tally more than forty thousand hawks in a single season.

▲ *Hawk counters post the tally for the day and the season at the hawk-watch at Cape May, N.J., one of the premiere migration points in North America.*

Weather and Hawk Flights

More than sixty years of observations have shown that weather is the single biggest force affecting hawk migration. In autumn, the best conditions generally follow the passage of cold frontal systems, which produce blustery north or northwest winds for a day or two following the frontal passage. The sudden drop in temperature may spur the birds south, but the winds themselves—deflected upward by mountain ridges—are probably the biggest reason for the heavy flights, since they allow the hawks to glide for long distances with little effort.

As the cold front moves east, high pressure builds in behind it. The wind drops as the high passes overhead, but in the days that follow, the winds pick up again, this time out of the south or southwest. Hawk will use these breezes as well, although

they must, naturally, fly on the south side of the ridge to take advantage of them. Depending on their location, most lookouts experience their heaviest flights on either northerly or southerly winds, but rarely both.

Some hawks are more dependent on weather conditions than others. Accipiters, falcons, and the larger buteos seem to need a stiff wind to get them moving, while northern harriers apparently do not. Broad-winged hawks are perhaps the least affected by wind conditions, moving from thermal to thermal with little regard to following ridges, and often traveling on hazy, almost windless days, or days when the wind is from the "wrong" quarter, such as southeast. Consequently, the bulk of the broadwings flight skips the mountains, traveling crosscountry on thermals, and whether or not their path intersects a hawkwatch is a matter of luck.

In spring, ideal weather conditions are completely different. The days immediately before a frontal passage, not after, are the prime time, with gentle south winds and a low-pressure system approaching from the west. In either season, rain, snow, or fog generally means dismal counts.

Identifying Migrant Hawks

Identifying a distant hawk is an art, not a science, a skill that can be polished only by hours of observation and practice. An experienced hawk-watcher can read the subtlest of clues—the cant of a wing, the speed of the flap, or the proportions of the body—to make an identification at incredible distances.

There are shortcuts to this knowledge, however. One of the best is simply spending time with expert hawk-watchers at established migration sites. Most are friendly and eager to help beginners, since they remember when they, too, were novices.

▸▸ CHARACTERISTICS OF FLYING RAPTORS

The following lists the major identification points for the species most often seen at North American hawkwatches.

··· **TURKEY VULTURE**   Long wings, with silvery undersides, held up in shallow V; rocks from side to side. Red head on adults, gray on immatures.

··· **BLACK VULTURE**   Wings held flat, tail so short as to be invisible at long range. White wing patches at base of primaries. Black head in all ages.

··· **OSPREY**   Wings held in distinctive shallow M-shape; white undersides, dark above. Head often appears white from distance, and when seen from above or behind may be mistaken for bald eagle.

··· **WHITE-TAILED KITE**   Delicate, pale gray bird with falconlike proportions; often hovers while hunting. Wings held in shallow dihedral.

··· **MISSISSIPPI KITE**   Also very falconlike in shape, but more casual and buoyant in the air than larger falcons. Light secondaries create pale line along trailing edge of wings on adults.

▶ *Osprey in flight.*

⋯ BALD EAGLE Large, heavy-bodied bird with planklike wings held flat. Head appears to stick as far forward as tail does behind. Immatures carry varying amounts (often considerable) of light mottling on back and undersides.

⋯ NORTHERN HARRIER Glides with shallow dihedral, flaps with deep, somewhat labored wingbeats. Wings and tail long and narrow; adult males pale gray with black wingtips, immatures and females rusty or brown. All plumages have light rump patch.

▶ *Male northern harriers are pale gray, while females and immatures are brown. All ages and sexes have a slight dihedral in the wings.*

··· **SHARP-SHINNED HAWK**   Dove-size, with squared-off tail; quick, snappy wingbeats; proportionately short head. Chest and belly of immatures appear "dirty." Alternates flapping with short glides.

··· **COOPER'S HAWK**   Longish wings; longer tail with rounded tip and heavier white band (usually); slower, deeper wingbeats than sharpshin; protruding head; pale chest of immature usually contrasts with darker head. Alternates flapping and gliding.

··· **NORTHERN GOSHAWK**   Crow-size accipiter with buteolike proportions. Tail appears short and wide, wings short and rounded. Underside of immature appears "dirty." Adults pale gray above and below.

··· **RED-SHOULDERED HAWK**   Buteo that flies like an accipiter, with stiff, mothlike flaps. Tail and wings appear longer than in most buteos. Pale crescents at base of primaries ("wing windows") obvious if bird is backlit. Often flies on lee side of ridges, out of heaviest wind.

··· **BROAD-WINGED HAWK**   Small, chunky buteo with deep wings that taper to a neat point. Adult tails are boldly banded in black; immatures brown with fine barring. Only eastern hawk to fly in large flocks, or "kettles".

··· **SWAINSON'S HAWK**   Long, finely tapered wings and long tail; wings held in shallow dihedral when soaring, crooked like osprey when gliding. Flight often resembles harrier. Normal-phase adult has distinct dark hood. Migrates in large flocks.

··· **RED-TAILED HAWK**   Heavy, angular buteo with bulging wings and short, wide tail. Dark belly band not always present; look also for dark markings along leading edge and at bend of wings. Brick-orange tail color only on adults, and only visible from above. Often hovers on motionless wings (kiting).

··· **FERRUGINOUS HAWK**   Large, eaglelike buteo, very pale underneath with rusty "leggings" (normal-phase adult). White wing patches and rump patch visible from above. Immature entirely pale below, with dark "commas" at bend of wings.

··· **ROUGH-LEGGED HAWK**   Long-winged buteo with highly variable plumage, from all-dark to pale; light-phase birds often have very heavy, black wing "commas" and black tail tip. Frequently hovers.

··· **GOLDEN EAGLE**   Large, all-dark bird with wide, flat wings and buteolike proportions; head appears smaller and shorter than that of bald eagle. Immatures have white wing patches (sometimes absent in eastern goldens) and white at base of tail; white disappears as bird matures. Brassy sheen on head and shoulders present in all ages.

··· **AMERICAN KESTREL**   Small falcon with buoyant flight; wings appear especially long and tapered. At distance, male's bluish upper wing surfaces and female's rusty wings visible. Frequently perches on utility wires; often hovers with rapid wingbeats.

··· MERLIN Medium-size, generally dark falcon (pale in prairies) with powerful wingbeats and direct, purposeful flight. Adult males bluish above; young and females brown, with pale throat and undertail. Does not hover.

▶ *Light-phase rough-legged hawks usually have a wide belly band and dark "wrist" markings.*

▶ *Golden eagle in flight.*

▶ *Dark wing lining feathers are diagnostic of prairie falcons.*

··· PRAIRIE FALCON Medium-size falcon with pale, sandy plumage. Dark axillaries ("wingpits"). From above, brown wings and body contrast with paler head and tail.

··· PEREGRINE FALCON Large, long-winged, long-tailed falcon; flight swift, with powerful wingbeats. In full soar can resemble broad-winged hawk. Adults appear pale gray above and light below; immatures brownish. Juveniles of tundra race have distinctive pale, golden crown.

 HAWK-WATCHING EQUIPMENT

WARM CLOTHES
Including gloves and wool cap for cold weather. For mountaintop lookouts, dress for weather 15 or 20 degrees colder than valley forecasts. Always take wind chills into account.

LOTS OF FOOD
Including thermos of hot beverage.

PILLOW OR PAD
To cushion rocks.

FOLDING CHAIR
For lakeside overlooks.

BINOCULARS

SPOTTING SCOPE
Tripod or gunstock mount.

SUNBLOCK OF AT LEAST 15 SPF
Use on face even in chilly weather.

HAT OR SUN VISOR

HAND-HELD "CLICKER" COUNTER

NOTEBOOK AND PENCIL
Pens fail to work at low temperatures.

FIELD GUIDE

WATER BOTTLE

INSECT REPELLENT
In warm weather.

Good field guides are invaluable for identifying hawks in the field. Most, however, concentrate on how hawks look when perched, or emphasize the sort of traditional field marks that are invisible at the distances usually encountered at hawkwatches.

HAWKS, by William S. Clark, illustrated by Brian K. Wheeler. Peterson Field Guide series, Houghton Mifflin Co., 1987. 198 pages, 24 color plates; maps, black-and-white photos. Uses traditional Peterson system for field identification to comprehensively cover all 39 breeding and accidental species in North America.

HAWKS IN FLIGHT, by Pete Dunne, illustrated by David Sibley, photos by Clay Sutton. Houghton Mifflin Co., 1988. 254 pages, line drawings, black-and-white photos. Nontraditional approach, but the best guide to identifying raptors in the air, using subtle clues of shape and behavior. Focuses mainly on migratory species.

A FIELD GUIDE TO THE BIRDS, by Roger Tory Peterson. Houghton Mifflin Co. Eastern volume: fourth edition, 1980. 384 pages. Western volume: third edition, 1990. 432 pages. Full color, range maps. Much revised and updated, these are the most popular general bird guides. Raptor identification information unsophisticated by current standards.

A FIELD GUIDE TO THE BIRDS OF NORTH AMERICA, second edition, National Geographic Society, 1987. 464 pages, full color, range maps. Most comprehensive general field guide to North American birds, but raptor-flight illustrations focus on color (difficult to see at distances) rather than shape.

THE AUDUBON SOCIETY MASTER GUIDE TO BIRDING, edited by John Farrand, Jr. Alfred A. Knopf, 1983. Three volumes, approximately 400 pages per volume. Uses color photographs and black-and-white illustrations; range maps.

FINDING NEW HAWKWATCHES

While the listing that follows includes more than 160 known hawk-watching sites, raptor experts agree that there are many more locations yet to be discovered, especially in the Midwest, southern Appalachians, Rocky Mountains, Southwest, and Pacific Coast.

To find potential hawk-watching sites, start with a good map. Raptors tend to follow landscape features like mountain ridges and lakeshores where they can find favorable winds, or can avoid long over-water crossings. Take the season into account; in autumn, hawks pile up along the northern shores of the Great Lakes, while in spring the flight is heaviest along the southern shores. Check south-pointing peninsulas in fall, north-pointing in spring.

Next, check the listing of hawkwatches to see if there are any known sites in the vicinity. Some excellent hawkwatch locations have been found by birders who decided to fill in a gap—exploring the region between previously discovered sites in an effort to trace the birds' flight path.

If you suspect there might be a migration corridor in the area, talk to local residents. They may have noticed a large, seasonal influx of raptors without ever recognizing their significance.

The last step is the most time-consuming—and the most fun. After doing your homework, get out in the field during peak migration periods to see whether or not the site is being used. This may mean giving up a good flight day at a known hawkwatch, but the rewards, should you locate a new spot, are well worth the sacrifice. There are undoubtedly still plenty of surprises out there, like the Rogers Pass/Bridger Mountains area in Montana. Only recently discovered, the region has the heaviest golden eagle migration known in the Lower 48 states.

If you do stumble across a new hawk migration point, keep accurate, detailed records, and contact the Hawk Migration Association of North America (HMANA) for information about submitting your annual data. Information from all hawkwatches, large and small, is necessary if raptor migration is to be understood and protected.

SELECTED HAWK-WATCHING LOCATIONS BY STATE AND PROVINCE

While some of these sites are nature reserves staffed daily through the season, most are small-scale volunteer efforts. Most sites are autumn-only; spring-only lookouts are marked*, and lookouts with significant spring *and* fall flights are marked **. Timing is indicated for Latin American sites where known. For complete regional information on hawk lookouts, contact the Hawk Migration Association of North America, listed in chapter 21 under "Raptor organizations."

NORTHEAST

MAINE
- South Harpswell
- York
- Waterford
- Mt. Agamenticus

NEW HAMPSHIRE
- Little Round Top (Bristol)
- Gap Mountain (Troy)
- Winchester
- Pack Monadnock
- Strafford
- Odiome Point (Rye)
- Meredith
- Jaffrey
- Small Hill (Nashua)

VERMONT
- Putney Mountain
- West Brattleboro
- Fuller Mountain
- White River Junction
- Garton
- Mt. Philo
- Brownell Mountain

MASSACHUSETTS
- North Adams
- Mt. Tom/Mt. Holyoke**
- Quabbin
- Hellcat Swamp (Plum Island)*
- Bolton Flats

continued

Mt. Wachusetts
Hancock
Pittsfield
Mt. Watatic
Granville*
Athol

RHODE ISLAND
Napatree Point
Sakonnet Point

CONNECTICUT
Quaker Ridge
East Shore Park
Botsford Hill
I-84 Overlook
Whippoorwill Hill
Lighthouse Point Park
Bridgewater
Huntington State Park
Kimball Hill

NEW YORK
Butler Sanctuary
Hook Mountain**
Braddock Bay Raptor Research*
Pelham Bay
Petersburg Pass
Hamburg
Fire Island
Mt. Peter**
Derby Hill Bird Observatory*
Franklin Mountain
Coot Hill*
Ripley

MID-ATLANTIC

PENNSYLVANIA
Hawk Mountain Sanctuary
Waggoner's Gap
Militia Hill
Sterret's Gap
Miller's Gap
Allegheny Front
Rocky Ridge
Penn State Hazleton Campus

Bake Oven Knob
Little Gap
Cornwall Fire Tower
Second Mountain
Tuscarora Summit
Ski Roundtop
Council Cup
Wildcat Rocks

NEW JERSEY
Cape May Point
Raccoon Ridge
Montclair Hawk Lookout Sanctuary**
Delaware Water Gap
Sandy Hook*
Boonton**
Sunrise Mountain
Scott's Mountain
Oko Jumbo

DELAWARE
Brandywine Creek State Park

MARYLAND
Washington Monument State Park
Fort Smallwood Park*

VIRGINIA
Harvey's Knob
Rockfish Gap
Kiptopeke
East River Mountain (also WV)
Short Hill Mountain
Mendota
Snickers Gap

WEST VIRGINIA
East River Mountain (also VA)
Bear Rocks
Hanging Rock

SOUTHERN APPALACHIANS

NORTH CAROLINA
Mahogany Rock Mountain

SOUTH CAROLINA
Bird Mountain

CENTRAL UNITED STATES

ILLINOIS
Mt. Hoy (Chicago)

INDIANA
Indiana Dunes

IOWA
Hitchcock Nature Reserve (Crescent)
Grammar Grove Wildlife Area
(Liscomb)
McBride Nature Area

MICHIGAN
Lake Erie Metro Park
Whitefish Point*
Brockway Mountain*
Point Huron

MINNESOTA
Hawk Ridge Nature Reserve

MISSOURI
St. Louis (seven sites near city)**

OHIO
Ottawa

WISCONSIN
Concordia University (Milwaukee)

GULF COAST

TEXAS
Bentsen State Park**
Hazel Bazemore County Park (Corpus
Christi)
Upper Coast Hawkwatch (Smith
Point)
Brazos Bend State Park

LOUISIANA
Cameron Parish
Baton Rouge**
Calcasieu Lake

MISSISSIPPI
Fort Hill
Knight's/Oxford

ROCKY MOUNTAINS, SOUTHWEST, & PACIFIC COAST

ALASKA
Dry Lake

ARIZONA
Grand Canyon (Lipan, Yaki Points)
Nankoweap Creek

CALIFORNIA
Golden Gate–Marin Headlands (Hawk
Hill/Pt. Diablo)
Carrizo Plains
Apple Valley

COLORADO
Dinosaur Ridge

MONTANA
Rogers Pass*
Bridger Mountains
Hauser Lake

NEVADA
Goshute Mountains
Toano Mountains*

NEW MEXICO
Manzano Mountains
Sandia Mountains**

UTAH
Wellsville Mountains

WASHINGTON
Cape Flattery (Makah Indian
Reservation)*
Diamond Head
Hart's Pass/Slate Peak

CANADA

ALBERTA
Mt. Lorette**

BRITISH COLUMBIA
Becher Bay Headlands

QUEBEC
Morgan Arboretum (Montreal)
Valleyfield (Montreal)*

continued

MANITOBA
  Patricia Beach Provincial Park
  St. Adolphe
  Windy Gates/Pembina
    Valley/Brown's Hill

ONTARIO
  Holiday Beach
  Hawk Cliff
  Grimsby/Beamer Memorial
    Conservation
  Cranberry Marsh (Whitby)

MEXICO

VERACRUZ
  Cardel**
  Xalapa*

CENTRAL AMERICA

GUATEMALA
  Izabal**

PANAMA
  Panama City**

SOUTH AMERICA

ARGENTINA
  Estancia Santa Teresa

BOLIVIA
  Concepción

BRAZIL
  Ilha do Cardoso

COLOMBIA
  Combeima Canyon

ECUADOR
  Estación Biológia Cuybeno
  Olón
  Salinas

VENEZUELA
  Paso de Portachuelo
  Parque Nacional Archipielago de Los
    Roques

HAWK-WATCH SITES GLOBALLY

Raptor study is an international undertaking, as this list of hawk migration sites shows. The numbers for each country reflect hawkwatches that have been registered under the Hawks Aloft Worldwide initiative, sponsored by Hawk Mountain Sanctuary.

COUNTRY	NUMBER OF SITES
EUROPE (99 SITES IN 20 COUNTRIES)	
Austria	3
Bulgaria	30
Croatia	1
Denmark	8
Finland	6
France	9
Germany	1
Hungary	4
Italy	4
Lithuania	1
Malta	1
Netherlands	4
Norway	1
Poland	4
Russia	13
(including area east of Ural Mts.)	

COUNTRY	NUMBER OF SITES
Slovenia	1
Spain	2
(including Gibraltar)	
Sweden	1
Switzerland	3
Ukraine	2

AFRICA (7 SITES IN 6 COUNTRIES)

Djibouti	1
Egypt	1
Kenya	1
Tanzania	2
Uganda	1
Zimbabwe	1

ASIA (28 SITES IN 13 COUNTRIES)

Bangladesh	1
People's Republic of China	4
(including Hong Kong)	
Pakistan	2
Tajikistan	1
Japan	1
Kazakhstan	4
South Korea	1
Lebanon	2
Nepal	1
Thailand	4
Turkey	3
(including area west of Bosporus)	
Saudi Arabia	1
Vietnam	3

AUSTRALASIA (1 SITE IN 1 COUNTRY)

Australia	1

SOUTH AMERICA (14 SITES IN 7 COUNTRIES)

Argentina	3
Bolivia	2
Brazil	1
Chile	2
Colombia	1
Ecuador	3
Venezuela	2

NORTH AMERICA (92 SITES IN 5 COUNTRIES)

Canada	15
Guatemala	2
Mexico	1
Panama	1
United States	73

(Source: Hawks Aloft Worldwide/Hawk Mountain Sanctuary, 1994)

SELECTED MIGRATION COUNTS

Abbreviations: TV—turkey vulture; BV—black vulture; OS—osprey; MK—Mississippi kite; WK—white-tailed (black-shouldered) kite; BE—bald eagle; NH—northern harrier; SS—sharp-shinned hawk; CO—Cooper's hawk; NG—northern goshawk; RS—red-shouldered hawk; BW—broad-winged hawk; RT—red-tailed hawk; SW—Swainson's hawk; RL—rough-legged hawk; FH—ferruginous hawk; ZT—zone-tailed hawk; GE—golden eagle; AK—American kestrel; ML—merlin; PrF—prairie falcon; PF—peregrine falcon. Unidentified raptors are not listed separately, but are included in totals.

SPRING HAWK COUNTS

SANDY HOOK, NJ

TV	191
OS	70
BE	2
NH	118
SS	1,911
CO	113
NG	2
RS	53

continued

BW	158
RT	105
SW	1
RL	1
AK	910
ML	214
PF	12
Other: American swallow-tailed kite	1

TOTAL: 3,862

(Year: 1991; Source: Cape May Bird Observatory)

BRADDOCK BAY RAPTOR RESEARCH, NY

TV	6,585
OS	311
BE	106
NH	875
SS	5,609
CO	673
NG	46
RS	867
BW	20,485
RT	4,027
SW	1
RL	435
GE	24
AK	683
ML	24
PF	9
Other: Gyrfalcon	1

TOTAL: 40,816

(Year: 1993; Source: Braddock Bay Raptor Research)

DERBY HILL BIRD OBSERVATORY, NY

TV	2,980
OS	414
BE	36
NH	1,134
SS	5,919
CO	504
NG	45
RS	1,029
BW	15,371
RT	7,313
RL	411

GE	27
AK	824
ML	13

TOTAL: 36,233

(Year: 1988; Source: Derby Hill Bird Observatory)

SANDIA MOUNTAINS, NM

TV	1,785
OS	70
BE	17
NH	85
SS	807
CO	1,050
NG	12
BW	6
RT	389
SW	59
FH	12
ZT	3
GE	338
AK	275
ML	5
PrF	28
PF	25

TOTAL: 5,346

(Year: 1992; Source: HawkWatch International)

ROGERS PASS, MT

BE	202
NH	3
SS	8
CO	1
NG	14
RT	25
RL	5
FH	5
GE	1,549
AK	1
ML	1
PrF	2

TOTAL: 1,898

(Year: 1993; Source: HawkWatch International)

FALL HAWK COUNTS

QUAKER RIDGE, CT

TV	453
OS	461
BE	12
NH	74
SS	2,128
CO	146
NG	13
RS	106
BW	7,823
RT	349
GE	5
AK	622
ML	39
PF	13

TOTAL: 12,224

(Year: 1991; Source: Audubon Nature Center)

FIRE ISLAND, NY

OS	278
NH	131
SS	639
CO	10
BW	1
RT	2
RL	1
AK	2,051
ML	1,092
PF	168

TOTAL: 4,406

(Year: 1991; Source: Fire Island Raptor Enumerators)

FRANKLIN MOUNTAIN HAWKWATCH, NY

TV	78
OS	36
BE	14
NH	57
SS	518
CO	26
NG	20
RS	215
BW	215
RT	1,529
RL	12
GE	60
AK	61
ML	2
PF	5

TOTAL: 2,851

(Year: 1991; Source: Franklin Mountain Hawkwatch)

MONTCLAIR HAWK LOOKOUT SANCTUARY, NJ

TV	609
OS	527
BE	13
NH	81
SS	2,579
CO	69
NG	6
RS	149
BW	9,936
RT	748
RL	2
GE	1
AK	695
ML	65
PF	26

TOTAL: 15,582

(Year: 1991; Source: Montclair Hawk Lookout Sanctuary)

CAPE MAY HAWKWATCH, NJ

TV	674
BV	66
OS	1,488
BE	86
NH	785
SS	8,207
CO	1,106

continued

NG	30
RS	152
BW	2,343
RT	624
SW	2
RL	1
GE	7
AK	5,872
ML	936
PF	429

TOTAL: 22,808

(Year: 1992; Source: Cape May Bird Observatory)

HAWK MOUNTAIN SANCTUARY, PA

TV	173
BV	43
OS	606
BE	70
NH	197
SS	5,678
CO	577
NG	55
RS	168
BW	5,854
RT	2,970
RL	9
GE	58
AK	634
ML	90
PF	44

TOTAL: 17,367

(Year: 1991; Source: Hawk Mountain Sanctuary Association)

HAWK RIDGE NATURE RESERVE, MN

TV	1,103
OS	281
MK	1
BE	361
NH	417
SS	16,018
CO	155
NG	569
RS	3
BW	53,145
RT	7,160

SW	5
RL	319
GE	24
AK	1,628
ML	203
PrF	1
PF	25

TOTAL: 83,540

(Year: 1991; Source: Hawk Ridge Nature Reserve)

MANZANO MOUNTAINS, NM

TV	603
OS	31
BE	7
NH	48
SS	1,194
CO	943
NG	27
BW	1
RT	562
SW	7,300
FH	17
GE	120
AK	520
ML	23
PrF	27
PF	30

TOTAL: 11,889

(Year: 1993; Source: HawkWatch International)

GOSHUTE MOUNTAINS, NV

TV	270
OS	54
BE	26
NH	116
SS	2,849
CO	2,298
NG	120
BW	27
RT	1,826
SW	158
RL	7
FH	15
GE	316
AK	1,232

ML	19
PrF	26
PF	4

TOTAL: 9,962

(Year: 1993; Source: HawkWatch International)

BRIDGER MOUNTAINS, MT

TV	1
OS	5
BE	123
NH	42
SS	274
CO	122
NG	38
RT	65
RL	54
GE	1,698
AK	50
ML	7
PrF	10
PF	6

TOTAL 2,582

(Year: 1993; Source: HawkWatch International)

MARIN HEADLANDS, CA

TV	2,450
OS	32
WK	25
NH	463
SS	4,216
CO	1,466
RS	277
BW	249
SW	4
RT	4,102
FH	27

RL	22
GE	12
AK	252
ML	51
PrF	2
PF	44

TOTAL: 13,694

(Year: 1991; Source: Golden Gate Raptor Observatory)

VERACRUZ, MEXICO

TV	1,229,916
OS	493
MK	118
NH	120
SS	1,534
CO	424
RS	2
BW	1,185,180
RT	33
SW	448,000
ZT	4
GE	1
AK	10,136
ML	17
PF	177
Other: Hook-billed kite	67
American swallow-tailed kite	1
Plumbeous kite	1
Harris' hawk	6
Unidentified raptor	133,260

TOTAL: 3,309,790

(Year: 1994; Source: Ernesto Ruelas Inzunza)

Hawk migration in much of Asia remains a mystery, but some intriguing hints have come to light. In the fall of 1991, noted raptor expert William Clark spent several weeks observing the migration of raptors in Beidaihe, China, along the western edge of Bohai Bay. While the numbers of individuals were not high, the variety—twenty-five species—far exceeds that found at most North American hawkwatches.

SPECIES	NUMBER	SPECIES	NUMBER
OSPREY	5	GRAY-FACED BUZZARD	11
ORIENTAL HONEY-BUZZARD	39	SHORT-TOED EAGLE	1
BLACK KITE	44	GREATER SPOTTED EAGLE	5
CINEREOUS VULTURE	1	IMPERIAL EAGLE	4
STRIPED HARRIER	137	GOLDEN EAGLE	1
NORTHERN (HEN) HARRIER	66	EURASIAN KESTREL	40
PIED HARRIER	32	LESSER KESTREL	3
NORTHERN GOSHAWK	100	AMUR FALCON	633
EURASIAN SPARROWHAWK	386	EURASIAN HOBBY	14
LESSER SPARROWHAWK	146	MERLIN	4
CHINESE GOSHAWK	2	PEREGRINE FALCON	1
COMMON BUZZARD	1,815		
ROUGH-LEGGED BUZZARD	1		
UPLAND BUZZARD	1	TOTAL	3,493

WATCHING WINTERING RAPTORS

Winter is one of the best times to find certain raptors, especially arctic species that have migrated south for the season. Furthermore, because trees are bare in most places, resident raptors will be easier to spot. Unlike watching migrants, winter hawk-watching is usually a motorized activity, spent cruising back roads and scanning distant treetops.

In many area, the number of wintering raptors can be spectacular; parts of the southern Plains and Southwest are famous for their large numbers of wintering buteos and eagles. Farmland across the northern third of the United States attracts migrant rough-legged hawks, and also affords the rare chance to see a gyrfalcon.

Early morning is the best time for winter hawk-watching. Buteos like red-tailed and rough-legged hawks often perch near the tops of dead trees for an hour or two after sunrise, perhaps trying to absorb some of the meager heat from the winter sun. Drive slowly, examining any suspicious lump in fencerows and windbreaks. The white breast of a redtail is an especially noticeable beacon when it catches the morning sunlight—so much so that inexperienced observers may mistake a perched redtail for a white gyrfalcon or snowy owl at first.

Utility poles and wires are a preferred perch—in some western regions almost the *only* perch—for wintering raptors. Some, like roughlegs, may allow a close approach in a vehicle; but others, like kestrels, are nervous and flighty, so it is usually best to stop some distance away, rather than attempt to pass by without spooking the bird.

Marshes, either freshwater or tidal, are also excellent locations for winter hawk-watching. In addition to buteos, marshes attract harriers, American kestrels, and bald eagles—not to mention short-eared owls, which often hunt at dusk and dawn in the company of harriers.

Bald eagles gather in huge winter concentrations in a number of places across North America, including the thousands of eagles that gather for the winter salmon run on Alaska's Chilkat River. For a listing of winter eagle concentrations, see chapter 16.

Watching Raptors in the Breeding Season

Generally speaking, it is both harder and less advisable to watch raptors during the breeding season. Many species become secretive during the nesting period, and excessive activity near the nest may cause the adults to abandon the site.

However, government wildlife agencies sometimes set up viewing areas that allow visitors to watch nesting peregrine falcons and bald eagles from a safe distance. In urban settings, peregrine falcon nests on skyscrapers have even been fitted with video cameras, and the image transmitted live on closed-circuit television. In one city, a local cable TV station even created a "peregrine channel," so subscribers could tune in to watch the nest from the comfort of their living rooms!

Helping Raptors

Man-made Nesting Sites

▸▸▸ Kestrel Nest Boxes

Because natural tree cavities are relatively rare, artificial nest boxes are usually a simple, effective way to bolster the populations of hole-nesting birds. While only one North American raptor, the American kestrel, routinely uses cavities, the bird is widespread and easy to attract to nest boxes.

Kestrels are open-country birds, most common in farmland, mixed grasslands, and woodlots, and in arid or desert habitats. They adapt easily to humans, and can often be found in or near suburban neighborhoods, or hunting along roads. They have even been known to nest in towns and small cities, hunting for mice and house sparrows.

A kestrel box is simply a greatly enlarged version of the traditional bluebird nest box. The outside dimensions are about twenty inches high by nine inches side to side and front to back, with a three-inch entrance hole.

For durability, protection against predators like raccoons, and insulation against heat and cold, use one-inch-thick pine lumber, and assemble the box with galvanized wood screws rather than nails, which eventually loosen. A single eight-foot length of 1-by-10 lumber will provide enough wood for one box.

Because the box must be cleaned out after each nesting season, be sure to hinge the roof so it can be raised; this also makes it easy to evict house sparrows, starlings, or mice that may set up housekeeping inside. To keep predators out, drive a wood screw down through the roof into the front of the box to hold it shut. Finally, add about three inches of wood shavings or pine needles to the floor of the box, mimicking the rotted wood inside a natural cavity. This also makes the box much easier to clean.

The biggest key to success is where the box is placed. Kestrels usually nest ten to thirty feet above the ground, in a fairly open site with high perches such as utility wires. The easiest alternative is to wire or screw the box into the trunk of a tree in a fencerow, although be sure to pick a dead tree or one without low branches, since kestrels like an unobstructed approach. Face the box to the east or south, so the hole is away from the prevailing wind and rain.

Because kestrels begin selecting a nest site in very early spring, be sure the box is erected by late winter—early February in parts of the North. Check it every week, and remove any nesting material brought in by sparrows or starlings—kestrels add nothing to the box, and will lay their eggs directly on the wood chips. Once the kestrels have accepted the box, do not disturb them until the chicks have fledged.

▸▸▸ OSPREY AND EAGLE NEST PLATFORMS

People have known for generations that ospreys—called "fish hawks" in the nineteenth century—will nest on artificial platforms. Forgiving of human disturbance, ospreys will build on a variety of man-made structures, including channel markers and duck blinds, and many rural communities erected old wagon wheels mounted on high poles as an inducement to nesting ospreys.

After coastal osprey populations crashed in the 1960s as a result of pesticide use, there was renewed interest in nesting platforms as a way of increasing breeding success among ospreys. Many natural sites (especially dead trees) and man-made objects are unstable, while a properly constructed and placed nest platform offers security from accidents and predators.

Ideally, osprey platforms are built on utility poles sunk into shallow water, although they may also be attached to topped, delimbed trees. Poles for coastal locations should be tall enough that the nest is twenty feet above the water, while researchers have found that inland nests should be higher than the surrounding trees. To prevent raccoons from destroying the nest, place a band of metal flashing at least three feet wide head-high around the pole or tree trunk, or use a cone-shaped predator baffle. Such antipredator guards are essential if the pole is to be erected on land.

While the best platforms are specially built from cedar boards and exterior-grade plywood, inexpensive alternatives include wooden shipping pallets, heavywire mesh baskets, and large truck tires with plywood floors. Most of these, however, lack durability.

▶ *Construct nest box from untreated 1-inch-thick lumber, and mount on a pole or unobstructed tree trunk 10-20 feet high, with the entrance facing south or east. Mount predator guard on pole.*

Kestrel Nest Box

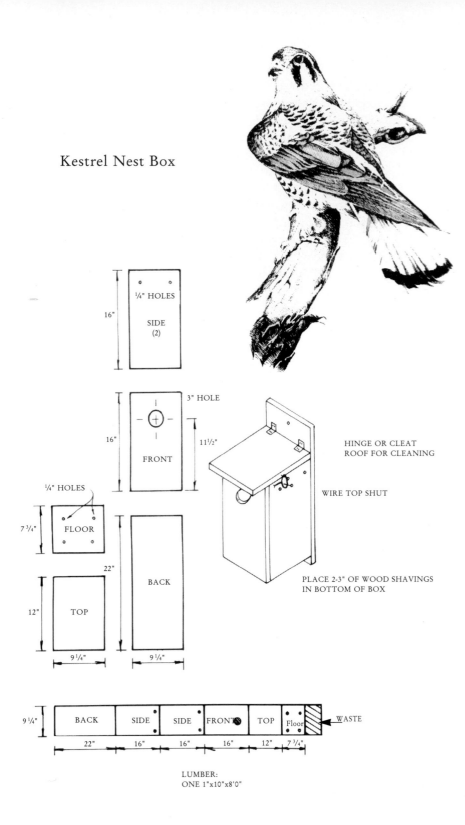

¼" HOLES

SIDE
(2)

16"

3" HOLE

16"

11½"

FRONT

¼" HOLES

7 ¾"

FLOOR

22"

BACK

12"

TOP

9¼"

9¼"

HINGE OR CLEAT
ROOF FOR CLEANING

WIRE TOP SHUT

PLACE 2-3" OF WOOD SHAVINGS
IN BOTTOM OF BOX

BACK	SIDE	SIDE	FRONT	TOP	Floor	WASTE

9¼"

22"   16"   16"   16"   12"   7 ¾"

LUMBER:
ONE 1"x10"x8'0"

(Adapted from Woodworking for Wildlife: Homes for Birds and Mammals, *Henderson, 1984.)*

Osprey Nest Platform

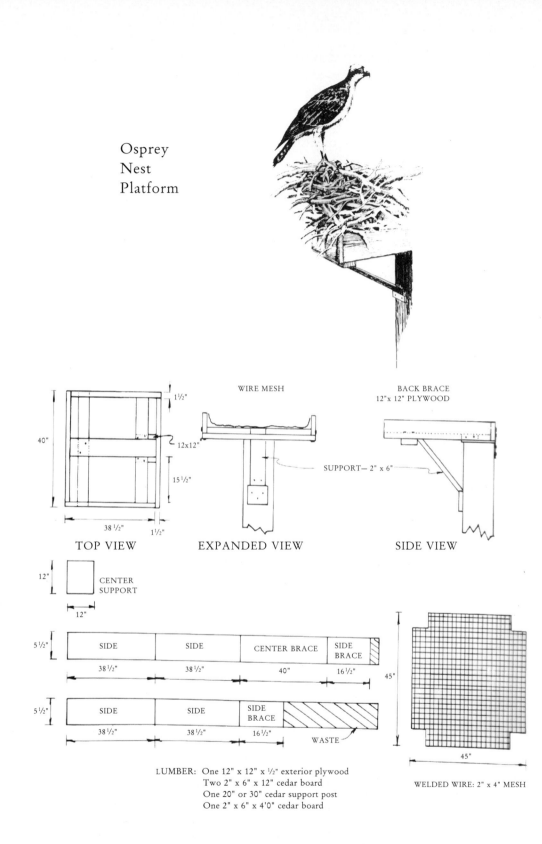

1½"

40"

12x12"

15½"

38½"   1½"

TOP VIEW

WIRE MESH

SUPPORT— 2" x 6"

EXPANDED VIEW

BACK BRACE
12"x 12" PLYWOOD

SIDE VIEW

12"   CENTER SUPPORT

12"

5½"

SIDE	SIDE	CENTER BRACE	SIDE BRACE
38½"	38½"	40"	16½"

45"

5½"

SIDE	SIDE	SIDE BRACE	WASTE
38½"	38½"	16½"	

45"

WELDED WIRE: 2" x 4" MESH

LUMBER: One 12" x 12" x ½" exterior plywood
Two 2" x 6" x 12" cedar board
One 20" or 30" cedar support post
One 2" x 6" x 4'0" cedar board

(From Woodworking for Wildlife: Homes for Birds and Mammals, *Henderson, 1984.)*

Osprey nest platforms are occasionally used by bald eagles. If the platform is being erected especially for eagles, the overall dimensions of the base should be increased about twenty-five percent to allow for the larger nest most eagles build. Natural eagle nest sites tend to be high trees near the water's edge, with a commanding view of the surrounding landscape. Choose a site for an artificial platform with these requirements in mind.

▸▸ OTHER RAPTOR NEST STRUCTURES

While it is known that various North American raptors will use artificial platforms and other nest structures, relatively little work has been done to determine the best designs and circumstances.

Eastern buteos like red-tailed hawks and broad-winged hawks usually have little trouble finding appropriate natural nest sites, but western species like ferruginous and Swainson's hawks, living in areas where grazing or agriculture has reduced the number of large trees, may benefit from artificial platforms erected on poles.

Some experimental work has also been done on creating artificial ledges or cliff cavities for prairie and peregrine falcons. Because such work requires rock-climbing skills and, depending on the situation, a knowledge of explosives, it is obviously best left to the experts.

BANDING

Banding—placing numbered, lightweight metal alloy bands around the legs of captured birds—has given science more information about raptor migration, life span, and natural history than almost any other technique.

▸▸ "ADOPTING" RAPTORS

Following the lead of whale conservation organizations, some raptor-research groups now raise money by soliciting "adoptions" of hawks captured for banding.

◂ *Using pliers, a biologist carefully locks the flange on a numbered aluminum band around the leg of a red-tailed hawk.*

The fee varies with the rarity of the species, from as low as ten or fifteen dollars for common raptors like sharp-shinned hawks or kestrels to several hundred dollars for eagles or peregrine falcons. Sponsors receive a certificate with the vital information about the bird—its species and sex, date caught, band number, and so forth. If the bird is ever recaptured or recovered, another certificate is sent with that information. Raptor adoptions are particularly popular as gifts, and as classroom education projects.

In the East, the Cape May Bird Observatory runs "Project Wind Seine," which also includes songbirds, owls, and marked butterflies, while in the Rocky Mountains, HawkWatch International sponsors its Adopt-a-Hawk program, which provides a certificate with a photo of the "adopted" raptor. For more information, contact these groups at the addresses listed later in this chapter under "Raptor organizations."

▲ *With a toss, an injured immature bald eagle is released following its recovery at a rehabilitation facility in Illinois.*

▸▸▸ WHAT TO DO WITH A BANDED RAPTOR

Placing a band on a bird is only half the battle. If the effort is to pay off, the band number must be reported months or years later, when the bird is recovered.

While some banded raptors are recaptured by scientists, most recoveries are made by lay people who discover a dead or injured hawk. There is no need to remove the band—even on small species like kestrels, the number is easy to read, and removing the band may mar or destroy some of the numbers. This is especially true of the heavier bands used for larger raptors, which feature a crimped joint that is difficult to open.

On a sheet of paper write your full name, address, and telephone number; the complete band number and whether the bird was banded on the left or right leg; the species, age, and sex of the hawk (if known); and the date and exact location where the bird was found. If you could determine the cause of death—for instance, being struck by a car along a highway—include that as well. It is not necessary to send the band itself.

Each band is marked with a cryptic address: AVISE BIRD BAND WRITE WASH D.C. on the smallest raptor bands, a more complete address on those for larger species. While the post office each year delivers hundreds of reports from around the world addressed simply to BIRD BAND WASH D.C., it is better to send it to this complete address: Department of the Interior, U.S. Fish and Wildlife Service, Bird Banding Laboratory, Laurel, MD 20811.

Some research projects also involve the use of color markers, streamers, dyes, or wing tags. Certain raptors, especially young falcons and eagles being released in hacking projects, may also carry additional colored, plastic bands with a separate set of numbers and letters. Such markers can often be read from a distance with binoculars or a spotting scope, although you must be certain that none of the numbers is obscured by feathers or the hawk's position. If you find or spot one of these marked birds, send complete information about the sighting to the federal Bird Banding Lab at the address above.

CLOSE ENCOUNTERS

▸▸▸ RAPTORS AT THE BIRD FEEDER

Almost everyone who feeds birds at a backyard feeder has had the experience. You hear piercing alarm calls from outside, and glance through the window just in time to see a brown blur streak through the yard, impaling a house finch or junco. The local sharp-shinned hawk has made another kill.

For many people, seeing a hawk at the feeder represents the closest brush with predation they will ever have. Experienced naturalists are inclined to view such incidents as the normal way of life in the wild, and are grateful for the chance to witness a natural drama so close to home. Not everyone is so thrilled by the event, however. Casual bird-watchers, or those with little contact with the outdoors, tend to react with anger or anguish at the death of "their" birds.

Most feeder attacks occur during fall and winter, when the majority of people feed backyard birds. The two species usually involved are sharp-shinned and Cooper's hawks—the former about the size of a jay or dove, the latter somewhat bigger, about pigeon- or crow-size. Brownish immatures are most often seen, although adults, with blue-gray backs and rusty under parts, also hunt in yards.

When a hawk attacks, the small birds may burst into flight or dive into thick cover, screaming alarm calls to warn the rest of the flock. They may stay away (or remain hidden) for quite some time after the hawk departs, although usually they resume feeding in a remarkably short while.

If the attacks become regular, or if there is little good escape cover nearby, the flocks may desert a feeding station entirely. If this happens, be patient; the hawk usually switches hunting grounds after a few days in the hope of finding better pickings, and the small birds should return. To minimize the impact of hawks, be sure to place feeders close to good cover—conifers, thickets, evergreen shrubs like rhododendrons, and so forth. Songbirds will also feel more secure if there is a larger area of forest or thicket near the yard, rather than just a few small shrubs around the house.

▸▸▸ What To Do with an Injured Raptor

Each year, thousands of sick and injured raptors are discovered by people—birds that have been hit by vehicles, shot, or poisoned, or that are the victims of collisions with buildings, wires, and even trees. Whether or not an injured raptor survives often depends on the care and handling it receives shortly after being found.

Federal and state laws wisely prohibit the keeping of even injured wild birds, unless one has a special possession permit. Penalties can be severe, including heavy fines and potential jail time, and are meant to prevent people from making pets out of wild animals. It is generally permissible to rescue an injured raptor, however, provided it is immediately turned over to a licensed wildlife rehabilitator or conservation officer. Contact your state or provincial wildlife agency for the name and number of the nearest rehabilitation center.

If you find a sick or injured raptor, avoid causing any unduo stress. Often, the simplest and easiest way to capture an injured hawk is with a large towel. Walk slowly toward the bird, holding the towel in front of you; frequently, the hawk will stand its ground, leaning backward with talons at the ready. Drop the towel over the bird, gathering it up gently, and be careful to keep the feet away from your hands, arms, or body. Because a hawk can grab easily through the towel, be sure to wear heavy gloves. Hawks that have been struck by vehicles may be stunned, and can be picked up with gloves, then wrapped in a towel.

Place the hawk in a large cardboard box, with an old towel on the bottom for traction, and keep the lid closed. The darkness will calm the bird and keep it from trying to escape, while the smooth, solid cardboard will not damage its plumage. Put the box in a warm, quiet place away from drafts, and do not disturb the hawk any more than necessary.

Under no circumstances should you put the hawk in a wire bird or animal cage—the hawk will struggle to escape, breaking its flight feathers in the mesh. A hawk with many broken feathers must be kept in captivity until its new plumage molts in, a process that takes months, even if its original injury heals quickly. Nor should you attempt to set broken bones or treat any of the hawk's injuries yourself, for in doing so you may only worsen the situation. Well-meaning individuals often try to bandage birds using adhesive medical tape, for example, hopelessly gumming up the hawk's feathers.

In an emergency—if you are unable to take the hawk to a licensed rehabilitator within twenty-four hours—try feeding the bird pieces of raw, red muscle meat, such as fresh beef. For a hawk the size of a redtail, cut the meat into finger-size strips, dip them in water, and place them in the box. An even better alternative is freshly killed mice, but be certain there is no chance the rodents may have ingested poison. Pet-store mice are ideal, but use brown or gray mice rather than the standard white, which many wild raptors do not immediately recognize as prey. Provide water in a shallow dish that cannot easily be tipped, but do not try to give water with a dropper, or by force—the hawk may easily inhale it.

Small accipiters like sharp-shinned hawks often strike windows while chasing songbirds at backyard feeders. Most stunned hawks recover within a short time without human assistance, but if the bird has not moved at the end of an hour or so, place it in a cardboard box and contact a rehabilitation center.

▲ *Captured for banding, a sharp-shinned hawk's bill is measured as part of a study on size differences.*

BIRDLIFE INTERNATIONAL (FORMERLY INTERNATIONAL COUNCIL FOR BIRD PRESERVATION)

Wellbrook Ct., Girton Road
Cambridge CB3 ONA United
Kingdom
Focuses on protection and research concerning rare birds worldwide.

BRADDOCK BAY RAPTOR RESEARCH

432 Manitou Beach Rd.
Hilton, NY 14468
(716) 392-5685
Conducts hawk counts and banding along Lake Ontario.

CAPE MAY BIRD OBSERVATORY

P.O. Box 3
Cape May Point, NJ 08212
(609) 884-2736
Conducts fall hawk counts on Cape May Point.

CENTER FOR THE STUDY OF TROPICAL BIRDS

218 Conway
San Antonio, TX 78209-1716

CORNELL LAB OF ORNITHOLOGY

159 Sapsucker Woods Rd.
Ithaca, NY 14850

DERBY HILL BIRD OBSERVATORY

Onondaga Audubon Society
Box 620
Syracuse, NY 13201
Conducts spring hawk counts along Lake Ontario.

GEORGE MIKSCH SUTTON AVIAN RESEARCH CENTER

P.O. Box 2007
Bartlesville, OK 74005
Instrumental in reintroducing southern bald eagles.

GOLDEN GATE RAPTOR OBSERVATORY

Building 201, Fort Mason
San Francisco, CA 94123
Conducts hawk counts and banding.

HAWK MIGRATION ASSOCIATION OF NORTH AMERICA

c/o Seth Kellogg, Membership
Secretary
377 Loomis St.
Southwick, MA 01077
Coordinates data collection at hundreds of hawkwatch sites in U.S., Canada, and Central America.

HAWK MOUNTAIN SANCTUARY ASSOCIATION

RR2 Box 191
Kempton, PA 19529-9449
(610) 756-6961
Conducts hawk counts, research on Kittatinny Ridge.

HAWK RIDGE NATURE RESERVE

Duluth Audubon Society
c/o Dept. of Biology, University of
Minnesota-UMD
Duluth, MN 55812
Conducts hawk counts along Lake Superior.

HAWKWATCH INTERNATIONAL

P.O. Box 660
Salt Lake City, UT 84110-0660
(801) 524-8511 or (800) 726-HAWK
Conducts hawk counts, banding at several sites in western U.S.

INTERNATIONAL OSPREY FOUNDATION

P.O. Box 250
Sanibel, FL 33957

INTERNATIONAL WILDLIFE REHABILITATION COUNCIL

4437 Central Place, B-4
Suisan, CA 94585

MANOMET BIRD OBSERVATORY

P.O. Box 1770
Manomet, MA 02345

MACDONALD RAPTOR RESEARCH CENTER

McGill University
Ste.-Anne-de-Bellevue
Quebec H9X 1C0 Canada

continued

NATIONAL FOUNDATION TO PROTECT AMERICA'S EAGLES
P.O. Box 120206
Nashville, TN 37212

NORTH AMERICAN FALCONER'S ASSOCIATION
c/o Larry Miller
305 Long Ave.
North Aurora, IL 60542

NORTHEAST HAWKWATCH
c/o Gerald Mersereau
P.O. Box 321
Tarriffville, CT 06081
Coordinates hawkwatches in New England.

PADRE ISLAND SURVEY
3410 E. Columbia
Meridian, ID 83642

THE PEREGRINE FUND
WORLD CENTER FOR BIRDS OF PREY
5666 W. Flying Hawk Lane
Boise, ID 83709
Research, captive propagation of endangered raptors.

PREDATORY BIRD RESEARCH GROUP
University of California
Santa Cruz, CA 95064

THE RAPTOR CENTER
University of Minnesota
1920 Fitch Ave.
St. Paul, MN 55108

THE RAPTOR EDUCATION FOUNDATION
21901 E. Hampden Ave.
Aurora, CO 80013

RAPTOR RESEARCH FOUNDATION INC.
12805 St. Croix Trail
Hastings, MN 55033

RAPTOR SOCIETY OF METROPOLITAN WASHINGTON
Box 482
Annandale, VA 22003

SASKATCHEWAN COOPERATIVE FALCON PROJECT
Dept. of Veterinary Anatomy
University of Saskatchewan
Saskatoon, Saskatchewan S7N 0W0
Canada

SOCIETY FOR THE PRESERVATION OF BIRDS OF PREY
P.O. Box 66070
Los Angeles, CA 90066

VERMONT RAPTOR CENTER
Vermont Institute of Natural Science
Church Hill Road
Woodstock, VT 05091

APPENDIX I

RAPTOR WORDS AND TERMS

Because they are such potent emblems of strength, freedom, and predatory tendencies, raptors have been part of human language almost from the start. In many cases, words and terms that originally pertained to raptors have taken on entirely unrelated meanings; in others, they grew from the same ancient roots as the names of hawks, eagles, and falcons—a man's "aquiline" nose, or a greedy person's "rapacious" behavior.

TERM	DEFINITION

ACCIPITRINE

adj. raptorial. [From L. *accipiter,* a hawk.]

AQUILINE

adj. 1. eaglelike. 2. hooked or curved, like an eagle's beak. [From L. *aquilinus,* eaglelike.]

BUZZARD

noun 1. any of several soaring hawks of the genus *Buteo.* 2. *slang,* any of several cathartid vultures of the New World. 3. *slang,* old, unpleasant man. [From F. *busard,* hawk.]

EAGLE

noun 1. any of several species of large, day-flying birds of prey. 2. silver military insignia in the shape of eagles, worn by colonels (U.S. Army, Air Force, Marine Corps) and captains (U.S. Navy). 3. ten-dollar gold coin formerly issued by U.S. government. 4. golf score of two below par on a hole. [From L. *aquila,* dark-colored; ME *egle.*]

EAGLE-EYED

adj. possessing keen eyesight.

FALCATE

adj. curved or sickle-shaped. [From L. *falcatus,* as a sickle.]

FALCON

noun 1. any of several day-flying birds of prey marked by notched bills and long wings and tails. 2. *in falcon ry,* the female of any species of falcon. 3. small cannon. [From LL *falcon* < L. *falx,* sickle.]

FALCONER

noun one who hunts with trained birds of prey, esp. falcons. [From ME *falkenar.*]

FALCONET

noun 1. any of several small Old World falcons. 2. a light cannon.

FALCONRY

noun sport of hunting with trained hawks, eagles, or, esp., falcons.

HARRIER

noun 1. any of several species of day-flying birds of prey with distinct facial disks. 2. one that harries or torments. 3. cross-country runner. 4. small hound used to hunt hares. [From OE *hergian,* harass.]

HARRY

verb 1. to harass or torment. 2. to plunder in war. [From OE *hergian,* harass.]

HAWK

noun 1. any of a variety of day-flying birds characterized by hooked beaks and curved claws. 2. several species of night-flying, insectivorous birds such as the nighthawk, unrelated to true raptors. 3. one who preys upon others. 4. a person who advocates the use of force in foreign policy; a war hawk. 5. a masonry tool for holding plaster. [From ME *hauke,* OE *hafoc,* hawk.]

HAWK

verb 1. to hunt on the wing. 2. to hunt using hawks or falcons; to participate in the sport of falconry. 3. to clear the throat loudly. 4. to sell door-to-door, or by peddling on the street.

HAWKED

adj. having been sold door-to-door.

HAWKER

noun one who sells goods door-to-door; a peddler.

HAWKEYE

noun nickname for a resident of Iowa.

HAWKEYED

adj. having exceptionally keen eyesight.

PEREGRINATE

verb to journey, esp. on foot. [From L. *peregrinatus,* travel abroad.]

PEREGRINE

adj. foreign, or of a foreign land. [From L. *peregrinus,* foreign.]

RAPACIOUS

adj. predatory or greedy; given to seizing or taking. [From L. *rapax,* greedy.]

RAPT

adj. 1. deeply absorbed; engrossed. 2. moved by deep emotion. [From L. *raptus,* seized.]

RAPTORIAL

adj. 1. preying upon other animals; predatory. 2. adapted for seizing prey, as in claws. 3. belonging to the orders Falconiformes or Strigiformes, the hawks and owls. [From L. *raptor,* one who seizes by force.]

RAPTURE

noun state of ecstasy or profound joy. [From L. *raptus,* seized.]

VULTURE

noun 1. any of several species of carrion-feeding birds, generally marked by naked heads. 2. *slang,* one with ghoulish tastes or tendencies. [From ME *vultur* < L. *vulturus,* tearer.]

VULTURINE

adj. pertaining to or resembling a vulture in habits or appearance.

As with most of the English language, the common names given to raptors have ancient roots that stretch back into many European and Native American tongues.

APLOMADO
From the Spanish *aplomado*, "lead-colored," referring to the color of the back (from the Latin *plumbum*, "lead.").

BUZZARD
From the French *busard*, "soaring hawk."

CARACARA
Apparently South American Indian in origin, mimicking the raptor's call.

CONDOR
From the Spanish *condor*, which in turn comes from the Peruvian name *cuntur*.

EAGLE
From the French *aigle*, based on the Latin *aquila*, "eagle."

FALCON
From the Latin *falx* or *falcis*, "sickle," referring to the curved talons and beak.

GOSHAWK
From Old Norse *gas-hauker*, "goose-hawk."

GYRFALCON
Origins unclear. Among the possibilities are the German words *ger*, "spear" or *gir*, "greedy"; Latin *gyro*, "to spiral"; Greek *hieros*, "sacred"; or Old Norse *verthr*, "worthy"

HARRIER
Old English *hergian*, "to harass."

HAWK
Anglo-Saxon *hafoc*, "hawk."

KESTREL
From French *crecerelle*, "noisy bell," or *crecelle*, "to ring," referring to the Eurasian species' call.

KITE
From Anglo-Saxon *cyta*, in turn from the Aryan root *skut*, "to go swiftly."

MERLIN
From Old English name *marlion*, or French name *esmerillon*.

OSPREY
From the Latin name *ossifragus*, "bone-breaker," a name correctly applied to lammergeiers, not ospreys.

PEREGRINE
From Latin *peregrinus*, meaning "wanderer" or "foreign"; root of the word "pilgrim."

VULTURE
From the Latin *vulturus*, "tearer."

ORIGINS OF GENUS NAMES OF NORTH AMERICAN RAPTORS

Genus and specific names are given to an organism by the person who makes the fist meticulous description of it for science. Almost all have their roots in the classical languages of Greek or Latin.

ACCIPITER
Latin name for a hawk, possibly stemming from *accipere*, "to take."

AQUILA
Latin name for an eagle, although possibly from Latin *aquilus*, a dark brown bird.

BUTEO
Latin name for a hawk.

BUTEOGALLUS
Combination of Latin *buteo*, "hawk," and *gallus*, "chicken."

CATHARTES
From Greek *kathartes*, "purifier."

CHONDROHIERAX
From Greek *chondros*, "cartilaginous" and *hierakos*, "hawk."

continued

CIRCUS
From Greek *kirkos,* "to circle."

CORAGYPS
From Greek *korax,* "a raven," and *gyps,* "a vulture."

ELANOIDES
Combination of Greek *elanos,* "a kite," and *oideos,* "similar to or resembling."

ELANUS
Latin name for a kite.

FALCO
As with falcon, from Latin *falx,* "sickle."

GYMNOGYPS
Greek *gymnos,* "naked," and *gyps,* "vulture."

HALIAEETUS
Greek *halos,* "sea," and *aetos,* "eagle." The Greek word *haliaetos* refers to the osprey rather than the eagle.

ICTINIA
From Greek *iktinos,* "a kite."

PANDION
A god in Greek mythology.

PARABUTEO
Combines Greek *para,* "besides," and Latin *buteo,* "a hawk." In other words, "nearly a buteo."

POLYBORUS (FORMER GENUS NAME OF CARACARA)
Combination of Greek *poly,* "many," and *borus,* "gluttonous."

RHOSTRHAMUS
Combines Latin *rostrum,* "beak," with Greek *hamus,* "hooked."

(*Sources: Primarily Ernest A. Choate,* Dictionary American Bird Names; *William S. Clark,* Hawks.)

SPANISH NAMES FOR RAPTORS

Most raptor species that occur in Canada and the United States are also found in Latin America, as either residents or seasonal migrants. But while English names have been standardized by the American Ornithologists' Union, Spanish bird names have not, and they vary widely from region or region, or country to country. These come from Veracruz, site of the world's greatest raptor migration.

ENGLISH	SPANISH	ENGLISH	SPANISH
BLACK VULTURE	CARROÑERO COMÚN	SHARP-SHINNED HAWK	GAVILÁN PECHIRRUFO MENOR
TURKEY VULTURE	AURA COMÚN	COOPER'S HAWK	GAVILÁN PECHIRRUFO MAJOR
OSPREY	AGUILA PESCADORA	HARRIS' HAWK	AGUILILLA ROJINEGRA
WHITE-TAILED KITE	MILANO COLIBLANCO	RED-SHOULDERED HAWK	AGUILILLA PECHIRRO-JIZA
SNAIL KITE	MILANO CARACOLERO		
MISSISSIPPI KITE	MILANO MIGRATORIO	BROAD-WINGED HAWK	AGUILILLA MIGRATORIA MENOR
BALD EAGLE	AGUILA CABECIBLANCA		
NORTHERN HARRIER	AGUILILLA RASTRERA	SWAINSON'S HAWK	AGUILILLA MIGRATORIA MAJOR

continued

ENGLISH	SPANISH
WHITE-TAILED HAWK	AGUILILLA COLIBLANCA
ZONE-TAILED HAWK	AGUILILLA AURA
RED-TAILED HAWK	AGUILILLA COLIRRUFA
CRESTED CARACARA	CARACARA COMÚN
AMERICAN KESTREL	HALCÓN CERNÍCALO

ENGLISH	SPANISH
MERLIN	HALCÓN ESMEREJON
APLOMADO FALCON	HALCÓN FAJADO
PRAIRIE FALCON	HALCÓN PÁLIDO
PEREGRINE FALCON	HALCÓN PEREGRINO

(Source: Martinez-Gomez, 1992)

FORMER NAMES FOR RAPTORS

Today, the official English and scientific names of North American birds are set by a committee of professionals, the American Ornithologists' Union. But in centuries past, each region had its own, often highly descriptive, names for raptors, causing a great deal of confusion. This is a sampling for several North American species; some of the names, including pigeon hawk, marsh hawk, and sparrowhawk, were in official use until the 1970s.

SPECIES	FORMER NAMES
BLACK VULTURE	Carrion crow, black buzzard, Jim Crow
TURKEY VULTURE	Turkey buzzard, red-headed buzzard
OSPREY	Fish hawk, fish eagle, sea eagle, fishing eagle, sea hawk, little eagle
BALD EAGLE	White-tailed eagle, American eagle, Bird of Washington (immature, named by Audubon), black eagle, gray eagle, sea eagle, Bird of Freedom, white-headed eagle
GOLDEN EAGLE	Brown eagle, black eagle, gray eagle, mountain eagle, ring-tailed eagle, jackrabbit eagle, royal eagle
AMERICAN SWALLOW-TAILED KITE	Fork-tailed kite, swallow hawk, wasp hawk, snake hawk

SPECIES	FORMER NAMES
MISSISSIPPI KITE	Mosquito hawk, American kite, blue snake-hawk, hovering kite, blue kite, snake-killer hawk, locust-eater, spot-tailed hobby
NORTHERN HARRIER	Marsh hawk, blue hawk (adult male), bog hawk, mouse hawk, frog hawk, snake hawk, rabbit hawk, mole hawk, white-rumped hawk
SHARP-SHINNED HAWK	Little blue darter, chicken hawk, bullet hawk, pigeon hawk, partridge hawk, fowl hawk, slate-colored hawk
COOPER'S HAWK	Big blue darter, chicken hawk, big bullet hawk, hen hawk, black-capped hawk, quail hawk, partridge hawk, pigeon hawk, long-tailed hen hawk, swift hawk, blue hawk
GOSHAWK	Blue partridge hawk, blue hen hawk, blue darter, chicken hawk, dove hawk, gray hawk

continued

SPECIES	FORMER NAMES	SPECIES	FORMER NAMES

RED-SHOULDERED HAWK

Red-bellied hawk, winter hawk, winter falcon, singing hawk, hen hawk, red-shouldered buzzard

RED-TAILED HAWK

Red hawk, chicken hawk, squealing hawk, white-breasted buzzard, buzzard hawk, Black Warrior (Harlan's hawk subspecies)

SWAINSON'S HAWK

Grasshopper hawk, gopher hawk, prairie hawk, prairie buzzard, black hawk, brown hawk

ROUGH-LEGGED HAWK

Mouse hawk, hen hawk, squalling hawk, black hawk, black-bellied hawk, rough-legged buzzard, hen hawk

AMERICAN KESTREL

Sparrowhawk, windhover, killy-hawk, grasshopper hawk, grasshopper falcon, house hawk, rusty-crowned falcon

MERLIN

Pigeon hawk, *le petit caporal*, Little Corporal, blue bullet hawk

GYRFALCON

Dark phase—Labrador falcon, black falcon; white phase—winter falcon, white hawk, winterer, white winter hawk, Greenland falcon

PEREGRINE FALCON

Duck hawk, great-footed hawk, wandering falcon, rock falcon, rock hawk, stone hawk, ledge hawk, big blue hawk, blue bullet hawk, black-cheeked hawk, mountain falcon

(Sources: Primarily Hausman, 1966; Terres, 1980; also Bolen and Flores, 1993)

 # RAPTORS NAMED FOR PEOPLE

During the Golden Age of North American ornithology in the nineteenth century, many newly discovered birds were named to honor patrons, friends, distinguished scientists, and even spouses and children. Although the practice is frowned upon today (in part because the names tell nothing descriptive about the birds), some of the old names survive.

COOPER'S HAWK

Named in 1828 for New York ornithologist William Cooper, who collected a specimen of this accipiter for French-born scientist Charles Lucien Bonaparte.

FUERTES' HAWK

Southern Plains race of red-tailed hawk; named for early-twentieth-century bird artist Louis Agassiz Fuertes by his former student George Miksch Sutton.

HARLAN'S HAWK

Dark northwestern subspecies of red-tailed hawk, once considered a separate species; named in 1831 by John James Audubon for his friend, Philadelphia physician Richard Harlan.

HARRIS' HAWK

Named by Audubon to honor his friend and patron Edward Harris, who was also namesake of the Harris' sparrow.

KRIDER'S HAWK

Pale prairie race of red-tailed hawk; named in 1873 by Bernard A. Hoopes to honor John Krider of Iowa, who collected the first pair for science.

PEALE'S FALCON

Dark, northwestern Pacific subspecies of peregrine falcon; named in 1873 for Titian Peale, an early-nineteenth-century naturalist, by Robert Ridgway.

SWAINSON'S HAWK

Named in 1838 by Bonaparte to honor his friend, English ornithologist William Swainson (for whom Swainson's thrush and warbler are also named).

HONORIFIC NAMES NO LONGER IN USE

AUDUBON'S CARACARA
Former name of crested caracara.

BIRD OF WASHINGTON (WASHINGTON'S EAGLE)
Immature bald eagle, named by Audubon in the belief it was a new species.

RICHARDSON'S PIGEON HAWK
Former name for pale prairie subspecies of merlin.

SENNETT'S WHITE-TAILED HAWK
Former name for white-tailed hawk.

SUCKLEY'S PIGEON HAWK
Former name for dark Pacific coastal race of merlin.

RAPTORS IN HIEROGLYPHICS

KING VULTURE
Incorporated in several Maya glyphic symbols, including glyph for *ahau*, both a day sign and rank of a king.

EAGLE AND VULTURE
Day symbols in Aztec calendar.

EGYPTIAN VULTURE
Hieroglyphic sign *a* in ancient Egypt.

EURASIAN GRIFFON
Hieroglyphic signs for *mwt, mut, nr* in ancient Egypt.

FALCON
Hieroglyphic symbol in ancient Egypt, used both phonetically and to represent royalty.

While not as popular as large mammals like bears, elk, and bison, raptors have been chosen as namesakes for many towns and geographic features across North America. As this list of placenames shows, eagles are the clear preference when it comes to naming a spot after a raptor.

BALD EAGLE (PA—2 SITES)
BALD EAGLE MOUNTAIN (PA)
BLACK EAGLE (MT)
BLACK HAWK (ONT., SD)
BUZZARDS BAY (MA)
BUZZARDS CROSSROADS (NC)
CAPE FALCON (OR)
EAGLE (AL, CO, ID, NE, NY, PA)
EAGLE BAY (NY)
EAGLE BEND (MN)
EAGLE BRIDGE (NY)
EAGLE BUTTE (SD)
EAGLE CAP (OR)
EAGLE CENTER (NY)
EAGLE CITY (OK)
EAGLE CRAGS (CA)
EAGLE CREEK (IN, MT, OR, SASK., TN)
EAGLE FALLS (NY)
EAGLE FOUNDRY (PA)
EAGLE FURNACE (TN)
EAGLE GROVE (IA)
EAGLEHEAD LAKE (ONT.)
EAGLE HARBOR (MD, MI, NY)

EAGLEHURST (PA)
EAGLE ISLAND (MANT.)
EAGLE LAKE (CA, FL, ME—2 SITES, ONT.—2 SITES, TX, WI)
EAGLE MILLS (AR, NC, NY)
EAGLE MOUNTAIN (CA, MN)
EAGLE MOUNTAIN LAKE (TX)
EAGLE NEST (NM, NY)
EAGLE PASS (AZ, TX)
EAGLE PEAK (CA—2 SITES, ID, MT, MN, TX)
EAGLE POINT (OR, PA, NY)
EAGLE RIVER (AK, B.C., MI, NEWFL., ONT., WI, YUKON)
EAGLE ROCK (NC, PA, VA)
EAGLE SPRINGS (NC)
EAGLE SUMMIT (AK)
EAGLES MERE (PA)
EAGLETAIL MOUNTAINS (AZ)
EAGLETOWN (NC, OK)
EAGLE VALLEY (NY)
EAGLE VILLAGE (AK, IN)
EAGLEVILLE (CA, CT, MO, NY—2 SITES, PA, TN)
FALCON (CO, NC, TN, TX)

FALCONER (NY)
FALCONERVILLE (VA)
FALCON ISLAND (ONT.)
FALCON LAKE (MANT., TX)
FALCON MANOR (NY)
GRAY HAWK (KY)
GREY EAGLE (MN)
HAWK (NC)
HAWKEYE (NY, PA)
HAWK HILL LAKE (NORTHWEST TERRITORIES)
HAWK INLET (AK)
HAWK JUNCTION (ONT.)
HAWK LAKE (ONT.)
HAWK RUN (PA)
HAWKS (MI)
HAWKSBILL MOUNTAIN (VA)
HAWKS SPRINGS (WY)
IMPERIAL EAGLE CHANNEL (B.C.)
KITTY HAWK (NC)
LITTLE EAGLE (SD)
OSPREY (FL)
THUNDER HAWK (SD)

Appendix II
Diurnal Raptors of the World

Range abbreviations: NA—North America; CA—Central America; SA—South America; EUR—Europe; AS—Asia; AF—Africa; AUS—Australia; NG—New Guinea; OC—Oceania; COS—cosmopolitan (Primary source: Clements, *Birds of the World: A Check List,* 4th edition.)

COMMON NAME	SCIENTIFIC NAME (GENUS/SPECIES)	BREEDING RANGE
▼		
ORDER FALCONIFORMES		
FAMILY CATHARTIDAE		
NEW WORLD VULTURES		
Black vulture	*Coragyps atratus*	NA–SA
Turkey vulture	*Cathartes aura*	NA–SA
Lesser yellow-headed vulture	*C. burrovianus*	CA–SA
Greater yellow-headed vulture	*C. melambrotus*	SA
King vulture	*Sacoramphus papa*	CA–SA
California condor	*Gymnogyps californianus*	Calif. (extirpated; reintroduced to wild)
Andean condor	*Vultur gryphus*	SA
▼		
FAMILY PANDIONIDAE		
OSPREYS		
Osprey	*Pandion haliaetus*	COS
▼		
FAMILY ACCIPITRIDAE		
KITES AND ALLIES		
African cuckoo-falcon	*Aviceda cuculoides*	AF
Madagascar cuckoo-falcon	*A. madagascariensis*	Madagascar
Jerdon's baza	*A. jerdoni*	s.e.AS
Pacific baza	*A. subcristata*	AUS–NG region
Black baza	*A. leuphotes*	AS
Gray-headed kite	*Leptodon cayanensis*	CA–SA
White-collared kite	*L. forbesi*	SA
Hook-billed kite	*Chondrohierax uncinatus*	CA–SA
Long-tailed honey-buzzard	*Henicopernis longicauda*	NG
Black honey-buzzard	*H. infuscata*	NG (New Britain Is.)
European honey-buzzard	*Pernis apivorus*	EUR–AS

COMMON NAME	SCIENTIFIC NAME (GENUS/SPECIES)	BREEDING RANGE
Oriental honey-buzzard	*P. ptilorhynchus*	AS
Barred honey-buzzard	*P. celebensis*	Philippines
American swallow-tailed kite	*Elanoides forficatus*	s.e.NA–SA
Bat hawk	*Macheiramphus alcinus*	AF–s.e.AS–NG
Pearl kite	*Gampsonyx swainsonii*	CA–SA
Black-shouldered kite	*Elanus caeruleus*	AF–AS–NG
Australian kite	*E. axillaris*	AUS
White-tailed kite	*E. leucurus*	s.NA–SA
Letter-winged kite	*E. scriptus*	AUS
Scissor-tailed kite	*Chelictinia riocourii*	AF
Snail kite	*Rostrhamus sociabilis*	Florida; CA–SA
Slender-billed kite	*R. hamatus*	CA–SA
Double-toothed kite	*Harpagus bidentatus*	CA–SA
Rufous-thighed kite	*H. diodon*	SA
Mississippi kite	*Ictinia mississippiensis*	s.NA
Plumbeous kite	*I. plumbea*	CA–SA
Square-tailed kite	*Lophoictinia isura*	AUS
Black-breasted kite	*Hamirostra melanosternon*	AUS
Red kite	*Milvus milvus*	EUR
Black kite	*M. migrans*	AF–EUR–AS–AUS
Black-eared kite	*M. lineatus*	AS
Whistling kite	*Haliastur sphenurus*	AUS–NG
Brahminy kite	*H. indus*	AS–AUS

SEA-EAGLES

White-bellied sea-eagle	*Haliaeetus leucogaster*	AS–AUS
Solomon sea-eagle	*H. sanfordi*	OC (Solomon Is.)
African fish-eagle	*H. vocifer*	AF
Madagascar fish-eagle	*H. vociferoides*	Madagascar
Pallas' fish-eagle	*H. leucoryphus*	AS
White-tailed eagle	*H. albicilla*	n.EUR–n.AS
Bald eagle	*H. leucocephalus*	NA
Stellar's sea-eagle	*H. pelagicus*	n.w.AS
Lesser fish-eagle	*Ichthyophaga humilis*	AS
Gray-headed fish-eagle	*I. ichthyaetus*	AS

OLD WORLD VULTURES

Palm-nut vulture	*Gypohierax angolensis*	AF

COMMON NAME	SCIENTIFIC NAME (GENUS/SPECIES)	BREEDING RANGE
Lammergeier	*Gypaetus barbatus*	EUR–AS–AF
Egyptian vulture	*Neophron percnopterus*	s.EUR–AS–AF
Hooded vulture	*Necrosyrtes monachus*	AF
White-backed vulture	*Gyps africanus*	AF
White-rumped vulture	*G. bengalensis*	AS
Long-billed vulture	*G. indicus*	AS
Rueppell's griffon	*G. rueppellii*	AF
Himalayan griffon	*G. himalayensis*	AS
Eurasian griffon	*G. fulvus*	s.EUR–n.AF–AS
Cape griffon	*G. coprotheres*	s.AF
Cinereous vulture	*Aegypius monachus*	s.EUR–AS
Lappet-faced vulture	*Torgos tracheliotus*	AF
White-headed vulture	*Trigonoceps occipitalis*	AF
Red-headed vulture	*Sarcogyps calvus*	AS

SNAKE-EAGLES

Short-toed eagle	*Circaetus gallicus*	AF–AS–EUR
Black-chested snake-eagle	*C. pectoralis*	AF
Brown snake-eagle	*C. cinereus*	AF
Fasciated snake-eagle	*C. fasciolatus*	AF
Banded snake-eagle	*C. cinerascens*	AF
Bateleur	*Terathopius ecaudatus*	AF
Crested serpent-eagle	*Spilornis cheela*	AS
Nicobar serpent-eagle	*S. minimus*	AS (Nicobar Is.)
Mountain serpent-eagle	*S. kinabaluensis*	AS (Borneo)
Sulawesi serpent-eagle	*S. rufipectus*	AS (Sulawesi Is.)
Philippine serpent-eagle	*S. holospilus*	Philippines
Andaman serpent-eagle	*S. elgini*	AS (Andaman Is.)
Congo serpent-eagle	*Dryotriorchis spectabilis*	AF
Madagascar serpent-eagle	*Eutriorchis astur*	Madagascar

HARRIERS

Western marsh-harrier	*Circus aeruginosus*	EUR–AS
African marsh-harrier	*C. ranivoris*	AF
Eastern marsh-harrier	*C. spilonotus*	AS
Swamp harrier	*C. approximans*	AUS–OC

COMMON NAME	SCIENTIFIC NAME (GENUS/SPECIES)	BREEDING RANGE
Reunion harrier	*C. maillardi*	Madagascar, nearby islands
Long-winged harrier	*C. buffoni*	SA
Spotted harrier	*C. assimilis*	AUS
Black harrier	*C. maurus*	AF
Northern harrier	*C. cyaneus*	NA–EUR–n.AS
Cinereous harrier	*C. cinereus*	SA
Pallid harrier	*C. macrourus*	AS
Pied harrier	*C. melanoleucos*	AS
Montagu's harrier	*C. pygargus*	EUR–n.AS
HARRIER-HAWKS		
African harrier-hawk	*Polyboroides typus*	AF
Madagascar harrier-hawk	*P. radiatus*	Madagascar
Lizard buzzard	*Kaupifalco monogrammicus*	AF
CHANTING-GOSHAWKS		
Dark chanting-goshawk	*Melierax metabates*	AF
Eastern chanting-goshawk	*M. poliopterus*	AF
Pale chanting-goshawk	*M. canorus*	AF
Gabar goshawk	*M. gabar*	AF
ACCIPITERS AND ALLIES		
Gray-bellied goshawk	*Accipiter poliogaster*	SA
Crested goshawk	*A. trivirgatus*	AS, Philippines
Sulawesi goshawk	*A. griseiceps*	AS (Sulawesi Is.)
Red-chested goshawk	*A. toussenelli*	AF
African goshawk	*A. tachiro*	AF
Chestnut-flanked sparrowhawk	*A. castanilius*	AF
Shikra	*A. badius*	AF
Nicobar sparrowhawk	*A. butleri*	AS (Nicobar Is.)
Levant sparrowhawk	*A. brevipes*	EUR–w.AS
Chinese goshawk	*A. soloensis*	AS
Frances' goshawk	*A. francesii*	Madagascar
Spot-tailed goshawk	*A. trinotatus*	AS (Sulawesi Is.)

continued

COMMON NAME	SCIENTIFIC NAME (GENUS/SPECIES)	BREEDING RANGE
Gray goshawk	A. novaehollandiae	AUS–NG region
Brown goshawk	A. fasciatus	AUS–NG
Black-mantled goshawk	A. melanochlamys	NG
Pied goshawk	A. albogularis	OC (Solomon Is.)
Fiji goshawk	A. rufitorques	OC (Fiji)
White-bellied goshawk	A. haplochrous	OC (New Caledonia)
Moluccan goshawk	A. henicogrammus	AS (Moluccan Is.)
Slaty-mantled goshawk	A. luteoschistaceus	NG (New Britain Is.)
Imitator sparrowhawk	A. imitator	OC (Solomon Is.)
Gray-headed goshawk	A. poliocephalus	NG
New Britain goshawk	A. princeps	NG (New Britain Is.)
Tiny hawk	A. superciliosus	CA–SA
Semicollared hawk	A. collaris	SA
Red-thighed sparrowhawk	A. erythropus	AF
Little sparrowhawk	A. minullus	AF
Japanese sparrowhawk	A. gularis	e.AS
Besra	A. virgatus	AS
Small sparrowhawk	A. nanus	AS (Sulawesi Is.)
Rufous-necked sparrowhawk	A. erythrauchen	AS (Moluccan Is.)
Collared sparrowhawk	A. cirrocephalus	AUS–NG
New Britain sparrowhawk	A. brachyurus	NG (New Britain Is.)
Vinous-breasted sparrowhawk	A. rhodogaster	AS (Moluccan Is.)
Madagascar sparrowhawk	A. madagascariensis	Madagascar
Ovampo sparrowhawk	A. ovampensis	AF
Eurasian sparrowhawk	A. nisus	EUR–n.AS
Rufous-chested sparrowhawk	A. rufiventris	AF
Sharp-shinned hawk	A. striatus	NA
White-breasted hawk	A. chionogaster	CA
Plain-breasted hawk	A. ventralis	SA
Rufous-thighed hawk	A. erythronemius	SA
Cooper's hawk	A. cooperii	NA–CA
Gundlach's hawk	A. gundlachi	Cuba
Bicolored hawk	A. bicolor	CA–SA

COMMON NAME	SCIENTIFIC NAME (GENUS/SPECIES)	BREEDING RANGE
Black goshawk	*A. melanoleucos*	AF
Henst's goshawk	*A. henstii*	Madagascar
Northern goshawk	*A. gentilis*	NA–EUR–n.AS
Meyer's goshawk	*A. meyerianus*	NG region
Chestnut-shouldered goshawk	*Erythrotriorchis buergersi*	NG
Red goshawk	*E. radiatus*	AUS
Doria's goshawk	*Megatriorchis doriae*	NG
Long-tailed hawk	*Urotriorchis macrourus*	AF
BUTEOS AND ALLIES		
Grasshopper buzzard	*Butastur rufipennis*	AF
White-eyed buzzard	*B. teesa*	AS
Rufous-winged buzzard	*B. liventer*	AS
Gray-faced buzzard	*B. indicus*	AS
Crane hawk	*Geranospiza caerulescens*	CA–SA
Plumbeous hawk	*Leucopternis plumbea*	CA–SA
Slate-colored hawk	*L. schistacea*	SA
Barred hawk	*L. princeps*	CA–SA
Black-faced hawk	*L. melanops*	SA
White-browed hawk	*L. kuhli*	SA
White-necked hawk	*L. lacernulata*	Brazil
Semiplumbeous hawk	*L. semiplumbea*	CA–SA
White hawk	*L. albicollis*	CA–SA
Gray-backed hawk	*L. occidentalis*	Ecuador
Mantled hawk	*L. polionota*	SA
Rufous crab-hawk	*Buteogallus aequinoctialis*	SA
Common black-hawk	*B. anthracinus*	s.w.U.S.–CA–SA
Mangrove black-hawk	*B. subtilis*	CA–SA
Great black-hawk	*B. urubitinga*	CA–SA
Savanna hawk	*B. meriodionalis*	CA–SA
Harris' hawk	*Parabuteo unicinctus*	s.w.U.S.–CA–SA
Black-collared hawk	*Busarellus nigricollis*	CA–SA
Black-chested buzzard-eagle	*Geranoaetus melanoleucus*	SA
Solitary eagle	*Harpyhaliaetus solitarius*	CA–SA
Crowned eagle	*H. coronatus*	SA
Gray hawk	*Asturina plagiata*	s.w.U.S.–CA–SA
Gray-lined hawk	*A. nitida*	CA–SA

continued

COMMON NAME	SCIENTIFIC NAME (GENUS/SPECIES)	BREEDING RANGE
Roadside hawk	*Buteo magnirostris*	CA–SA
Red-shouldered hawk	*B. lineatus*	NA
Ridgway's hawk	*B. ridgwayi*	Hispaniola
Broad-winged hawk	*B. platypterus*	NA
White-rumped hawk	*B. leucorrhous*	SA
Short-tailed hawk	*B. brachyurus*	Florida–CA–SA
White-throated hawk	*B. albigula*	SA
Swainson's hawk	*B. swainsoni*	NA
White-tailed hawk	*B. albicaudatus*	s.w.U.S.–CA–SA
Galapagos hawk	*B. galapagoensis*	Galapagos Is.
Red-backed hawk	*B. polyosoma*	SA
Puna hawk	*B. poecilochrous*	SA
Zone-tailed hawk	*B. albonotatus*	s.w.U.S.–CA–SA
Hawaiian hawk	*B. solitarius*	Hawaii
Red-tailed hawk	*B. jamaicensis*	NA–CA
Rufous-tailed hawk	*B. ventralis*	SA
Common buzzard	*B. buteo*	EUR–AS
Mountain buzzard	*B. oreophilus*	AF
Madagascar buzzard	*B. brachypterus*	Madagascar
Long-legged buzzard	*B. rufinus*	EUR–AS–AF
Upland buzzard	*B. hemilasius*	AS
Ferruginous hawk	*B. regalis*	NA
Rough-legged hawk	*B. lagopus*	n.NA–n.EUR–n.AS
Red-necked buzzard	*B. auguralis*	AF
Augur buzzard	*B. augur*	AF
Archer's buzzard	*B. archeri*	Somalia
Jackal buzzard	*B. rufofuscus*	AF

TROPICAL EAGLES

Crested eagle	*Morphnus guianensis*	CA–SA
Harpy eagle	*Harpia harpyja*	CA–SA
New Guinea eagle	*Harpyopsis novaeguineae*	NG
Philippine (monkey-eating) eagle	*Pithecophaga jefferyi*	Philippines
Black eagle	*Ictnaetus malayensis*	AS

BOOTED EAGLES

Lesser spotted eagle	*Aquila pomarina*	EUR–AS

| SCIENTIFIC NAME (GENUS/SPECIES) | BREEDING RANGE

COMMON NAME	SCIENTIFIC NAME (GENUS/SPECIES)	BREEDING RANGE
Greater spotted eagle	*A. clanga*	EUR–AS
Tawny-eagle	*A. rapax*	AF–w.AS
Steppe eagle	*A. nipalensis*	AS
Spanish eagle	*A. adalberti*	Spain
Imperial eagle	*A. heliaca*	EUR–AS
Wahlberg's eagle	*A. wahlbergi*	AF
Gurney's eagle	*A. gurneyi*	NG region
Golden eagle	*A. chrysaetos*	NA–EUR–AS
Wedge-tailed eagle	*A. audax*	AUS–NG
Verreaux's eagle	*A. verreauxii*	AF

HAWK-EAGLES

Bonelli's eagle	*Hieraaetus fasciatus*	EUR–AS
African hawk-eagle	*H. spilogaster*	AF
Booted eagle	*H. pennatus*	EUR–AF–s.AS
Little eagle	*H. morphnoides*	AUS–NG
Ayres' hawk-eagle	*H. ayresii*	AF
Rufous-bellied eagle	*H. kienerii*	s.AS
Martial eagle	*Polemaetus bellicosus*	AF
Black-and-white hawk-eagle	*Spizastur melanoleucus*	CA–SA
Long-crested eagle	*Lophaetus occipitalis*	AF
Cassin's hawk-eagle	*Spizaetus africanus*	AF
Changeable hawk-eagle	*S. cirrhatus*	AS
Mountain hawk-eagle	*S. nipalensis*	AS
Blyth's hawk-eagle	*S. alboniger*	Malaysia
Javan hawk-eagle	*S. bartelsi*	AS (Java)
Sulawesi hawk-eagle	*S. lanceolatus*	AS (Sulawesi Is.)
Philippine hawk-eagle	*S. philippensis*	Philippines
Wallace's hawk-eagle	*S. nanus*	Malaysia
Black hawk-eagle	*S. tyrannus*	CA–SA
Ornate hawk-eagle	*S. ornatus*	CA–SA
Crowned hawk-eagle	*Stephanoaetus coronatus*	AF
Black-and-chestnut eagle	*Oroaetus isidori*	SA

▼

FAMILY SAGITTARIIDAE
SECRETARY-BIRDS

Secretary-bird	*Sagittarius serpentarius*	AF

continued

COMMON NAME	SCIENTIFIC NAME (GENUS/SPECIES)	BREEDING RANGE
FAMILY FALCONIDAE		
CARACARAS AND ALLIES		
Black caracara	*Daptrius ater*	SA
Red-throated caracara	*D. americanus*	CA–SA
Carunculated caracara	*Phalcoboenus carunculatus*	SA
Mountain caracara	*P. megalopterus*	SA
White-throated caracara	*P. albogularis*	SA
Striated caracara	*P. australis*	s.SA
Guadalupe caracara	*Caracara lutosus*	Baja Calif. (extinct)
Crested caracara	*C. plancus*	s.NA–CA–SA
Yellow-headed caracara	*Milvago chimachima*	CA–SA
Chimango caracara	*M. chimango*	SA
Laughing falcon	*Herpetotheres chachinnans*	CA–SA
FOREST-FALCONS		
Barred forest-falcon	*Micrastur ruficollis*	CA–SA
Plumbeous forest-falcon	*M. plumbeus*	SA
Lined forest-falcon	*M. gilvicollis*	SA
Slaty-backed forest-falcon	*M. mirandollei*	CA–SA
Collared forest-falcon	*M. semitorquatus*	CA–SA
Buckley's forest-falcon	*M. buckleyi*	SA
FALCONETS		
Spot-winged falconet	*Spiziapteryx circumcinctus*	SA
Pygmy falcon	*Polihierax semitorquatus*	AF
White-rumped falcon	*P. insignis*	s.AS
Collared falconet	*Microhierax caerulescens*	AS
Black-thighed falconet	*M. fringillarius*	Malaysia
White-fronted falconet	*M. latifrons*	Borneo
Philippine falconet	*M. erythrogenys*	Philippines
Pied falconet	*M. melanoleucus*	AS
TRUE FALCONS		
Brown falcon	*Falco berigora*	AUS–NG
Lesser kestrel	*F. naumanni*	EUR–n.AF–AS
Eurasian kestrel	*F. tinnunculus*	EUR–AF–AS
Newton's kestrel	*F. newtoni*	Madagascar
Mauritius kestrel	*F. punctatus*	AF (Mauritius Is.)

COMMON NAME	SCIENTIFIC NAME (GENUS/SPECIES)	BREEDING RANGE
Seychelles kestrel	*F. araea*	AF (Seychelles Is.)
Spotted kestrel	*F. moluccensis*	Java region
Australian kestrel	*F. cenchroides*	AUS
American kestrel	*F. sparverius*	NA–CA–SA
Greater kestrel	*F. rupicoloides*	AF
Fox kestrel	*F. alopex*	AF
Gray kestrel	*F. ardosiaceus*	AF
Dickinson's kestrel	*F. dickinsoni*	AF
Barred kestrel	*F. zoniventris*	Madagascar
Red-necked falcon	*F. chicquera*	AF
Red-footed falcon	*F. vespertinus*	EUR–AS
Amur falcon	*F. amurensis*	AS
Eleonora's falcon	*F. eleonorae*	Mediterranean basin
Sooty falcon	*F. concolor*	AF
Aplomado falcon	*F. femoralis*	CA–SA
Merlin	*F. columbarius*	n.NA–n.EUR–n.AS
Bat falcon	*F. rufigularis*	CA–SA
Eurasian hobby	*F. subbuteo*	EUR–AS
African hobby	*F. cuvieri*	AF
Oriental hobby	*F. severus*	AS–NG
Australian hobby	*F. longipennis*	AUS
New Zealand falcon	*F. novaezeelandiae*	New Zealand
Gray falcon	*F. hypoleucos*	AUS
Black falcon	*F. subniger*	AUS
Prairie falcon	*F. mexicanus*	NA
Lanner falcon	*F. biarmicus*	s.EUR–AF–AS
Lagger falcon	*F. jugger*	AS
Saker falcon	*F. cherrug*	e.EUR–c.AS
Altai falcon	*F. altaicus*	AS
Gyrfalcon	*F. rusticolus*	NA–EUR–AS (Arctic)
Peregrine falcon	*F. peregrinus*	COS
Barbary falcon	*F. pelegrinoides*	n.AF
Orange-breasted falcon	*F. deiroleucus*	CA–SA
Taita falcon	*F. fasciinucha*	AF

(Source: Primarily Clements, Birds of the World: A Checklist, *fourth edition, 1991)*

SELECTED BIBLIOGRAPHY

Abreu, Manuel Vasconcelos. "The Migration of Raptors Through Portugal," In *Raptors in the Modern World*. Edited by B.-U. Meyburg and R. D. Chancellor. Berlin: World Working Group on Birds of Prey, 1989.

Andrews, Michael. *The Flight of the Condor*. Boston: Little, Brown and Co., 1982.

Anonymous. "Breeding Success Signals Hope for Philippine Eagles," *Focus* (World Wildlife Fund), Vol. 16 (July–August 1994) 3.

Attenborough, David. *The First Eden*. Boston: Little, Brown and Co., 1987.

Baker, J. A. *The Peregrine*. New York: Harper & Row, 1967.

Bates, Craig D., Janet A. Hamber, and Martha J. Lee. "The California Condor and California Indians," *American Indian Art Magazine* (Winter 1993) 40–47.

Beebe, Frank L. *A Falconry Manual*. Surrey, British Columbia: Hancock House Publishing, 1984.

Bent, Arthur Cleveland. *Life Histories of North American Birds of Prey*, Vols. 1 and 2. Washington, DC: United States National Museum, 1937 and 1938. Reprint ed., Dover Publishing, New York, 1961.

Bildstein, Keith. "Corn Cob Manipulation in Northern Harriers," *Wilson Bulletin*, Vol. 92 (1980) 128–30.

————. "Causes and Consequences of Reverse Sexual Dimorphism in Raptors: The Head Start Hypothesis," *Journal of Raptor Research*, Vol. 26 (Sept. 1992) 115–23.

————, Jim Brett, Laurie Goodrich, and Cathy Viverette. "Shooting Galleries: Migrant Raptors in Jeopardy," *American Bird*s, Vol. 47 (Spring 1993) 38–43.

Bird, David M., chief ed. *Biology and Management of Bald Eagles and Ospreys*. Ste.-Anne-de-Bellevue, Quebec: Harpell Press, 1983.

Blodget, Bradford, William J. Davis, and Mark Pokras. "Bald Eagle Survives Two Years in Wild with One Foot," *Journal of Field Ornithology*, Vol. 61 (Winter 1990), 76–78.

Bolen, Eric, and Dan Flores. *The Mississippi Kite*. Austin, TX: University of Texas Press, 1993.

Bollengier, Rene M., et al. *Eastern Peregrine Falcon Recovery Plan*. Revised draft. Washington, DC: U.S. Fish and Wildlife Service, 1979.

Brett, James J. *The Mountain and the Migration*. Kutztown, PA: Hawk Mountain Sanctuary, 1986.

Brinker, David F., and T. C. Erdman. "Characteristics of Autumn Red-tailed Hawk Migration Through Wisconsin." In *Proceedings of Hawk Migration Conference IV*. Edited by Michael Harwood. Hawk Migration Association of North America, 1985.

Brockman, H. J., and C. J. Barnard. "Kleptoparasitism in Birds," *Animal Behavior*, Vol. 27 (May 1979) 487–514.

Broun, Maurice. *Hawks Aloft: The Story of Hawk Mountain*. Cornwall, NY: Cornwall Press, 1948.

Brown, Leslie. *Eagles of the World*. New York: Universe Books, 1977.

————, and Dean Amadon. *Eagles, Hawks and Falcons of the World*, Vols. 1 and 2. Reprint ed. Secaucus, NJ: Wellfleet Press, 1989.

Cade, Tom J. *Falcons of the World*. Ithaca, NY: Cornell University Press, 1982.

—————, J. H. Enderson, C. G. Thelander, and C. M. White. *Peregrine Falcon Populations: Their Management and Recovery*. Boise, ID: The Peregrine Fund, 1988.

Callopy, Michael W. "Regional Report: Southeast," *The Eyas,* Vol. 12 (Fall 1989) 26–29.

Cameron, Matt, and Penny Olsen. "Significance of caching in *Falco:* Evidence from a pair of Peregrine Falcons, *Falco peregrinus*." In *Australian Raptor Studies*. Edited by Penny Olsen. Victoria, Australia: Australasian Raptor Association, 1993.

Champagne, Duane, ed. *The Native North American Almanac*. Detroit: Gale Research Inc., 1994.

Choate, Ernest A. *The Dictionary of American Bird Names*. Rev. ed. Boston: Harvard Common Press, 1985.

Clapp, R. B., M. K. Klimkiewicz, and J. H. Kennard. "Longevity Records of North American Birds: Gaviidae through Alcidae," *Journal of Field Ornithology,* Vol. 53 (Spring 1982) 81–124.

Clark, William S., and Brian K. Wheeler. *Field Guide to Hawks*. Boston: Houghton Mifflin Co., 1987.

—————, Peter H. Bloom, and Lynn W. Oliphant. "Aplomado Falcon Steals Prey from Little Blue Heron," *Journal of Field Ornithology,* Vol. 60 (Summer 1989), 380–1.

—————. "Raptor Counts at Beidaihe, China, Fall 1991," *HMANA Hawk Migration Studies,* Vol. 17 (Oct. 1992) 14–16.

Clements, James. *Birds of the World: A Checklist*. Fourth ed. Vista, CA: Ibis Publishing, 1991.

Clinton-Eitniear, Jack. "Status Report: The Harpy Eagle," *The Eyas,* Vol. 10 (Fall 1987) 30–31.

Cochran, William W. "Ocean Migration of Peregrine Falcons: Is the Adult Male Pelagic?" In *Proceedings of Hawk Migration Conference IV*. Edited by Michael Harwood. Hawk Migration Association of North America, 1985.

Collar, N. J., and S. N. Stuart. *Threatened Birds of Africa and Related Islands*. Third ed. Cambridge, England: ICBP/IUCN, 1985.

Collar, N. J., and P. Andrew. *Birds to Watch: The ICBP World Checklist of Threatened Birds*. ICBP Technical Publication No. 8. Washington, DC: Smithsonian Institution Press, 1988.

Collar, N. J., et al. *Threatened Birds of the Americas: The ICBP/IUCN Red Data Book*. Third ed. Washington, DC: Smithsonian Institution Press, 1992.

Craig, Robert J., E. S. Mitchell, and J. E. Mitchell. "Time and Energy Budgets of Bald Eagles Wintering Along the Connecticut River," *Journal of Field Ornithology,* Vol. 59 (Winter 1988) 22–32.

Craighead, John J., and Frank C. Craighead. *Hawks, Owls and Wildlife*. Harrisburg, PA: Stackpole Books, 1956. Reprint ed. by Dover Publishing, New York, 1969.

Crocoll, S. T., and J. W. Parker. "Breeding Biology of Broad-Winged Hawks and Red-Shouldered Hawks in Western New York," *Journal of Raptor Research,* Vol. 23 (Winter 1989) 125–39.

DeBlieu, Jan. *Meant to be Wild*. Golden, CO: Fulcrum Publishing, 1991.

Diamond, Jared. "Bob Dylan and Moas' Ghosts," *Natural History* (Oct. 1990) 26–31.

Dorst, Jean. *The Life of Birds*. New York: Columbia University Press, 1974.

Dunne, Pete, David Sibley, and Clay Sutton. *Hawks in Flight*. Boston: Houghton Mifflin Co., 1988.

Ehrlich, Paul A., David S. Dobkin, and Darryl Wheye. *The Birder's Handbook*. New York: Simon & Schuster, 1988.

Farquhar, C. C. "White-tailed Hawk." In *The Birds of North America*, No. 30. Edited by A. Poole and F. Gill. Philadelphia: The Academy of Natural Science, and Washington, DC: American Ornithologists' Union, 1992.

Feduccia, Alan. *The Age of Birds*, Cambridge, MA: Harvard University Press, 1980.

———. "The Great Dinosaur Debate," *Living Bird*, Vol. 13 (Autumn 1994) 28–33.

Fenton, M. Brock. *Bats*. New York: Facts on File, 1992.

———. "Raptors and Bats: Threats and Opportunities," *Animal Behavior*, Vol. 48 (1994) 9–18.

Fernandez, Marie. "Aplomado Falcons Return to Southwest," *Fish and Wildlife News* (Jan. 1994) 13.

Friedman, R., and P. J. Munday. "The Use of 'Restaurants' for the Survival of Vultures in South Africa." In *Vulture Biology and Management*. Edited by Sanford R. Wilbur and Jerome A. Jackson. Berkeley, CA: University of California Press, 1983.

Garber, Gail. "Endangered Species Update: The Mauritius Kestrel," *RaptorWatch*, Vol. 6 (Summer 1992) 6.

Gill, Frank B. *Ornithology*. New York: W. H. Freeman and Co., 1990.

Goldstein, David L., and Neal G. Smith. "Response to Kirkley" (fasting by migrant Swainson's hawks), *Journal of Raptor Research*, Vol. 25 (Fall 1991) 87–88.

Goodrich, Laurie, et. al. "An Invitation to Join Hawks Aloft Worldwide: Hawk Mountain Sanctuary's Raptor Migration Atlas Project," *HMANA Migration Studies* (Feb. 1994) 7–9.

Graham, Frank H. "Kite vs. Stork," *Audubon*, Vol. 92 (May 1990) 104-10.

Grinnell, George Bird. *Blackfoot Lodge Tales*. Lincoln, NE: University of Nebraska Press, 1962.

Grossman, Mary Louise, and John Hamlet. *Birds of Prey of the World*. New York: Bonanza Books, 1964.

Hamerstrom, Frances. *Harrier: Hawk of the Marshes*. Washington, DC: Smithsonian Institution Press, 1986.

Harrison, Hal H. *A Field Guide to Birds' Nests in the United States East of the Mississippi River*. Boston: Houghton Mifflin Co., 1975.

———. *A Field Guide to Western Birds' Nests*. Boston: Houghton Mifflin Co., 1979.

Hausman, Leon Augustus. *Birds of Prey of Northeastern North America*. Peterborough, NH: Richard R. Smith Publishers, 1966.

Henderson, Carrol. "Regional Report: Midwest," *The Eyas*, Vol. 10 (Fall 1987) 8–15.

———. *Woodworking for Wildlife: Homes for Birds and Mammals*. St. Paul, MN: Minnesota Department of Natural Resources, 1984.

Houston, C. Stuart, G. A. Fox, and R. D. Crawford. "Unhatched Eggs in Swainson's Hawk Nests," *Journal of Field Ornithology*, Vol. 62 (Autumn 1991) 479–85.

Houston, David C. "To the Vultures Belong the Spoils," *Natural History*, Vol. 103 (Sept. 1994) 34–41.

Howard, Norman. *Northern Tales*. New York: Pantheon Books, 1990.

Johnsgard, Paul A. *Hawks, Eagles & Falcons of North America*. Washington, DC: Smithsonian Institution Press, 1990.

Johnston, Richard F., ed. *Current Ornithology*, Vol. 2. New York: Plenum Press, 1985.

Jorde, D. G., and G. R. Lingle. "Kleptoparasitism in Bald Eagles Wintering in Southcentral Nebraska," *Journal of Field Ornithology*, Vol. 59 (Spring 1988) 183–88.

Kerlinger, Paul. *Flight Strategies of Migrating Hawks*. Chicago: University of Chicago Press, 1989.

————, and Jim Brett. "Hawk Mountain Sanctuary: A Case Study of Birder Visitation and Birding Economics at a Private Refuge." In *Wildlife and Recreationists: Coexistence Through Management and Research*. Edited by R. Knight and K. J. Gutzwiller. Washington, DC: Island Press, 1994.

Kirkley, John S. "Do Migrant Swainson's Hawks Fast En Route to Argentina?" *Journal of Raptor Research*, Vol. 25 (Fall 1991) 82–86.

Klimkiewicz, M. Kathleen, and Anthony G. Futcher. "Longevity Records of North American Birds, Supplement 1," *Journal of Field Ornithology*, Vol. 60 (Autumn 1989) 469–94.

Kruger, Erich. "Contaminant Bio-accumulation and Raptors," *RaptorWatch*. Vol. 8 (Summer 1994) 20–21.

Langrand, O., and B.-U. Meyburg. "Range, Status and Biology of the Madagascar Sea Eagle." In *Raptors in the Modern World*. Edited by B.-U. Meyburg and R. D. Chancellor. Berlin: World Working Group on Birds of Prey, 1989.

Lee, David S., and Walter R. Spofford. "Nesting of Golden Eagles in the Central and Southern Appalachians," *Wilson Bulletin*, Vol. 102 (4) 693–98.

Lenhart, Cynthia. "Is History Repeating Itself?" (sharp-shinned hawk declines), *Hawk Mountain News*, No. 76 (Spring 1992) 3–4.

MacRae, Diann. "Overwater Migration of Raptors: A Review of the Literature." In *Proceedings of Hawk Migration Conference IV*. Edited by Michael Harwood. Hawk Migration Association of North America, 1985.

Manosa, Santi, and Pedro J. Codero. "Seasonal and Sexual Variation in the Diet of the Common Buzzard in Northeast Spain," *Journal of Raptor Research*, Vol. 26 (Dec. 1992) 235–37.

Martínez-Gómez, Juan Esteban. "Raptor Conservation in Veracruz, Mexico," *Journal of Raptor Research*, Vol. 26 (3) 181–88.

Meyburg, B.-U. "The Spanish Eagle: Its Biology, Status and Conservation." In *Raptors in the Modern World*. Edited by B.-U. Meyburg and R. D. Chancellor. Berlin: World Working Group on Birds of Prey, 1989.

————, et al. "Observations on the Endangered Java Hawk Eagle." In *Raptors in the Modern World*. Edited by B.-U. Meyburg and R. D. Chancellor. Berlin: World Working Group on Birds of Prey, 1989.

Mountfort, Guy. *Rare Birds of the World*. Lexington, MA: The Stephen Greene Press, 1988.

Negro, J. J., et al. "Kleptoparasitism and Cannibalism in a Colony of Lesser Kestrels," *Journal of Raptor Research*, Vol. 26 (Dec. 1992) 225–28.

Newton, Ian. *Population Ecology of Raptors*. Vermillion, SD: Buteo Books, 1979.

————, and R. D. Chancellor, eds. *Conservation Studies on Raptors*. Cambridge, England: International Council on Bird Preservation, 1985.

————. *The Sparrowhawk*. Calton, England: T. & A.D. Poyser Ltd., 1986.

————, and Penny Olsen, eds. *Birds of Prey.* New York: Facts on File, 1990.

Nye, Peter. "A Second Chance for Our National Symbol," *The Conservationist,* (July-August 1990) 16–23.

Olendorff, Richard. *Status, Biology and Management of Ferruginous Hawks: A Review.* Washington, DC: U.S. Department of the Interior, Bureau of Land Management, 1993.

Palmer, Ralph S., ed. *Handbook of North American Birds,* Vols. 4 and 5. New Haven: Yale University Press, 1988.

Parkhurst, J. A., and R. P. Brooks. "American Kestrels Eat Trout Fingerlings," *Journal of Field Ornithology,* Vol. 59 (Summer 1988) 286–87.

Pendleton, Beth, A. Giron, et al. *Raptor Management Techniques Manual.* Washington, DC: National Wildlife Federation, 1987.

Peterson, Roger Tory. *Birds Over America.* New York: Dodd, Mead and Co., 1950.

Philips, Mark. "Urban Falcons Return to Baltimore High-rise for 14th Year," Endangered *Species Technical Bulletin,* Vol. 18 (No. 2 1993) 18.

Poole, Alan F. *Ospreys: A Natural and Unnatural History.* New York: Cambridge University Press, 1989.

Preston, C. R., and R. D. Beane. "Red-tailed Hawk (*Buteo jamaicensis*)." In *The Birds of North America,* No. 52. Edited by A. Poole and F. Gill. Philadelphia: The Academy of Natural Science, and Washington, DC: American Ornithologists' Union, 1993.

Proctor, Noble S., and Patrick J. Lynch. *Manual of Ornithology.* New Haven: Yale University Press, 1993.

Reeves, Doug. "State Report: Iowa," *The Eyas,* Vol. 11 (Winter 1988) 6–8.

Restani, Marco. "Resource Partitioning Among the Three *Buteo* Species in the Centennial Valley, Montana," *Condor,* Vol. 93 (Nov. 1991) 1007–09.

Rick, Pat V. "The Fossil History of Vultures: A World Perspective." In *Vulture Biology and Management.* Edited by Sanford R. Wilbur and Jerome A. Jackson. Berkeley, CA: University of California Press, 1983.

Rosenfield, Robert N., and Michael W. Gratson. "Food Brought by Broad-winged Hawks to a Wisconsin Nest," *Journal of Field Ornithology,* Vol. 55 (Spring 1984) 246–47.

————, and J. Bielefeldt. "Cooper's Hawk (*Accipiter cooperii*)." In *The Birds of North America,* No. 75. Edited by A. Poole and F. Gill. Philadelphia: The Academy of Natural Science, and Washington, DC: American Ornithologists' Union, 1993.

Rowell, Galen. "Falcon Rescue," *National Geographic,* Vol. 179 (April 1991) 106–115.

Russell, Robert W. "Nocturnal Flight by Migrant 'Diurnal' Raptors," *Journal of Field Ornithology,* Vol. 62 (Autumn 1991) 505–08.

Senner, Stanley E., and Mark R. Fuller. "Status and Conservation of North American Raptors Migrating to the Neotropics." In *Raptors in the Modern World.* Edited by B.-U. Meyburg and R. D. Chancellor. Berlin: World Working Group on Birds of Prey, 1989.

Schüz, Ernest, and Claus König. "Old World Vultures and Man." In *Vulture Biology and Management.* Edited by Sanford R. Wilbur and Jerome A. Jackson. Berkeley, CA: University of California Press, 1983.

Simons, Dwight D. "Interactions Between California Condors and Humans in Prehistoric Far Western North America." In *Vulture Biology and Management.* Edited by Sanford R.

Wilbur and Jerome A. Jackson. Berkeley, CA: University of California Press, 1983.

Smith, Jeff P., S. W. Hoffman, and J. A. Gessaman. "Regional Size Differences Among Fall Migrant Accipiters in North America," *Journal of Field Ornithology,* Vol. 61 (Spring 1990) 192–200.

Snyder, Noel, and Helen Snyder. *Birds of Prey: Natural History and Conservation of North American Raptors.* Stillwater, MN: Voyageur Press, 1991.

Sodhi, N. S., et al. "Merlin (*Falcon columbarius*)." In *The Birds of North America,* No. 44. Edited by A. Poole and F. Gill. Philadelphia: The Academy of Natural Science, and Washington, DC: American Ornithologists' Union, 1993.

Spofford, Walter R., and Dean Amadon. "Live Prey to Young Raptors—Incidental or Adaptive?" *Journal of Raptor Research,* Vol. 27 (Dec. 1993) 180–84.

Squires, J. R., S. H. Anderson, and R. Oakleaf. "Food Habits of Nesting Prairie Falcons in Campbell Co., Wyoming," *Journal of Raptor Research,* Vol. 23 (Winter 1989) 157–67.

Stefanek, Patrick R., et al. "Nestling Red-tailed Hawk in Occupied Bald Eagle Nest," *Journal of Raptor Research,* Vol. 26 (March 1992) 40–41.

Suttles, Wayne, ed. *Handbook of North American Indians,* Vol. 7. Washington, DC: Smithsonian Institution Press, 1990.

Sutton, George M. *Birds of Pennsylvania.* Harrisburg, PA: J. H. McFarland Co., 1928.

Sykes, Paul W., Jr. "Recent Population Trend of the Snail Kite in Florida and Its Relationship to Water Levels," *Journal of Field Ornithology,* Vol. 54 (Summer 1983) 237–46.

————. "A Closer Look: Snail Kite," *Birding,* Vol. 26 (April 1994) 118–22.

Tallman, Marjorie. *Dictionary of American Folklore.* New York: Philosophical Library, 1959.

Tennesen, Michael. *Flight of the Falcon.* Toronto: Key Porter Books, 1992.

Terres, John K. *The Audubon Society Encyclopedia of North American Birds.* New York: Alfred A. Knopf, 1980.

Thurow, T. L., and C. M. White. "Nest Site Relationship Between the Ferruginous Hawk and Swainson's Hawk," *Journal of Field Ornithology,* Vol. 54 (Autumn 1983) 401–06.

Titus, K., and J. A. Mosher. "Selection of Nest Tree Species by Red-shouldered and Broad-winged Hawks in Two Temperate Forest Regions," *Journal of Field Ornithology,* Vol. 58 (Summer 1987) 274–83.

Toland, Brian. "Food Habits and Hunting Success of Cooper's Hawks in Missouri," *Journal of Field Ornithology,* Vol. 56 (Autumn 1985) 419–22.

Tripp, Edward. *Crowell's Handbook of Classical Mythology.* New York: Thomas Crowell Co., 1970.

Tucker, Priscilla. *The Return of the Bald Eagle.* Harrisburg, PA: Stackpole Books, 1994.

Watson, J. "Status of the Golden Eagle, *Aquila chrysaetos*," *Bird Conservation International.* Vol. 2 (Sept. 1992) 175–83.

Weishu, Hsu. "Preliminary Report on the China Raptor Watch in Hebei Province." In *Raptors in the Modern World.* Edited by B.-U. Meyburg and R. D. Chancellor. Berlin: World Working Group on Birds of Prey, 1989.

Welty, Joel C., and Luis Baptista. *The Life of Birds.* Fourth ed. Philadelphia: W. B. Saunders, 1988.

Hawk Mountain *(continued)*
    314*illus.*, 322*t*
Hawk Ridge Nature Reserve, 341*t*
hawks. *See names of individual
    species*
Hawks Aloft Worldwide, 221
Hawks (Clark), 320*t*
Hawks in Flight (Dunne), 320*t*
hawk watching, 312–321, 319*t*,
    320*t*, 321–329*t*, 330–331
HawkWatch International, 337,
    341*t*
"hen harrier." *See* northern harrier
Henst's goshawk, 357*t*
Hesperornis, 36
Himalayan griffon, 96*t*, 354*t*
hippoboscid flies, 214*illus.*, 214–215
honey-buzzards, 16*t*, 74*t*, 157*t*, 221
hooded vulture, 40*illus.*, 354*t*
hook-billed kite, 11, 14*t*, 19, 352*t*
    color phases, 34*t*
    eye color changes, 74*t*
    feeding adaptations, 157*t*
    primary food, 154*t*
    sexual plumage differences, 63*t*
    subspecies, 25*t*
Hoopes, Bernard A., 348*t*
"hunger panic," 92
hunting techniques, 158, 159*illus.*,
    160*illus.*

identification guides, 320*t*
imitator goshawk, 356*t*
imitator sparrowhawk, 236*t*
imperial eagle, 18*t*, 359*t*
    breeding habitat, 109*t*
    courtship behavior, 112*t*
    endangered or threatened
        status, 231*t*
    nest sites, 121*t*
    reproductive information, 141*t*
    subspecies, 29*t*
    vocalizations, 103*t*
    weight, 56*t*
    wintering areas, 206*t*
imprinting, 142–144, 243, 245,
    253*illus.*
International Council for Bird

Preservation, 235, 341*t*
International Osprey Foundation,
    341*t*
International Wildlife
    Rehabilitation Council, 341*t*

jackal buzzard, 358*t*
Japanese sparrowhawk, 200*t*, 201*t*,
    356*t*
Javan hawk-eagle, 218, 237*t*, 238*t*,
    359*t*
Jerdson's baza, 352*t*

Kerlinger, Dr. Paul, 310
kestrel nest boxes, 332–333
king vulture, 19, 70, 78, 154*t*, 288,
    349*t*, 352*t*
kites, 11, 11*illus.*, 16*t*, 19*illus.*,
    352–353*t*
Krider, John, 348*t*
Krider's hawk, 24, 348*t*

lagger falcon, 361*t*
lammergeier, 14, 17*t*, 172*illus.*, 173, 354*t*
    breeding habitat, 109*t*
    courtship behavior, 112*t*
    eye color changes, 74*t*
    feeding adaptations, 157*t*
    nest sites, 120*t*
    primary food, 154*t*
    reproductive information, 140*t*
    subspecies, 28*t*
    vocalizations, 103*t*
    weight, 55*t*
    wintering areas, 206*t*
lanner falcon, 18*t*, 361*t*
    breeding habitat, 110*t*
    courtship behavior, 112*t*
    nest sites, 121*t*, 122*t*
    reproductive information, 141*t*
    sexual plumage differences, 66*t*
    subspecies, 29*t*
    used in falconry, 300
    weight, 57*t*
    wintering areas, 207*t*
lappet-faced vulture, 100, 354*t*
laughing falcon, 152–153, 155*t*, 360*t*
lesser fish-eagle, 353*t*
lesser kestrel, 18*t*, 94, 360*t*
    breeding habitat, 110*t*

    colonial nesting, 96*t*
    endangered or threatened
        status, 237*t*
    flocking behavior, 97*t*
    nest sites, 121*t*, 122*t*
    sexual plumage differences, 54*t*
    weight, 56*t*
    wintering areas, 207*t*
lesser spotted eagle, 18*t*, 358*t*
    breeding habitat, 109*t*
    courtship behavior, 112*t*
    eye color changes, 74*t*
    flocking behavior, 97*t*
    nest sites, 121*t*
    reproductive information,
        137*t*, 141*t*
    subspecies, 28*t*
    weight, 56*t*
    wintering areas, 206*t*
lesser yellow-headed vulture, 352*t*
letter-winged kite, 96*t*, 353*t*
Levant marsh-harrier, 121*t*
Levant sparrowhawk, 17*t*, 28*t*, 355*t*
    breeding habitat, 109*t*
    flocking behavior, 97*t*
    sexual plumage differences, 65*t*
    weight, 56*t*
    wintering areas, 206*t*
Life Histories series (Bent), 305
lined forest-falcon, 360*t*
Linnaeus, Carolus, 4
little eagle, 359*t*
little sparrowhawk, 356*t*
lizard buzzard, 355*t*
long-billed vulture, 96*t*, 354*t*
long-crested eagle, 359*t*
long-legged buzzard, 17*t*, 358*t*
    breeding habitat, 109*t*
    color phases, 35*t*
    nest sites, 121*t*
    reproductive information, 141*t*
    subspecies, 28*t*
    weight, 56*t*
    wintering areas, 206*t*
long-tailed hawk, 357*t*

PHOTOGRAPH LIST

The photographs on the pages listed below have been printed by permission:

Rob Curtis: 9*t*, 31*t*, 40, 89, 95, 153, 211, 223, 238*t*, 319

Jeff Foott: 9*b*, 69, 70, 77*inset*, 81*t*, 99, 114*t*, 135, 145, 147, 149*t*, 159, 163, 169, 216, 251, 263, 318*b*

Michael Francis: 98, 124, 126, 222, 244, 247, 256, 261

Tim Gallagher: 60*t*

Daybreak Imagery: 11, 12, 129, 134, 137, 225*t*, 260, 337

Rick Kline: 3, 31*b*, 33, 53, 84, 92, 100, 130, 143*t*, 160, 167, 174, 182, 191, 242, 272, 318*t*

Bill Marchel: 172*t*, 302, 304

The Metropolitan Museum of Art: 286, 290, 291, 293, 301

Arthur Morris: 8, 13, 24, 30, 47, 49, 82, 103*t*, 123, 162, 171, 188, 200, 208, 230, 238*b*, 267*t*, 306, 307, 309, 313, 315, 316*b*

Stacia A. Navoy: 149*b*

The Peregrine Fund: 241, 274, 278

Rick Poley: 19, 81*b*, 258

Lee Rentz: 133, 181

Dennis Sheridan: 280

Millard H. Sharp: 114*b*

U.S. Fish & Wildlife Service: 71, 77, 224, 249, 270, 279

Mike Wallace: 88, 253

Scott Weidensaul: vii, 2, 21, 50, 61, 73, 75, 79, 86, 90, 116, 143*b*, 178, 189, 210, 214, 218, 219, 220, 225*b*, 227, 299, 305, 314, 316*t*, 336, 340

Windrush Photos: 7, 117, 172*b*